Sopher Mahir

Northwest Semitic Studies Presented to
Stanislav Segert

edited by
Edward M. Cook

Winona Lake, Indiana
EISENBRAUNS
1990

Library of Congress Cataloging-in-Publication Data

Sopher Mahir : Northwest Semitic studies presented to Stanislav Segert
/ edited by Edward M. Cook.
p. cm.
"Bibliography of the writings of Stanislav Segert": p.
ISBN 0-931464-56-0
1. Semitic languages, Northwest. 2. Bible. O.T.—Language, style.
3. Segert, S. (Stanislav) I. Cook, Edward M. II. Segert, S. (Stanislav)
PJ4121.S67 1990
492—dc20 90-2924
CIP

Table of Contents

ACKNOWLEDGEMENTS

Circumstances often cooperate to make the editor's task (and life) difficult, but there are also people who make it easier, and I would like to thank them here. Dr. Matthew L. Jaffe of the University of California Press was very liberal in the early stages of this project with advice, encouragement, and good cheer; he is represented herein as the translator of Prof. Fronzaroli's contribution. Ms. Sharon Brown of the *MAARAV* staff has provided, as is her wont, loyal, diligent, and practical support. Dr. Bruce Zuckerman's acceptance of this *Festschrift* as a special double number of *MAARAV* has enabled it finally to see the light of day; and the contributors, who have faithfully endured a gap longer than expected between submission and publication, have demonstrated a courtesy equal to their intellectual prowess. The honoree himself, Prof. Segert, freely made available his personal bibliographical records for publication, assuring a comprehensive and accurate chronicle of a life in scholarship. Finally, I thank my wife, Laura, and children, Elizabeth and Tristan—all of whom rejoice at the approaching end of the editor's preoccupation with his task. I rejoice in them.

Edward M. Cook

Cincinnati
July 10, 1989

PHOTO: EYE ON THE WORLD

MAARAV 5–6 (Spring, 1990): 7–10

STANISLAV SEGERT: AN APPRECIATION

For many scholars and students, Stanislav Segert is a name that appears on several important volumes on the bookshelf—the "special" bookshelf that contains books consulted with greater frequency than others. Increasingly, for a new generation of graduate students, the name "Segert" is as well known as Aqhat, Keret, Baal, and Kothar-wa-Khasis—for his *Basic Grammar of the Ugaritic Language* (1984) is the new textbook of choice for beginning classes in Ugaritic studies.

But "Segert" is no mere name, nor yet a chthonic or fertility deity—although, with well over 500 items and counting in his bibliography, I am not sure that the word "fertile" has not been used. This fall (1989), Stanislav Segert, scholar and teacher, marks twenty years of teaching at UCLA—an astonishing figure when one reflects that his academic career began more than twenty years before his appearance in Westwood.

Not that Segert is ready to number years with El. He was born May 4, 1921, in Prague, Czechoslovakia, to Antonin Segert and Marie Segertova (*nee* Zvolska). It is interesting that among his early occupations was a short stint as an accountant for the Central Bank of the Czech Savings Association—which may have something to do with his penchant for systematization. More importantly, he was ordained a minister of the Evangelical Church of Czech Brethren in 1943, a fact which will surprise no one familiar with his integrity and gentle, pastoral approach to teaching and scholarship.

In April 1947 he received his doctorate from Charles University in Prague, while teaching at the John Huss Evangelical Theological Faculty (since 1950 Comenius Faculty). In 1951 he joined the faculty at Charles University and added to this in 1952 the position of Research Associate in Semitic Philology at the Oriental Institute of the Czechoslovak Academy. An important part of this phase of his career was his membership on the Editorial Board of the Czech journal *Archiv Orientální*, in whose pages he was able to comment on almost every significant book and trend in Old Testament and Semitic studies in the '50s and '60s.

In 1966 he became Visiting Associate Professor at the Oriental Institute of the University of Chicago and in 1968–69 Visiting Professor at the Johns Hopkins University. In July 1969 he began teaching as Visiting Professor at UCLA, a prelude to his appointment as full professor in September, 1970. From that time he has brought to his American students a rich tradition of Continental learning and a commitment to the study of the North-West Semitic languages and literatures.

I would not leave unmentioned his wife, Dr. Jarmila Segertova—certainly the first wife to receive a dedication in Imperial Aramaic (*Altaramäische Grammatik*, p. 7)—or his two children, Eva and Jan, who have followed their learned parents into academic careers—Eva in political science (Ph.D., UCLA) and Jan in physics (Ph.D., Princeton).

Thus the external career; internally, Prof. Segert's interests and contributions can be read off from his massive bibliography in this volume. I think he has touched on every topic related to the study of the North-West Semitic languages; besides writing grammars of Ugaritic, Phoenician, and Ancient Aramaic (and Syriac, unpublished), he has done *the* definitive treatment of the Mesha stele, and made important contributions to our knowledge of Hebrew poetry, the history of the alphabet, comparative Semitic lexicography, and the Dead Sea Scrolls. No doubt many scholars could echo Dr. Dennis Pardee's comment, in a review of the Aramaic and Phoenician grammars: "If only he could be persuaded to make an analogous contribution to Hebrew studies by providing a modern replacement of Gesenius/Kautsch/Bergsträsser!" (*JNES* 37 [1978]: 198).

In person, Segert is the most modest of men. He is not capable of patting himself on the back or of stabbing anyone else in theirs. In class, he does not intimidate, does not criticize; he is able to turn even the most ill-conceived comment or question into an opportunity for learning.

For true learning, a concentration on the *res ipsa*, the object of study, is at the center of Segert's work. His courtesy flows not simply from an unspoken ideal of charity, but from a conviction that progress towards truth can only be made by scholars working together. In a memorandum on book reviewing distributed to his students in the fall of 1979, Segert wrote:

> The more critical the review is, the more effort the reviewer has to devote to both the exact and as possible objective presentation of the facts, the clearest statement of his opinions and the most understanding and tactful and least personal expression of his critical or even negative judgments. Such attitude leaves the door open for further fruitful discussion. A matter-of-fact reasoning may help both the author—especially if he prepares a new edition of his book—and the reviewer; and, what is even more important, it may stimulate further study of the problem and perhaps even lead to its satisfactory solution. On the other hand, a personal attack or vilification, or ridiculizing of the book, can stop a fruitful exchange of opinions and deflect the discussion from scholarly matters and problems to petty bickering.

Ecce homo. There you have the man himself, both scholar and gentleman.

Segert is no *Fachnarr.* He is well informed in current affairs; his judgment on internal American politics, world politics, and especially East European matters is trenchant. He possesses an excellent sense of humor and is a witty *raconteur.* I vividly remember an entertaining afternoon when Prof. Segert took the Hebrew Literature class to the campus ice-cream shop to commemorate the end of the quarter and regaled us with stories, reminiscences, and ice-cream.

No appreciation of Stanislav Segert would be complete without a mention of Segert the polyglot. He has remarked facetiously that for him "ESL" means English as a *seventh* language; no one who has heard the distinctive Segert idiolect would disagree. Besides English and his native Czech, he speaks and reads German, French, Russian, and Hebrew, and has at least a reading knowledge of Italian and Spanish. He has published articles in Latin, and has a complete mastery of Classical Greek—all this besides his acknowledged preeminence in the field of ancient Semitic languages. He is capable of illustrating or adorning a point with an apt quotation from Czeslaw Milosz or from Plautus, charitably translated for the unlearned. Although it cannot be said that Segert's polyglossia and general erudition serve as a model for his students—no doctoral candidate could aspire to such ability without nervous collapse—it does bring near a vision of life on the

Mount Zaphon of scholarship, where the gods allow happy mortals to hold converse with them.

Stanislav Segert's career continues apace. The *sopher mahir* has promised us, among other things, an *editio maior* of his Ugaritic grammar and, importantly, a book on the alphabet. They will be significant works, and will make a place for themselves on our "special" shelf. May his days continue to be filled with the pleasure of work well done—and ours with learning.

Edward M. Cook
Ph.D., UCLA, 1986

MAARAV 5–6 (Spring, 1990): 11–21

À PROPOS DE MILKOU, MILQART ET MILKᶜASHTART

Pierre Bordreuil
CNRS, PARIS, FRANCE

Le sens formel de l'appellatif divin Milqart, phonétiquement l'aboutissement du syntagme sémitique M L K Q R T est clair:[1] c'est "le roi de la ville." La généralisation de sa notoriété dans le monde phénicien du premier millénaire amène à s'interroger sur l'évolution du sens de ce syntagme à partir d'une donnée nouvelle sur le dieu Milkou du deuxième millénaire, apparue en 1986 dans une tablette alphabétique d'Ougarit.[2]

On pourra ainsi mettre en relation sur un point précis l'Ougarit et la Phénicie du premier millénaire, dont les langues sont maintenant mieux connues grâce aux travaux du Professeur Stanislav Segert.

I. DONNÉES OUGARITIQUES

A. *La Ville Ougaritienne de ᶜAthtartou*

C'est à Ougarit qu'apparaît pour la première fois un dieu *mlk* qui pourrait être qualifié de poliade car il figure dans un récit

1. Voir en dernier lieu S. Ribichini, "*Poenus advena*, gli dei fenici e l'interpretazione classica," *Collezione di studi fenici* 19 (Rome, 1985): 41–50; G. C. Heider, *The Cult of Molek: A Reassessment* (JSOTSup 43; Sheffield: Almond, 1985): 1–92; C. Bonnet, *Melqart: Cultes et mythes de l'Héraklès tyrien en Méditerranée*, thèse de doctorat Université de Liège, faculté de philosophie et lettres, année académique 1986–87; *Studia Phoenicia VIII*, Leuven-Namut, 1988; je remercie vivement l'auteur de m'avoir communiqué son manuscrit et de m'avoir permis de l'utiliser.

2. Voir A. Caquot dans *CRAI* (1986): 438; P. Bordreuil dans *Akkadica* 50 (1986): 28 et *CRAI* (1987): 298.

mythologique[3] énumérant des divinités d'Ougarit et d'ailleurs dont plusieurs sont déterminées géographiquement. Cette détermination est patente: pour Daganou *ttlh*: "à Touttoul" (1.15), ville de la vallée de l'Euphrate, pour Kotharou *kptrh*: "à Kaftor" (1.41), peut-être la Crète, pour Athtartou *mrh*: "à Mari" (1.78), ville du Moyen-Euphrate et pour Milkou *ʿṯtrth*: "à ʿAthtarot" (1.41) interprétée par certains comme l'Aštarot biblique, aujourd'hui Tell Aštarah dans le sud syrien près de l'antique ʾEdrei qui est aujourd'hui Deraʿa.[4] Chaque détermination géographique est indiquée dans ce texte par la désinence locative *-h* (= à), mais une seconde mention de *mlk* dans un fragment du même mythe situe ce dieu *bʿṯtrt* "dans ʿAthtarot."[5]

Une nouvelle attestation de ce dieu "localisé" se trouve dans la liste RS 1986/2235 qui dénombre des rations d'orges destinées à des ânes dont les propriétaires sont indiqués. Rompant avec treize lignes d'énumération monotone le texte mentionne:

(14) *ṯlṯ.ddm.šʿrm.l.ḥmrm*	Trois paniers d'orges pour les ânes des forgerons[6]
(15) *dt.tblm.*	
(16) *ḫmš.ʿšr.dd.l.ššw.ršp*	Quinze paniers pour les chevaux de Rašapou
(17) *ḫmš.ddm.l.ššw.mlk.ʿṯtrt*	Cinq paniers pour les chevaux de Milkou de ʿAthtartou

L'élément nouveau est le séparateur qui apparaît entre *mlk* et *ʿṯtrt*; on ne lit plus comme sur les deux textes précédents respectivement "Milkou *à* ʿAthtartou" ou "Milkou *dans* ʿAthtartou," mais "Milkou *de* ʿAthtartou." Nous trouvons certainement ici le premier exemple de liaison génitivale entre le théonyme Milkou et un nom de ville.

Si la présence de villes (Touttoul, Mari) et de contrées lointaines (Kaftor) sur la tablette mythologique citée plus haut pouvait conforter l'identification de ʿAṯtartou avec la ʿAshtarot biblique, située

3. RS 24.244 = *Ugaritica* V:7 = *KTU* 1.100; sur Malik à Ebla et à Mari, voir G. C. Heider (N 1): 93–113; sur Milkou à Ougarit, voir pp. 113–141.

4. P. Xella, *I testi rituali di Ugarit—I testi* (Rome, 1981): 235; Heider (N 1): 115s; D. Pardee, *Les textes para-mythologiques, avec une notice archéologique par J. C. C. Courtois* (Ras Shamra-Ougarit IV; Paris, 1987): 84ss.; Bonnet (N 1): 98s.

5. RS 24.251 = *Ugaritica* V:8 = *KTU* 1.107; Bonnet (N 1): 314s.

6. Voir P. Bordreuil, *CRAI* (N 2): 299; littéralement les "frappeurs," d'après le sens conservé en arabe, cp. Tubal Caïn à Gen 4:22.

dans le sud syrien et plus proche d'Ougarit que ne le sont Mari et la Crète, il n'en est pas de même de la tablette RS 86/2235 qui consigne les rations destinées à quelques dizaines d'ânes. Il est évident que le contenu de cette liste se réfère à un circuit de distribution interne à l'Ougarit et que *ᶜṯtrt* doit y être recherchée plutôt qu'à quelques centaines de kilomètres des frontières où l'on aurait pris la peine d'acheminer cinq (!) paniers de céréales. Si, de surcroît, la liste néglige de localiser Rašapou n'est-ce pas que sa grande popularité dans le royaume rendait une telle indication superflue?

L'argument principal, plaidant en faveur d'une localisation intra-ougaritienne de la ville de ᶜAṯtartou, est l'attestation de l'existence de *gt ᶜṯtrt* (PRU II 40 [KTU 4.125]:6) où l'on peut voir un toponyme théophore de cette déesse. A côté de déterminations anthroponymiques qui sont les plus fréquentes, et deux cas où *gt* est déterminé par le gentilice *mlkym* (PRU II 26 rev.2 [KTU 4.126]:19; CTA 74 [KTU 4.99]:5) qui désigne à l'évidence les habitants de la ville de *mlk*, il existe d'autres cas où *gt* est déterminé par un toponyme proprement dit, tel que *ilštmᶜ* (PRU II 153 [KTU 1.80]:1), *ṯbq* (PRU II 84 [KTU 4.213]:5), *yknᶜm* (PRU II 61:15 = KTU 4.307:21), *mᶜrb* (PRU II 61 [KTU 4.307]:3) auquel s'ajoutent *mᶜrby* (PRU II 84 [KTU 4.213]:8) et la graphie erronnée *mᶜbr* (PRU II 98 [KTU 4.243]:12); *gt bir* (PRU V 13 [KTU 4.636]:2) et PRU V 168:4 (= KTU 4.397:13) clôt cette liste provisoire.

De tels *gt* appartenant à la communauté villageoise des Milkiens, à d'autres villages et à la reine, dont un *gt* contenait cent cinquante oliviers (PRU II 9 [KTU 4.143]:1), devaient correspondre à la mise en valeur d'une superficie appréciable, comme le confirme un texte alphabétique d'Ougarit que consigne l'adjonction d'un ou de plusieurs *šdm* à un *gt* dans une opération d'achat ou de remembrement de parcelles (PRU II 104 [KTU 4.110]:14, 16 etc.).

L'interprétation toponymique peut aussi convenir pour *ᶜṯtrt* de RS 24.252 (KTU 1.108):

il.yṯb.bᶜṯtrt	. . . Le dieu qui siège à ᶜAṯtartou,
il.ṯpṭ.bhd rᶜy	. . . qui règne avec Haddou le berger,[7]

mais il est difficile de voir dans le séquence *ᶜṯtrt-hdrᶜy* les noms respectifs de ᶜAštarot et de ᵓEdrei, résidences du roi ᶜOg d'après

7. *Ugaritica* V:2 [*KTU* 1.108]:13; Heider (N 1): 118–122; avis contraire dans Pardee (N 4): 94s.

Jos 12:4. Le premier de ces noms avait d'abord permis de localiser *ʿṯtrt* dans le sud syrien, mais on a vu plus haut que cette ville est à rechercher dans la province ougaritaine, ce que confirment les lignes 25s. de ce texte en appelant les bénédictions divines *btk.ʾugrt* "au sein d'Ougarit." Une telle mention n'est guère compréhensible si la ville de *ʿṯtrt* est éloignée du territoire de l'Ougarit. De plus, le texte biblique qui orthographie *ʾedreʿi*, ne correspond pas exactement à l'ougaritique *hdrʿy*. D'autre part, l'allusion de la ligne 18 au succès que Rapʾiou demandera à Baʿlou n'évoquerait-elle pas une concertation entre le dieu Rapiʾou de la ligne 1 et Haddou le berger qui règnent ensemble d'après la ligne 3? Notons enfin que, dans l'inscription araméenne de Tell Fekheryé quelques siècles plus tard, les "pâturages" (*rʿy*) feront partie des dons de Haddou (*hd*)[8], et ce dieu qui accorde la pâture doit être ici l'héritier du dieu d'Ougarit *hd rʿy*: "Haddou le berger."

Peut-être pourrait-on concilier l'interprétation "transjordanienne" et notre localisation "ougaritienne" en supposant que le nom de ʿAthtartou a pu être donné à cette localité de l'Ougarit en référence à la ʿAshtarot transjordanienne, assurément connue des ougaritains. Une telle équivalence pourrait être illustrée par un épisode de la légende de Keret dont le héros, pour sacrifier aux divinités des tyriens et des sidoniens, ne se rend certainement pas à Tyr et à Sidon, mais auprès de sanctuaires moins éloignés et consacrés aussi aux cultes tyrien et sidonien.

Il n'est pas invraisemblable de penser que, dans un royaume aussi étendu que l'Ougarit, les agglomérations provinciales devaient abriter le culte de divinités pourvues ou nom de détermination géographique dans les mythes ougaritains que nous connaissons. L'exemple le plus clair est probablement celui de ʿAnat de la localité septentrionale de Salḫu où le roi se rend en personne pour "voir" la déesse (RIH 77/10 B 1.9).

B. *Le dieu Milkou à Ougarit*

Aux trois textes alphabétiques déjà cités qui localisent Milkou à ʿAṯtartou, s'ajoutent quelques textes syllabiques, listes de théonymes appelées encore "panthéons,"[9] comme RS 24.309[10] et RS

8. A. Abou-Assaf, P. Bordreuil, A. R. Millard, *La statue de Tell Fekheryé et son inscription bilingue assyro-araméenne* (Paris, 1982): 1.2.

9. Heider (N 1): 116s.

10. *Ugaritica* V: 216, 1.81.

24.264+280.[11] RS 20.24[12] en fait un pluriel (MALIK.MEŠ) équivalent de l'ougaritique *mlkm*, lui-même attesté dans la version ougaritique de ce panthéon que donne CTA 29 et dans le texte de présages RIH 78/14.[13]

Le nom propre *aḫat-milku* a été porté par deux reines d'Ougarit, apparemment ainsi nommées en référence directe au roi humain, encore vivant ou déjà trépassé, dont elles étaient proches. Or une référence directe à un roi humain suppose une vocalisation *malku* et non pas *milku* qui désignerait en réalité le dieu Milkou;[14] cette nuance importante ne traduirait-elle pas l'existence d'un lien entre la dynastie régnant à Ougarit et le culte du dieu Milkou?[15]

Depuis une quinzaine d'années notre connaissance du culte des ancêtres royaux d'Ougarit a progressé grâce à la tablette RS 34.126 qui présente le processus d'intégration du roi défunt dans la hiérarchie des Rephaim.[16] Une confirmation était apportée peu après par la tablette RIH 77/8A hélas très mutilée,[17] qui présente le syntagme *rpi yqr* à ligne 14′. Il ne fait guère de doute que Yaqarou, l'ancêtre fondateur de la royauté d'Ougarit, est désigné dans ce dernier texte comme l'un des Rephaim.

Or le début de RS 24.252, dont on vient de parler à propos de la ville de ᶜAthtartou, présente à la suite les titres *rpi, mlk ᶜlm, gṯr* et *yqr*. Une analyse très fine de ce texte, dont je ne m'écarte que pour la localisation de ᶜAthtartou sur le terrain, vient de conclure à la "présence dans ces deux premiers versets, d'un faisceau très touffu de références et d'allusions: *Rapi'u* donnerait à *Milku* la fonction de 'guérisseur'; *malku ᶜalami* 'roi de l'Eternité' serait un titre de *Rapi'u* et en même temps ferait allusion à *Milku* le roi de l'au-delà; *gaṯaru* 'fort' serait un titre de *Rapi'u* et en même temps ferait

11. *Ugaritica* VII: 3, 1.32.

12. *Ugaritica* V: 45, 1.32.

13. *Syria* LVII (1980): 352 verso 1.4′.

14. Voir J. L. Cunchillos, "Una carta paradigmatica de Ugarit (*KTU* 2.11)," dans *El Misterio de la Palabra, Homenaje al profesor L. Alonso-Schökel* (Valence-Madrid, 1983): 61–74 (p. 70). Il faut ajouter ce nom et *mlkytn* (*PRU* II 20 [*KTU* 2.15]: ll.2 et 8 et *PRU* II 34 [*KTU* 4.264]: 2, à la liste présentée par Heider (N 1): 133–137; voir aussi Pardee (N 4): 87 et n. 41.

15. De même à Tyr: voir Bonnet (N 1): 328. Au premier millénaire on connaît un sceau phénicien au nom de ᵓḥtmlk; il représente une femme assise sur un trône, devant laquelle une autre femme se tient, lui servant à boire: F. Vattioni, "I sigilli ebraici," *Biblica* 50 (1969): 357–388 (p. 367, no. 63).

16. Voir en dernier lieu P. Bordreuil et D. Pardee, "Le rituel funéraire ougaritique RS 34.126," *Syria* LIX (1982): 121–128.

17. *Syria* LVI (1979): 302.

allusion à la divinité ougaritique *Gaṯaru* qui est l'équivalent de la divinité *Milk/Melk*-hourrite; *yaqaru* 'honorable' serait un titre de *Rapi'u* et en même temps ferait allusion au membre des Rephaim et roi fondateur de la dynastie ougaritique: *Yaqaru.*"[18] Ce vers énumérait ainsi "une série de titres du roi du royaume des morts, *Milku*: il est qualifié du titre ancien de *Rapi'u* 'guérisseur'; de *malku ᶜalami* 'roi d'éternité,' en l'occurence des ancêtres qui ont passé dans l'éternité; . . . et de *yaqaru* 'précieux, honorable,' comme le premier des rois d'Ougarit morts et divinisés."[19]

Le dieu Milkou, roi du royaume des morts, était donc particulièrement vénéré à ᶜAthtartou, ville de l'Ougarit qu'il reste encore à localiser. Ce syntagme /*mlk* + nom de ville/, permettrait-il à son tour d'expliquer le nom d'autres dieux poliades du premier millénaire, du type *mlk* + *qrt* (= ville)?

II. DONNÉES PHÉNICIENNES

Les attestations du théonyme Milk dans l'onomastique ouest-sémitique du premier millénaire ne nous renseignent guère sur les caractéristiques de ce dieu. Dans le domaine phénicien, à côté du sceau de *ᵓḥtmlk* dont on a déjà parlé, il existe à Chypre comme à Ougarit le nom *mlkytn.*[20] En Transjordanie les sceaux moabites aux noms de *mlkyᶜzr* et *gdmlk*, les sceaux ammonites aux noms de *mqnmlk, pdmlk* et *yrmlk* et vraisemblablement la bulle édomite au nom de *mlklbᶜ*[21] manifestent à la fois la permanence de ce théonyme et peut-être la faveur particulière qu'il connaissait dans un région proche de celle où régnait encore le dieu Milk de ᶜAshtarot.

18. Pardee (N 4): 83–96; voir aussi Heider (N 1): 123.

19. Pardee (N 4): 93.

20. Voir O. Masson et M. Sznycer, *Recherches sur les Phéniciens à Chypre* (Genève-Paris, 1972): 131.

21. Voir P. Bordreuil, *Catalogue des sceaux ouest-sémitiques inscrits de la Bibliothèque Nationale, du Musée du Louvre et du Musée biblique de Bible et Terre Sainte* (Paris, 1986): 59, no. 63 et n. 19., contre Heider (N 1): 169–172. Sur la bulle de *mlklbᶜ* voir E. Puech dans *Levant* IX (1977): 12s; Heider (N 1): 171. Ajouter maintenant aut *lmlk* de l'ostracon de Kh. ᶜOuzza: F. Israel, *Rev. bib. Ital.* 35 (1987): 337–356 (p. 339). Au contraire le sceau *lmlk ṣrm* appartenait au roi (humain) des Tyriens dont le titre est ici parallèle à celui du "roi des sidoniens": *mlk ṣdnm*. Les éléments du culte de Milqart présents sur ce sceau (*CRAI* [1986]: 298–305) manifestent vraisemblablement l'attachement de la dynastie au *mlk* (divin) de Tyr; voir G. Garbini, *I Fenici. Storia e religione* (Naples, 1980): 53–63; Bonnet (N 1): 319.

Il reste qu'au premier millénaire c'est la forme *mlk* + *qrt* alias Milqart qui forme l'essentiel de notre documentation.

A. *Le dieu Milk de la métropole tyrienne (Milqart)*

Si Milqart était vénéré à Tyr dès le Xème siècle d'après Ménandre d'Ephèse,[22] sa première attestation en même temps que sa plus ancienne représentation figurée, remontant vraisemblablement au IXème siècle, est sans doute la stèle de basalte du Musée d'Alep, appelée de ce fait le plus souvent "stèle de Milqart." Elle représente un personnage anthropoïde barbu debout, torse nu, passant à gauche, vêtu d'une sorte de pagne, coiffé d'une *lebbadeh* et portant sur l'épaule gauche une hache fenestrée.[23] Sur la base est gravée une inscription de quatre lignes dans laquelle le dédicant Bar Hadad remercie son seigneur Milqart pour l'exaucement qu'il lui a accordé. L'inscription est écrite en araméen et le dédicant s'intitule lui-même "Roi d'Aram," mais un original phénicien n'est pas á exclure,[24] en raison de la formule finale qui rappelle assez bien celle des inscriptions phéniciennes. Il s'agit de *kšm*^{c} *qlh* "car il a entendu sa voix," qui clôt habituellement les dédicaces phéniciennes d'Orient, à l'exception du suffixe possessif qui normalement ne serait pas noté en phénicien et pas en tout cas sous la forme *-h*.

Une telle analogie de structure avec les inscriptions phéniciennes n'est pas surprenante, car Milqart, bien que sa plus ancienne mention connue à ce jour appartienne ici au domaine araméen, est en fait un dieu phénicien et probablement d'origine tyrienne. C'est le traité d'Asarhaddon avec Baal roi de Tyr qui, au VIIème siècle en donne le plus ancien témoignage. Milqart, transcrit en assyrien *Mi-il-qa-ar-tu*, figure en effet au nombre des dieux tyriens qui sont les garants de ce traité.[25]

Revenant à la stèle de Milqart, force nous est de constater que cette stèle est rédigée en araméen par un roi araméen et qu'elle ne provient pas de Phénicie, mais de la région d'Alep. Le site de Breidj où elle a été mise au jour a livré beaucoup de matériel de réemploi mais on ignore si, quand et d'où elle a été amenée jusqu'au lieu où les archéologues devaient la retrouver il y a

22. Ribichini (N 1): 44s.

23. On trouvera une description dans Bonnet (N 1): 103.

24. J. C. L. Gibson, *Textbook of Syrian Semitic Inscriptions. Volume II: Aramaic Inscriptions* (Oxford: Clarendon, 1975): 2, no. 1.

25. E. Reiner dans *ANET*: 533s.

quelques décennies. Si son emplacement primitif était situé dans la région d'Alep, on pourrait penser que le culte de Milqart a pu être adopté pour des raisons diplomatiques par le royaume d'Alep désireux de se concilier les bonnes grâces de la métropole insulaire.[26] Cette stèle a-t-elle fait partie quelque temps d'un butin guerrier abandonné en ce lieu ou dans les environs? Le nom de *br rḥb* "fils de Rehob," lu dans la titulature du dédicant[27] désigne Bar Hadad comme un dynaste araméen dont le territoire était situé dans la Beqaᶜa libanaise. Or, si la stèle de Milqart était primitivement dressée dans un temple du *bt rḥb*, lui même situé à quelqes dizaines de kilomètres de Tyr, elle a pu être emportée comme trophée, abandonnée dans la région de Breidj et réemployée éventuellement par la suite. Une telle option rendrait compte du caractère araméen de l'inscription, de la titulature et du nom de Bar Hadad, de l'appartenance de ce "roi d'Aram" au monde des royaumes araméens, et de la vénération d'un dieu—dont on connaît le caractère tyrien—represénté ici *grosso modo* sous l'aspect d'un dieu phénicien.

B. *La signification de Qart*

Si l'étendue géographique de l'Ougarit peut contribuer à expliquer l'existence d'un culte provincial de Milkou, la situation était certainement très différente dans une ville phénicienne telle que Tyr au début du premier millénaire, limitée qu'elle était à l'agglomération urbaine et à un arrière-pays de dimensions réduites. Cette situation particulière devait amener inévitablement l'accession à la tête du panthéon local d'un dieu poliade, et la notoriété de ce dernier devait suivre inévitablement les heurs et malheurs de la ville. Dans le cas de Tyr, le culte de son dieu devait essaimer outremer, au hasard de l'expansion coloniale, mais pouvait aussi être adopté outremont dans la Beqaᶜa, où pourrait se situer, comme on l'a dit, l'emplacement primitif de la stèle de Milqart.

1. *Qart = Tyr.* Cette interprétation qui vient immédiatement à l'esprit était assurément celle des tyriens du VIIème siècle qui

26. Bonnet (N 1): 104s. W. T. Pitard, "The Identity of the Bir-Hadad of the Melqart Stela," *BASOR* 272 (1988): 3–21 considère cette stèle comme un monument nord-syrien.

27. P. Bordreuil et J. Teixidor, "Nouvel examen de l'inscription de Bar Hadad," *Aula Orientalis* 1 (1983): 271–276.

considéraient le dieu Milqartu invoqué dans le traité d'Asarhaddon comme le Milk (*mlk*) de la ville (*qrt*) (de Tyr), héritier vraisemblable d'un Milkou tyrien du deuxième millénaire et que CIS I 122 appellera quelques siècles plus tard *bʿl ṣr*.

(a) A la même époque, dans l'inscription phénicienne de Karatépé,[28] Azitawadda dit expressément: "J'ai construit cette ville (*hqrt z*) et je lui ai donné le nom d'Azitawadiya (*ʾztwdy*)." Il s'agit bien sûr de la capitale du royaume à laquelle le monarque a donné son nom et sous le nom de *qrt*, les tyriens désignaient certainement aussi leur propre métropole.

(b) Un second argument en faveur de l'interprétation tyrienne de *qrt* est le nom même de sa fille africaine Carthage dont le nom sémitique *qrtḥdšt* (= *qartḥadašt*, littéralement "Villeneuve") renvoie évidemment à la métropole tyrienne.[29] On sait d'autre part, grâce à plusieurs témoignages[30] que les Carthaginois avaient conservé une conscience très vive de leurs origines tyriennes.

2. *Qart hors de l'aire tyrienne.* S'il est certain à Carthage et probable ailleurs que le théonyme Milqart se référait au dieu tyrien, on ne peut affirmer que toutes les attestations connues dans le monde phénico-punique en ont toujours conservé le souvenir. Au syntagme primitif a succédé selon toute vraisemblance un nom propre désormais insécable dont on ne percevait plus partout les éléments proprement tyriennes. Sinon, comment expliquer la séquence *mlqrt bʿl ṣr*[31] réaffirmant ces racines et surtout l'apparition, tard dans le premier millénaire, d'un nouveau syntagme *mlqrt bṣr* qui témoigne clairement d'une séparation sémantique entre le nom même de Milqart et la ville de Tyr? En effet, si l'identification primitive de *qrt* avec la ville de Tyr était encore vivace, la mention *bṣr* "à Tyr" demeurerait ici superflue et même redondante. Or, plusieurs attestations montrent qu'on prenait bien soin de préciser qu'il s'agissait, le cas échéant, du Milqart de Tyr.[32]

On pourrait alors supposer qu'à l'instar de Tyr plusieurs cités phéniciennes avaient forgé un syntagme, composé du nom d'un

28. En dernier lieu voir J. C. L. Gibson, *Textbook of Syrian Semitic Inscriptions. Volume III: Phoenician Inscriptions* (Oxford: Clarendon, 1982): no. 15.

29. Voir la discussion dans Bonnet (N 1): 320.

30. Bonnet (N 1): 128; voir aussi P. Bordreuil et A. Ferjaoui, "A propos des 'fils de Tyr' et des 'fils de Carthage'," *Studia Phoenicia* VII (1988): 137–142.

31. *CIS* I 122.

32. Voir en particulier la tessère portant *lmlqrt bṣr* publiée par H. Seyrig dans *Syria* XXVIII (1951): 225–228, dont il existe plusieurs autres exemplaires inédits ainsi qu'un poids du Musée du Louvre qui porte la même inscription (voir BAALIM V: II 4, *Syria* 65 [1988]: 43).

dieu *mlk* (= Milkou, éventuellement roi divin) local et de *qrt* désignant la ville (= *Qart*) elle-même sans qu'il soit besoin de voir dans ce théonyme une quelconque référence au Milqart tyrien. Pour accepter une telle solution, il faudrait disposer d'attestations du syntagme /*mlqrt* + nom de lieu/, ce qui n'existe pas (encore?) en l'état actuel de nos connaissances. Il est étonnant de constater par exemple que la version grecque de l'inscription bilingue d'Arados[33] est dédiée à Hermès-Héraklès et que la version phénicienne dédiée à *ʾrm wmlqrt* "à Hermès et à Milqart" ne signale aucune détermination géographique de ce dernier dieu. S'agit-il vraiment du Milqart tyrien ou d'une adaptation locale? Se distinguaient-ils l'un de l'autre et comment? Autant de questions actuellement sans réponse.

3. *Milqart-Herakles-Milkʿashtart.* Si l'inscription précédente ne nous permet pas de préciser les rapports existant entre le Milqart proprement tyrien et le dieu du même nom connu ailleurs en Méditerranée, l'équivalence qu'elle établit entre Héraklès et Milqart est significative car attestée en Phénicie proprement dite. Confirmant la présentation par Diodore de l'Héraklès de Tyr qui veille sur les colons partis outremer,[34] elle concrétise l'analogie perçue par les grecs entre Milqart le dieu "mortel," "réveillé" de la mort et "le héros par excellence, Héraklès le seul . . . promu au rang d'olympien," ayant fait l'expérience de la vie et de la mort.[35]

Son iconographie de type hérakléen,[36] autant que la présence dans son nom de l'élément *mlk* amènent à s'interroger sur les rapports de Milkʿashtart, dieu d'Oumm el ʿAmed près de Tyr, avec le théonyme Milqart. On pourrait penser, à partir du *mlk.ʿṯtrt* d'Ougarit, que l'élément *ʿštrt* dans *mlkʿštrt* est un toponyme correspondant à l'élément *qrt* dans *mlqrt*; *mlkʿštrt* serait ainsi l'équivalent de *mlqrt*. Cette explication ne peut être complètement écartée mais les probables représentations de la déesse *ʿštrt* en ce lieu[37] et sa présence dans l'inscription de Maʿṣoub donnent à penser que *ʿštrt* doit plutôt être ici le nom même de la déesse Astarté.

L'essai d'explication le plus vraisemblable en l'état actuel de nos connaissances semble être la réinterprétation au niveau théologique

33. En dernier lieu J. P. Rey-Coquais, *Arados et sa Pérée* (Paris, 1974): 25.

34. G. Bunnens, "Aspects religieux de l'expansion phénicienne," *Studia Phoenicia* IV (1986): 119–125 (p. 121).

35. Bonnet (N 1): 319.

36. S. Ribichini, *RSO* 50 (1976): 43–55; S. Ribichini et P. Xella, *RSF* 7 (1979): 145–158.

37. Voir la documentation dans Bonnet (N 1): 97.

ou populaire du nom de Milkᶜashtart comme l'expression théocrasique de l'union de Milqart et d'Astarté.[38] On pourrait même aller plus loin et se demander si une telle présentation de Milqart subordonné à Astarté, déterminé par elle, n'a pas été rendue possible, ou en tout cas facilitée, par le fait que Milqart, pour employer la terminologie de Philon de Byblos, appartenait aux "dieux mortels" et qu'Astarté appartenait aux "dieux immortels." Ce n'est peut-être pas par hasard si Echmoun semble aussi être déterminé par Astarté dans le nom *ᵓšmnᶜštrt.*[39] En effet, identifié à Asklépios, il fait, comme Milqart, partie de ces dieux mortels appelés encore "héros divins."

Entre, d'une part, Milkou d'Ougarit, déterminé par *ᶜṯtrh, bᶜṯtrt* et maintenant par *ᶜṯtrt* et, d'autre part, *mlkᶜštrt* des Echelles de Tyr, pourrait n'avoir existé qu'une homonymie purement formelle, le premier syntagme désignant le toponyme ᶜAthtartou-ᶜAshtarot et le second désignant le théonyme ᶜAshtart. Une réinterprétation théologique ultérieure aurait fait alors du Milkou de la ville de ᶜAshtarot le Milk de la déesse Astarté.

Ce qu'on connaît maintenant du Milkou ougaritien au deuxième millénaire et qui correspondait peut-être aux croyances tyriennes contemporaines, le caractère du Milqart tyrien lui-même, dieu tourné à la fois vers les morts et vers les vivants et le caractère hérakléen de Milkᶜashtart, constituent un fil conducteur permettant de penser que la succession de *mlk.ᶜṯtrt* à *mlkᶜštrt* en passant par *mlqrt* devait pourtant revêtir une signification plus profonde. En l'état actuel de notre documentation on ne peut guère en dire plus et en particulier renoncer encore à trouver la raison pour laquelle on assiste à une résurgence de *mlk.ᶜṯtrt* sous la forme *mlkᶜštrt*, en aval d'un parcours souterrain long d'un bon millénaire.

38. Bonnet (N 1): 99, citant S. Ribichini et P. Xella.
39. Voir Heider (N 1): 180s.

MAARAV 5–6 (Spring, 1990): 23–32

CYBERNETICA MESOPOTAMICA[1]

GIORGIO BUCCELLATI
UNIVERSITY OF CALIFORNIA, LOS ANGELES

Under the watchful eye of its patron deity, Nisaba, the art of writing has progressed along paths that only the gods could have foreseen some 5000 years ago. By most standards, we have come to associate "history" with the evidence provided primarily by the written record, and "prehistory" with the evidence provided exclusively by the archaeological record. By the same standards, we may be tempted to envisage our age as the beginning of a third major phase in human history. The computer holds a status, vis-à-vis writing, quite analogous to what writing held vis-à-vis pre-literate or pre-scribal information techniques, and as such it may be heralding a major transition in human development into some sort of "post-history." But just as we are being weaned from Nisaba's maternal cares, and as we are trading clay for silicone, we seem to be growing in our commitment to the past, to the domain over which she has ruled for so long. It seems ironical to say that no Mesopotamian ever knew as much about his cultural past as we know today, but there is much that is true in this assertion: while our accent in speaking their language may be at best abominable, which Mesopotamian scribe could ever have had access to as full a gamut of text types, and from as many different periods, as we do today?

The reasons why the computer is of such dramatic consequence as to lead us slowly beyond the realm of Nisaba are much more

1. The text of this paper follows that of an oral presentation given at the national meeting of the American Oriental Society in Los Angeles in March, 1987. I dedicate it with friendship to Stanislav Segert, with a special personal recollection of our first acquaintance in Chicago, at a time when he was pioneering the use of the computer on a research project he had undertaken with I. J. Gelb.

than just greater ease or increased efficiency. Not that ease and efficiency are unimportant: most of us have become apt at using the computer for both word-processing and, perhaps to a more limited extent, for data base management—two functions which have certainly made a convert of many a skeptic in recent years. But the major impact to be felt in the very immediate future is in the way in which we *conceptualize* both the data and the utilization we can make of it. I would like to address here some aspects of these changes. I will do this in a rather minor key, because I will deal with the practical dimension rather than with theoretical issues. Specifically, I would like first to speak about the general scope of our project; second, to explain the notion of distribution disks; and third, to illustrate the specific disks which are currently available.

I started applying data processing techniques to Mesopotamian materials back in the age of dinosaurs—1968, to be precise. The dinosaurs were the large mainframe computers: no thought, then, of microcomputers and of general widespread use of magnetic media. By 1972 we had progressed, with the support of funds from the Research Committee of the Academic Senate at UCLA, to a point where we felt ready for a major grant application from NEH, which we in fact received. Under the terms of the grants we were to produce a computerized data base of Old Babylonian letters: this was accomplished over a period of 5 years, but we were then faced with the problem of distribution. Printouts of the basic sign concordance ran upwards of 10,000 pages; morphological concordances which we had completed for sections of the data base were even larger: the sheer physical volume was such that any type of standard publication was out of the question. Thus I kept making available to interested colleagues tapes and portions of the printouts upon request, and gave much thought to ways of compressing the data through editorial compacting of one type or another. I started within Undena a book series under the title *Cybernetica Mesopotamica* which was to make available the intended results, and began publishing portions of the data sets as well as some of the analysis.

With the advent and the widespread use of microcomputers, the situation changed drastically. We could plan on distributing data on magnetic media, which would not only be much more realistic economically, but also allow the interactive type of utilization of the data that constitutes a major difference vis-à-vis paper-base products. Through the major support of the Ambassador International Cultural Foundation I was able to begin using microcomputers for archaeological field work, and in fact we were the first to bring "microcomputers" to Syria for data entry in the field. This was back in 1981, when micro-computers were all but micro in size (although they were certainly so in power): unimaginable as it may seem today, IBM was not yet in the market at the time. The work on archaeological materials has resulted in a very complex and comprehensive system of coding and analysis especially for stratigraphic information: this changes in essential ways the mechanism for arriving at strategy decisions during the excavations, by providing much greater capillary control on stratigraphic details; it also adds a whole new dimension of objectivity to the record, since it makes it possible to publish, if one so chooses, the full range of observations made in the field, without the selectivity that has otherwise been necessary in archaeological publications. This is what I call the "global record," which we are in the process of implementing at both Terqa and Tell Mozan—but which I have no time to illustrate here.

If I have referred to it at all, it is because the archaeological component is as essential, conceptually, to the overall scope of *Cybernetica Mesopotamica* as the philological one, and shares in much the same way the technical problems attendant to the formalization of the data and the manner of distribution. I will however concentrate, for the rest of my paper, on the philological dimension alone. Work on this has been made possible recently through the support of the David and Lucile Packard Foundation: under the terms of this grant we are currently concentrating on the texts of Ebla, and hope to be able to continue subsequently with the Old Babylonian letters (prepared especially by John Hayes, Paul Gaebelein and Yoshi Kobayashi), the Middle Assyrian corpus (prepared by Claudio Saporetti), and the Akkadian of the West (prepared by John Hayes and Thomas Finley)—all of which were already available on the mainframe computer and have to be harmonized and revised thoroughly for distribution on floppy disks.

The study of the Ebla texts is of obvious significance. My own work on these texts along the lines described here follows the mandate I was given within the framework of the International Committee established by the University of Rome, and will grow apace with the work done by Alfonso Archi and the epigraphic staff of the Expedition. In this respect I benefitted especially from the presence of Lucio Milano at UCLA where he served for two years as Visiting Professor. Through our collaboration with him and our other Italian colleagues we have been adding texts as yet unpublished to our data base. As a result, not only is the preparatory work for publication made easier for the editor, but also we can hope to have the data pertaining to future volumes of the *Archivi Reali di Ebla* very quickly available in the format which I am describing.

The second part of my paper deals with the general concept of distribution disks. To disseminate data in disk form is an obvious step to take, given the current general availability of personal computers. Yet there are some significant considerations to be made. While computer use is widespread, it is not necessarily so as yet for computer literacy. By this I mean that in a broad sense computer use is generally limited to its lowest common denominator: in an undergraduate class of 60 which I taught recently, some 40 students produced their papers on word processors; but when I made class notes available on disk, only two students took advantage of the opportunity. A similar ratio might obtain among the intended users of *Cybernetica Mesopotamica*. In distributing data on disk, we aim therefore not only to serve, but also to stimulate, a need.

At this point, my first goal is to make the *primary data* available in a *cohesive and well-structured* format. The second goal is to provide *programs* that will allow an effective *interactive use* of the data.

As for the data: The most basic format of our distribution disks is that of graphemic transliteration. While this may appear simple enough, real problems arise as soon as one tries to build a data base that goes beyond one type of text: harmonization is critical if one is to develop a uniform approach to data retrieval, as for instance with sign concordances. In addition, standard transliterations are hybrid systems which include other levels of representation besides graphemics. We have tried to give as full and as precise a representation of the graphemic level as possible: the resulting encoding system seems to us sufficiently transparent to be accessible to Assyriologists, but at the same time sufficiently differentiated to account for all relevant graphemic phenomena. These data can be used with any conventional word-processor, utilizing at a minimum such simple but powerful functions as word or character searches. To minimize potential problems, only basic ASCII characters (essentially, those that are visible on the keyboard) are used in the primary encoding, so that for instance special characters such as *šin* are represented by a sequence of two characters (s and circumflex in this particular case). Separate programs are provided for those who wish to change their data to either show on the screen or print on paper special characters, including cuneiform.

Certain sets of data will be coded for aspects other than graphemic, and issued as such on separate disks. For instance, the royal letters of Babylon had been fully encoded on the mainframe computer for morpho-lexical analysis by John Hayes, myself and others, and have also been analyzed for historical categories by Patricia Oliansky and others. Morpho-lexical analysis of the personal names from Ebla had been started under the supervision of I. J. Gelb, and will now be continued in collaboration with Alfonso Archi, Pelio Fronzaroli and Lucio Milano by James Platt, Joseph Pagan, Mark Arrington and myself. The encoding manual for morpho-lexical categories, which I have prepared, corresponds in some measure to a compacted version of Akkadian grammar.

The full use of the data will however be done in an interactive environment through some type of programs. The format of our data files is so clearly defined that those adept at it can more easily use them in their programming. But we will at the same time make available a number of our own programs which will allow various types of manipulation of the data. Some are simple utility programs which allow to format or manipulate the texts in different ways for various types of personal use. Some are more complex interactive programs that allow, for instance, to derive selective indices within or across disk boundaries. More complex programs yet will allow in depth analysis with, for instance, a statistical base. Finally, we also recommend certain commercial programs that seem especially useful for interfacing with our data. Some programs will be made available routinely on data disks, but program disks as such will also be issued periodically, and will contain updated versions of all major non-commercial programs available directly from us. One direct result of this approach will be, I hope, an effective contribution to real computer literacy, in the sense, for instance, that these programs may be used not only for our own data disks, but also for data being prepared for publication or simply being studied by individual scholars and students.

An ancillary type of disks will contain secondary literature. On the one hand, we will distribute on disk the text portion of some of the volumes which are being published in book form by Undena. The first example is *Mozan 1*, which will be available shortly. These disks will contain exactly the same text as the printed version, but without formatting commands, so that most word processors will be able to access them. They will thus serve primarily the purpose of greater convenience in scanning through the text portion. A different type of secondary literature will consist of compilations of secondary literature prepared specifically for disk use, whether or not they are also made available at the same time in paper format. One such example is an extensive annotated bibliography on Akkadian grammar, which I have in advanced state of preparation.

As for some practical aspects. Each disk contains one major body of texts, generally corresponding in scope to a book size publication. We are restricting for now our distribution disks to MS-DOS format. Besides the data themselves in graphemic format, there are a number of introductory files, and supplementary files—which I will explain in a moment in connection with three distribution disks which are currently available. While we retain the copyright on the disks to protect them from abuse, there is no limitation on copying and at $1 per disk even the initial distribution price is nominal. Even though in some cases there is room left on the disks, we will in general maintain this correlation between disks and bodies of data: the cost of a disk is a negligible factor, and distribution of, as well as bibliographical references to, disks are easier if such a correlation is maintained. Where necessary, we will use archival compacting to store larger data files that belong together on one disk. At any rate, disks should be considered on the same level as book publications, with an autonomous bibliographical validity of their own.

I will come now to an illustration of specific examples of distribution disks, using three titles which are currently available. The *first* one (*CMT* 1) contains all texts from Terqa excavated through the fourth season, as well as a new edition of all known Khana texts: the texts have been established and annotated by Olivier Rouault, Amanda Podany, and myself. The *second* disk (*CMT* 2) contains the Middle Assyrian Laws as established by Claudio Saporetti. The *third* disk contains indices of all words, numerals and names from *ARET2*, and has been established by James Platt, Joseph Pagan and Mark Arrington.

I have subdivided the distribution disks into five major categories: the data, subdivided in turn into texts (*CMT*) and archaeological materials (*CMA*), the programs (*CMP*), the secondary literature (*CMB*) and the indices (*CMX*). Within these categories, disks will be numbered sequentially without concern for further subtypes, as I had tried to do originally in the first prospectus of *Cybernetica Mesopotamica.* The reason for the elaborate structure envisaged there was to bring out the structural relationships among the various components, which I had at that time anticipated would be numerous. The kind but firm criticism which has recently been made by Edzard of this approach misses, I think, this point and yet, I could have shown validity of the overall system only if the various parts had in fact come to fruition. Now that we can rely on disks for a much more effective and inexpensive distribution of the data, the paper base collection *Cybernetica Mesopotamica* will be limited only to a few representative volumes of data, and otherwise to analytical titles. The electronic files on the other hand will consist exclusively of data and of programs which, when combined, will produce interactively the kind of results that were envisaged as separate series within the paper base collection.

Disks will be further labeled with a letter that will mark the particular edition or "generation" represented in that particular disk. Because of the ease of updating, and because distribution disks will be produced on demand thereby including always the latest "generation," it is important that this be made part of the formal disk "title." The table of contents of a disk, or "directory," is shown as Fig. 1. This is actually a sort of template, a list of all possible files that may occur on a disk, but in practice only some will be found on any given disk. The first file can be activated by pressing an exclamation mark on the keyboard: this will provide basic start-up information, and will proceed to read, as desired, all other introductory files on the disk. Introductory files are marked by a prefix enclosed within two hyphens: files with the prefix C contain information about the system *Cybernetica Mesopotamica* as a whole; prefix D refers to the data contained on that particular disk; prefix E refers to encoding rules, i.e. it provides the encoding manual for the data given: prefix F refers to the file formatting characteristics used in the disk; prefix G refers to general overviews of the data, such as statistical summaries or compositional analysis;

prefix I refers to indices and prefix P to programs: while separate indices files are redundant because they can be generated through the use of programs provided, they are occasionally included for the benefit of those who are not as yet fully familiar with the operation of the computer. (It is for the same reason that I have avoided using subdirectories and have resorted instead to the use of file prefixes.)

The second set of files, each beginning with a letter T for text (or A for Artifacts in the case of archaeological data) contains the data. Normally, each file will correspond to a single text, although this is not required. Files are labeled sequentially, and the label is repeated on the first line of the file itself, followed by the actual bibliographical reference to the text itself.

As indicated, utility programs allow various types of reformatting. For instance, one program merges the individual data files into a single large file, and adds the bibliographical reference in front of each line: while this makes the size of the file considerably larger, and makes it less manageable for certain operations or certain word processors, it may in other cases serve a useful purpose, for instance for global searches within the corpus. Another program changes the two character clusters (e.g. s and circumflex for shin) into single characters while yet another (not fully implemented yet) will provide the possibility of converting a normal transliteration into standardized cuneiform characters, without re-entering the data. Two cuneiform programs are planned to work in conjunction with two commercially available programs which already provide a number of other advantages a relatively low cost (Lettrix and Multi-Lingual Scholar).

-C-FILES

FILES ON CM DIRECTORIES (March 21, 1987)

CM directories may contain any one of the following files

!.EXE	gives first orientation and reads introductory files
-C-	(prefix for general files about Cybernetica Mesopotamica)
-C—PREF	brief preface to system as a whole
-C-FILES	describes introductory files (=i.e., this file)

-C-INTR	describes Cybernetica Mesopotamica as a system
-C-SIGNS	cuneiform signs with unknown reading, not in standard lists
-C-TITLS	catalog of titles in Cybernetica Mesopotamica
-C-UTIL	utility programs available for further use of data bases
-D-	(prefix for files dealing with data on this disk)
-D—PREF	brief preface to data base on this disk
-D—VERS	synopsis of characteristics of version on this disk
-D-BIBL	list of references sorted in bibliographical order
-D-CATEG	identification of data items by provenience, date, type, etc.
-D-EPIGR	documents as artifacts (field numbers, archaeological settings)
-D-HARMO	harmonization principles and changes from established edition
-D-INTRO	general introduction to data base included in this disk
-D-NOTES	notes on specific, unique passages
-D-REF	list of references sorted in the order of the data
-D-REFCO	concordance between data files and references
-E-	(prefix for files with information about encoding)
-E-TG	encoding manual for texts, graphemic format
-E-TM	encoding manual for texts, morphological format
-F-	(prefix for files which explain file format for data files)
-F-G	data entry format for texts, connected graphemic version
-F-GI	output format for texts, alphabetical list of items
-F-GO	output format for texts, alphabetical list of occurrences
-F-GT	same as -F-G, but with volume label on each text line
-G-	(prefix for general information outside current scope)
-G-COMPS	compositional analysis of basic data unit (e.g., text outline)
-G-TAB	tabulation of numeric data (e.g. summaries of entries by type)
-I-Xxxa	(prefix for files with indices to data files) X - CME data files (A, S or T) xx - volume (1 though 99) a - version (a through z)
-I-Xxxa#.GI	numerals: lexical items with totals
-I-Xxxa#.GO	occurrences with references
-I-XxxaD.GI	divine names: lexical items with totals
-I-XxxaD.GO	occurrences with references
-I-XxxaG.GI	geographical names: lexical items with totals

-I-XxxaG.GO	occurrences with references
-I-XxxaN.GI	names (various): lexical items with totals
-I-XxxaN.GO	occurrences with references
-I-XxxaP.GI	personal names: lexical items with totals
-I-XxxaP.GO	occurrences with references
-I-XxxaW.GI	words (other than above): lexical items with totals
-I-XxxaW.GO	occurrences with references

-P-	(prefix for program files)
-P-xxxxx.XPL	explains goals and procedures for program "xxxxx" (e.g., ADDT)
-P-ADDT	adds publication titles to individual records
-P-NDXO	establishes lexical items by lexical items
-P-NDXI	establishes lexical items by items
-P-REMT	removes publication titles from individual records

Xxxa(-zz). data files labeled as follows:

- X CME (Cybernetica Mesopotamica, Electronic files)
  - A - archaeological materials
  - S - secondary literature
  - T - texts
- xx sequential number of CMX disk (from -1 to 99)
  - A1 to T99
- a generation of CMX disk (from A to Z)
  - A1a to T99z
- (-zz) sequential number of files for given disk (optional)
  - A1a-01 to T99z999
- -(—) extension identifying type of data
  - G - graphemic version
  - GO - graphemic index of occurrences

T1A-01.G

T	CME (Cybernetica Mesopotamica, Electronic Files)
1	disk number
A	generation
-01	text number
.G	extension specifying format

MAARAV 5–6 (Spring, 1990): 33–48

ʾĔDAYIN/TOTE—ANATOMY OF A SEMITISM IN JEWISH GREEK

RANDALL BUTH
SUMMER INSTITUTE OF LINGUISTICS, POB 44456, NAIROBI

It is with pleasure that I offer this study[1] to a man of truly wide interests and impressive achievements. The topic is rooted in Aramaic studies but stretches beyond them into the linguistic backgrounds of the Gospels and Jewish Greek. These are a few of the areas in which Professor Segert has taught and published.

1. Introduction

The history and functions of the words אדין *ʾĕdayin* and באדין *bēdayin* contribute to the character of Imperial Aramaic and reflect linguistic processes that have not often been addressed in Aramaic studies. This paper will try and elucidate why the use of *ʾĕdayin* developed in Imperial Aramaic and also how it was used in conjunction with *bēdayin* in Biblical Aramaic. From those results we will look at the use of the words in Qumran and then use this Aramaic perspective as a background for outlining facts and theories concerning Hebrew and Aramaic sources to the Gospels and Jewish Greek during the Second Temple period. Some of the conclusions are far-reaching and show that this simple word "then" is a significant touchstone for source criticism. It is like a fingerprint

1. This study develops an idea first presented in Buth, "Perspectives in Gospel Discourse Studies," *Selected Technical Articles Related to Translation* 6 (Dallas: Summer Institute of Linguistics, 1981). I would like to thank David Bivin for helpful comments on this present paper. All responsibility remains with the author.

that distinguishes Aramaic from Hebrew. "Then" points toward a Hebrew background for Mark and Luke but demonstrates some kind of Aramaic connection for Matthew.

2. *ᵓĔDAYIN* in Old Aramaic

The Aramaic inscriptions from 900 B.C.E. to 700 B.C.E. are remarkable for their lack of *ᵓĕdayin*, "then." By and large, the inscriptions either use *wa-* "and," *pa-* "and, in addition," or no conjunction at all at the beginning of a clause. This is similar to other languages of the period like Hebrew, Phoenician, Moabite, and Ugaritic which did not commonly use either an adverb "then" or a cognate to *ᵓĕdayin* as a narrative conjunction. Old Aramaic knew earlier forms of *ᵓĕdayin* (e.g., *ᵓzy*, Ashur ostracon, line 14), but it was very restricted in comparison with Imperial Aramaic.

3. The Need for 'Then' in Imperial Aramaic

As Aramaic became widely used as a diplomatic and administrative language in the middle of the first millennium B.C.E. some profound structural changes occurred. Contact with Assyro-Akkadian[2] resulted in different word order rules for Aramaic. Aramaic used a Verb-Subject-Object order in the Old period and only allowed one element to precede the verb. In Imperial Aramaic the language is still basically VSO, but more than one element is allowed to precede the verb, verbs are sometimes withheld until the end of the clause, and single elements before the verb are much more frequent than in Old Aramaic.

In Old Aramaic sequentiality is generally correlated to verb-initial clauses. That is, the normal, sequential progression of events in a narrative was described with verb-initial clauses. The advancement of the narrative was broken by putting some element before the verb. This distinction was compromised in the Imperial dialect. Frequently, SVO clauses were used for events that were sequential in the narrative and otherwise "foregrounded"[3] or part of the main

2. See R. Buth, *Aramaic Word Order From the Perspectives of Functional Grammar and Discourse Analysis* (Ph.D. dissertation, UCLA, 1987).

3. "Foreground" refers to a pragmatic parameter that strongly correlates with a semantic distinction of "the next event in the narrative." "Pragmatic" refers to a

line of events. Consequently, the overall system of the language would be more clearly marked if another marker was added to word order in order to mark sequentiality and foreground: hence the introduction of "then" to the repertoire of common Aramaic conjunctions. In fact, *ʾĕdayin/bēdayin* were not the only words so used. In the Ahiqar narrative from Elephantine one finds *qrbtʾ*[4] and the Aramaic text of the Behistun inscription records *ʾḥr*, which Ahiqar also uses (ll. 8, 11). These different words reflect independent development within Aramaic dialects. For Jewish Aramaic, it was the words *ʾĕdayin/bēdayin* that were used to reinforce the marking of sequentiality.

4. Two Words for 'Then' in Biblical Aramaic

The need to mark sequentiality more clearly explains why a word for "then" is used in Biblical Aramaic (BA) but it does not explain why two words were used. The answer to this comes from positing another parameter: "more closely connected in predictability-consequentiality." "Predictability" refers to events that are culturally more expected. For an example, compare the following:

(1) He knocked on the door. (Predictably) The woman opened.
(2) He knocked on the door. (Unpredictably) The house collapsed.

The first example is culturally more predictable than the second. In English, the first example could have signalled this closer connection by joining the clauses together with "and."

"Consequentiality" is also often connected with predictablity in a marking system. In the second example, if "and" was used between the clauses the closer connection would signal the second event as a direct consequence of the first.

It is possible to propose several possible functions to explain the difference between *ʾĕdayin* and *bēdayin* in Biblical Aramaic. We will look at several texts in order to show that other functions and structural devices like the beginning of a paragraph, more thematic

communication situation in which an author may choose to mark a clause "as though it were the next event in the story" even though on strict semantic grounds it does not represent a temporal advancement from the last clause.

4. Cf. A. Cowley, *Aramaic Papyri of the Fifth Century B.C.* (Oxford: Clarendon, 1923), and F. Rosenthal, *An Aramaic Handbook* I/2 (Wiesbaden: Harrassowitz, 1967): 14.

events, new subjects, subject-initial clauses, verb-initial clauses, perfect-suffix verbs, participles, or subordinate clauses do not affect the choice of *ʾĕdayin* or *bēdayin.* Etymology suggests that a function related to a "closer connection" will prove correct. After all, within a clause, the preposition *bə* normally marks case relationships for which English uses "in" and "with."

Verb Forms with ʾĕdayin and bēdayin

Verb forms in the clauses do not distinguish or explain the use of *ʾĕdayin* and *bēdayin* since both words for "then" can be used with the basic verb forms.

Perfect verbs with *ʾĕdayin*: Dan 2:15, 17, 19, 19, 25, 48; 3:24; 4:16; 5:6; 6:7, 12, 15, 19, 22, 7:19; Ezr 4:23, 5:4, 9, 16; 6:13. With *bēdayin*: Dan 2:14, 35, 46; 3:13, 13, 19, 21, 26, 30; 5:3, 13, 24, 29, 6:13, 14, 16, 17, 24, 26; 7:1; Ezr 4:24; 5:2; 6:1.

Participles with *ʾĕdayin*: Dan 5:8, 9; 6:6. With *bēdayin*: Dan 3:3, 26, 4:4; 5:17 (Masoretic text, but should be read as a suffix-verb according to 6:14), 7:11.

Participle with *hwy*, "to be," with *ʾĕdayin*: Dan 6:4, 5. With *bēdayin*: none.

Imperfect with *ʾĕdayin*: Ezr 5:5 *ytybwn* (future-modal meaning). With *bēdayin*: Dan 6:20 *yqwm* (simple past, cf. *ytwb* 4:31–33).

Word Order

Various word orders do not explain why one form of *ʾĕdayin* is chosen over the other. (However, the relative frequencies of *ʾĕdayin*/*bēdayin* do correspond to what may be expected from what is know about the functions of the word orders; see below.)

Verb-Subject order with *ʾĕdayin*: Dan 5:8; 6:19; Ezr 5:9 (no explicit subject). With *bēdayin* Dan 2:35; 3:3, 26, 26; 4:4; 5:3, 17, 29; 6:13 (no explicit subject), 6:14 (no explicit subject); Ezr 4:24; 5:2.

Subject-Verb order with *ʾĕdayin*: Dan 2:19; 3:24; 6:4, 5, 6, 7, 12; Ezr 5:16. With *bēdayin*: Dan 2:14, 46, 3:13, 13, 19, 21, 30; 5:13; 6:16, 17, 26; Ezr 6:1.

(Noun)-(X)-Verb order with *ʾĕdayin*: Dan 2:17, 19, 25, 48; 4:16; 5:6, 9; 6:15, 22; 7:19; Ezr 4:23, 5:4; 6:13. With *bēdayin*: Dan 2:14; 5:24; 6:20, 24; 7:1, 11.

Subordination

The words *ʾĕdayin* and *bēdayin* were given the meanings "when, as, because" by Hayyim Rosén.[5] He claimed that the "adverb . . . has thus become subordinative." This was part of a proposal to reinterpret radically the verb morphology of the Aramaic of Daniel and should be rejected. It is clear that *ʾĕdayin* and *bēdayin* do not mark subordinate clauses of a narrative but, on the contrary, connect clauses that are part of the main event line of the story. More to the point in this article, one cannot say that just one of the two words for "then" is a subordinating temporal conjunction, "when," and the other is not. We have two examples of successive *ʾĕdayin* and *bēdayin* which cannot be taken as subordinate:

אדין לדניאל . . . רזא גלי
אדין דניאל ברך לאלה שמיא

Then to Daniel . . . the secret was revealed.
Then Daniel blessed the God of heaven. (Dan 2:19)

באדין נבוכדנצר . . . אמר להיתיה . . .
באדין גבריא אלך היתיו . . .

Then Nebuchadnezzar . . . commanded to bring . . .
Then the men were brought in . . . (Dan 3:13)

Neither of these clauses is subordinate to the other.

Paragraph-initial clauses

The clauses in Dan 3:13 above, with *bēdayin*, do not seem to be marking new paragraphs and certainly this is not a function in distinction to *ʾĕdayin.*

Change of Subject

Both *ʾedayin* and *bēdayin* are used with different subjects from the previous clause. They can also be used when continuing the same subject, though this use of "then" may imply a unit break,

5. Rosen, "On the Use of the Tenses in the Aramaic of Daniel," *JSS* 6 (1961): 189.

i.e., a new paragraph (*ʾĕdayin*: Dan 2:17, 48; 6:7, 19; *bēdayin*: Dan 2:14; 3:30; 7:1).

More Thematic versus Less Thematic

Thematicity is a difficult parameter to assess because it is "pragmatic" and not "semantic."[6] That is, it would reflect the evaluation of the author and not an identifiable semantic or syntactic feature. One must ask whether *bēdayin* really marks clauses as "more thematic" than the *ʾĕdayin* clauses, or vice versa. Many clauses would fit such an analysis but there are some problem texts that have a more probable solution. For example, Ezra 4:23–24 uses both *ʾĕdayin* and *bēdayin*, *ʾĕdayin* introducing the actual events while *bēdayin* only introduces a statement that the work was stagnant for a certain time. (That is, it is less transitive, durative-stative, and negative, and thus unlikely to be part of the main event-line of the story.)

אדין מן די פרשגן . . . קרי . . . אזלו . . . ובטלו . . .
באדין בטלת עבידת בית אלהא . . . והות בטלא

Then when the letter . . . was read . . . they went . . . and stopped . . .
Then ceased the-work-of-the-temple (Sub.) . . . and was ceasing for . . .

A better explanation than "thematicity" for Ezr 4:23–24 is that the *bēdayin* marks an outcome/result as "closely connected."

Another example of reversed thematicity comes from Dan 6:22–24:

אדין דניאל עם מלכא מלל . . .
באדין מלכא שגיא טאב עלוהי

Then Daniel with-the-king spoke . . .
Then the king, greatly it-pleased him.

6. In fact, after preliminary work on the discourse grammar of BA I orally proposed an analysis based on thematicity in a paper at the SBL Pacific Coast Regional meeting, March, 1982. It is not accepted here.

In the context, the reply of Daniel is a significant event and this significance is probably reflected in the verb-final word order.[7] However, 6:24, in relation to 6:22, is quite expected, predictable, and not likely to marked as *more* thematic than 6:22. But 6:24 has *bēdayin.*

Although I conclude that *bēdayin* is not directly marking prominence (and such a case for *ʾĕdayin* is even less likely), it needs to be pointed out that there is a natural prominence to the final event of a narrative chain.[8] So one might expect that a particle used to mark more closely related events would often be used on events that could be argued to more thematic or more prominent. Consequently, most clauses with *bēdayin* in Daniel and Ezra happen to fit as "more thematic," though that is not what it is marking.

More Closely Connected

Within this short article we will not take the time to examine every context of a clause with *bēdayin* or *ʾĕdayin.* Instead, we will state a conclusion that seems satisfactory from contextual examinations, linguistic viability, etymological considerations, and a statistical profile.

Both *ʾĕdayin* and *bēdayin* at the beginning of a clause mark the clause as temporally sequential. In addition, *bēdayin* marks the clause as "more closely connected," either in the sense of being "more predictable, more expected," or in the sense of being a "more direct" result, response, or outcome of the previous event(s).

As for a *contextual* examination, one can argue that this fits all of the occurrences in Biblical Aramaic. However, it must be admitted that most cases are not provable. The context would often allow an author either to mark a clause as "closely connected," or not mark it. The importance of this device for the reader is that it shows how the author intended to link the events of the story together.

The *linguistic* viability of such a parameter of "narrative closeness" can be demonstrated by mentioning that many languages

7. Cf. Buth (N 2), *passim.*

8. Such a prominence theory is developed in J. Beekman, J. Callow, and J. Kopesec, *Semantic Structure of Written Communication* (unpublished manuscript in "fifth edition," 1981), available through the Summer Institute of Linguistics, Dallas.

have connectors that mark consequence or outcome in narrative. For example, in Greek one finds *oun* "therefore" and *ōste* "so that" in narrative, while in English one finds "so" and "so then." This is not to suggest that English or Greek use their connectors in the same manner or frequencies as Aramaic, only that the marking of "more direct consequence" occurs.

Etymologically, it has been pointed out above that *bēdayin* includes a morpheme for "in/with," which might imply a closer connection than the word without it.

Finally, the *statistical* profile with word order was suggestive. The clauses with non-Subject material placed before the verb break up the flow of VSO-structured clauses. They can be expected to be not as closely connected, since new topicalization will be part of the reason for the intervening material. This turns out to be true. Fourteen such clauses used *ʾĕdayin* while only five used *bēdayin*, although the two words are equally frequent in BA (28 *ʾĕdayin*, 29 *bēdayin*). On the other hand, verb-initial clauses, which do not mark any topicalization, which put an event in the foreground as "sequential" and which more directly advance the narrative, have only three examples with *ʾĕdayin* but 12 with *bēdayin*. One does not expect identical overlap with the parameters that affect word order and the parameters that affect *ʾĕdayin/bēdayin*. What is helpful is that a predicted tendency and correlation occurs. Of course, such small numbers are not decisive for the proposal, only supportive.

5. Greek Translation Practice

Having shown the need for developing a connector for sequentiality and proposed an explanation for the *ʾĕdayin/bēdayin* distinction, we need to call attention to Greek translation practice, since this will affect our discussion of the Gospels and Semitisms in Greek.

Simply put, Greek translators used *tote* for both *ʾĕdayin* and *bēdayin*. The precise details become a little complicated because of textual problems with LXX, Theodotion, Masoretic Text, and unpublished Qumran fragments. The figures published by McNeile[9] can still give us a clear picture even if they are necessarily approximate.

9. A. McNeile, "*Tote* in St. Matthew," *JTS* 12 (1911): 127–128.

> In Dan. ii iii v vi אדין or בידין occurs 45 times, these instances being represented as follows: *tote* LXX 32, Theod. 22; *kai* LXX 8, Theod. 20. Five times the LXX has no word to correspond with it, and Theod. once. Moreover the LXX has *tote* 8 times, and Theod. 3 times, where the particle is absent from the present Aramaic text. In Ezr. iv v vi it occurs 11 times in the Aramaic, in 10 of which the LXX has *tote*, and the remaining passage no corresponding word.[10]

This becomes significant for New Testament studies because *tote* is virtually non-existent in LXX translation from Hebrew narrative. We will look at some sample Greek material later to confirm that narrative *tote* is not Attic or Hellenistic Greek. First, we must complete the survey of the use of *ʾĕdayin* in Aramaic.

6. The Genesis Apocryphon

The manuscript discoveries in the Judean desert have provided scholarship with an Aramaic narrative from the century before the Gospels were written. The Genesis Apocryphon is the best text that we possess for studying the development of linguistic structures from Imperial and Biblical Aramaic into a later stage of literary Jewish Aramaic. Naturally, anyone who proposes Aramaic influence on the Greek Gospels must pay close attention to this scroll.

Some general comments are needed in order to evaluate the data. Only columns 2 and 19–22 provide extended context for studying narrative functions in the language. Furthermore, there is a noticeable distinction between the grammar of column 2 and columns 19–22. The word order of column 2 appears to be good example of Imperial Aramaic while columns 19–22 are very close to the word order that one finds in later Jewish Aramaic. This may represent different sources or different styles, but in any case, one must bear in mind the differences.

From the discussion on the function of "then" in Imperial Aramaic, one would expect to find differences in the function of "then" between column 2 and columns 19–22. The Aramaic dialects with a stricter VSO order and less ambiguous marking of foreground and sequentiality would be expected to make less use of narrative "then." This is the case, both in Qumran Aramaic and later Jewish Aramaic.

10. *Ibid.*: 128.

Column 2. *ʾĕdayin/bēdayin* occur six times in the first 19 lines of text. This gives an "Imperial" sound to the language, but three of the six are not simple narrative connectors. In line 1 *bēdayin* follows *hʾ* "behold." In line 11 *ʾĕdayin* occurs in the middle of the clause "greatly my heart upon me then was changed." In line 13 *bēdayin* serves in conjunction with a "when" clause: "when . . . , then . . ."

The three occurrences of narrative "then" are sequential, they probably correctly distinguish between *ʾĕdayin* and *bēdayin*, and they may begin paragraphs. At lines 3 and 19 *bēdayin* begins a new narrative unit that follows as a possible consequence from the preceding material (= "so then . . ."). Both of these places appear to have a blank space between narrative *then* and the preceding sentence. The blank space may serve to mark a new paragraph. The third narrative "then" occurs in line 8. Here, *ʾĕdayin* introduces a dramatic point in the narrative with verb-final word order where Lamech's wife assures him that he is the father of the child. (A blank space may not appear before this "then," though the manuscript is damaged.)

Columns 19–22. Column 19 does not contain a "then."

Bēdayin occurs in 20:21. It probably begins a paragraph, is preceded by a blank space, and introduces material that serves as an outcome or result of what preceded. It should also be pointed out that at 20:24 a "when" is not followed by "then" as in 2:12–13.

Column 21 does not contain a "then."

Column 22 has three examples of "then," two of which can be called narrative connectors.

ואברם באדין הוא יתב בחברון

And Abram at-that-time was dwelling in Hebron. (22:3)

In 22:3 *bēdayin* is not a narrative connector.

באדין קרב מלכא די סודם ואמר לאברם

So-then approached the-king of Sodom and said to Abram (22:18)

This begins a paragraph and follows a blank space in the manuscript.

אדין אמר אברם למלך סודם

Then said Abram to-the-king of Sodom (22:20)

This also follows a blank space and begins a paragraph. The use of *ʾĕdayin* instead of *bēdayin* appears purposeful, in accord with what we found in BA. Here, contrary to the request of the king of Sodom, Abram makes an oath and pledges to give him all of the booty. The introduction to the speech is a word-for-word translation of the Hebrew, with the exception of the addition of *ʾĕdayin*. The speech itself also follows the Hebrew text very closely.

7. *ʾĔdayin/Bēdayin* in Later Aramaic

By and large, narrative *ʾĕdayin/bēdayin* drops out of later Aramaic writings. This can be partly explained by the fact that Jewish Aramaic and Syriac are more consistent VSO languages than the old Imperial dialect. This does not mean that *ʾĕdayin* never occurs or that it has not left a trace. In the Old Syriac Gospel of Matthew one finds *hydyn* for *tote* and later Syriac has apparently fused natural Aramaic *ʾĕdayin* with Greek *de* "and, but" to produce *den*, a conjunction that behaves very much like Greek *de*, even to being placed after the first element of the clause.

8. *Tote* in Greek Narrative

In order for *tote* to be significant as a tool in source or text criticism of an ancient text it needs to be verified that it is not functioning as would be normal in Greek. It is easy to show that a narrative *tote* did not develop within Greek. For witnesses that are reasonably close to the New Testament we can look at Josephus (literary Greek, end of 1st century C.E.) and "The Martyrdom of Polycarp" (common Greek, middle 2nd century C.E.).

Josephus has left us two very long histories, *The Antiquities of the Jews* and *The Jewish War*. In both of them he uses *tote*, but not as a narrative conjunction. For example, in *Antiquities* 18:30 and 18:81 one finds *tote* near the beginning of a clause. These read *kai tote oun* "and then therefore" and *kai dē tote* "and indeed then." In neither case does *tote* stand alone as a conjunction but is an adverb supported by conjunctions. This is also clear at 18:91 where *tote* begins the clause: *tote de en tē Antōnia* . . . "*and* at-that-time in the Antonia fortress . . ." Greek *de* is the conjunction. The two other occurrences of *tote* in the first 100 sections of book

18 are at 67 and 78. In both places *tote* is far inside the clause. The same thing happens in *The Jewish War*, e.g., 1:91 *ginetai de kai tote kreittōn* "but he got the upper hand even this time . . ."

"The Martyrdom of Polycarp" is a relatively short narrative within a letter. The register of language is more colloquial than Josephus and is closer to the New Testament. Only one *tote* occurs in the book, at 12:3: *tote edoxen autois homothumadon epiboēsai* "then it seemed good to them all together to call . . ." This example is close to Matthew's use. However, because this is the only example in the book it is better to view this as asyndeton plus *tote* co-occurring in an isolated example rather than any kind of Aramaic influence. The lack of any other example of *tote* in the "Martyrdom" shows just how un-Greek narrative *tote* is.

9. *Tote* in the Gospels

The Gospel of John has eight occurrences of *tote* in the narrative framework. Of these, four are *tote oun*; two are *hōs* . . . *tote*; one is *hote* . . . *tote*, and one is *meta* . . . *tote*. The result is that John does not have one example of a narrative *tote* based strictly on an Aramaic paradigm. This fits all theories that state that John was originally written in Greek. It could provide circumstantial evidence that out of Hebrew, Aramaic, and Greek, Aramaic was not his mother-tongue or at least was not a major literary influence. Actually, all that it shows is that he had a reasonable control of Greek conjunctions.

Mark is even more remarkable than John. There is not one example of *tote* in the narrative framework of the gospel. This is surprising in the light of what is often written about Mark. Mark is the one noted for a "rough," "un-Greek" style and this has often been attributed to Aramaic. However, in the light of what is known about Aramaic narrative, Aramaic cannot be assumed to account for Mark's style. Hebrew remains a strong possibility, but Aramaic is out.

The lack of narrative *tote* in Mark does not simply result from a dislike of the word or ignorance of it. *Tote* occurs six times in the gospel (2:20, 3:27, 13:14, 21, 26, 27). All of these are within quoted speech and all would fit in Hebrew as well. It also happens that all six have parallels in either Matthew (3:27, 13:21, 27) or both Matthew and Luke. Wherever Mark did use the word in his gospel it found a place in synoptic tradition.

Luke raises several interesting points in regard to *tote*. First of all, Luke does not reflect Aramaic narrative style since *tote* only occurs twice in the narrative framework, at 21:10 and 24:45. The gospel is quite long so that two occurrences of *tote* at the beginning of a clause are compatible with a Hebrew-based source. In terms of narrative conjunctions one must reckon with the possibility of Hebrew source(s) while one must doubt any suggestion of Aramaic.

The conclusions based on the general structure of the narrative are even more reliable for Luke than for Mark since Luke uses *tote* more frequently in the quoted speech sections (Luke 5:35; 6:42; 11:24, 26; 13:26; 14:9, 10, 21; 16:16; 21:20, 21, 27; 23:30). It is clear that Luke did not remove *tote* from his sources out of antipathy towards the word. Within quoted speech he frequently uses the word, and at the beginning of clauses. However, most of these are in future contexts[11]: "at that time . . ." (5:35; 6:42; 11:26; 13:26; 14:9, 10; 23:30) or with some additional word or structure to make it more appropriate in Greek (5:35; 6:42; 14:9, 10; 16:16; 21:20, 27). Luke does not regularly use *tote* as a narrative conjunction patterned on Aramaic.

There is one suggestive use of *tote* in a parable: Luke 14:21, the parable of the "Great Supper." It is told in narrative format with a succession of past tense verbs. In v. 21 a new paragraph begins with "the lord of the house" becoming angry and giving an order. This development in the parable begins with *tote*. One would not expect *tote* if the story was literally translated from a Hebrew source. Likewise, one would not expect it in normal Greek. But one occurrence is not a lot of evidence for ascertaining a source language.[12] Tote does not prove that Aramaic was the original source language for the story but it does suggest the possibility.

In summary, throughout the whole gospel, Luke generally reflects Hebrew style in regard to narrative conjunctions (see above) and specifically does not reflect Aramaic narrative style, although it is possible that the story in Luke 14:16–24 may come from an Aramaic background.

11. The future context is quite Hebraic and matches a prophetic style.

12. Luke 14:18 *apo mias* "from one" has often been cited as an Aramaism (see M. Black, *An Aramaic Approach to the Gospels and Acts*[3] [Oxford: Clarendon, 1967]: 113, for a summary). However, it does not make good sense as either Aramaic or Hebrew and only partial sense as Syriac. It should be considered Koine Greek (cf. W. Arndt, F. Gingrich, F. Danker, *A Greek-English Lexicon of the New Testa-ment*[2] [Chicago: Univ. of Chicago, 1979]: 88). Underlying Hebrew or Aramaic could have been *kʾḥd*, "like one, with one accord."

Matthew is strikingly different from the other evangelists in his use of *tote*. There are about 90 occurrences of *tote* in the gospel, depending on textual readings. Of these, 52 are used at the beginning of a narrative clause and serve as a narrative conjunction. The difference from normal Greek and the other gospels is remarkable and has been noticed by many commentators. The obvious reason for such a frequency of narrative *tote* is Aramaic influence of some kind.

Before investigating the kind of influence reflected in Matthew, we need to look at narrative *tote* to see if it reflects Biblical-Imperial Aramaic or later Qumran Aramaic narrative. The frequency of *tote* in Matthew is more suggestive of Qumran Aramaic. The gospel of Matthew is a great deal longer than the stories of Daniel and Ezra yet they have about the same number of occurrences of narrative "then." Another correspondence with Qumran Aramaic is the common use of "then" at the beginning of paragraphs. Matthew frequently begins paragraphs with narrative *tote* (3:5, 13; 4:1, 5; 9:14; 11:20; 12:22, 38; 15:1, 12; 16:24; 17:19; 18:21; 19:13; 20:20; 22:15; 23:1, 26:3, 14, 31, 36, 45, 52; 27:3, 27, 38). Matthew also uses *tote* at a peak in a paragraph or as a concluding event (3:15; 4:10, 11; 8:26; 9:6, 29, 37; 12:13; 15:28; 16:12, 20; 17:13; 19:27; 22:21; 26:38, 50, 65, 67, 74; 27:9, 13, 26, 58; 28:10). This has a parallel in column 2:8 of the Genesis Apocryphon. Matthew rarely uses *tote* more than once in any paragraph unit, though it does occur (cf. 3:13–15, 4:10–11). Particularly towards the end of the gospel, Matthew uses *tote* to begin paragraphs that do not have some other device at the beginning of the unit like "genitive absolute" (26:6, 20, 26, 47; 27:1, 57; 28:11) or a time phrase (26:1, 17, 20; 27:1, 45, 57, 62; 28:1). It would be nice to have more Aramaic narrative material from the period with which to compare Matthew. With the material at hand we can conclude that Matthew is reasonably compatible with what is known from the Genesis Apocryphon.

10. *Tote* and Gospel Source Criticism

Mark and Luke. The lack of narrative *tote* in both Mark and Luke is a fact whose significance has been overlooked in gospel criticism. This paper cannot enter into the general question of Semitisms in the gospels. The sociolinguistic conditions of the first century and the Semitic character of the Greek in the gospels has made the question of Semitisms a perennial issue in gospel research. One of the Semitic features is the relation of *kai* to *de* as a clause conjunction. For Luke, this is particularly important because the ratio of *kai* to *de* in Acts is closer to the norms of Koine Greek than the gospel, while even in Acts the last half of the book has a lower *kai* to *de* ratio than the first half.[13] Unfortunately, most discussions have centered on "Aramaisms" in the gospels because of the old assumption that Aramaic was the only Semitic language in common use in the first century. With a broader knowledge of both Aramaic and Hebrew as a result of the Judean desert discoveries, it is possible to distinguish more accurately Aramaic narrative from Hebrew narrative, even in Greek translation. *Tote* is a diagnostic word of extreme importance for differentiating Hebrew and Aramaic narrative during this period.

The results from looking at *tote* are that any major Semitic sources for Mark and Luke should be Hebrew. Mark and Luke do not reflect reliance on Aramaic narratives. Likewise, they do not reflect the use of Matthew according to the Griesbach hypothesis (see below).

Matthean Sources. The evidence of *tote* in Matthew raises questions of relationship to Mark and Luke. The fact that both Mark and Luke use *tote* within quoted speech suggests that neither one used a text like the Greek of Matthew as a source. It is difficult to believe that Mark and Luke scrupulously omitted all narrative *tote*'s but left many *tote*'s in quoted speech and at the same time produced the Semitic-sounding narrative *kai*'s. One must conclude that common narrative tradition for the synoptic gospels did not have narrative *tote* and that the synoptic narrative tradition ultimately goes back to a Hebrew source, if a Semitic source is assumed.

The narrative *tote*'s in Matthew come from a "special source." Because narrative *tote* occurs throughout the gospel of Matthew, in triple tradition, double tradition, and Matthean material, we must conclude that it is a feature that Matthew himself has brought

13. Nigel Turner (*Grammar of New Testament Greek, Vol. 4: Style* [Edinburgh: Clark, 1976]: 58) gives the following figures for *kai:de*: Lucan "Q" 1.9:1; Lucan material 1.4:1, Luke parallel to Mark 1.2:1, selection from first half of Acts 1.0:1, selection from second half of Acts 0.6:1, "we" sections 0.5:1. This can be compared to 0.24:1 for Josephus, 0.5:1 for the Didache, 0.6:1 for Epictetus, and 0.92:1 for the papyri.

to the text. This tells us something about Matthew's background. On the basis of his use of *tote* it is very probable that Matthew knew Aramaic. Matthew has been influenced by Aramaic literary style. Probably Aramaic was his first or most developed language. Greek was not his primary language. This means a Palestinian milieu for the composition of the gospel and even a traditional "tax collector" background for the author are distinct possibilities. The view that Matthew is non-Jewish or monolingual in Greek becomes less probable. (This paper cannot pursue logical "possibilities" such as a non-Jewish author who knew Aramaic, Greek, and Hebrew.) Matthew chose to write his gospel in Greek and has made use of written Greek materials while at the same time exposing his own Aramaic literary background.

CONCLUSION

The importance of narrative *tote* to gospel criticism is clear. It is one of the facts that theories of gospel origins must take into account. Narrative *tote* or the lack of it is a good tool for source criticism because it is on the fringe of an author's conscious activity. It is part of the "glue" of a story that an author, at times almost subconsciously, adds while focusing on the content.

Matthew uses "Aramaic" narrative *tote* while Mark and Luke do not. Without evidence and strong explanations to the contrary, one must assume that common Semitic sources to the synoptic gospels were in Hebrew, that Matthew himself knew Aramaic, and that Matthew is responsible for adding the "Aramaic" narrative style to his gospel.

MAARAV 5-6 (Spring, 1990): 49-52

SUR *MDL* À UGARIT, EN IS 40,15 ET HAB 3,4

HENRI CAZELLES
BIBLIOTHEQUE OECUMENIQUE ET SCIENTIFIQUE D'ÉTUDES BIBLIQUES, PARIS, FRANCE

Comme l'avait recontrée notre distingué sémitisant dans ses études sur la grammaire ugaritique,[1] j'ai rencontré de mon côté cette racine, mais en tout autres circonstances. Il s'agissait de cerner de près les origines de la racine *rûaḥ, rḥ* à Ugarit. Ce dernier mot désigne certainement en plusieurs cas l'atmosphère extérieure à l'homme, sans qu'il s'agisse toujours pour autant du vent. En effet, lorsque la mort du héros Aqhat est au futur, non encore accomplie, il est dit que "son souffle (*npš*) sortira (*tṣi*) de lui comme *rḥ*." Une fois qu'il est mort, le narrateur passe de l'inaccompli à l'accompli: "son souffle est sorti (*yṣat*) comme (l'est) la *rḥ*." Sur l'opposition accompli/inaccompli à Ugarit, S. Segert nous a livré ses réflexions.[2] Elles étaient nuancées et, en ce qui concerne l'exemple susdit, il restait une incertitude car d'excellents spécialistes estiment que l'action porte sur l'action de "sortir" et non sur le fait pour la *npš* d' "être dehors ou dedans."

Ce qui m'a paru trancher le problème, c'est un autre passage tiré cette fois-ci du mythe de Baal. En CTA 5, v, 6–10, celui-ci est

1. S. Segert, *A Basic Grammar of the Ugaritic Language* (Berkeley: Univ. of California, 1984): 191 ("to saddle").

2. Segert, "Verbal Categories of Some Northwest Semitic Languages: A Didactical Approach," *Afroasiatic Linguistics* 2/5 (1975): 9: "The function of the perfect and imperfect tenses in the older prose of the Hebrew Bible can be described by the terms 'perfective' and 'imperfective,' denoting accomplished and non-accomplished actions. For such texts this interpretation seems to be more satisfactory than the conception of subjective aspect."

sommé par Môt de descendre sous terre, non seulement avec deux de ses filles, non seulement avec ses sept pages ou officiers (*ǵlmk*), et ses huit sangliers (*ḫnzr*), mais aussi avec ses nuages (*ʿrpt*), son *rḥ*,ses pluies (*mṭr*) et son *mdl.* Il était clair qu'il s'agissait là de personnes et de phénomènes extérieurs à Baal, et non d'une faculté interne comme son souffle.

Dès l'édition princeps, C. Virolleaud remarquait que, dans une pareille énumération de phénomènes atmosphériques, "le sens ne peut guère être autre que foudre ou tonnerre."[3] Mais quelle était la racine? Etait-ce directement ou par métaphore que *mdl* était ici un phénomène comme la pluie et les nuages? En 1974, A. Caquot et M. Sznycer, tout en traduisant par "foudre" (mais en italique, donc comme une approximation), notaient[4] que les uns avec J. de Moor rattachaient *mdl* à l'akkadien *mu-du-lu*, une sorte de verge, métaphore pour l'éclair servant de verge à ce "chevaucheur des nuées,"[5] que d'autres pensaient à des "seaux" avec Gaster, Driver, Jirku, Rin (hébreu *dlt*, racine *dl*(*l*), d'autres enfin à un "attelage" (Cassuto, Aistleitner) à cause du parallèle *mdl*/*ṣmd* dans l'équipage d'Ashérat en CTA 4, iv, 9, confirmé par la monture de Pughat en CTA 19, 57 (sur une ânesse).

En 1964, M. J. Dahood observait[6] que le sens de *Gespann,* "attelage," convenait mal au contexte; en 1986, R. M. Good fera une observation semblable pour la traduction *saddle*, "selle," invoquant une autre raison:[7] à l'époque du Bronze récent, celle d'Ugarit, on ne sellait pas les animaux, on les guidait seulement avec une corde. M. J. Dahood renvoyait à Isa 40, 15. La comparaison est heureuse puisqu'elle évitait de donner le sense inhabituel de "poussière"[8] au parallèle *šəḥāqîm* de *mar middəlî.* Non moins heureux est le renvoi à Num 24, 7 TM, car *yizzal mayim*

3. C. Virolleuad, *Syria* 15 (1934): 327.

4. A. Caquot et M. Sznycer, *Textes Ougaritiques. Vol. I: Mythes et Légendes* (Paris 1974): 170 note *r*; cf. p. 247.

5. J. de Moor, "Der *mdl* Baals im Ugaritischen," *ZAW* 78 (1966): 69–71: "wie eine Lanze stilisierten Blitz." On pense évidemment, bien que ce ne soit pas dit expressément dans cet article, à "la flamme de l'épée *mhpkt*" qui avec les Chérubins garde l'entrée de l'Eden en Gen 3, 24.

6. M. J. Dahood, *Mélanges Tisserant*, Vol. 1 (Rome 1964): 87.

7. R. M. Good, "Some Ugaritic Words Relating to Draught and Riding Animals," *UF* 16 (1984): 81.

8. Conservé cependent par D. Winton Thomas, "A Drop of a Bucket? Some Observations on the Hebrew Text of Isaiah 40, 15," dans *In Memoriam Paul Kahle* (BZAW 103; Berlin: Töpelmann, 1968): 214–221.

mdlyw du TM peut alors recevoir un sens acceptable. Nous restons dans les contextes de nuages et de pluie. Moins heureuse est la référence à une racine *dll*, "être bas": la préformante *m* sert à former des substantifs et des participes (*mdll*), non des racines verbales. *Mdl* est un bon trilittère; nous allons le retrouver en akkadien.

J. C. Greenfield a bien vu la difficulté lorsque, au lieu de recourir à un *dll*, il a proposé une métathese de *lmd*. Cette racine pourrait dire non seulement "enseigner" mais "lier." Il garde donc l'idée de "seller, atteler."[9]

En 1977–8, travaillant sur la seconde édition des *Canaanite Myths and Legends* de G. R. Driver, J. C. L. Gibson garde "saddle" pour les montures d'Ashérat et de Pughat; mais, lorsqu'il s'agit de Baal et do son équipage, il passe à "thunderbolts."[10] Pour ce dernier sens, il se réfère à l'akk. *mudulu*, "fouet, corde." Il semble distinguer deux racines, mais ne l'affirme pas. Il élimine tout rapprochement avec Zech 9, 9, mais en admet un avec Ps 135, 7. Il y est question en effet de nuages, d'éclairs (vocabulaire différent) et de *rûaḥ*.

Dans le même numéro des *Ugarit-Forschungen* où Good donnait ses raisons pour éliminer la traduction du verbe "to saddle," B. Margalit reprenait la question.[11] Good estimait que la relation du *mdl* verbe et du *mdl* substantif n'était pas claire. Il n'en repoussait pas pour autant l'idée que la corde ou laisse (*guide-rope*) par laquelle on conduisait un animal puisse être pensée comme un "éclair." Il suggérait de plus un rapprochement avec le difficile passage, Hab 3, 4. Dans un contexte de phénomènes lumineux et célestes, l'obscur *mydw lw* serait à lire *m(y)d(w)lw* et viendrait de la racine *mdl*. Margalit quant à lui estime que les deux *mdl* n'en font qu'un. Baal utiliserait un *mdl*, "harnais" (*riding gear*) à titre de coursier (*riding*) des nuages.

En 1986, Good revient à l'hypothèse de la métathèse *mdl*/*lmd* et remarque que la lettre *lamed* dans l'écriture du IIe millénaire a la forme d'une corde.[12] Comme le dessin de la lettre suppose une corde souple, il écarte l'hypothèse d'un "aiguillon pour les boeufs" (*ox-goad*). Il pense lui aussi à une corde pour âne, et ceci malgré le

9. J. C. Greenfield, "Ugaritic *mdl* and its Cognates," *Biblica* 45 (1964): 527–534.

10. J. C. L. Gibson, *Canaanite Myths and Legends* (Edinburgh: Clark, 1977): 150.

11. B. Margalit, "Lexicographical Notes on the Aqhat Epic," *UF* 16 (1984): 1335.

12. R. M. Good, "*Lamed*," *BASOR* 262 (1986): 89–90.

tentant *mlmd* de Jud 3, 31 où l'on voit d'habitude un aiguillon comme arme dans les mains de Shamgar.

La même année, W. G. E. Watson écarte l'hypothèse tant d'une racine *dll* que celle d'une métathèse. Il réétudie la *madalu/mudulu* akkadien,[13] pouvant produire en effet un texte d'Ebla[14] où l'on donne pour harnachement aux chevaux du roi, "une couverture (*aktum*)[15] et quatre *ma-da-LUM* pour deux équidés (IGI.NITA) du roi." Il garde, comme possibilité non prouvée, un rapprochement avec le *ṣerret šamami*, les "laisses du ciel" des textes akkadiens.[16]

Dans le voyage d'Ashérat avec son âne et son *mdl,* elle est accompagnée de la ou des divinité(s) secondaire(s) *qdš w Amrr*. Or celle(s)-ci "luisent comme une torche et comme une étoile" (CTA 4, iv, 15–18). De plus, dans les attributs de Baal convoqué par Môt, *mdl* est placé entre l'atmosphere et la pluie, non près des nuages. Nous sommes dans le lumineux, non dans l'obscur. Il semble donc bien que le sens métaphorique de *mdl* comme une corde, voire un fouet dont il dispose pour mener son attelage, soit déjà acquis à Ugarit. C'est un phénomène lumineux attribué au dieu de l'orage qui mène sa monture, chevauche les nuages, fait se durcir la laisse éclair/aiguillon. Il me semble tout à fait plausible que Isa 40, 15 (Dahood) et Hab 3, 4 (Good) aient conservé cette métaphore de phénomènes célestes sans qu'ils soient désormais bien compris.

13. W. G. E. Watson, "Unravelling Ugaritic *mdl*," *Studi epigrafici e linguistici* 3 (1986): 73–78. On trouvera à la note 5, p. 75, une bibliographie qui complète celle que nous donnons ici.

14. M. G. Biga et L. Milano, "Testi amministrativi. Assegnazioni di Tessuti," *Archivi reali di Ebla* IV/6 64 (XI, 19–XII, 7).

15. Cf. le *ktm* sémitique, "couvrir," Biga-Milano (N 14): note 22.

16. *CAD*, Ṣ: 134–137 et *AHW*: 1092, plus la note de R. Borger en *JCS* 18 (1961): 55, "Die Zitzen des Himmels (d.h. der Himmelskuh)."

MAARAV 5–6 (Spring, 1990): 53–67

THE ORTHOGRAPHY OF FINAL UNSTRESSED LONG VOWELS IN OLD AND IMPERIAL ARAMAIC[1]

EDWARD M. COOK
THE JOHNS HOPKINS UNIVERSITY, BALTIMORE, MD

The use of consonants to represent vowels in Old and Imperial Aramaic texts has always been a topic of great interest to Prof. Stanislav Segert.[2] It is hoped that this reconsideration of the subject, offered to him, will emulate his own creative and methodical treatments.

I. Since F. M. Cross and D. N. Freedman published their *Early Hebrew Orthography* in 1952, the prevailing view of Old Aramaic

1. References are sometimes made in this essay to Aramaic texts. For Old Aramaic texts, KAI was followed; for the Balaam text from Tell Deir ᶜAlla, J. Hoftijzer and G. van der Kooij, *Aramaic Texts from Deir ᶜAlla* (Leiden, 1976); for Tell Fekherye, A. Abou-Assaf, P. Bordreuil, and A. Millard, *La statue de Tell Fekherye et son inscription bilingue assyro-araméenne* (Paris, 1982). For Imperial Aramaic texts, the sources used are as follows: "Cowley"—A. E. Cowley, *Aramaic Papyri of the Fifth Century B.C.* (Oxford, 1923); "Driver"—G. R. Driver, *Aramaic Documents of the Fifth Century B.C.* (Oxford, 1957); Hermopolis Papyri—Bezalel Porten and Ada Yardeni, *Textbook of Aramaic Documents from Ancient Egypt, Vol. I: Letters* (Jerusalem, 1987); "Segal"—J. B. Segal, *Aramaic Texts from North Saqqara* (Oxford, 1987); "Kraeling"—E. Kraeling, *The Brooklyn Museum Aramaic Papyri* (New Haven, 1953). The term "Qumran Aramaic" is used to cover all the Aramaic texts recovered from the Judean desert; explicit quotations are from J. Fitzmyer and D. Harrington, *Manual of Palestinian Aramaic Texts* (Rome, 1978).

2. See "Vowel Letters in Early Aramaic," *JNES* 37 (1978): 111–114; "Altaramäische Schrift und Anfange des griechischen Alphabets," *Klio* 41 (1963): 38–57; *Altaramäische Grammatik* (Leipzig: VEB Verlag Enzyklopädie, 1975): 62–66.

orthography is that "the spelling of these inscriptions is characterized by the regular use of *matres lectionis* to indicate final vowels, the absence of medial vowel letters . . . , and the consistent representation of diphthongs by their consonantal element."[3] Although the Cross and Freedman synthesis has been criticized and adjusted somewhat with respect to the absence of medial vowel letters and the representation of diphthongs,[4] the representation of final long vowels by *matres lectionis* has been accepted virtually unopposed.

But a significant demurrer was registered by E. Y. Kutscher, who cited the spelling of the 3rd person masculine singular suffix on a masculine plural noun (*-wh*) and the 1st person plural perfect sufformative (*-n*). Both of these examples are followed by long vowels in later Aramaic (*-ōhī* and *-nā*, respectively),[5] and Kutscher asked, quite rightly, if long vowels are reconstructed in these positions for Proto-Aramaic, and they also appear as long in later Aramaic dialects, then why should we not assume they were there in Old Aramaic?[6]

L. A. Bange further argued that in ancient Hebrew and Aramaic orthography no final vowels were written if they were unstressed.[7]

3. Cross and Freedman, *Early Hebrew Orthography: A Study of the Epigraphic Evidence* (American Oriental Series 36; New Haven: American Oriental Society, 1952): 52.

4. See the discussion in Joseph Fitzmyer, "The Phases of the Aramaic Language," in *A Wandering Aramean: Collected Aramaic Essays* (SBLMS 25; Missoula, MT: Scholars Press, 1979): 63–65, and the literature cited there.

5. Kutscher, "Aramaic," in T. Sebeok, ed., *Current Trends in Linguistics 6: Linguistics in South West Asia and North Africa* (Mouton: The Hague, 1971): 349–350.

6. Kutscher's view is also put forth in his *Toledot Aramit* (Jerusalem: Akademon, 1972): 11, with the added example of *ʾnḥnh* [ʾanaḥnā] from Imperial Aramaic. T. Nöldeke suggested that certain long vowels in Imperial Aramaic were defectively written; cf. F. Rosenthal, *Die aramäistische Forschung seit Th. Nöldeke's Veröffentlichungen* (Leiden: Brill, 1939): 57. Kutscher's position, and the general topic of defective writing of final long vowels, is treated by S. F. Bennett, *Objective Pronominal Suffixes in Aramaic* (Yale Ph.D. dissertation, 1985): 8–18; Bennett nicely paraphrases Kutscher's argument given above as follows: "The difficulty for those arguing against defectively written long vowels in Old Aramaic is in explaining the presence of these long vowels in later Aramaic. . . . [O]ne does not often find a long vowel suddenly appearing where there was none before" (p. 12). Bennett does not identify phonological stress as a factor in the defective writing of final long vowels.

7. L. A. Bange, *A Study of the Use of Vowel-Letters in Alphabetic Consonantal Writing* (Munich: UNI-Druck, 1971): 105. Bange's suggestion was mentioned and criticized by S. F. Bennett in a paper titled "Long Vowels in Early Aramaic" delivered at the 1987 Society of Biblical Literature national meeting, Aramaic Studies section. My thanks to Dr. Bennett for sharing a copy of his paper with me, which has stimulated my own thinking on the subject.

As with the other theses in his book, which is a sustained critique of Cross and Freedman, Bange could hardly defend this suggestion without making some highly unlikely reconstructions of Old Aramaic phonology, such as placing the stress on the final syllable of the form *hmlkny* (Zakkur A 10) or on the final syllable of the 3rd masc. pl. perfect of the verb.[8] But recently, Klaus Beyer has again suggested that final long vowels were written consistently only when stressed; final unstressed long vowels were written "nur, wenn Missverständnisse zu befürchten sind."[9] The latter point was also made by Kutscher,[10] but only Beyer, as far as I know, has followed Bange in seeing the absence of stress as a factor in the defective writing of final long vowels. This essay is devoted to examining some typical Aramaic forms in the light of Beyer's suggestion.

II. A prominent set of unstressed final long vowels in Aramaic is the whole array of pronominal suffixes occurring after a long syllable.[11] On the basis of comparative reconstruction, such suffixes form three pairs with alternating *a*/*i* vocalism:

3rd sing. suffixes: [-hī] (masc.) [-hā] (fem.)

2nd sing. suffixes: [-kī] (fem.) [-kā] (masc.)

1st common suffixes: [-nī]: objective; [-ī]: possessive (sing.); [-nā] (pl.)

In Imperial Aramaic—the first stage of the language in which all forms are attested—the forms with *i* vocalism are all represented in

8. Bange (N 7): 79, 92.

9. Beyer, *Die aramäischen Texte vom Toten Meer* (Göttingen: Vandenhoeck & Ruprecht, 1984): 88.

10. Kutscher, "Aramaic" (N 5): 349.

11. The distribution of the different forms of the pronominal suffixes in Aramaic is usually said to differ according to whether they follow a consonant or a long vowel (see, e.g., Segert, *Grammatik* [N 2]: 168ff.). The development in fact seems to have been more complex. As a working hypothesis, I propose that in Proto-Aramaic, forms with final short vowel were attached to words ending in a short vowel (case vowel for nouns, *Bindevokal*/modal vowel for verbs), while forms with long vowel were attached to long syllables (CvC or Cv̄). This accounts for the differing distribution of forms on, for instance, the perfect and imperative: with the Peal 3rd masc. perfect + 3rd masc. suffix, all the dialects have reflexes of [qaṭalēh], which must go back to Proto-Aramaic [qaṭalíhi], from [qatala + hi]; but the parallel imperative forms in some dialects show [qṭulhī] (see, e.g., the examples in G. Dalman, *Grammatik des jüdisch-palästinischen Aramäisch*, 2nd ed. [Darmstadt: Wissenschaftliche Buchgesellschaft, 1981; orig. pub. 1927]: 375; cp. also [-awhī] and [-anhī], to be discussed below). After the apocope of final short vowels, the short-vowel forms were reinterpreted as [C + Vh] and spread by analogy to originally

the orthography by consonant plus *yod*, while the *ā* forms are unrepresented: *-hy* ~ *-h* (3rd sing.), *-ky* ~ *-k* (2nd sing.), *-ny* ~ *-n* (1st common). In Old Aramaic, [-nī] or [-ī] occurs with a *mater*, [-hī] without; [-kī] appears, it seems, with one in the Balaam text from Tell Deir ᶜAlla (*bᶜbky*, I:6). Are the forms in Old and Imperial Aramaic without a *mater* to be considered as in fact lacking a final vowel, or are they simply written defectively? The suffix pairs will be considered in the order given above.

1. *The 3rd singular suffixes.* One of the most puzzling (and typical) of Aramaic forms is the 3rd masc. sg. pronominal suffix attached to masc. pl. endings, spelled *-wh* in Old Aramaic texts, *-why* in Imperial Aramaic and its daughter Standard Literary Aramaic, and vocalized [-ōhī] (<**-awhī*) in Biblical Aramaic and in the Onqelos and Jonathan Targums. A number of suggestions have been offered to explain how a form like [-awhī] could derive from the expected proto-form [*-ayhu]. Cross and Freedman propose an evolution of [ayhu] > [ayu] > [aw], with the masc. suffix added yet again to yield [awh] or [aweh].[12] W. R. Garr, on the other hand, sees a development of [ayhu] > [awhu] (via assimilation) > [awhi] (via dissimilation).[13]

Both of these explanations founder on the fact that there is no evidence at all of any masc. pronominal suffix in Aramaic other than *-hi*/*hī*.[14] Although the topic needs to be discussed in greater detail,[15] we can say that the suffix [-hī] can be reconstructed after long syllables and [-hi] can be reconstructed after short vowels.[16]

---

closed forms, including the imperative. Since this analogical levelling spread unevenly, all the later dialects have irregular distributions of short and long forms.

The 1st person forms do not have a short/long opposition; the sing. always has long [-ī], the plural always long [-nā].

12. *Early Hebrew Orthography* (N 3): 29.

13. W. R. Garr, *Dialect Geography of Syria-Palestine, 1000-586 B.C.E.* (Philadelphia: Univ. of Pennsylvania, 1985): 107.

14. J. Barth, *Die Pronominalbildung in den semitischen Sprachen* (Leipzig: Hinrichs, 1913): 29.

15. See Bennett, *Suffixes* (N 6): 82ff.

16. Whenever the vowel quality of the masc. pron. suffix can be recovered from any of the later dialects, it is always *i*-class. The ending [-ēh], too, can best be explained by assuming an evolution in which the case vowel or *Bindevokal* was assimilated to the vowel of the suffix: -V(a,i,u)*hi* > *-ihi* > *-ih* (after the apocope of final short vowels) > *-ēh* (after the raising of vowels under word stress). The same process, of course, can be seen in the 3rd fem. and 2nd masc./fem. suffixes: -V*ha* > *-aha* > *-ah* (3rd fem.); -V*ka* > *-aka* > *-ak* (2nd masc.); -V*ki* > *-iki* > *-ik* (2nd fem.).

Hence a suffix [-hu] could not have been present to induce the assimilation Garr wants,[17] nor could a simple [-h] have been added to a putative [*-aw], as Cross and Freedman argue.

The quality of the final vowel is therefore certain. More important for our purposes, however, is the quantity of that vowel: Was it short or long? If it was short, it would have fallen off with the rest of the short vowels in some stage prior to Old Aramaic: [*-awhi] > [awh]—thus bringing us to Cross and Freedman's vocalization by a different route. All evidence from the later dialects, however, indicates that it was long. As noted above, Imperial Aramaic has *-why* virtually without exception, as do the dialects of Biblical Aramaic, Qumran Aramaic, and Targums Onkelos and Jonathan.[18] (Nabatean and Palmyrene are considered, for purposes of orthography, as varieties of Imperial Aramaic.) Jewish Palestinian Aramaic has *-wy* [ōy], obviously derived from [*-ōhī] via syncope of intervocalic *hē*. (Samaritan has *-yw* [o],[19] probably from [*-aw] < [*-áwī] < [*-awhī]; but no evidence remains of the vowel in question.) Syriac has *-why* [aw]; the orthography confirms that the vowel was originally long, but disappeared in pronunciation in the general loss of final unaccented vowels in the first few centuries of the Common Era.[20] Finally, one may cite the evidence of the Aramaic incantation written in cuneiform characters, where the suffix on masc. pl. occurs as *-a-a-'i-i*, probably pronounced /-ayhī/[21]; this Eastern Aramaic form differs from the

17. Unless the change is pushed back to Proto-Northwest-Semitic, when *-hu* was undoubtedly present, perhaps in complementary distribution with *-hi*. The form [-aw] < [-ayhu] might have competed in different registers of the language with [-ayhī]; the outcome may well have been a compound [-awhī]; similarly, in English the competing plural forms *childer* and *childen* yielded *children* (for the example and a discussion of "affix compounding" see H. H. Hock, *Principles of Historical Linguistics* [Berlin: Mouton de Gruyter, 1986]: 191).

18. A few cases of defective spelling (noted by Beyer [N 9]: 451) do not appreciably change the picture—certainly not enough to distinguish an entire dialect, as Beyer would have it ([N 9]: 53).

19. Cf. L. H. Vilsker, *Manuel d'Araméen Samaritain* (tr. J. Margain; Paris: CNRS, 1981): 52–53; and Beyer (N 9): 118 n. 1.

20. For a discussion of this process, see Beyer (N 9): 122–125. For Syriac, it might be possible to argue that a spoken pronunciation deriving from original [-awh] was mapped onto an essentially foreign orthography deriving from an [-awhī] dialect; but forms like *qṭlwhy* (3rd pl. perfect with 3rd masc. sing. suffix), pronounced [qaṭlūy], show that the *-hy* was originally present in "Proto-Syriac" in other positions, and therefore probably also in the form under discussion.

21. For the Uruk cuneiform Aramaic text, see C. H. Gordon, "The Aramaic Incantation in Cuneiform," *Archiv für Orientforschung* 12 (1937/39): 115–117.

Classical and Western Aramaic forms under discussion, but testifies to the length of the vowel.

In the later dialects, then, we have no evidence of any form deriving from a proto-form *[-awh].

The same evidence is available for final [-hī] after non-diphthongal long vowels, e.g., in the singular construct of some biradical nouns: *ʾbwh* "his father" (KAI 215:2), later *ʾbwhy* (Cowley 71:5), Syriac *ʾbwhy* [ʾabūy], etc.

Given, then, that the later dialects all testify to the presence of [-hī] as the masc. suffix after a long vowel/diphthong, the interpretation of Old Aramaic *-h* in that environment as representing [-h] is improbable. It could still be argued that since Old Aramaic had a number of traits not appearing in the later dialects (e.g., the preservation of the Proto-Semitic interdentals), [-h] after long vowel was one of them. But [-h] is not an early form of [-hī]—quite the reverse. We do not expect a suffix to add an unstressed vowel, but to drop one. It could be argued, in turn, that the unstressed vowel was dropped in the inscriptional dialect, just as it was dropped later on in, say, Syriac. If so, Old Aramaic anticipated a sound-change which was to not to become widespread in Aramaic for half a millennium. Surely this is unlikely. Finally, it may be argued that Old Aramaic is essentially a Western dialect, while Imperial Aramaic is essentially an Eastern one. The influence of the Imperial dialect—which had [-hī] after long vowels—determined the nature of the suffix for all later varieties of Aramaic and prevented the [-h] dialects from leaving any dialectal progeny. This too is possible; but the orthography *-wh* crosses dialect lines, being found far to the south at Tell Deir ʿAlla (*ʾlwh*, "to him," I:1) and to the east, in Assyrian territory, at Tell Fekherye (*mwh*, "his water," line 2). Without further evidence to the contrary, we must assume that *-wh* was the standard Aramaic orthography before the Persian period, that it signaled the same phonetic form in the inscriptions where it appeared, and that that form was [-awhī].

There is another example of the masc. sing.suffix which was probably written defectively in Old Aramaic. I refer to the suffix *-h* occurring on the "energic" forms of the imperfect: *yqtlnh* (Sefire I B 27), *yʿbrnh* (Sefire III 17). The former case J. Fitzmyer vocalizes [yiqtulinneh] in conformity with the vocalization in later dialects.[22] In Imperial Aramaic, however, one finds the spelling *-nhy* on

22. Joseph Fitzmyer, *The Aramaic Inscriptions of Sefire*[2] (Rome: PBI, 1967): 67.

forms of the imperfect without sufformatives (i.e, the 1st common pl., 2nd/3rd. masc. sg., 1st common sing; the spelling on forms with plural sufformatives, e.g., something like *-wnhy*, is not attested).[23] Beyer posits for Imperial Aramaic two energic forms, parallel to the two Arabic energic forms: [-an] on imperfects without sufformatives and [-nn(a)] on forms with sufformatives. To the first, consonantal, form, were added the series of long-vowel suffixes [-hī], [-hā], etc., to the latter, the short vowel series [-ih],[-ah], resulting in a complementary distribution *tqṭlnhy* [tiqṭulanhī] ~ *tqṭlnh* [tiqṭulūnnih]. Later—Beyer suggests the 3rd century B.C.E.—the short vowel series was leveled through, accounting for the vocalization of Biblical and Targumic Aramaic.[24] It is possible, in fact, that the levelling process began even earlier than Beyer thinks; we find forms like *ʾntnnh* (Cowley 35:5). In any case, it appears that the customary Imperial Aramaic plene writing of this suffix caught it before it disappeared, so we are justified in projecting the pronunciation [-anhī] or [-inhī] back into Old Aramaic forms such as Sefire *yqtlnh*, which probably should be vocalized [yaqtulanhī]. The orthographic resemblance to later forms is a by-product of the defective writing of the suffix.

The masculine singular form, then, after long vowels and consonants was [-hī]. What of the feminine form? It is always written *-h* in Old Aramaic (as in Sefire III 23 *kpryh wbʿlyh wgblh*). In Imperial Aramaic we find a few isolated spellings with *-hh* (*ʾḥthh*, Hermopolis 7:4) or *-hʾ* (*ʾḥwhʾ*, RES 1300:4).[25] In Qumran Aramaic, the spelling *-hʾ* is common,[26] as it is in the Onkelos/Jonathan Targums.[27] In Late Aramaic texts, the spelling is again *-h*, pronounced [-h]. The easiest way to account for this pattern of evidence is to assume that the final [-hā] was written defectively in the

23. For an excellent discussion of earlier views of this form, see Bennet, *Suffixes* (N 6): 82ff., and the literature cited there. For lists of forms, see, with Bennett, Beyer (N 9): 477; Segert, *Grammatik* (N 2): 312–317; J. M. Lindenberger, *The Aramaic Proverbs of Ahiqar* (Baltimore: Johns Hopkins Univ., 1983): 284–285. Except for the form cited below from Cowley 35, there are apparently *no* singular imperfect verbs with 3rd masc. sing. suffix spelled *-nh*; it is easy to get the impression from the literature that the *-nhy* suffixes are somehow anomalous in Imperial Aramaic, but they are the normal spelling for that morpheme.

24. Beyer (N 9): 477.

25. Cf. E. Y. Kutscher, "The Hermopolis Papyri," *Israel Oriental Studies* 1 (1971): 56.

26. Lists of attestations in Beyer (N 9): 450, 451.

27. Dalman (N 11): 203ff.

early texts, and plene in the Middle Aramaic texts; in Late Aramaic the apocope of final unstressed long vowels led to a "return" to the spelling *-h*, which reflected in this case phonetic reality. As with the 3rd masc. sing. suffix, the only way to avoid this conclusion is to posit some kind of dialect levelling in the Persian period based on Imperial Aramaic. In fact, it is likely that the influence of Imperial Aramaic *did* lead to some kind of dialect levelling, but there is no evidence that a preservation or restoration of final unstressed long vowels was among the features levelled through.[28]

2. *The 2nd sing. suffixes.* In Old Aramaic, only the 2nd masc. sing. suffix *-k* is attested.[29] In Imperial Aramaic, the 2nd fem. suffix makes its appearance, written *-ky*; the 2nd masc. sing. is still written *-k*. In all Middle and Late Aramaic texts the masc. is *-k* [-k]; the feminine is most often *-ky* in Middle Aramaic, and this spelling occasionally survives in Late Aramaic even when apocope of the final vowel yielded [-k] in practice.

In Qumran Aramaic, the 2nd sing. masc. suffix is mostly written *-k*, but, significantly, there are some spellings with *-kh*: [*q*]*wdmykh* (4QenGiants[a] 9:5), *mnkh* (1QGenAp 20:26), etc. Targumic Aramaic shows a development of [-kā] > [-k] alongside the preservation of [-nā] and [-hā], showing that in one dialect, at least, these suffixes did not pattern together. In sum, about the same picture is presented by the 2nd sing. suffixes, as by the 3rd sing. suffixes: general defective writing of [-Cā], followed by sporadic plene spellings in the Middle Aramaic period, followed by disappearance of the final vowel.

3. *1st common suffixes.* Essentially the same pattern is visible with the 1st person suffixes. The 1st sing. suffix [-nī] is written *-ny* wherever it appears in Aramaic, right up to the Late Aramaic period, and remains as a grapheme even when the final vowel has fallen away, as in Syriac (*qṭlny* [qaṭlan], "he killed me").

The treatment of [-nā] is different. For simplicity's sake, we may consider as a group all the 1st common plural morphs ending in

28. The best support for the general presence of final unstressed long vowels in Old Aramaic is those final unstressed long vowels that *were* written, such as *hmlkny* [hamlikánī] (Zakkur A 3) or *hˁmqw* [haˁmíqū] (Zakkur A 10), etc. If a sound change dropping final unstressed long vowels was underway in Old Aramaic, then (1) it was confined to the Western inscriptional dialect and (2) had, according to all our evidence, only affected final [-Cā] and the final vowel of [-awhī]. While this is possible, it is less contrived simply to assume defective writing.

29. R. Degen, *Altaramäische Grammatik des 10.-8. Jh.v.Chr.* (Wiesbaden: Deutsche Morganlandische Gesellschaft, 1969): 55, 57.

unstressed [-nā]: the independent personal pronoun, the sufformative of the perfect conjugation of the verb, and the pronominal suffix. The independent form does not appear in Old Aramaic; the verbal sufformative appears as *-n*, e.g., *ktbn* (Sefire I C 1), and the suffix likewise as *-n* (*mrʾn* in the Hazael ivory plaque found at Arslan Tash[30]). The independent personal pronoun is spelled *ʾnḥn* in some early Imperial Aramaic documents, (e.g., Hermopolis 4:5) and it is safe to assume that this spelling was taken over from Old Aramaic.

It will be recalled that this form was cited by Kutscher to support the idea of defectively written final long vowels. The fact that [-nā] (in the suffix and independent pronominal forms) occurs sporadically as *-nh* or *-nʾ* at Elephantine[31]—and regularly in later dialects—led him to ask, "How can we account for the emergence of this vowel except by assuming that it was original?"[32]

W. R. Garr, in his comments on the possessive suffix, says the following:

> The orthography of the suffix does not indicate whether the suffix was pronounced [na], with short [a], thereby anticipating the later common Aramaic suffix [nā], or [an], like the suffix in eastern Aramaic dialects which have lost final vowels. . . . The pronunciation may have been [na] or [an] in the early texts.[33]

Neither possibility mentioned by Garr is viable. If final short vowels were lost in Old Aramaic—as is generally admitted and as Garr himself believes[34]—then it is difficult to see how a [-na] form could exist. The [-an] vocalization, on the other hand, is difficult to reconcile with the evidence of the later dialects: Biblical, Qumran, and Targumic Aramaic all show *-nʾ* [-nā]; the Late Aramaic dialects

30. Text in J. C. L. Gibson, *Textbook of Syrian Semitic Inscriptions, Volume II: Aramaic Inscriptions* (Oxford: Clarendon, 1975): 4–5.

31. Most frequently in the independent personal pronoun *ʾnḥnh*, e.g., in Cowley 27:1. The most frequent spelling in Biblical and Qumran Aramaic is *ʾnḥnʾ*. The plene spelling of the pronominal suffix is rare (see Beyer [N 9]: 450 for the possessive forms) and is unattested for the verbal sufformative; see, however, the form *zbnhy* [zabbinā́hī] (Kraeling 3:5) which shows, minimally, that the vowel was still present before a suffix, and therefore must have been there at some earlier stage.

32. Kutscher, "Aramaic" (N 5): 350.

33. Garr (N 13): 104. Garr's footnotes to this statement refer us to Kutscher's remarks alluded to above; but Kutscher believed that the final vowel was long [ā], not short.

34. Garr (N 13): 62–63.

all show [-an], [-n], or -[nan], but all these are obviously a result of the tendency in this period to drop or nunate all final unstressed long vowels. As with the forms mentioned above, the most straightforward explanation is simply that final unstressed [-nā] was written defectively in Old Aramaic, and increasingly less so in Imperial Aramaic and the later dialects.[35]

III. The same conclusion, buttressed by the same array of evidence (with the same limitations), applies, *mutatis mutandis*, to the 2nd sing. sufformatives of the verbal perfect. In Old Aramaic, the sufformative is always written *-t* (e.g., Sefire I B 38: *šqrt*) and the same is true of Imperial Aramaic. Only in Qumran Aramaic and in Targumic Aramaic do we find a final [-tā] indicated in the consonantal text: *-th* or *-tᵓ*.[36] In Biblical Aramaic, the final vowel is also indicated by the punctuation, and in Samaritan Aramaic the reading tradition preserves final [-tā], although it is not always written. Vowelless forms are found in Late Aramaic and sporadically in Biblical and Targumic Aramaic. These forms can best be explained as a result of the apocope of unstressed final vowels, a common enough phenomenon in these relatively late dialects.

It is possible, again, that the forms with final vowel were the result of language contact (e.g., from Hebrew or Arabic). In general, however, in contact situations, Aramaic seems to have induced forms in other languages instead of receiving them.

The 2nd fem. sing. perfect sufformative [-tī] is absent in Old Aramaic, but written *-ty* in Imperial Aramaic (e.g., *ᶜbdty*, Cowley 14:6). It is difficult to find any examples in Qumran Aramaic, but there is *hwyt* "you were" (Mur 19 ar, line 5); the paucity of

35. The development of this suffix demands more space than this essay allows. For the objective suffixes, the reader is referred to the relevant pages of Bennett (N 6). Briefly, the development of the 1st common plural morpheme must have been as follows: In Imperial Aramaic, the pronoun [ᵓanáḥnā] was commonly written *ᵓnḥnh*, probably by graphic assimilation to the 1st common singular *ᵓnh*. Gradually, in the literary dialects derived from Imperial Aramaic, the final [-nā] in all forms was writen plene. In later dialects, there is found a tendency to end-stop the unstressed syllable with *nun*; early Syriac *ᵓanaḥnan* yields *ḥnan* in standard Syriac; Babylonian Talmudic Aramaic, Mandaic, Galilean, Samaritan, and Christian Palestinian *ᵓanan* arose by a no doubt similar process. In verbal forms the syllable was either nunated (Galilean *qṭlnn*) or dropped (Syriac *qṭln*); likewise in suffixal forms. All the endings in the later dialects can be derived from original [-nā] by normal processes well attested in those dialects.

36. For attestations, see Beyer (N 9): 470 for Qumran Aramaic, Dalman (N 11): 260ff. for Targumic Aramaic.

evidence does not allow any firm conclusions on the pronunciation. Targumic Aramaic always has simple *-t*, which could mean this vowel had already apocopated there, but may simply reflect the Babylonian redaction. Syriac orthography preserves final *-ty*, although the pronunciation does not; likewise Christian Palestinian Aramaic.

The graphemic opposition, then, between -[tā] and [-tī] (the 2nd fem. sufformative) is visible in Imperial Aramaic as in the pronominal suffixes: The unstressed -*Cā* is not indicated by a *mater lectionis*, while unstressed -*Cī* is indicated with final *yod.*[37]

IV. For the 2nd masc. independent personal pronoun, a proto-Aramaic form [ʾántā] is likely; penultimate stress is reconstructed because the final [-ā] tended to apocopate in later dialects. Old Aramaic always has *ʾt* (e.g., Sefire III 20), Imperial Aramaic *ʾnt*. As with the other cases discussed, it is in Qumran Aramaic and Biblical Aramaic that the plene spelling *ʾnth* begins to be common.[38] It might be natural to assume that the independent pronoun and the verbal sufformative patterned together, and in several dialects the presence or absence of final vowel in the two morphs takes a parallel course; e.g. Syriac [qaṭalt] ~ [ʾat(t)], Qumran Aramaic *qṭlth* ~ *ʾnth.*[39] But in Targumic Aramaic verbal [-tā] co-exists with independent [ʾat], as in Biblical Aramaic the Qere [ʾant] (Ketiv *ʾnth*) occurs with [-tā]; such a phenomenon lends credence to the idea that the perfect sufformative [-tā] in these dialects is restored from forms with suffixes by a four-part analogy such as [qatalū́hī]:[qatálū]::[qataltā́hī]: X; X = [qataltā]. We would expect the independent and suffixed pronouns to pattern together. Nevertheless, such an analogy is unlikely since, by and large, foundational forms for analogies tend to be the common and basic forms, not the derived ones, such as the suffixed verbs above.[40] Possibly the *ʾt* forms in Onkelos/Jonathan are a product of the Eastern redaction of those works.

The 2nd fem. sing. [ʾántī] is unattested in Old Aramaic. In Imperial Aramaic, sometimes *ʾnt* is found (e.g., Kraeling 6:8), but the plene spelling *ʾnty* is most common (e.g., Cowley 8:9). The

37. For attestations of the 2nd fem. perfect of the verb in Imperial Aramaic, cf. Beyer (N 9): 470.

38. Locations of attested forms are given in Beyer (N 9): 518.

39. For attestations of the 2nd masc. independent pronoun, see Beyer (N 9): 518.

40. Cf. Hock (N 17): 213ff.

Qumran Aramaic forms are rare and present no unified spelling: *ʾnt* (Mur 21 ar, recto, col. 2, line 12; early 2nd century C.E.?), *ʾty* (Mur 19 ar, recto, col. 2, line 17, first century C.E.?), but *ʾt* in the same document (recto, col. 1, line 5). The form *ʾt* [ʾat] is generalized for all 2nd sing. pronouns in the later period, although Syriac has graphemic *ʾnty* [ʾat], and Samaritan retains *ʾty* [atti].

Overall, it is likely that Beyer is right in his claim that, judging from the orthography of the Qumran Aramaic texts, final unstressed long vowels were still present in the early centuries C.E., and *a fortiori* in Old and Imperial Aramaic.

V. Having established, then, at least the possibility of defective writing of final unstressed long vowels, I now pass to a discussion of some miscellaneous forms where the possibility also exists.

1. The demonstrative pronoun *ʾl*. This form, which appears in the Zakkur inscription (A 9, 16) and in Samalian (Hadad 29) is arguably [ʾḗlle] written defectively.[41] In Imperial Aramaic the equivalent form is written *ʾlh*, and in Biblical Aramaic and Hebrew the final vowel is unstressed.[42] The relationship of this demonstrative to *ʾln* of Sefire is moot; the nunation of final unstressed long vowels, so characteristic of later Aramaic, is unlikely to have been operative as early as the 8th century B.C.E. The final *-n* of the Sefire pronoun may have been a deictic formative element as in [dek] ~ [dikken].[43]

2. The demonstrative pronoun *zn*. It has been claimed that the demonstrative *zn* in Samalian and in the Taima inscription (KAI 228:4) is a defective writing of *znh*, also found at Samal and elsewhere in Old Aramaic.[44] In the vocalized traditions of Aramaic, however, the final syllable of *dnh* is always stressed. Yet, in Middle Aramaic the form *dn* appears, looking for all the world like *dnh* with final vowel apocope—and note also the relic form *dnn*, with the nunation sometimes added to unstressed final vowels

41. Segert, *Grammatik* (N 2): 176.

42. In Ezra 5:15 the Qere is [ʾēl], the Ketiv *ʾlh*. The Qere—no doubt originating in a genuine old variant—shows that this orthography survived in a few cases in Imperial Aramaic.

43. Segert, *Grammatik* (N 2): 176.

44. Segert, *Grammatik* (N 2): 176; Bennett (N 6): 16–17; P.-E. Dion, *La langue de Ya'udi* (Ottawa: Éditions SR): 63. H. Schaeder argued that *zn*, as a Canaanite-derived defective writing for *znh*, in fact served as a model for the defective writings of final [-nā] (*Iranische Beiträge I* [Halle: Niemeyer, 1930]: 239–240). Although Schaeder deserves credit for noticing the problem, his solution is unlikely.

in the Late Aramaic period.[45] It is possible, then, that [ḏínā], with penultimate stress, was original, and the final-stress form was a product of later scribes.

3. The word *lm* in the Deir ᶜAlla plaster text. In Combination I, line 4, the phrase *lm tṣm wtbkh* means "Why do you fast and weep?" If the word *lm* was pronounced [lámmā], as in Biblical Hebrew, then this is an example of unstressed final long vowel written defectively. (But note the form *lmh* in the Ashur ostracon [KAI 233:20].)

4. Two verbal forms in the Hadad inscription.[46] In Hadad 30, the sentence *qm ᶜyny ᵓw dlḥ* means something like "my eye/s is/are fixed or blurred." The verbal forms, however, seem to be all wrong; for the singular fem. perfect, one expects a form with final *-t* (this would apply as well to the passive participial forms postulated by Gibson[47]). But, if the verbs are read as feminine dual/plural perfects (*ᶜyn* should be so construed in Semitic), vocalized [qámā, daláḥā], then it is possible that the final unstressed [ā] was written defectively.

5. The feminine plural jussive. J. Huehnergard has recently argued that the feminine plural jussive in Old Aramaic was not vocalized *[yvqtvlan] as in later Aramaic, but *[yvqtvlna], as in Arabic.[48] Huehnergard's reconstruction is convincing, and only the following statement is likely to need revision in view of the evidence presented herein:

> The final vowel of Proto-West-Semitic **yvqtvlna* must be reconstructed as anceps. It seems likely that if the Old Aramaic reflex had been **yvqtvlnā*, with long *-a*, the form would have been written with final *-h*.[49]

45. For further examples of nunation, see Beyer (N 9): 149. Although most of the nunated examples Beyer gives did originally have unstressed final long vowel, some of them did not: e.g., *kᵓn* "here" < [kā]; *hnwn* "they (m.)" < [hennū́]; the proper name *yhwdn* < [yhūdā́]. Perhaps some of the exceptions are really examples of a spread of the deictic element *-n*; but not all of them can be, and the temporal and grammatical extent of the phenomenon remain unclear.

46. This suggestion comes from Prof. Stephen A. Kaufman, verbal communication.

47. Gibson (N 30): 76.

48. J. Huehnergard, "The Feminine Plural Jussive in Old Aramaic," *ZDMG* 137 (1987): 266–277.

49. *Ibid.*: 274.

In Hebrew and Arabic, where the proposed form is preserved, the final vowel is unstressed. If, according to the view defended here, final unstressed long vowels were written defectively, then the Old Aramaic form may indeed have been *[yvqtv́lnā]. It is impossible to be sure, however, since the proposed form left no reflexes in later dialects.

6. Two adverbs with penultimate stress preserved in Imperial and Biblical Aramaic. The adverb *ʾsprnʾ* "exactly, perfectly" (< Persian *uspṛnā*) occurs seven times in Ezra (5:8, 6:8, 12, 13; 7:17, 21, 26) and twice in Imperial Aramaic—both times spelled *ʾsprn*,[50] with final [-nā] written defectively. Similarly, the adverb *knmʾ* (Ezra 5:9, 11), with penultimate stress, appears in Imperial Aramaic as *knm*.[51]

SUMMARY

All the available evidence suggests that final unstressed long vowels in Old and Imperial Aramaic could be, and often were, written defectively. This is especially true of final -*Cā*; only in the Middle Aramaic period do we have full orthographic evidence for the existence of these vowels. Rejection of this evidence entails the assumption that the long vowels in question fell away in Old Aramaic, reappeared (or survived) in Imperial Aramaic and its daughter literary dialects, then fell away again in a general *Abfall* of unstressed final long vowels at a later time. An adjustment of the orthographical orthodoxy enables philology to dispense with the first step.

Granted that this is true, we can see that the development of Aramaic orthography was not as simple as it once appeared to be. Instead of a simple linear development from "no *matres lectionis*" to "final vowel *matres*" to "final vowel *matres* plus some medial *matres*" a truer picture of the development would be from "no *matres*" directly to "some final and medial *matres*, often chosen to disambiguate forms." The Tell Fekherye Aramaic inscription from the 9th century B.C.E., replete with medial *matres*, shows that the "rigid laws" claimed for the orthographic development by Cross and Freedman[52] were not so rigid.

50. In the Abydos lion-weight (KAI 263) and in Driver 10:4.

51. In Driver 8:3, Segal 2:3, 21:5, and the Kandahar inscription (KAI 279:5).

52. Cross and Freedman, *Early Hebrew Orthography* (N 3): 60.

We have argued above that unstressed final long vowels could be written defectively, particularly if the vowel was *-ā*. Why should this be? Perhaps because the vowels *i* and *u* have homoorganic consonants readily at hand to express them, *y* and *w*, respectively. When a grammatical contrast had to be indicated graphically, as we have seen, the *i* member was chosen for such marking. The vowel *a*, on the other hand, has no such "natural" consonant to signal it.

It is hoped that the focus herein on the *graphemic* function of vowel-indicating consonant letters would stimulate inquiry into further possible graphemic spellings in Old Aramaic—such as the possibility that final *alep* for the emphatic state and final *hē* for the feminine nominal absolute ending both indicate [ā], but were differentiated graphemically—as argued by Prof. Stanislav Segert.[53]

53. Segert, *Grammatik* (N 2): 190.

MAARAV 5–6 (Spring, 1990): 69–87

QOHELETH AND NORTHERN HEBREW

JAMES R. DAVILA
TULANE UNIVERSITY, NEW ORLEANS, LOUISIANA

The purpose of this article is to re-examine the problem of the language of Qoheleth, with a special view to a theory which has been proposed before, but never thoroughly treated in published form, namely that Qoheleth has been influenced by a northern dialect of ancient Hebrew. It is with great pleasure that I dedicate this study to my esteemed teacher Stanislav Segert.

I will begin by discussing the two most significant theories which have been proposed to date to explain the linguistic peculiarities of Qoheleth—the Phoenician provenance theory and the Aramaic translation hypothesis. Then I will present evidence that Qoheleth was written in, or influenced by, a northern Hebrew dialect.

1. QOHELETH AND PHOENICIAN

In a series of articles beginning in 1952, Mitchell Dahood proposed the novel theory that the linguistic peculiarities of the book of Qoheleth are primarily due to Phoenician influence.[1] He states, "The book of Ecclesiastes was originally composed by an author who wrote in Hebrew but who employed Phoenician orthography,

1. M. Dahood, "Canaanite-Phoenician Influence in Qoheleth," *Biblica* 33 (1962): 30–52, 191–221; "The Language of Qoheleth," *CBQ* 14 (1952): 227–232; "Qoheleth and Recent Discoveries," *Biblica* 39 (1958): 302–318; "Qoheleth and Northwest Semitic Philology," *Biblica* 43 (1962): 349–365; "Canaanite Words and Qoheleth 10, 20," *Biblica* 47 (1966): 210–212; "The Phoenician Background of Qoheleth," *Biblica* 47 (1966): 264–282.

and whose composition shows heavy Canaanite-Phoenician literary influence."[2] This theory has elicited considerable response.[3]

The first part of this paper will evaluate the major elements of Dahood's thesis. I will examine them under three headings: orthography, morphology and syntax, and vocabulary. Space considerations preclude an analysis of his arguments based on cultural allusions.

Orthography. A keystone of Dahood's thesis is that Qoheleth "employed Phoenician orthography," i.e., the original text of the book was written without medial or final vowel letters. He argues that many of the textual variants found both in Hebrew manuscripts and the ancient versions are best explained by positing an original text without *matres lectionis.*

But there is a major weakness in his reasoning. The Latin Vulgate and the Syriac Peshitta were translated well into the Common Era, and were based on the Masoretic text substantially as we have it now (with some Septuagintal influence). Normally the Septuagint allows us to reach back to an earlier form of the text, but in the case of Qoheleth the Greek translation is that of Aquila, and is thus quite late.[4] The manuscript discoveries from Qumran, Masada, and elsewhere show that, while there was a plethora of variant biblical texts in circulation in Palestine before and during the Herodian period, not long after this they were systematically suppressed and the rabbinic (i.e., a proto-Masoretic) recension was made the standard.[5] By the time the versions arose the rabbinic text was the main one available. While it is true that these later versions preserve some earlier readings, radically different recensions of the text were no longer used. In addition, it has been pointed out by both R. Gordis and C. Whitley that ortho-

2. Dahood, "Influence" (N 1): 32.

3. R. Gordis, "Was Koheleth a Phoenician?" *JBL* 74 (1955): 103–114; "Qoheleth and Qumran—A Study of Style," *Biblica* 41 (1960): 395–410; *Koheleth—The Man and his World*[3] (New York: Schocken, 1968): 416–417. H. L. Ginsberg, "Koheleth 12:4 in the Light of Ugaritic," *Syria* 33 (1956): 99–101; *Koheleth Interpreted: A New Commentary on the Torah, the Prophets, and the Holy Writings* (Hebrew; Tel Aviv/Jerusalem: Newman, 1961): 42–49; C. F. Whitley, *Koheleth: His Language and Thought* (BZAW 148; Berlin/New York: de Gruyter, 1979).

4. R. Klein, *The Text of the Old Testament* (Philadelphia: Fortress, 1974): 6.

5. F. M. Cross, "The History of the Biblical Text in the Light of Discoveries in the Judaean Desert," in F. M. Cross and S. Talmon, eds., *Qumran and the History of the Biblical Text* (Cambridge: Harvard Univ., 1975): 183–188.

graphic practices were still in flux at the time of the composition of Qoheleth.[6]

Now to specifics. A number of Dahood's examples admit to far simpler explanations. Nine of them are textual variants due to the presence or absence of an internal *yod* or *waw*.[7] But the use of these vowel letters is irregular in the MT, and internal vowel letters do not seem to have been completely fixed in the early rabbinic recension.[8] Three more examples involve a simple *yod*/*waw* confusion—a very common error in the period of the Qumran texts.[9] The last of these also involves a haplography. With an original text *wlbyrʾh ʾt* the scribe's eye skipped from the first *ʾalep* to the second. This, along with the *yod*/*waw* confusion, led to MT *wlbwr ʾt*. There is no need to posit *wlbrʾt* as the original text.[10] Other haplographies may appear in 9:3 in the phrase *zh rʿ* for *zh hrʿ*,[11] in 12:12 *wlhg hrbh* for *wlhgh hrbh*,[12] and in 7:6, where the LXX reading *kql* is a haplography of MT *ky kql*.

The variations between the singular and plural construct of *mʿśh* and *mrʾh* do seem to be *Hörfehler*, contra Dahood.[13] In Esther and 1–2 Chronicles, post-exilic books which were never written in the Phoenician orthography, the word *mʿśh* is used in the singular or plural construct nine times.[14] Of these, five are inverted (from singular in MT to plural, or from plural in MT to singular) in the LXX and Vg.[15] Again, there is no need to assume Phoenician orthography to explain this type of variant.

The cases involving the phrase *kl ʾšr hyh* (1:16; 2:7, 9; 4:16)—as well as *ʾšr hyh, hyh*, and *ʾšr nʿśh* (1:10, 13; 2:7)—are similar. The verbs appear sometimes in the plural, sometimes in the singular in

6. Gordis, "Was Koheleth" (N 3): 105–109; Whitley (N 3): 112–114.

7. *hṣdk*/*hṣdyk* 3:16; *ʾylw*/*ʾlw* 4:10; *rglyk*/*rglk* 4:17; *ydk*/*ydyk* 7:18; *mʾrk*/*mʾryk* 8:12; *mškbk*/*mškbyk* 10:20; *ydk*/*ydyk* 11:6; *bwrʾyk*/*bwrʾk* 12:1; *wyšb*/*wyšwb* (proposed) 12:6.

8. W. F. Albright, "New Light on Early Recensions of the Hebrew Bible," in Cross and Talmon (N 5): 141–142. For examples of mixed *plene* and defective writing in the MT and in early manuscript discoveries, see Whitley (N 3): 112–114.

9. *hwʾ*/*hyʾ* 2:24; *mmny* (as the Phoenician form of the 3 m.s. pronominal suffix) 2:25; *wlbyrʾh ʾt*/*wlbwr ʾt* 9:1.

10. Dahood, "Influence" (N 1): 41.

11. Ibid.

12. Haplography proposed by Whitley (N 3): 104.

13. Dahood, "Influence" (N 1): 40, on Qoh 5:5; 7:3; 8:11, 14; 11:5, 9.

14. Est 10:2; 1 Chr 9:31; 23:28; 2 Chr 3:10; 4:5, 6; 17:4; 32:19; 34:25.

15. 1 Chr 9:31; 23:28; 2 Chr 4:6; 17:4; 32:19; 4:5 is uncertain.

the manuscripts and versions. But this is also true of constructions involving a finite verb with subject *kl ʾšr* where the subject can be construed as a singular or plural, elsewhere in the post-exilic literature: *kl ʾšr yntn* (Esth 2:13), *kl ʾšr nʿśh* (Esth 4:1), *kl ʾšr hyh ʿm lbbh* (2 Chr 9:1), *whyh kl npš ḥyh ʾšr*, and *ʾl kl ʾšr ybwʾ* (Ezek 47:9). Of these five examples, the subject is read as plural against the MT singular three times in the LXX and once in the Vg.[16] Clearly the translators felt free to change the grammatical number of such constructions.

Some of his other examples are simply unconvincing. The variants *zô/zeh/zôh* are all easily derived from an original consonantal *zh*. Likewise, the variant *zʾt* for *zh* is a scribal correction.[17] The reading *ʾt* for the second person masculine singular pronoun is insignificant by itself, since, as Dahood mentions, this spelling appears elsewhere in the MT.[18] The LXX reading of *ʾēt* as the pronoun is interesting, but could be a misunderstanding due to the frequent use of the pronoun in Qoheleth. Confusion between the roots *rʾh* and *yrʾ* are unsurprising,[19] and changes in verbal number[20] are not uncommon in translations.

The rest of his examples involve variants in the final *matres lectionis*.[21] But one of these is merely a III-*ʾalep*/III*y* root confusion, very common in late Hebrew.[22] Whitley's suggestion to emend *ʾz* in 2:15 to *ʾy* is better than reading *ʾy zh*.[23] This leaves Dahood with six examples with which to support his thesis that Qoheleth was written in Phoenician orthography. They are not enough to demonstrate such a startling claim.

16. LXX: Est 4:1 (L text); 2 Chr 9:1; Ezk 47:9 (second example). Vulgate: 2 Chr 9:1. The Vulgate translations of the first two examples are too paraphrastic for it to be clear whether the singular or plural was in the mind of the translator.

17. Qoh 2:2, 24. Dahood, "Influence" (N 1): 37, 38. Cf. Gordis, "Was Koheleth" (N 3): 109.

18. Dahood, "Influence" (N 1): 40. Cf. Gordis, "Was Koheleth" (N 3): 109.

19. Qoh 12:5. Dahood, "Influence" (N 1): 42.

20. *yplw/ypl* 4:10. Dahood, "Influence" (N 1): 38.

21. *ʾz/ʾy zh* 2:15 (Dahood, "Influence" [N 1]: 205); *kl ʿmt/ky lʿmt* 5:15; *ky mh/kmh* 6:8 (Dahood, "Recent" [N 1]: 304); *mh š/mš* 7:24; *yšnʾ ʾny/yšnh ʾny* 8:1–2; *zbwby/zbwb* 10:1; *ʾny py/ʾnpy* 8:12; *bšty/bšt* 10:17 (Dahood, "Recent" [N 1]: 304).

22. Qoh 8:1–2. See M. H. Segal, *A Grammar of Mishnaic Hebrew* (Oxford: Clarendon, 1980): 90 (§198), and S. J. du Plessis, "Aspects of Morphological Peculiarities of the Language of Qoheleth" in I. H. Eybers *et al.*, eds., *De Fructu Oris Sui* (Leiden: Brill, 1971): 177–178.

23. Whitley (N 3): 24–25.

Morphology and Syntax. Dahood presents many grammatical arguments to establish that Qoheleth has a Phoenician provenance. I will comment on and categorize most of these as space permits. First are the features I find convincing as indicators of Phoenician influence. One is the use of the infinitive absolute with a personal pronoun to express a finite verb. This occurs in the Canaanizing Amarna letters, the Ugaritic texts, and the Phoenician inscriptions,[24] as well as in Qoheleth. This feature will be discussed further in section 3 below.

Another good argument is the usage of the preposition *ʿl* for comparison in 1:16 and *b-* as "from" in 5:14. The preposition *mn* almost always performs these functions in classical Hebrew, as well as in Mishnaic Hebrew and Aramaic. On the contrary *mn* is absent in Phoenician. Qoheleth does use *mn* most of the time.

Many features which Dahood cites can be paralleled in Aramaic or Mishnaic Hebrew as well. The nominal forms *mšlḥt* and *nḥt* also appear in Aramaic.[25] So does the conjunction *ʾl* (*ʾillû*).[26] His first four examples under the morphology heading (*hm* used as the feminine plural pronominal suffix, *zōh* as the demonstrative pronoun, *š* as the relative pronoun, and *mh š-* as the indefinite pronoun) are normal features of the Mishnaic dialect. The same is true of *my* and *mh* used as indefinite pronouns (syntax no. 9).[27]

A number of his examples are relatively normal Hebrew constructions which do not require Phoenician influence to be explained. These include *l* + the infinitive construct used as a future (no. 2), the conjunction *lmh* meaning "lest" (no. 8, cf. 1 Sam 19:17), and the independent personal pronoun plus *ʾšr* in a relative clause (no. 11).

24. See W. L. Moran, "The Use of the Canaanite Infinitive Absolute as a Finite Verb in the Amarna Letters from Byblos," *JCS* 4 (1950): 169–172; J. Oberman, "Does Amarna Bear on Karatepe?" *JCS* 6 (1952): 58–61; Moran, "Does Amarna Bear on Karatepe—An Answer," *JCS* 6 (1952): 76-80; C. H. Gordon, *UT*: 68 (§9.25); Gordon, "Azitawadd's Phoenician Inscription," *JNES* 8 (1949): 108–115; H. L. Ginsberg, "Ugaritico-Phoenicia," *JANES* 5 (1973): 134–147.

25. See Dahood's own discussion in "Influence" (N 1): 46; also Gordis, "Was Koheleth" (N 3): 109; *DISO*: 177.

26. Note that the word *ʾl* in the Ahiram inscription may be vocalized *ʾūlê* (cp. Hebrew *ʾūlay*); J. C. L. Gibson, *Textbook of Syrian Semitic Inscriptions. Vol. 3: Phoenician Inscriptions* (Oxford: Clarendon, 1982): 15.

27. Gordis, "Was Koheleth" (N 3): 110–111, and Segal (N 22): 41 (§§71–72), 42 (§§77–78), 204–205 (§422), 209 (§436). Gordis also compares Qoheleth's *ʾdn* and *ʾdnh* with Mishnaic Hebrew's *ʿădayin* ("Was Koheleth" [N 3]: 111).

One of his major claims is that the chaotic use of the definite article follows the Phoenician usage. But his Neo-Punic examples of the non-syncopation of the article are not strong proof of his case.[28] Neo-Punic was contaminated by other languages, and contains uses of the article not found in Phoenician.[29] It would be more convincing if there were Phoenician examples of this phenomenon.

T. Lambdin has suggested that the definite article follows predictable rules in the various Phoenician dialects.[30] He argues that there is syncope of *h* after prepositions, on *nomina recta* of construct phrases, and sometimes after *ʾyt* and *w* (but consistently in each dialect). Let us examine Qoheleth's use of the article with these criteria in mind.

1. Post-prepositionally: The article is usually, but not always, syncopated after the prepositions *b, l,* and *k*.[31] It is not syncopated after other prepositions.[32]

2. Construct phrases: no syncopation. Examples are *mqwm hmšpṭ* (3:16) and *lbny hʾdm* (2:3).

3. *ʾyt* and *w*: While syncopation after these varies among the Phoenician dialects, Qoheleth should consistently follow the rules of the Phoenician dialect to which he was exposed in his use of Hebrew *ʾt* and *w*. In fact, he is not consistent. The article appears after *ʾt* in *ʾt hʿnyn* (3:10), and *ʾt hkl, ʾt hʿwlm* (3:11), but is missing in *ʾt nrdp* (3:15). Likewise, the article after *w* is retained in *whḥy* (7:2) and *whḥkmym* (9:1), but may be syncopated in *wḥsrwn* (1:15) and *wdʿt* (1:16).

In short, Qoheleth's use of the article remains chaotic. It follows no consistent rules, even those of Phoenician. Of course, Lambdin's position is controversial,[33] and may not be correct. If so, Dahood's argument is considerably stronger.

Vocabulary. In this category Dahood presents the strongest support for his case. He gives a number of examples of convincing

28. Dahood, "Influence" (N 1): 45–46.

29. E.g., the article is placed before proper nouns. See *KAI* 150:2, 152:1, 153:2.

30. "The Junctural Origin of the West Semitic Definite Article," in H. Goedicke, ed., *Near Eastern Studies in Honor of William Foxwell Albright* (Baltimore: Johns Hopkins, 1971): 326–330. J. Huehnergard has noted further data in support of Lambdin's theory in the Aramaic inscription from Tell Fakhariyah; see his review of A. Abou-Assaf, P. Bordreuil, and A. Millard, *La Statue de Tell Fekherye et son inscription bilingue assyro-araméenne* in *BASOR* 261 (1986): 93.

31. E.g., 1:11; 2:11; 9:12. Contrast 8:1.

32. E.g., *tḥt hšmš* 1:3; *ʾl hym* 1:7; *ʾḥry hmlk* 2:12.

33. See, e.g., Gibson (N 26): xix.

Canaanite words and usages in Qoheleth. But it is not superfluous to point out that Hebrew is itself a Canaanite dialect. This is where his methodological weakness comes in. To demonstrate his case he must show that many common Canaanite-Phoenician usages occur in Qoheleth and these are *contrary* to classical Hebrew. It is not enough to show that rare words in our text have Canaanite parallels. This is to be expected. Even less impressive are the examples which also have parallels in Mishnaic Hebrew or Aramaic. These may merely be common to Northwest Semitic.

The following table lists a group of words which are used commonly in Phoenician, but have different synonyms in classical Hebrew. These are compared with the usages of Qoheleth and of Mishnaic Hebrew.

Phoenician	*Hebrew*	*Qoheleth*	*Mishnaic Hebrew*
ʾdm "man" (preferred)	*ʾyš* (preferred)	*ʾdm* (49), *ʾyš* (7)	*ʾdm/ʾyš*
ʾnk "I"	*ʾny/ʾnky*	*ʾny* (only)	*ʾny* (only)
ḥrṣ "gold"	*zhb* (preferred)	*zhb* (2)	*zhb*
ytn "to give"	*ntn*	*ntn* (only)	*ntn*
kwn "to be"	*hyh*	*hyh* (only)	*hyh*
nʿm "good"	*ṭwb*	*ṭwb*	*ṭwb*
pʿl "to do/make"	*ʿśh* (preferred)	*ʿśh* (28)	*ʿśh* (preferred)
rb "great"	*gdl* (preferred)	*gdl* (8), *rb* (4)	*gdl/rb*
ʾš (rel. pron.)	*ʾšr* (preferred)	*š* (67), *ʾšr* (89)	*š*
šʾr "flesh"	*bśr* (preferred)	*bśr* (3)	*bśr* (preferred)
št "year"	*šnh*	*šnh*	*šnh*

These results are significant. The words *ʾny, ntn, hyh,* and *ʿśh* are all used frequently in Qoheleth, but their Phoenician counterparts never appear. The same is true for the rarer words *zhb, ṭwb, bśr,* and *šnh.* As for the exceptions, *rb* is used normally rather than *gdl* in Aramaic, commonly in Mishnaic Hebrew, and sometimes in Biblical Hebrew. Likewise, *š* replaces *ʾšr* in the Mishnaic dialect, and *ʾdm* becomes more common. In addition, the word *ʾdm* is used more widely in pre-exilic Hebrew inscriptions, which suggests that it was more frequent in the common speech.[34] The agreements between Qoheleth and Mishnaic Hebrew indicate a close relationship between the two. This text gives no evidence of Phoenician influence.

34. See *KAI* 191:2; 194:6–7, where *ʾdm* is used as an indefinite pronoun. This is pointed out by G. B. Sarfatti, "Hebrew Inscriptions of the First Temple Period: A Survey and Some Linguistic Comments," *MAARAV* 3 (1982): 74–75.

I will also comment on representative examples of his vocabulary items.[35] First among them are what appear to be genuine Canaanite-Phoenician terms or usages which do not appear elsewhere in Biblical Hebrew. These include *tḥt hšmš* (1:3, etc.), *ʾrk rwḥ* (7:8), *šmn rwqḥ* (10:1), the pairing of *ymk* and *ydlp* (10:18), and *bʿly ʾspwt* (12:11). Sometimes Ugaritic or Phoenician seems to illuminate obscurities in the text. The word *glgl* seems to have the Phoenician meaning "vase" in 12:6. Dahood points out quite correctly that Ugaritic *kṯr* shows that *kšrwn* (2:21) cannot be an Aramaic borrowing, or else it would be spelled **ktrwn*.[36]

Most of his other examples are not as good. Many of them are infrequently used Hebrew words or roots which also appear in Canaanite-Phoenician. These include *ksyl* (2:15), *lḥš* (10:11), *bʿl hknpym* (10:20), the numerical sequence *lšbʿ*. . . *lšmwnh* (11:12), and *bnwt hšyr* (12:4). The last is an example of a common usage of *bn/bt* to mean "a member of the class of" (see, e.g., Gen 6:4, 11:5; 2 Kgs 4:1). His reference to the use of *šm* meaning "good name" is puzzling. It has a similar usage in classical Hebrew and Akkadian.[37]

Dahood mentions a number of other words appearing in Mishnaic Hebrew and/or Aramaic, as well as in Canaanite-Phoenician. Some of these are *byt ʿwlm* "tomb," the root *šlṭ* (if it does, in fact, appear in Ugaritic), the word *rʿwt*, the root *mlḥ* "clever," and the words *śwq* and *kd*.[38] This suggests several possible sources for linguistic influence on Qoheleth.

In this section I have shown that Dahood's arguments for an original Phoenician orthography fall short of proof. Likewise many of the examples for Canaanite-Phoenician influence on Qoheleth's morphology, syntax, and vocabulary are methodologically faulty, or have other parallels in classical or Mishnaic Hebrew or Aramaic. Nevertheless, he has pointed out a number of features best paralleled in Phoenician.

35. All examples cited in the rest of this section are discussed by Dahood in "Influence" (N 1): 201–219 in the order of their occurrence in Qoheleth.

36. "Influence" (N 1): 206.

37. E.g., 2 Sam 8:13. For Akkadian, see *AHW šumu(m)* A 11, and *awīlum* B.2c (*awīl šumim*). I wish to thank Daniel Fleming for pointing out this Akkadian meaning to me. R. Gordis points out that this meaning is also found in the Mishnah ("Was Koheleth" [N 3]: 111).

38. Gordis, "Was Koheleth" (N 3): 111, 112.

2. QOHELETH AND ARAMAIC

While Aramaic influence on the language of Qoheleth has been recognized for a long time,[39] the more radical theory, that our Hebrew Qoheleth is a translation of an Aramaic document, has been defended by F. Zimmermann, C. C. Torrey, and H. L. Ginsberg.[40] This theory has been subject to a great deal of criticism and has not been generally accepted.[41] I have little to add to this consensus, so I will briefly summarize the weaknesses and contributions of the translation hypothesis.

A basic assumption of the theory is that the translator often completely misunderstood the Aramaic text before him. But it is generally agreed that too many egregious blunders must be attributed to the translator for the argument to be convincing.[42]

Ginsberg replies that the LXX is full of mistakes which directly parallel the errors he and Zimmermann postulate for the translation of Qoheleth. He singles out the LXX and Hebrew of Hosea as an example.[43] But this is not entirely fair. The MT of Hosea is notoriously corrupt, and it is frequently impossible for modern scholars to make sense of it. How much less might we expect an ancient Alexandrian who had none of the research tools Ginsberg mentions, and who was not a native speaker of Hebrew, to translate it coherently. Qoheleth is a different matter. Neither Zimmermann nor Ginsberg gives any indication that the putative Aramaic *Vorlage* of the book was full of textual corruptions. Given the

39. E.g., C. F. Keil and F. Delitzsch, *Commentary on the Old Testament. Vol. 6: Proverbs, Ecclesiastes, Song of Songs* (Grand Rapids: Eerdmans, 1980): 190–199. S. R. Driver, *Introduction to the Literature of the Old Testament* (New York: Scribner's, 1916): 303–304; P. M. Wagner, *Die lexikalischen und grammatikalischen Aramäismen im alttestamentlichen Hebraisch* (BZAW 96; Berlin: Töpelmann, 1966): 139–148.

40. F. Zimmermann, "The Aramaic Provenance of Qoheleth," *JQR* 36 (1945–46): 17–45; "The Question of Hebrew in Qoheleth," *JQR* 40 (1949–50): 79–102. C. C. Torrey, "The Question of the Original Language of Koheleth," *JQR* 39 (1948–49): 151–160. H. L. Ginsberg, *Studies in Qoheleth* (New York: Jewish Theological Seminary of America, 1950); *Koheleth Interpreted* (N 3): 30–42.

41. See R. Gordis, "The Original Language of Qoheleth," *JQR* 37 (1946–47): 67–84; "The Translation Theory of Qoheleth Re-Examined," *JQR* 40 (1949–50): 103–116; "Koheleth—Hebrew or Aramaic?" *JBL* 71 (1952): 93–109; *Koheleth* (N 3): 413–414; Whitley (N 3): 106–110.

42. Gordis, "Original Language" (N 41): 70; Whitley (N 3): 106–107.

43. *Studies* (N 41): 37–38.

short time between composition and translation this seems most unlikely. Nor is it reasonable to assume that the translator did not know Aramaic well, at a time when it seems to have been the normal language of commerce in Palestine. Our evidence for widespread use of Hebrew at this time is not as clear,[44] but in any case, most of the mistakes postulated by this theory involve misunderstandings of the Aramaic original.

Perhaps the strongest argument for an Aramaic original is the irregular use of the definite article in Qoheleth. It is suggested that this is due to a breakdown in the distinction between the *status absolutus* and *status emphaticus* in Aramaic.[45] To some degree this is subject to the criticism given above. But it may be granted that if the distinction was being lost in Aramaic such confusions might appear in a translation into Hebrew. But is this the simplest explanation? We have seen above that Dahood used the same problem to argue for Phoenician influence, and that his argument may be equally valid. Likewise Gordis has pointed out that the article is used irregularly in Mishnaic Hebrew.[46] It is probably easiest to assume that Aramaic *influenced* the use of the article in late Hebrew, including Qoheleth.[47]

Another argument adduced in favor of the translation theory is that the pronoun *hwʾ* and the Aramaic root *hwy* were confused several times by the translator.[48] But again we are faced with a translator who cannot read his own language. The question of whether a pronoun or a perfect form of the verb "to be" is more appropriate in a late Hebrew context is frequently a very subtle exegetical point. Other interpretations of all of these passages have been proposed.[49] Likewise, many of the "mistranslations" proposed can be explained in other, less violent ways.[50]

Finally, there is the question of when this translation took place. Ginsberg is firm here: "Only the Maccabean age enters into con-

44. On Hebrew and Aramaic at this time see J. Naveh and J. Greenfield, "Hebrew and Aramaic in the Persian Period" in W. D. Davies and L. Finkelstein (eds.), *The Cambridge History of Judaism.* Vol. 1: *The Persian Period* (Cambridge: Cambridge Univ., 1984) 115–29.

45. Zimmermann, "Aramaic Provenance" (N 41): 20–23.

46. "Original Language" (N 41): 82; cf. Segal, *Grammar* (N 22): 180–185 (§§373–378).

47. Cf. Whitley (N 3): 110.

48. Zimmermann, "Aramaic Provenance" (N 41): 33–36.

49. Whitley (N 3): 34, 46–47, 60, 64. Gordis, "Original Language" (N 41): 79–80; "Translation Theory" (N 41): 112.

50. See the works of Gordis and Whitley cited in N 41.

sideration. There is no period subsequent to the third century B.C.E. when an Aramaic work was likely both to be translated into Hebrew and to become canonical."[51] Dahood pointed out that this requires that the book be translated and removed to the Qumran community in only 17 years.[52] It would surely have taken longer than this for the book to have been translated, canonized (with the original being lost!), and adopted by the Essenes. In short, the Aramaic translation hypothesis is not supported by the data.

This is not to imply that the theory has made no contribution. It has been valuable in pointing out the undeniable Aramaic flavor of Qoheleth. The irregular use of the article is ambiguous, but may be indirectly due to Aramaic influence. Aramaic vocabulary in the book, such as *ᶜbd* (9:1) and *yhwᵓ* (11:3), have been emphasized by this theory. The same is true of loan translations, e.g., *lbd* (from Aramaic *lḥd* in 7:29,[53] and prepositions patterned after Aramaic models. Any attempt to explain the language of Qoheleth must take this Aramaic background into account.

3. QOHELETH AND NORTHERN HEBREW

In reviewing the positions of Dahood, Zimmermann, and Ginsberg, I have argued that both theories carried their claims too far, but that both have valid contributions to make. The language of Qoheleth has both a Phoenician and an Aramaic flavor. Any theory concerning the dialect used in Qoheleth should explain both of these facts. A theory has been proposed having the potential to do so. It has been suggested by C. H. Gordon that Qoheleth in particular, and post-exilic Hebrew prose in general, was influenced by North Israelite Hebrew.[54] Although we have little information about northern Hebrew, it is reasonable to suppose that it had more in common with both Phoenician and Aramaic than did Judean Hebrew, since Israel was closer to Phoenicia and Aram.

Mishnaic Hebrew is a third dialect which shares many elements with the language of Qoheleth. In some ways, to state this is only

51. *Studies* (N 41): 44–45.

52. "Recent" (N 1): 303–304.

53. Zimmermann, "Aramaic Provenance" (N 41): 19–20.

54. *Ugaritic Literature* (Rome: PBI, 1949): 133; "North Israelite Influence on Postexilic Hebrew," *IEJ* 5 (1955): 85–88. Cf. S. Segert, *A Grammar of Phoenician and Punic* (München: Beck, 1976): 22.

to push the problem back a step, since we must then ask whence came Mishnaic Hebrew. Some of the differences between it and classical Hebrew can be explained by internal developments or Aramaic influence, but others may be the result of influence by other Canaanite dialects. M. Segal suggests that northern Hebrew influenced the Mishnaic dialect.[55] Other features were at home in Transjordanian dialects.[56] In short, isoglosses between Qoheleth and Mishnaic Hebrew may be marks of a non-Judean dialect, rather than simply late features.

In the rest of this article I will present some connections between the language of Qoheleth and the scattered remains of northern Hebrew. First, I will review the evidence we have available for the northern dialects.

Our most important evidence for northern Hebrew comes from epigraphic materials. The Gezer Calendar (late 10th century B.C.E.) and the Samaria ostraca (early 8th century B.C.E.) form the largest part of the northern corpus,[57] although a few other Hebrew documents are known from this area.[58] These texts give us the valuable information that the diphthongs **aw* and **ay* had contracted in the north by the 10th century B.C.E.[59] Unfortunately, this does not help us determine the provenance of Qoheleth, since the diphthongs in Judean Hebrew also contracted sometime after the exile.

It has been argued that a small corpus of texts in the Hebrew Bible originated in the north, and still bears traces of the northern dialect. These include Ephraimite narratives in the books of Judges and Kings, particularly the Elijah-Elisha cycle, Hosea, and the

55. On the nature and affinities of Mishnaic Hebrew see his valuable discussion in *Grammar* (N 22): 1–20. On northern Hebrew influence, see Segal: 12, 41, 42–43, 103.

56. E.g., the masc. pl. ending *-în* was found in Moabite (Segal, *Grammar* [N 22]: 126, §281) and the dialect of the plaster inscriptions from Deir ᶜAllā. See J. Hackett, *The Balaam Text from Deir ᶜAllā* (HSM 31; Chico: Scholars, 1980): 115.

57. For discussions and bibliography see *KAI*: 2.181-185; J. C. L. Gibson, *Textbook of Syrian Semitic Inscriptions. Vol. I: Hebrew and Moabite Inscriptions* (Oxford: Clarendon, 1971): 1–20. The standard edition of the Samaria Ostraca is G. A. Reisner, C. S. Fisher, and D. G. Lyon, *Harvard Excavations at Samaria. I: Text* (Cambridge, MA: Harvard Univ., 1924): 227–246.

58. Particularly the *brk* fragment (*KAI* 188), the *byt ḥrn* sherd, and the *ʾšr* inscription (see B. Maisler, "Two Hebrew Ostraca from Tell Qasîle," *JNES* 10 [1951]: 265–267, pl. XI; E. Carmon, *Inscriptions Reveal* [Catalogue of the Israel Museum; Jerusalem: Israel Museum, 1972]: nos. 41–43.

59. F. M. Cross and D. N. Freedman, *Early Hebrew Orthography* (AOS 36; New Haven: American Oriental Society, 1952): 45, 47, 57.

Song of Songs.[60] Hosea prophesied in the northern kingdom, so his book is a logical place to look for "northernisms." The Ephraimite narratives in the Deuteronomistic History also come ultimately from the north. The Song of Songs shares several linguistic peculiarities with these other texts, and shows a distinct interest in the north ("Lebanon," 4:8, 15; 7:5; "Tirzah," 6:4). The northern origin of this material cannot be conclusively proven, but it will be accepted as a working hypothesis in this paper.[61] In the following

60. W. F. Albright, "Archaic Survivals in the Text of Canticles" in *Hebrew and Semitic Studies Presented to Godfrey Rolles Driver* (Oxford: Clarendon, 1963): 1–7; C. F. Burney, *The Book of Judges with Introduction and Notes on the Hebrew Text of the Book of Kings* (New York: KTAV, 1970): 2.207–215; Driver, *Introduction* (N 39): 188, 448–450; Segal, *Grammar* (N 22): §§15, 72, 78, 228. Daniel C. Fredericks has been kind enough to furnish me with some pages from his unpublished doctoral dissertation ("A Reevaluation of Qoheleth's Language and Its Bearing on the Date of the Book: A Grammatical, Lexical, and Methodological Reconsideration" [Univ. of Liverpool, 1982]), which discuss this material in relation to the language of Qoheleth. He independently points out some of the parallels suggested in the third part of the present paper, i.e., Morphology nos. 1 (aside from the epigraphic evidence) and 2, and Syntax nos. 1, 3, and 4. His work furnished me with two examples I had missed, namely under Syntax no. 3, Qoh 1:7 and no. 4, Qoh 4:12. He also mentions the following "northern" features in Qoheleth: *ʾet* plus nominative, Qoh 4:3; *qətīlāh* as a verbal noun form; *yəgīʿat* Qoh 12:12; construction of typically BH masc. pl. as fem. pl., *tʿngt* Qoh 2:87, *bḥwrwt* Qoh 11:9, 12:1; reduced diphthong, *î* Qoh 4:10, 10:16. Fredericks does not accept the theory of northern influence on Qoheleth due to the texts outside of northern Hebrew which show alleged "northernisms." Briefly, I would reply that most of these cases are found in the post-exilic period, when northern and other dialects were thoroughly intermingled with Jerusalemite Hebrew (see the conclusion of this paper).

61. On the "Shibboleth" incident in Jdg 12:1–6, see Burney (N 60): 1.328.

The content, scope, and even existence of the E document have been debated in recent years. Those who accept E as a continuous narrative source argue that it developed in the north, primarily on the basis of the theology of the E material. I am not yet convinced of either assertion, and feel that it is better to try to establish some of the features of northern Hebrew, and then analyze the E material to see if linguistic arguments bolster the literary-critical ones. For this reason I will not include E among the "northern" texts examined here. For discussion and bibliography, see A. W. Jenks, *The Elohist and North Israelite Traditions* (SBLMS 22; Missoula: Scholars, 1977). I see no connection between Qoheleth's exclusive use of *ʾlhym* and the same usage of *ʾlhym* in the E document. Qoheleth simply avoids the personal name *yhwh* because his view of God is largely impersonal.

It is generally agreed that much of the book of Deuteronomy and the Deuteronomistic History was transmitted in a northern circle, but the text as we have it is written in the Jerusalemite prose which pervades most of the Hebrew Bible. If the priests of Anathoth were in fact responsible for preserving and editing these traditions, perhaps they wrote in the nearby Jerusalem "literary" dialect, even though the traditions themselves were northern. For a recent discussion, see R. W.

discussion I divide the evidence reviewed into the categories morphology, syntax, and vocabulary.

Morphology

(1) The relative pronoun *š*. As noted above, this form of the relative appears 67 times in Qoheleth, more than any other book of the Hebrew Bible. It appears in the following northern biblical texts: Judg 5:7 (twice); 6:17; 7:12; 8:26; 2 Kgs 6:11 (*mšlnw*),[62] and 28 times in the Song of Songs except the title. It also occurs occasionally in exilic and post-exilic texts (Jon 1:7, 12; 4:10; Lam 2:15, 16; 4:9; 5:9; Ezra 8:20; 1 Chr 5:20; 27:27), as well as 19 times in the Psalms, probably in Gen 6:3, and possibly in Gen 49:10.

There is only one certain occurrence of the relative pronoun in a northern inscription, namely the *ʾšr* fragment from Samaria.[63] The word divider following the *r* makes its interpretation virtually certain. A monumental inscription such as this could be expected to have a formal character, and thus to be influenced by the Jerusalem literary dialect (cf. *ʾšr* in the Mesha stele, *KAI* 181: 29), and so my case is not seriously undermined by this appearance of *ʾšr*.

There are several possible occurrences of *š* in other northern epigraphic texts. The earliest is the alphabetic cuneiform tablet from Taanach. According to F. M. Cross, it reads as follows: *kkbʾ lpʿm / kpr š yḥtk l / dw* "Kôkaba to Puʿm / The fee fixed (has been) remitted to / him."[64] If Cross is correct, we have an instance

Wilson, *Prophecy and Society in Ancient Israel* (Philadelphia: Fortress, 1980): 231–235, 297–301, as well as all of chapter 4.

It has been suggested that the book of Job had a northern provenance (D. N. Freedman, "Orthographic Peculiarities in the Book of Job," *Eretz-Israel* 9 [1969]: 35–44). The argument is based on the orthography of the book, which indicates that the diphthongs were contracted. That Job was written in a non-Jerusalemite dialect seems clear, but it may have been Transjordanian rather than northern. Note, e.g., that the diphthongs in Moabite were in the process of contracting, or had already contracted, by the ninth century B.C.E. (Cross and Freedman [N 59]: 42–43). More work needs to be done to establish the dialectal background of Job.

62. The MT is preferable to *mglny* of the versions (*lectio facilior*) and to the emendation *mklnw* (difficult on epigraphic grounds). See J. A. Montgomery and H. S. Gehman, *The Books of Kings* (ICC; Edinburgh: Clark, 1951, 1976): 382–383.

63. See N 58.

64. "The Canaanite Cuneiform Tablet from Taanach," *BASOR* 190 (1968): 41–46. For another interpretation see D. R. Hillers, "An Alphabetic Cuneiform Tablet from Taanach," *BASOR* 173 (1964): 45–50.

of the relative pronoun *š* used in northern Israel in the late 13th or early 12th century B.C.E.

From around 600 B.C.E. comes a seal written in Ammonite script: . . . / *ʾbndb š nd/r lʿšt bṣdn/tbrkh* [PN son of] Abinadab, (this is) what he vowed to Ashtart (?) in Sidon. May she bless him." K. P. Jackson raises the possibility that this seal may be written in northern Israelite, but by an Ammonite scribe, since another Ammonite text has the relative pronoun *ʾš*.[65] More information is necessary before the provenance of the seal can be established.

A hematite weight, discovered in the vicinity of Samaria, bears the inscription *rbʿ šl* / *rbʿ nṣp*. This was incorrectly interpreted "quarter of a quarter of a *nṣp*," but the weight of the object is 2.54 grams, approximately 1/4 of a *nṣp*. It seems best to take the *šl* as an abbreviation of some sort.[66]

It is generally agreed that Phoenician *ʾš* and Hebrew *š* are related.[67] The evidence presented here suggests that *š* was used mainly in the north, possibly under Phoenician influence, and that from the exile on it spread to Judean Hebrew. It replaced *ʾšr* in the Mishnaic dialect.

(2) *zôh*/*zô* as a fem. sing. demonstrative pronoun. This form appears as the fem. sing. demonstrative six times in Qoheleth, always as *zôh*. It is found in northern biblical texts four times (Jdg 18:4; 1 Kgs 14:5; 2 Kgs 6:19 [*zôh*]; and Hos 7:16 [*zô*]) and has been compared to Aramaic *dâ*.[68] *Zôh* is also found in 2 Sam 11:25 and Ezek 40:45.[69] It becomes common in Mishnaic Hebrew. The demonstrative pronoun is not found in any northern inscription.

(3) The feminine nominal ending *-t*. Dahood pointed out that we find feminine nouns with **t* endings in Qoheleth which usually

65. *The Ammonite Language of the Iron Age* (HSM 27; Chico: Scholars, 1983): 77–80. On the script, see L. G. Herr, *The Scripts of Ancient Northwest Semitic Seals* (HSM 18; Missoula: Scholars, 1978): 71, 77, fig. 40.

66. R. Y. B. Scott, "Shekel Fraction Markings on Hebrew Weights," *BASOR* 173 (1964): 53–64; Burney (N 60): 2.208–209; Driver, *Introduction* (N 39): 449. For the original lively controversy over the object see *Palestine Exploration Fund Quarterly Statement 1894*: 220–231, 284–287.

67. E.g., Burney (N 60): 2.208. For another viewpoint, see S. Gevirtz, "On the Etymology of the Phoenician Particle *ʾš*," *JNES* 16 (1967): 124–127. Cf. G. Bergsträsser, "Das hebräische Prefix Š," *ZAW* 29 (1909): 40–56.

68. Burney (N 60): 2.208.

69. *zô* is used in Ps 132:12 as a relative pronoun. Cf. *zû* in Ex 15:13, 16 and *z* in the Ahiram inscription (KAI 1).

end in *-*at* (> *āh*) in classical Hebrew. His examples are *mtt* (3:13; 5:18), *nḥt* (4:6; 6:5; 9:17), *mšlḥt* (8:8), and *mʾt* (8:12). He notes that this noun formation is common in Phoenician, and gives many examples.[70]

At least one parallel can be found in a northern biblical text. The word *mlʾt* appears as an absolute nominal form in Song of Songs 5:12. Whether it be related to *məlēʾāh* "fullness" or **milluʾāh* (appears only in construct) "setting (of a jewel),"[71] the ending *-t* is unusual. The Samaria ostraca offer additional support. The word for "year" in these texts is always *št*, i.e., *šat*(*t*) vs. *šānāh* in Biblical Hebrew. The same is true in Phoenician. The word is *šnh* in Qoheleth, but it is likely that *-t* and *-at* were used with some variation in the north. We know that the ending *-*at* (> *āh*) existed there from *pšt* (*pištā*) "flax" in the Gezer Calendar (l. 3). The *-t* ending also becomes more common in Mishnaic Hebrew.[72]

Syntax

(1) The infinitive absolute plus a personal pronoun used as a finite verb.[73] This construction appears in Qoh 4:2 and possibly 9:15.[74] The only other place it is used in biblical or epigraphic Hebrew is in Est 9:1. The example(s) in Qoheleth require discussion. This is essentially a second millennium B.C.E. feature, since it is found in Ugaritic and Amarna Canaanite.[75] The appearances in Phoenician may be conscious archaizing. But it is also possible that this archaic idiom was preserved in Phoenician and northern Hebrew long after it had died out in the rest of Northwest Semitic. I find the use of the infinitive absolute in Est 9:1 baffling. Could it have been picked up in the mixing of dialects in the post-exilic period? It is not found in Mishnaic Hebrew or Aramaic.

(2) *my* and *mh* used as indefinite pronouns. The pronoun *my* is used indefinitely in Qoh 5:9 and 9:4. In northern biblical texts the same usage occurs in Jdg 7:3 and Hos 14:10. Elsewhere in the Hebrew Bible it is found 14 times (three post-exilic).[76] Dahood

70. "Influence" (N 1): 46–47; "Recent" (N 1): 306.

71. BDB: 571.

72. Segal, *Grammar* (N 22): 125 (§277).

73. C. H. Gordon suggests this is a northern feature (*Ugaritic Literature* [N 54]: 133, "North Israelite Influence" [N 54]: 85).

74. Dahood, "Influence" (N 1): 50.

75. See N 28.

76. Zech 4:10; Ezra 1:3=2 Chr 36:23; Gen 19:2; Exod 24:14; 32:26, 33; 2 Sam 20:11; 1 Kgs 1:20, 27; Jer 49:19=50:44; Prov 9:4=16.

notes that this interrogative pronoun is used indefinitely in Phoenician. Gordis replies that the same is true of Mishnaic Hebrew.[77] Aramaic *mn* is indefinite in *KAI* 225:5 and 226:8.[78]

The indefinite use of *mh* occurs in Qoh 1:9 and 3:15. In northern texts it appears in Jdg 9:48; 2 Kgs 2:9; 4:2; Song 5:8, as well as six times in post-exilic texts and eight times elsewhere;[79] *mh* is also used indefinitely in the phrase *mh š* (Qoh 1:9; 3:15, 22; 6:10; 7:24; 8:7; 10:14). Dahood suggests that *mᵓš* in the Kilamuwa inscription is comparable. Although possible, this is not universally accepted.[80] In Aramaic, *mh* plus the relative pronoun is used indefinitely.

The interrogative pronouns do not appear in northern epigraphic Hebrew. This indefinite use of *my* and *mh* may be an idiom favored in the north, which became more popular in the post-exilic period.

(3) Non-syncopation of the article. Two instances of non-syncopation of the article after a proclitic particle have been singled out as a northern feature, one in the Elisha narratives (*bhśdh*, 2 Kgs 7:12),[81] and the other in the Song of Songs (*šhmlk* 1:12).[82] The feature occurs four times in Qoheleth (1:7; 6:10; 8:1; 10:3).

(4) Anticipatory pronominal suffix. Constructions with the pronoun suffix anticipating the object are found in Qoh 2:21 *wlᵓdm šlᵓ ᶜml bw ytnnw ḥlqw* "and to a man who did not toil for it he must give his portion," and Qoh 4:12 *wᵓm ytqpw hᵓḥd* "and though one may prevail over the one (alone) . . ." The same type of construction appears twice in the Elijah-Elisha cycle, and has been called a northern feature, akin to the Syriac usage.[83]

Vocabulary. Since our knowledge of the northern dialect(s) of Hebrew is so sketchy, my comments here must be considered very provisional. We do not have the data to do a thorough dialectal comparison, as is more feasible, for example, between Phoenician and Biblical Hebrew. Therefore I will make no attempt to construct a chart like that given above (p. 75) and will limit myself to a few observations.

77. "Influence" (N 1): 195–196. Cf. N 25 above.

78. This was pointed out to me by J. Huehnergard.

79. Post-exilic: Zech 1:9, 15:34; 5:5; Est 2:11, 8:1; Neh 2:12, 16. Other: 1 Kgs 3:5; Num 23:3; 1 Sam 19:3, 20:4; 2 Sam 18:22, 23, 29; Amos 4:13.

80. Dahood, "Influence" (N 1): 45. Cf. Gevirtz, "Etymology" (N 67).

81. Burney (N 60): 209; Driver, *Introduction* (N 39): 188 note.

82. Fredericks, "Qoheleth's Language" (N 60): 33.

83. Burney (N 60): 209. 1 Kgs 19:21 *bšlm hbśr*; 1 Kgs 21:13 *wyᶜdhw . . . nbwt*.

First, there are two words in Qoheleth which have been termed Aramaisms, but which also appear in northern biblical texts. They are *ḥwrym* "nobles" in *bn ḥwrym* (Qoh 10:17) and *mdynh* "province" (Qoh 2:8; 5:7). The word *ḥwrym* occurs in 1 Kgs 21:8, 11 (as well as in post-exilic texts, Isaiah, and Jeremiah);[84] *mdynh* occurs in 1 Kgs 20:14, 15, 17, 19 (elsewhere only from the exile on: Ezk 19:8; Lam 1:1; Est [37 occurrences]; Dan 8:2, 11:24; Ezra 2:1; Neh 1:3; 7:6; 11:3). Both terms have been considered northernisms in Kings.[85] Dahood cites an Ugaritic proper name, *bn ḥrm*, as parallel to the first.[86] But the Ugaritic meaning and derivation is unknown, and a parallel from the late second millennium is of doubtful value for establishing first millennium dialectal relationships. *Bn ḥwryn* appears also in Mishnaic Hebrew.[87] Dahood also proposes that *mdnt* in CTA 3 ii 6 is the same word, with a shift in meaning comparable to that of *mmlkt* in Phoenician, and that the same meaning fits in Qoh 2:8.[88] This suggestion is vulnerable to the same chronological objection, and should be established with more evidence.

The word *kd* "pitcher" is found in Qoh 12:6. Elsewhere it occurs only in northern texts (Jdg 7:16 [twice], 19, 20; 1 Kgs 17:12, 14, 16; 18:34), and in Gen 24 (nine times), a passage set in a northern location ("Aram-Naharaim," v. 10), whose inhabitants are speakers of Aramaic (Gen 31:47). It is also known from Aramaic, Mishnaic Hebrew, and, as Dahood notes, Greek transcriptions of Punic.[89] It may be a word peculiar to the northern dialect, although I cannot suggest a southern synonym for it.

Lastly, the word *rʿwt* "longing, pursuit" (Qoh 1:14; 2:11, 17, 26; 4:4, 6; 6:9) is generally considered an Aramaism (from the root **rḍy*, Hebrew *rṣy*, Aramaic *rʿy*). Dahood notes that it may have been borrowed into Phoenician as well.[90] Gordis suggests that the Aramaic root was borrowed into Hebrew early, and cites as evidence Hos 12:2a *ʾprym rʿh rwḥ wrdp qdym* "Ephraim chases the

84. Neh 2:16; 4:8, 13; 5:7; 6:17; 7:5; 13:17; Isa 34:12; Jer 27:20; 39:6. Isa 34–35 is usually considered post-exilic as well: O. Eissfeldt, *The Old Testament: An Introduction* (New York: Harper & Row, 1965): 327–328.

85. Burney (N 60): 209; Driver, *Introduction* (N 39): 188.

86. "Recent" (N 1): 311.

87. Gordis, "Qoheleth and Qumran" (N 3): 410.

88. Dahood, "Phoenician Background" (N 1): 267–268.

89. "Influence" (N 1): 216.

90. "Influence" (N 1): 203–204.

wind and pursues the east wind."[91] Note that Hosea is within our northern corpus. The meaning "pursue, desire" certainly parallels *rdp* "pursue" better than "shepherd," and the comparison to Qoheleth's *rʿwt rwḥ* and *rʿywn rwḥ* is striking. There is one orthographic problem. The reflex of the consonant **ḏ* was written with a *qop* at this time in Aramaic (cf. *KAI* 216:3 *ʾrqʾ*, ca. 730 B.C.E.). But how would it have been heard and spelled in pre-exilic Hebrew? The fact that it later merges with *ʿayin* in Aramaic at least allows the possibility that it would have been written with *ʿayin* in Hebrew. Thus it is possible that the root *rʿy* was borrowed into northern Hebrew (and perhaps Phoenician) early on, and that this is reflected in Qoheleth.

CONCLUSION

In this study I have presented evidence that the Hebrew of Qoheleth was influenced by a northern dialect of Hebrew, and have further suggested that northern influence would help explain the Phoenician and Aramaic coloring of Qoheleth. The close relationship between Qoheleth and Mishnaic Hebrew is certainly due to the fact that they are both late, but it seems likely that northern influence may explain some of the features they share. We have evidence for a great mixture of dialects in the post-exilic period in the environs of Jerusalem (Neh 13:23–27). There are good indications that the dialect of Qoheleth was influenced by northern Hebrew, and we can only hope that further discoveries will give us more information in this regard.[92]

91. "Qoheleth and Qumran" (N 3): 409.

92. I would like to thank James Kugel for suggesting that an analysis of the connections between northern Hebrew and the language of Qoheleth would be worthwhile. Versions of this article were presented in the Hebrew 200 seminar at Harvard University in 1984, and in the Northwest Semitic Epigraphy group at the 1986 annual meeting of the Society of Biblical Literature. The following works relating to northern Hebrew have become available to me since the writing of this article in 1986: James Barr, "Hebrew Orthography and the Book of Job," *JSS* 30 (1985) 1–33; W. Randall Garr, *Dialect Geography of Syria-Palestine, 1000–586 B.C.E.* (Philadelphia: University of Pennsylvania, 1985); Gary A. Rendsburg, "Morphological Evidence for Regional Dialects in Ancient Hebrew" (unpublished); "The Northern Origin of the 'Last Words of David' (2 Sam 23, 1–7)," *Biblica* 69 (1988) 113–121. Also see my review of Daniel C. Fredericks, *Qoheleth's Language: Re-evaluating Its Nature and Date* (Lewiston/Queenston: Mellen, 1988), forthcoming in *JAOS*.

MAARAV 5–6 (Spring, 1990): 89–109

THE SYNTAX OF OMENS IN UGARITIC*

M. Dietrich and O. Loretz
FORSCHERGRUPPE UGARIT-FORSCHUNG, MÜNSTER

Translated by Richard White
OXFORD CENTRE FOR HEBREW STUDIES

Contents

* Abbreviations: KTRIH = Keilalphabetische Texte aus Ras Ibn Hani; *MUg*: E. Verreet, *Modi Ugaritici: eine morpho-syntaktische Abhandlung über das Modalsystem im Ugaritischen* (Diss.), Leuven, 1986; *PU* K. Aartun, *Die Partikeln des Ugaritischen* (AOAT 21/1.2), 1974, 1978.

INTRODUCTION

During the 24th campaign at Ras Shamra in autumn 1961 the remains of a priestly library came to light in the centre of the "South Acropolis." The texts found in this library were primarily religious ones written in Ugaritic, Akkadian, and Hurrian. Despite extensive research since their initial publication by Ch. Virolleaud,[1] E. Laroche,[2] and A. Herdner,[3] we are still a long way from our goal of understanding the language and content of these difficult texts. This also applies to the two texts which contain a number of

1. "Les nouveaux textes mythologiques et liturgiques de Ras Shamra (XXIVe Campagne, 1961)," *Ugaritica* 5 (1968): 545–606.

2. "Documents en langue hourrite provenant de Ras Shamra," *Ugaritica* 5 (1968): 447–544 ("III: Textes hourrites en cunéiformes alphebétiques," pp. 496–518).

3. A. Herdner, "Nouveaux textes alphabétiques de Ras Shamra—XXIVe Campagne, 1961," *Ugaritica* 7 (1978): 1–74.

birth omens based on human and animal foetuses: RS 24.247+ . . . (= *KTU* 1.103+145)[4] and RS 24.302 (= *KTU* 1.140).[5]

In 1978 the number of texts in this genre was increased; during the fourth season at Ras Ibn Hani, the so-called "Summer Palace of the Kings of Ugarit" at Ras Ibn Hani, the Franco-Syrian team of archaeologists came across a broken tablet RIH 78/14 (= *KTRIH* 1.14) which contains omens based on meteorological, lunar, and stellar observations. The text was first published and interpreted by P. Bordreuil and A. Caquot.[6]

While preparing a translation for the collection *Texte aus der Umwelt des Alten Testaments*[7] we studied these three texts and presented the results in Volume 2 (Part 1), *Deutungen der Zukunft in Briefen, Orakeln und Omina.*[8] At the same time we wrote a detailed philological and literary-historical commentary which is due to appear shortly.[9]

In the course of our studies we established that despite the fact they were found in different locations the three omen texts have a number of striking common features which permit (even require) them to be assessed together. This applies even more to the following formal features which brink *KTU* 1.103+145 and *KTRIH* 1.14 particularly close together than to their common literary genre as collections of omens: the writing can only be described as crude; where there is enough space the signs are large, where space is limited they are smaller. The line guide (individual omens are separated from one another by a cross-line) is a straight line the length of the intended text; with over-long lines the scribe did not hesitate to use the righthand edge of the tablet as a writing surface or to extend lines from the obverse to the next available free space on the reverse. This creates the impression that the scribe wrote out the text for his personal use. The obvious deduction that this is the work of an unpracticed scribe—a trainee, for example—would not be appropriate because the usual indications (e.g., scribal

4. Herdner (N 3): 44–60.

5. Herdner (N 3): 60–62.

6. "Les textes en cunéiformes alphabétiques découvertes en 1978 à Ibn Hani," *Syria* 57 (1980): 343–373: p. 352 with photograph on p. 369 (Fig. 5).

7. Gütersloh, 1984ff., ed. O. Kaiser.

8. Gütersloh, 1986: 94–99.

9. M. Dietrich and O. Loretz, *Keilalphabetische Omina aus Ugarit und Ras Ibn Hani* (Abhandlungen zur Literatur Alt-Syrien-Palästinas 2), Münster, 1989.

errors) are missing.[10] The two texts must then have been written by the same scribe who was an expert in the "science" of omens.

Matters are quite different with regard to *KTU* 1.140; here we have only the lower lefthand corner of a tablet which was considerably narrower than *KTU* 1.103+145 and *KTRIH* 1.14 and which was written with a fine ductus as the beginning of lines clearly shows. Thus *KTU* 1.140 is in all probability to be attributed to another scribe.

It must be admitted that these epigraphic criteria alone are scarcely enough to set *KTU* 1.103+145 and *KTRIH* 1.14 apart from *KTU* 1.140—they can be easily countered by pleading chance. But since syntactic phenomena also argue for such a grouping a syntactic study of all three texts is set out below. At the same time this will enable us to present a syntactic analysis of the omen texts as a discreet group. Because of the many problems peculiar to the language of these texts such a study will doubtless be of interest to all those concerned with the grammar of Ugaritic.

In order to make concise reference to the texts under discussion we have provided them with particular sigla for this study: A = *KTU* 1.103+145, B = *KTU* 1.140 and C = *KTRIH* 1.14.

We have taken "syntax" as our subject with particular regard to our contribution to a Segert *Festschrift*: During his stay in Münster in the summer of 1983, Stanislav Segert provided much stimulus for our thoughts on Ugaritic lexicography and grammar. He has also underlined his reputation as an Ugaritologist with his recently published *Basic Grammar of the Ugaritic Language*.[11] With the following reflections we hape to provide him with additional material for his own valuable research.

TRANSLITERATION AND TRANSLATION OF THE TEXTS

Before we begin our description of the syntax it seems advisable to provide the texts which we are analyzing. We present them with a suggested translation.

10. The only "mistake" in all three texts seems to have been an extra divider in *mt*{.}*n* (A 6).

11. Stanislav Segert, *A Basic Grammar of the Ugaritic Language, with Selected Texts and Glossary* (Berkeley: Univ. of California, 1984).

Text A (KTU 103+145)

1 w* ttṣin[X X]ṣ*/l*dat.abn.madtn tqln bḥwt
2 ᶜlh nḥ*/ṭ*[X X]y*aṯr yld.bhmth tᶜm*q*n*
3 w* mšš*[X X.rġ]b*n ykn b ḥwt
4 w in*[X X X X X X].ḥw*tn tḫlq
5 w* [qrbh.]p*t*ḥ*.r*ġbn ykn b ḥwt
6 [w] i*[n bh] a*p* w ḫr apm.ḥwtn*[tḫlq] m*ṯ{.}n rgm
7 [w] i*n*.[X X X X] m*lkn yiḫd ḥw*[t ib.]m*rḥy mlk tdlln
8 [X]Xh.mX[X X X X(X)]Xm*ḫt.bhmtn [tḫlq(?)]
9 w* in šq.š*[ma]l*b*h.mlkn y*[. . .]
10 w* in qṣr [šm]a*l.mlk[n . . . ḥwt(?) i]b*
11 w* qrn šir* [l(?)] p*ith.šm*[al mlkn . . . ḥwt (?)] i*b
12 ṭḥl.in.bh.[r]ġ*bn.y*[kn b ḥwt]
13 mlkn.l ypq š*[p]ḥ X[. . .] m*ṯt* [rgm]
14 w* in uškm bh*.ḏr*[ᶜḥwt hyt] y*ḥ*s*l*
15 w* in.krᶜ yd*h [šmal mlkn (?)] y*ḫlq.bhmt*[ib(?)]
16 [w] i*n*[. . .]X.ibn yḫlq bhmt ḥ*w*t
17 [. . .]ḥ*.ṯnn ᶜz yuḫd ib mlk
18 [. . .]ibn(?)] y*ḫlq.mṯn.rgm*
19 [. . .]rġb.w tp.mṣqt*
20 [. . .]t*ᶜzzn
21 [. . .]r*n
22 [. . .i]bh
23 [. . .]tpš*[. . .]
(Rest of obverse broken off)

(Beginning of reverse broken off)
24 [X X X X X X].l* [. . .]
25 [w qrn š(?)]i*r.l kr*[. . .]
26 w* in*.šq ymn.bh*[. . .]
27 w* in.ḫrṣp.b kr*[ᶜydh . . .]
28 w in.krᶜ ydh y*[mn . . . mlkn]
29 l* ypq špḥ [. . .]
30 w in.ḫr apm.kl[. . .]
31 w in.lšn bh.r[. . .]
32 špth.tḥ(!)yt.kr*[t . . .]X[. . .]
33 pnh.pn.irn.uX[X (X) X X X X X]b*/d* tqṣrn
34 ymy.bᶜlhn bhm*[tn tḫlq(?)]
35 w in.udn.ymn.b*[h ibn y]šdd ḥwt
36 [hyt w y]ḥslnn

37 w* ini.udn šmal.b*[h].m*l*k*n*.y*šdd ḥwt ib*
38 w* yḥslnn [. . .]
39 w* qṣrt.pˤnh.bˤln yǵtr* [ḫ]rd.w uḫr
40 y.ykly r*š*p*
41 w* a*p*h*.k* a*p*. ˤṣr*.ilm tbˤr*n*.ḥwt
42 [hyt.ḥwt.h]y*.št.w ydu [. . .]
43 [X X X X X X X X].l rišh.ḏrˤ*[.]m*lk hwt
44 [yḥsl.X X X X]ḫ*
45 [w lbh b š]b*rh.yṣu.špš*n*.tpšlt ḥwth yḫll
46 [X X X X X].mlkn.yd.ḫrdh.yddll
47 [X X X X]X.ušrh.mrḥy.mlk tnšan t
48 [dll]n* b ydh
49 [w bh] l* aṯrt.ˤnh.w ˤnh b lṣbh
50 [ibn y]r*ps ḥwt
51 [w l]b*h.b ph.yṣu.ibn.yspu ḥwt
52 w* i*[n.]p*ˤnt.bh.ḫrdn.yhpk.l mlk
53 w i*[n.]lšnh.ḥwtn tprš
54 b X[X]z* ḥrh.b pith.mlkn.yšlm l ibh
55 w i*[n.]k*bm.bh.ḏrˤ.ḥwt.hyt.yḥsl
56 w ˤq*[l(?)].ilm.tbˤrn ḥwt.hyt
57 w ˤnh*[b l]ṣvh.mlkn.yˤzz ˤl ḫpṯh
58 w ḥr w* s̄*r*.bh.mlkn ybˤr ibh
59 w in yd š*m*a*l* bh.ḥwt ib tḫlq

TRANSLATION

1. And (if) . . . [on it(:the foetus) he/it (:the foetus) has no . . .], (then) there will be . . . of the stone (weight), (then) a large number (of the inhabitants) in the land will fall.

2. (If) on/over it (:the foetus)..[. . .] follows, (then) the young of its (:the house/country) animals will be strong.

3. And (if) [there is] a . . . [on it (:the foetus)], (then) famine will prevail in the land.

4. And (if) [it (:the foetus) has] no [. . .], (then) the land will perish.

5. And [(if) its (:the foetus) body] is open, (then) famine will prevail in the land.

6. [And (if) it (:the foetus) has [neither] nose nor nostrils, (then) the land will [perish]; ditto.

7. [And (if) it (:the foetus) has] no [. . .], (then) the king will conquer the land [of the enemy (?)]; (then) the lances of the king will subjugate (the enemy).

8. [(If)] its (:the foetus) . . . is [. . .], (then) the cattle will [perish (?).]
9. And (if) it (:the foetus) has n[o le]ft leg, (then) the king will [. . .].
10. And (if there is) no [lef]t ankle (there), (then) the king will [conquer/devastate(?) the land of the] enemy.
11. And (if) there is a "horn of flesh" [on] the le[ft] (side of) its (:the foetus) forehead, [(then) the king will conquer/devastate(?) the land(?)] of the enemy.
12. If there is no spleen in it (:the foetus), (then) famine will [prevail in the land;]
13. (then) the king will have no descendant(s); [(then) will . . ;] dit[to].
14. [And (if)] there are no testicles on it (:the foetus), (then) the "see[d" of this land will] be destroyed.
15. And (if) its (:the foetus) [left] forearm is not (there), (then) [the king(?) will] destroy the animals [of the enemy(?)].
16. [And (if) . . .] is not (there), [(then) will . . .]; (then) the enemy will destroy the animals of the land.
17. [And (if) . . . ,] (then) the powerful deputy will seize the enemy of the king.
18. [And (if) . . . , (then) the enemy(?) will] perish; ditto.
19. [And (if) . . . , (then)] famine (will prevail) and affliction (will be) visible.
20. [And (if) . . . , (then) the . . .] will have strength.
21. [And (if) . . . , (then) the . . .] will[. . .].
22. [And (if) . . . , (then) will . . .] his enemy/enemies [. . .].
23. [And (if) . . . , (then) will . . .] . . . [. . .].
(Rest of obverse broken off)

(Beginning of reverse broken off)
24. [And (if) . . .] . . . on (?) [. . . (is), (then) . . .].
25. [And (if there is)] a "[horn of] flesh" on the[/its (:the foetus)] collar bone (?), [(then) . . .].
26. And (if) is (:the foetus) has no right leg, [(then) . . .].
27. And (if) [there is] no wrist (?) on [its (:the foetus)] forea[rm], [(then) . . .].
28. And (if) its (:the foetus) right forearm is not (there), [(then) . . . the king will]
29. have no descendants.
30. And (if) there are no nostrils, (then) all the [. . . will].

31. And (if) there is no tongue in it (:the foetus), (then) [. . .].
32. (If) its (:the foetus) lower lip is shor[t, (then) . . .].
33. (If) its (:the foetus) face is (like) the face of a puppy, (then) will . . . [. . .]
34. shorten the days of its master; (then) the animals will [perish(?)].
35. And (if) it (:the foetus) has no right ear, (then) [the enemy will] lay waste [this] land
36. [and] devastate it.
37. And (if) it (:the foetus) has no left ear, (then) the king will lay waste the land of the enemy
38. and devastate it.
39. And (if) there is shortness of one of its (:the foetus) feet/legs, (then) the master will be killed, by the guard and the descendants
40. will be destroyed.
41. And (if) its (:the foetus) nose (is like) the beak of a bird, (then) the gods will desert this land;
42. [(then)] abandonment and neglect (will) threaten [th]is [land].
43. [And (if) (there is/are) . . .] on its (:the foetus) head, (then) the "seed" of this king
44. [will be destroyed; (then) . . .] . . .
45. [And (if) its (:the foetus) innards] come out of its anus, (then) the "sun" will be pierced in the baseness of its land.
46. [And (if) . . .], (then) the king will be subjugated by his guard.
47. [And (if) its (:the foetus) penis (is) [. . .], (then) the lances of the king will be raised, they will
48. [subjuga]te by his hand.
49. [And (if) in it (:the foetus)] one of its (:the foetus) eyes is on the back and its (other) eye is on the temple,
50. [(then) the enemy will] crush the land.
51. [And (if)] its (:the foetus) innards come out of its mouth, (then) the enemy will consume the land.
52. And (if) there are n[o] feet/legs on it (:the foetus), (then) the kings' guard will turn away.
53. And (if) its (:the foetus) tongue is n[ot (there)], (then) the land will be annihilated.
54. (If) . . . its (:the foetus) entrails are on its (:the foetus) forehead, (then) the king will repay his enemy completely.
55. And (if) no intestines are in it (:the foetus), (then) the "seed" of this land will be destroyed.
56. And (if) it (:the foetus) is crip[pled(?)], (then) the gods will desert this land.

57. And (if) its (:the foetus) (two) eyes are on its temples, (then) the king will have power over his ḫpṯ-mercenaries.
58. And (if) there are entrails and intestines (for extispicy) in it (:the foetus), (then) the king will destroy his enemy/enemies.
59. And (if) there is no left hand on it (:the foetus), (then) the land of the enemy will perish.

Text B (*KTU* 1.140)

(Beginning of obverse broken off)
1 *k*[*tld aṯt*
2 *ḥw*[*t*

---

3 *k tld** [*aṯt*
4 *y*^{c}*zz* ^{c}*l**]
5 *k tld a**[*ṯt*
6 *ḥwt ib t**[*ḫlq*
(Reverse:)
7 *k tld a*[*ṯt*
8 ^{c}*ḏrt tk*[*n*(?)

---

9 *k tld a**/*ṯt*
10 *mrḥy** [*mlk . . . mlk*]
11 *l yp*[*q špḥ*

---

12 *bh y**[
13 *tḥ**[

---

14 *k** [*tld aṯt*
(Rest of reverse broken off)

TRANSLATION

(Beginning of obverse broken off)
1 If [a woman bears . . .]
2 (then) the lan[d will . . .]

---

3 If [a woman] bears[: . . . , (then) will . . .]
4 have power over [. . .].

---

5 If a w[oman] bears [: . . . ,]
6 (then) the land of the enemy will [perish . . .].

(Reverse:)

7 If a w[oman] bears [: . . . ,]

8 (then) there will [be(?)] help [. . .].

---

9 If a w[oman] bears [: . . . ,]

10 (then) the lances [of the king will . . .], (then) [the king]

11 will ha[ve] no [descendant(s) . . .].

---

12 (And if) on it (:the foetus) .[. . . is,]

13 (then) [will] . . . [. . .].

---

14 I[f a woman bears: . . .]

(Rest of reverse broken off)

Text C (*KTRIH* 1.14)

(Beginning of obverse broken off)

1 [hm.X X X X X X X X]X.l* X[X X X X]X X.* b*h*m*[tn.] t*ḫ*l*q*

---

2 [hm.yrḫ(?) X X X].* b* ḥdṯ yrḫ.bnšm

3 [X X X X X X X X]n*.thbẓn

---

4 [hm.bṯ]l*ṯ*.*ym*.yh.yrḫ.kslm.mlkm.tbṣrn*

---

5 [h]m* ṯlṯ.id.ynphy.yrḫ.b yrḫ.aḫrm

6 [ǵrp]lt.mẓrn ylk

---

7 [hm.]k*bkb.yql.b ṯlṯm.ym.mlkn.l*.y*[i]ḫd* / i*b*h*

(Reverse:)

8 [hm.X]X X X X X X ṯ* X y*[X X]X.X X X.ṯlṯ

9 [X X]X X X X X[X X X]X[X X X]m*

---

10 h*m.b* ḥd*ṯ*.y*r*ḫ*.w* [q]d*r*.*i*r*šn.ykn

11 w* X X X.l*.y*X[ ]

---

12 hm.yrḫ.b ʿl*[yh].w pḥm

13 nʿmn.yḫs*r*.*l*h*

---

14 [hm.]y*rḫ.b ʿlyh.y*r*q

15 [X X X X X(X)]b*hmtn.tḫlq

---

16 [hm.yrḫ.b ᶜ]l*yh.* w pḥm
17 [X X X X X X X X X X X]w* qbṣt
18 [bhmt(?) X X X X LX X X X X X] [ ]

(Rest of reverse broken off)

TRANSLATION

(Beginning of obverse broken off)
1 [If . . . ,] (then) the animals will perish.

---

2 [If . . .] there is a new moon, (then) the inhabitants will
3 [. . .]and be removed.
4 [If on the thi]rd day(?) there is faintness of the moon on both sides, (then) the kings will remain at a far distance,

---

5 [I]f they are visible three times one after another month by month,
6 (then) clouds (will appear), rain will fall.

---

7 [If] a star falls on the thirtieth day (of the month), (then) the king will not seize his enemy.

(Reverse:)
8 [If . . .] . . . [. . .] . . . three
9 [. . .] . . . , (then) . . .

---

10 If there is new moon and darkness (prevails), (then) need will exist.
11 and . . . will not . . .

---

12 If the moon is at [its] rising and redness (is visible),
13 (then) he/it will lack agreeableness.

---

14 [If] the moon at its rising is yellow,
15 [(then) . . . will (prevail), and] the animals will perish.

---

16 [If the moon is at] its [ri]sing and redness (is visible),
17 [. . . (then) . . . (will) . . .] and collecting
18 [of the animals (?) (will be necessary) . . .] [ ]

(Rest of reverse broken off)

1. Structure of the Omens

An omen is composed of two main sections: protasis and apodosis which function as parallel coordinated main clauses. Without exception[12] the two are joined asyndetically.

2. Protasis

2.1 Introduction of the Protasis

The normal conditional particle *hm* "if"[13] is used only in C to introduce the protasis: C 5, 10, 12. In C 1, 2, 4, 7, 8, 14, 16 *hm* "if" is broken off but should nonetheless be assumed if all the omens had the same structure. In B the protasis is introduced by *k* "that; because, for; when; if"[14]: B 1, 3, 5, 7, 9, 14. B 12 begins without a particle just like some of the omens in A: A 2, 8(?), 12, 32, 33, 54. At other places where its text will permit a conclusion, A does not have a conditional particle and introduces the protasis with the simple copula *w* "and" for which we should infer conditional force ("and (if)"): A 1, 3, 4, 5, [6], [7], 9, 10, 11, 14, 15, [16], [25], 26, 27, 28, 30, 31, 35, 39, 41, [45], [49], [51], 52, 53, 55, 56, 57, 58, 59. Since even the first omen (A 1) is introduced merely with *w* "and" one might guess that tablet A was preceded by at least one other tablet, the first omen of which contained a complete text, i.e., including *hm* "if" or *k* "that; because, for; if."

2.2 Syntactic Structure of the Protasis

2.2.1 Preliminary Remarks

Where preserved, the protasis generally consists of a single clause, e.g., *w in lšn bh* "and (if) there is no tongue in it" (A 31); only on four occasions do we encounter one with two clauses—here the two clauses are joined with the copula *w* "and": [*w bh*] *l* aṯrt ˁnh wˁnh b lṣbh* "[and (if) in it] one of its eyes (is) on the back and its (other) eye (is) on its temple" (A 49); *h*m b* ḥd*ṯ* y*r*ḫ* w** [*q*]*d*r** "if (there is) a new moon and darkness (prevails)" (C 10); *hm yrḫ b ˁl**[*yh*] *w pḥm* "if the moon (is) at [its] rising and redness (is visible)" (C 12, 16).

So far as their state of preservation will allow us to recognize them, the majority of protases are constructed as nominal clauses: 12 verbal clauses against 38 nominal clauses.

12. PU 2: 95f.; MUg: 18.1.
13. PU 2: 93f.; MUg: 18.1.
14. PU 2: 93f.; MUg: 18.1.

2.2.2 Protasis as Verbal Clause

2.2.2.1 Preliminary Remarks

Word order in conditional clauses is not uniform as becomes clear from the position of subject, predicate, and direct and indirect objects:

2.2.2.2 Position of the Subject

The subject is placed *first* in A 45 ([*lbh*] "its innards"), 51 ([*l*]*b*h* "its innards"), C 5 (*yh yrḫ* "the faintness of the moon," implicitly), 7 (*k*bkb* "a star"), 14 (*y*rḫ* "the moon"). It is placed *second* in A 2 ([. . .]), B [1], [3], 5, 7, 9, [14] (in each case *aṯt* "a woman").

2.2.2.3 Position of the Predicate

The verb is put in the indicative of the prefix conjugation (/*yaq-tulu*/) and occupies the first position in B [1], 3, 5, 7, 9, [14] (in each case *tld* "she bears"). It stands in the second position in C 5 (*ynphy* "becomes visible"—in fact this is the third position after the implied subject and an adverb), 7 (*yql* "he falls"). It comes third and last in A 2 (*y*aṯr* "follows"), 45 (*yṣu* "goes out"), 51 (*yṣu* "goes out"), C 14 (*yrq* "is yellow").

2.2.2.4 Position of Direct and Indirect Objects

Usually the objects stand at the end of the clause, i.e., in third position. This also applies to the direct objects in B (1, 3, 5, 7, 9, 14—which are however all broken off) and to the indirect objects in C 5 (*yrḫ b yrḫ aḫrm* "one after another, month by month"), 7 (*b ṯlṯm ym* "on the thirtieth day (of the month)") which function as temporal adverbs. Exceptions are the indirect objects in A 45 ([*b š*]*b*rh* "from its anus"), 51 (*b ph* "from its mouth"), C 14 (*b ʿlyh* "at its rising") which are placed second and in A 2 (*ʿlh* "on/over it") which is in fact in the first position. The latter seems also to be the case for the protasis in B 12 which is only partially preserved (*bh* "in it").

2.2.2.5 Conclusions

For the clause structure of the verbal protases the following possibilities emerge:

subject—(adverb)—predicate—indirect object: 2× (C)
subject—indirect object—predicate: 3× (A, C)
predicate—subject—[object]: 6× (B)
indirect object—[subject]—predicate: 1× (A; cf. B 12)

2.2.3 Protasis as Nominal Clause

2.2.3.1 Preliminary Remarks

As a general rule conditional nominal clauses consist of one member and are made up of subject and indirect object. Only in five out of 38 examples, so far as the tablets will permit us to recognize them, does the nominal clause have two members and includes a predicate. There is thus a far greater regularity in word order than with the verbal clause.

2.2.3.2 Position of the Subject

The subject is a substantive, either independent or expanded with a genitive, in A 39 (*qṣrt pʿnh* "shortness of its feet/legs (is found)"), C 10 ([*q*]*d***r** "darkness (prevails)"), 12, 16 (in each case *pḥm* "redness (is visible)"), with negation in A 30 (*in ḫr apm* "there are no nostrils"), 53 (*i**[*n*] *lšnh* "its tongue (is) not") and an independent adjective in A 56 (*ʿq**[*l*] "(is) crippled").

In two cases a double subject is specified: A 6 (*a***p w ḫr apm* "nose and nostrils") and 58 (*ḥr w** *š***r** "intestines and entrails (for extispicy)").

When a predicate is present the subject—with or without an appositional addition—precedes, without exception: A 5, 12, 32 (with an adjective), 33, 41. Generally this also applies when an indirect object is used as the subject—whether in the negative with *in* "is not," with an appositional expansion or linked with a genitive: A 9, 10, 11, 12, 14, 15, 25, 26, 27, 28, 31, 35, 37, 49 (second part), 52, 54, 55, 57, 58 (two subjects), 59, C 4, 10 (implicit subject), 12, 16. There are three exceptions to this rule, see 2.2.3.4.

2.2.3.3 Position of the Predicate

Of the five two-member nominal clauses three have a substantive as predicate (A 12: *in* "is not"; 33: *pn irn* "the face of a puppy"; 41: *k** *a***p** *ʿṣr** "like a bird's beak") while two have an adjective (A 5: *p***t***ḥ** "open"; 32: *kr**[*t*] "short"). These come after the subject.

2.2.3.4 Position of the Indirect Object

The three exceptions against the 21 cases which obey the general rule that the indirect object stands in the last position—in A 12 (*ṭḥl in bh* "(there is) no spleen in it") it even appears after the subject and predicate)—are A 6 (*i**[*n bh*] *a***p** *w ḫr apm* "there (are) no nose and nostrils in it"), 49 ([*bh*] *l** *aṯrt ʿnh* "[on it] one of its eyes (is) on the back") and C 4 ([*bṯ*]*l***ṯ** *ym** *yh yrḫ kslm* "on the third day there is faintness of the moon on both sides"). Only A 6 is uncertain.

2.2.3.5 Conclusions

The following possibilities exist for nominal protases:

subject—(apposition): 10× (A, C)
subject—(subject—apposition)—indirect object: 20× (A, C)
subject—predicate—(indirect object): 5× (A)
indirect object—(indirect object)—subject—(subject)—indirect object: 3× (A, C)

2.3 Results

As a verbal clause the protasis is consistently made up of only two members: subject and predicate. In texts A and C this word order is fixed and is to be explained as the adoption of Babylonian clause structure. Text B on the other hand has the Canaanite word order where the subject follows the predicate. It follows that the direct object (all instances of which are broken off) stood in the next position. The indirect objects in texts A and C can occupy any position.

In a protasis constructed as a nominal clause—because of the state of preservation of our texts this can only be demonstrated for A and C—the subject, with or without negation or expansion, is also almost invariably placed at the beginning of the clause and it generally contains one member (30×); only rarely (5×) is it supplied with a nominal predicate. With only two exceptions the indirect object comes at the end of the clause (21×).

3. Apodosis

3.1 Introduction of the Apodosis

So far as the examples preserved will permit us to judge, the apodosis is without exception connected asyndetically to the protasis. There is no syntactic marker to indicate the beginning of the apodosis (the *n*-affix on singular absolute subjects can scarcely indicate this, see 3.2.2.4 and 3.2.3.2).

3.2 Syntactic Structure of the Apodosis

3.2.1 Preliminary Remarks

In the majority of cases apodoses consist of a single clause (e.g., *ḥwt ib tḫlq* "the enemy's land will perish," A 59, B 6; or *mlkn ybʿr ibh* "the king will destroy his enemy/enemies," A 58). There are 33 certain and 10 doubtful cases.

In 10 certain and one probable case the apodosis has two clauses. Of these, nine (A 1, 6, 7, 18, 41f., B 10f., C 6) are joined by asyndeton (e.g., *m*lkn yiḫd ḥw*[t ib] m*rḥy mlk tdlln* "the king will conquer the land of the enemy, the king's laces will subdue," A 7) while two (A 19, C 10f.) are connected by the copula *w* "and" (e.g., *rǵb w tp mṣqt** "famine (will prevail) and affliction (will be) visible," A 19). To this group belong also those two cases where the second clause contains the asyndetically co-ordinated remark *mṯn rgm* "repetition of the text (of the preceding apodosis)" because it implies the clause of the preceding apodosis (A 6, 18).

The apodoses of A 33f., 39f., and C 17f. contain three clauses (in the last mentioned there could even be space for four). A 33f. and C 17f. are only partially preserved and provide no certain clues as to how their clauses might be related. In C 17f. the single member nominal clause *qbṣt* [*bhmt*(?)] "collecting [the animals (?) (will be necessary)]" could have been the second clause connected by the copula *w* "and" to a preceding one, which is broken off. Thus, only in A 39f. are the relationships clear; all three clauses are joined asyndetically: *bʿln yǵtr** [*ḫ*]*rd w uḫry ykly r*š*p* "the master will be killed; guard and descendants will be destroyed; Ršp (will prevail)."

Apart from the badly preserved apodosis in C 17f., in which there could originally have been four complete clauses, there is only one four*clause*apodosis—in A 12f.—unfortunately its third clause is missing: [*r*]*ǵ*bn y**[*kn b ḥwt*] *mlkn l ypq š**[*p*]*ḥ* X[. . .] *m*ṯ*n* [*rgm*] "famine will prevail in the land; the king will have no descendants; .[. . .]; repetition of the text (of the preceding apodosis)."

Most of what can be said about the structure of apodosis clauses applies to verbal clauses, to the extent that the state of preservation of the passage in question will permit a fairly certain judgment. There are 59 verbal clauses against a mere seven nominal clauses. Three times the nominal expression *mṯn rgm* "repetition of the text" is found at the end of an apodosis and on each occasion it refers to the verbal clause of the preceding omen. Hence the number of verbal clauses strictly speaking rises to 62. We begin our analysis of the apodoses with the nominal clauses.

3.2.2 Apodosis with Nominal Clauses

3.2.2.1 Preliminary Remarks

Of the seven nominal concluding clauses two form an independent apodosis (A 19) while five are individual members of apodoses which otherwise consist of two or three verbal clauses (A 1, 41f.,

C 6; similarly 39f.). In C 17f. there is no means of identifying how it is related to its context. There is thus no apodosis which is made up of only a simple nominal clause. This means that, with the exception of A 19, the nominal clauses are really only accessories to the verbal clauses which come before and after them (A 39f., 41f., similarly A 1, C 6).

With regard to the construction of the nominal clauses it should be remarked that six have one member and one has two members.

3.2.2.2 Single Member Nominal Clauses

The single member nominal clauses have only substantives as their subject. These either stand alone (*rǵb* "famine (will prevail)," A 19; *r*š*p* "Ršp (will prevail)," A 40; [*ǵrp*]*lt* "clouds (will appear)," C 6) or are connected to a genitive ([ ]*ṣ*/l*dat abn* " . . . of the stone (weight) (will be)," A 1; *tp mṣqt** "the appearance of affliction (will be)," A 19 and possibly *qbṣt* [*bhmt*(?)] "collecting [of the animals (?) (will be necessary)]," C 17f.).

3.2.2.3 Two Member Nominal Clauses

Only one example of a two member nominal clause is attested (A 42). Its two following predicates (infinitives) are joined with the copula *w* "and": [*ḫwt h*]*y* št w ydu* "this land (will suffer) abandonment and neglect," A 42.

3.2.2.4 Conclusions

In the apodoses, which are primarily verbal, the nominal clause plays an insignificant role. In the protases the opposite can be observed (see 2.2.1).

For nominal apodoses the following constructions are found:

subject—(subject): 6× (A, C)

subject—predicate—predicate: 1× (A)

So far as can be ascertained, the *n*-affix, which is attached to the subject of verbal clauses (see 3.2.3.2) is not found in nominal clauses.

3.2.3 Apodosis with Verbal Clauses

3.2.3.1 Preliminary Remarks

In contrast to the word order in verbal protases (2.2.2) that of the 59 (or 62) verbal apodoses is surprisingly uniform as the following description will show.

3.2.3.2 Position of the Subject

In each case there is only one subject per clause. It appears with or without expansion and always takes the first position in the clause. When it is singular and in the absolute state it takes the affix *-n*.[15] This brings to mind the definite article in Hurrian.[16] It would scarcely be credible to equate this *-n* with the first person plural pronominal suffix ("our"). The following examples should be noted: *ibn* "the enemy" (A 16, [18], [35], [50], 51), *i*r*šn* "the need" (C 10), *bhmtn* "the animals" (A 8, 34, C 1, 15), *bᶜln* "the master" (A 39), *ḥwtn* "the land" (A 4, 6, 53), *ḫrdn* "the watchman" (A 52), *madtn* "the large number" (A 1), *mẓrn* "the rain" (C 6), *mlkn* "the king" (A 7, 9, 10, [11], 13, [15], [28], 37, 46, 54, 57, 58, C 7), *nᶜmn* "the agreeableness" (C 13), *rǵbn* "the famine" (A 3, 5, 12), *špš*n** "the sun, the Great King" (A 45) and *ṯnn ᶜz* "the strong deputy" (A 17). As soon as the singular subject stands in the construct state and is expanded with a genitive this affix is dropped: *ḏrᶜ ḥwt hyt* "the seed of this land" (A 14, 55), *ḏrᶜ* m*lk hwt* "the seed of this king" (A 43) and *ḥwt ib* "the land of the enemy" (A 59).

Notably, text B does not recognize this suffix as the only appropriate example B 8 (*ᶜḏrt* "the help") indicates. In all other apodoses any subject which could have taken the *n*-affix is not preserved.

Subjects in the plural show no peculiarities: *ilm* "the gods" (A 41, 56), *bnšm* "the inhabitants" (C 2), *mlkm* "the kings" (C 4), in the construct: *yld bhmth* "the young of his/her animals" (A 2) and *mrḥy mlk* "the lances of the king" (A 7, 47).

3.2.3.3 Position of the Predicate

The predicate is in full grammatical congruence with the subject (there is only one example of a *constructio ad sensum*: A 1, *madtn tqln* "the large number will fall"). It follows the subject in the indicative and is separated from it only by an adverb (see 3.2.3.5).

In five apodoses there are two verbs connected to a single subject (with or without the copula *w* "and"): *yšdd . . . wyḥslnn* "will lay waste . . . will devastate it" (A 35f., 37f.), *yǵtr* . . . ykly* "will be

15. According to J. Hoftijzer, "Quodlibet Ugariticum" in G. V. Driel, *et al.*, eds., *Zikir Šumim, Kraus Festschrift* (Leiden: Brill, 1982): 121–123, this *-n* should be interpreted as a sort of *-n-apodoseos* and by K. Aartun (PU 1: 61–65; PU 2: 169) as an emphatic element.

16. To be pronounced as *-ne*, see I. M. Diakonoff, *Hurrisch und Urartäisch* (Munich, 1971): 87 and table 2.

killed . . . destroyed" (A 39f.), *tnšan t*[*dll*]*n** "will be raised, destroyed" (A 47f.) and [. . .]*n** *w thbẓn* "will be [. . .]ed and removed" (C 3).

The singular forms of the finite verbs—whether in the ground, doubled, passive doubled,[17] or passive stems (G, D, Dt, N)—are for the masculine: *yiḫd* "will seize" (A 7), *l** *y**[*i*]*ḫ***d** "will not seize" (C 7), *yuḫd* "will seize" (A 17), *ybʿr* "will destroy" (A 58), *yddll* "will be subjugated" (A 46), *ylk* "will come, fall" (C 6), *yhpk* "will turn" (A 52), *yḥslnn* "will destroy it" (A 36, 38), *yḥsl* "will be destroyed" (A 14, [44], 55), *yḫll* "will be pierced" (A 45), *y*ḫlq* "will perish" (A 18), "will destroy" (A 15, 16), *yḫs*r** "will lack" (C 13), *l ypq* "will not maintain" (A 13, 29, B 11), *ykly* "will be destroyed" (A 40), *ykn* "will exist" (A 3, 5, 12, C 10), *yspu* "will consume" (A 51), *yʿzz* "will have strength" (A 57, B 4), *yǵtr* "will be killed" (A 39), [*y*]*r*ps* "will crush" (A 50), *yšdd* "will devastate" (A 35, 37), *yšlm* "will completely repay" (A 54); on two occasions nothing but the conjugational prefix is preserved: *y**[. . .] "will [. . .]" (A 9, *l** *y**[. . .] "will not [. . .]" (C 11).

The feminine forms are: *tḫlq* "will perish" (A 4, 6, [8], [34], 59, B 6, C 1, 15), *tk*[*n*] "will exist" (B 8) and *tprš* "will be scattered" (A 53).

The plurals have the form /*taqtulū*/*āna*/: *tbʿrn* "will abandon" (A 41, 56), *tbṣrn* "will remain distant" (C 4), *tdlln* "will subjugate" (A 7, 47f.), *thbẓn* "will be removed" (C 3), *tnšan* "will be raised (fem.)" (A 47), *t*ʿzzn* "will have strength" (A 20), *tʿm*q*n** "will be strong" (A 2), *tqln* "will fall" (A 1), *tqṣrn* "will shorten" (A 33); in two places only the end of a verbal form is preserved: [. . .]*r*n*/*n** "they will [. . .]" (A 21, C 3).

3.2.3.4 Position of the Direct and Indirect Objects

Both direct and indirect objects are consistently placed immediately after the predicate, i.e., in the last position in the clause—for the objective suffix *-nn* in *yḥslnn* "will destroy it" (A 36, 38) this is self-evident. The following direct objects are found: *ib mlk* "the king's enemy" (A 17), *ibh* "his enemy" (A 22, 58, C 7), *bhmt ib* "the enemy's animals" (A 15), *bhmt ḥ*w*t* "the country's animals" (A 16), *ḥwt* "the land" (A 50, 51, B 2), *ḥwt ib* "the enemy's land" (A 7, 10, 11, 37), *ḥwt hyt* "this land" (A 35, 41f., 56), *ymy bʿlhn* "their master's days" (A 34) and *špḥ* "descendant(s)" (A 13, 29,

17. *ydll* < *ydtll* "he will be subjugated," A 46.

B [11]). The indirect objects are *b ḥwt* "in the land" (A 1, 3, 5, [12]), *b ydh* "in his hand" (A 48), *l*h** "for him/it" (C 13), *l ibh* "for his enemy" (A 54), *l mlk* "from the king" (A 52), *ˁl ḫpṯh* "over his 'freed ones'" (A 57); on one occasion the noun in question has not been preserved: *ˁl**[. . .] "on [. . .]" (B 4).

3.2.3.5 Position of Adverbial Phrases
In the following three cases nouns, in the adverbial accusative standing immediately before the predicate, describe the manner or the circumstance of the action: [*ḫ*]*rd w uḫry* "by the (hand of the) guards and descendant(s)" (A 39f.), *yd ḫrdh* "by the hand of his guard" (A 46) and *tpšlt ḥwth* "in the baseness (of the inhabitants) of his land" (A 45).

3.2.3.6 Conclusions
So far as the state of preservation of the tablets will permit us to draw such a conclusion, the apodosis consistently shows the following form in the overwhelming majority of cases when it is constructed as a verbal clause:

Subject—(adverb)—predicate—(predicate)—direct/indirect object

3.3 Results
Nominal clauses are rarely used in apodoses (7×) and apparently serve only to describe the accompanying circumstances of the verbal clauses to which they are attached. Only in A 19 do we find a purely nominal double concluding clause. On the other hand the verbal clause is very popular (59 or 62 times). In contrast to the protases the extremely uniform structure of the apodoses, which take the form: subject—predicate—object, is surprising.

Text B seems to contain only verbal clauses. But it is impossible to make a certain pronouncement because the preserved length of the lines is very short.

CONCLUDING REMARKS

In the introduction it was pointed out on the basis of epigraphic features that *KTU* 1.103+145 and *KTRIH* 1.14 stand particularly close together and that *KTU* 1.140 stands on its own.

This argument can now be strengthened with the following syntactic observations: *KTU* 1.140 introduces the protasis with the particle *k* "if" (*KTRIH* 1.14 with *hm* "if," *KTU* 1.103+145 with *w* "and (if)"), see 2.1; the indicative verb forms of the protasis stand before the subject (in *KTU* 1.103+145 and *KTRIH* 1.14 after the subject), see 2.2.2 and 2.3; there are no nominal protases (in *KTU* 1.103+145 and *KTRIH* 1.14 the nominal clause predominates), see 2.2.3; the absolute subject of the apodosis in the singular is not given prominence by the addition of the *n*-affix (in *KTU* 1.103+145 and *KTRIH* 1.14 this is always the case), see 3.2.3.2.

Possibly still further criteria for the exceptional position of *KTU* 1.140 against *KTU* 1.103+145 and *KTRIH* 1.14 would have been forthcoming if the text had come down to us in a more complete form (see, e.g., 3.3).

If there are now syntactic reasons in addition to the epigraphic evidence that *KTU* 1.103+145 and *KTRIH* 1.14 may be said to have been written by the same scribe, then the fact that they were found in different locations ("South Acropolis" and "Summer Palace") is all the more surprising. Thus at some time before the fall of the city *KTRIH* 1.14 must have found its way from the Priests' Library to the "Summer Palace" of Ras Ibn Hani.[18]

18. Since completing the manuscript of this article, we have continued our research on the omens, and have improved substantially our interpretation of the texts. We refer especially to KTU 1.103 + 145 (Text A here) line 1 and the consequences for a new look at this text. Our observations on syntax are not significantly affected by this more recent work, except in relation to that line. Because of the large number of alterations that would be involved, we have not been able to take account of these new results here. We therefore refer the reader to our study of the omens in *Die keilalphabetischen Omina aus Ugarit und Ras Ibn Hani* in the series Abhandlungen zur Literatur Alt-Syrien-Palästinas (ALASP) 2 (Münster: UGARIT-Verlag, 1989; ISBN 3-92710-05-7).

MAARAV 5–6 (Spring, 1990): 111–125

FORMS OF THE DUAL IN THE TEXTS OF EBLA*

PELIO FRONZAROLI
UNIVERSITY OF FLORENCE, ITALY

TRANSLATED BY MATTHEW L. JAFFE

If some verbal forms[1] and two forms of the pronoun suffix[2] are excluded, the attestations of the dual are exclusively nominal as far as they have been identified in the texts of Ebla.

*The present work was carried out with a contribution of CNR ("Research for the Common Semitic Lexicon"). The unedited texts are cited with the permission of Paolo Matthiae, director of the Italian Archaeological Mission in Syria. Besides the usual abbreviations, the following are to be noted: *ARET* = *Archivi Reali di Ebla. Testi* (2: D. O. Edzard, *Verwaltungstexte verschiedenen Inhalts*, Rome, 1981; 5: D. O. Edzard, *Hymnen, Beschwörungen und Verwandtes,* Rome, 1984); *BaE* = L. Cagni (ed.), *Il bilinguismo a Ebla*, Naples, 1984; *BFE* = M. Krebernik, *Die Beschwörungen aus Fara und Ebla,* Hildesheim: Olms, 1984; *LdE* = L. Cagni (ed.), *La lingua di Ebla,* Naples, 1981; *MAS-GELLAS* = *Groupe d'Études de Linguistique et de Littératures Arabes et Sudarabiques. Matériaux Arabes et Sudarabiques* (Paris); *MEE* = *Materiali epigrafici di Ebla* (2: G. Pettinato, *Testi amministrativi della biblioteca L. 2769*, Naples, 1980; 4: G. Pettinato, *Testi lessicali bilingui della biblioteca L. 2769*, Naples, 1982); *QuSem* = *Quaderni di Semitistica* (13: P. Fronzaroli (ed.), *Studies on the Language of Ebla,* Florence, 1984).

1. *da-za-a* (Gelb, "Ebla and the Kish Civilization," *LdE*: 36: dual or plural; Fronzaroli, "Per una valutazione della morfologia eblaita," *Studi Eblaiti* 5 (1982): 109 and n. 40; Krebernik, *BFE*: 134: singular); *gi-ra-ba* (Krebernik, *BFE*: 192f.); *ib-šè-a-ma* (Edzard, *ARET* 2: 128: dual or plural); PI-*ti-a* (Edzard, *ARET* 5: 25); *sa-ba-du-na*, *si-⟨ba-⟩du-na* (Krebernik, *BFE*: 115f.); *si-ba* (Krebernik, *BFE*: 133f.; Edzard, *ARET* 5: 27: plural imperative, or else nominal form); *(wa-)li-da* (Krebernik, *BFE*: 192f.).

2. *-gú-ma-a* (von Soden, *LdE:* 360: *-kumā*; Fronzaroli, "Morfologia" (N 1): 98; *-na-a*, *-ne-a* (Krebernik, *BFE*: 114f.). The writing *-gu-ná* (*ARET* 2: 105, s.v. *En-na-gú-na*) does not exist; see Fronzaroli, "Morfologia" (N 1): 97 n. 11: *En-na-gu-nu*[!].

The recognizable forms have given place to diverse interpretations. Some scholars have admitted the existence of a diptotic inflection;[3] others have maintained that the orthography preserved in the texts indicate a unique termination which would have been used for either the nominative or for the genitive-accusative.[4] It remains doubtful, furthermore, if the available signs are sufficient to prove the existence of nunation.[5] It seems therefore opportune to systematically examine the documentation, either clarifying the problems inherent in the nominal inflection, or for verifying the existence of pronominal and verbal forms.

1. INFLECTION OF THE NOUN

1.1 BILINGUAL LEXICAL LISTS

In the bilingual lexical lists the forms of the dual have been known for some time. Owing to the existence of variants (like *si-li-sa*![6] for *si-li-sa-a* functioning as nominative, *i-da* for *i-da-a* functioning as genitive-accusative) some scholars suppose that the two signs that characterize the dual, *-Ca* and *-Ca-a*, would be used without functional difference. It appears, therefore, opportune to reexamine the documentation.

For this purpose it is necessary to distinguish the two lists, TM.75.G.2000+ (=A) and TM.75.G.2001+ (=B) from the other copies and from the extracts. In list A (and for which we can judge from the sole writing *ga-na-a*, also in list B) the form of the nominative dual (syllabograms of the type *-Ca*) is kept distinct from the form of the genitive-accusative dual (syllabograms of the type *-Ca-a*). This function of the two writings appears clear from the following attestations:

3. Gelb (N 1): 31; Fronzaroli, "Morfologia" (N 1): 103f.; see also Edzard, "Sumerisch 1 bis 10 in Ebla," *Studi Eblaiti* 3 (1980): 126 (*-ā(n)*).

4. Krebernik, "Zu Syllabar und Orthographie der lexikalischen Texte aus Ebla. Teil 1," *ZA* 72 (1982): 223; *BFE*: 314 n. 67; cf. also Krecher, "Sumerische und nichtsumerische Schicht in der Schriftkultur von Ebla," *BaE*: 152 and n. 93.

5. See especially Krecher, "Schicht" (N 4): 152 n. 93.

6. The reading *si-li-sa*! (followed by Krebernik, "Syllabar 1" [N 4]: 223; "Zu Syllabar und Orthographie der lexikalischen Texte aus Ebla.Teil 2 (Glossar)," *ZA* 73 (1983): 30) is given in *MEE* 4: 28. In fact the gloss of TM.75.G.2001 + v. I 34 has to be read *si-li-sa-⸢a⸣* (collation 1979); for this reason the variant is not indicated in Fronzaroli, "Morfologia" (N 1): 103.

(a)	*da-la-za*	(= á-e-gi$_4$-gi$_4$, A v. I 13f.; B r. X′ 2f.)
	ga-ba-a	(= íb, A v. XII 26f.; B v. IV 24f.)
	ḫu-ba-ra	(= gù-dim-dim, A r. V 25f.)
	ma-ba-da-ʾà	(= giš-giškim-ti, A. r. XIII 29f.; var. *ma-ba-da-a*, B r. VII′ 23f.)
	ma-ba-da-ra	(= giš-IŠ-II, A r. X 20f.; var. [*m*]*a*-[*ba*]-*da-la*, B r. IV′ 14)
	ma-ba-ga-da	(= še-KA-KA, A v. V 18f., B r. XIII′ 19)
	mar-ʾa_x*-za*	(= á-e-daḫ, A v. 1 15f.; var. *mar-a-za*, B r. X′ 4f.)
	mar-ba-a	(= giš-RU-RU, A r. XI 54f.; B r. VI′ 3)
	mu-ba-a	(= giš-GIL-dím, A r. XIV 13f.; B r. VIII′ 12f.)
	si-li-sa-a	(= an-ki, A v. IX 27f.; B v. I 34: *si-li-sa-*⌜*a*⌝)
	za-la-sa	(= ù-sar, B v. XII 43f.)
	zu-zu-a	(= ti-gi-núm, A v. XIII 35f.)[7]
(b)	*dal-da-bù-um a-na-a*	(= igi-dar, A v. VII 19f.)
	ga-nu a-li ga-na-a	(= ga-nu$_{11}$, A v. XVIII 27f.; B v. X 3f.)
	ḫu-ma-zu a-na-a	(= igi-du$_8$-du$_8$, A v. VII 14f.)
	ma-wu i-da-a	(= a-šu-luḫ, A v. IV 6f.; B r XII′ 17: *m*[*a-w*]*u i-*[*da-a*])
	na-si-ì a-na-a	(= igi-íl, A v. VII 32f.)
	šè-a-du ma-ḫa-rí a-na-a	(= igi-kù-dub-igi-gar, A v. VII 40f.)[8]

7. The following glosses have been interpreted as forms of the dual: *da-la-za* (Krebernik, "Syllabar 2" (N 6): 20; for a different opinion, Hecker, "Doppelt t-erweiterte Formen oder: der eblaitische Infinitiv," *BaE*: 209; *ga-ba-a* (Krecher, "Schicht" [N 4]: 157); *ma-ba-da-ʾà* (Edzard, "Sumerisch 1 bis 10" [N 3]: 126; Krebernik, "Syllabar 2" (N 6): 17; cf. Krecher, "Schicht" [N 4]: 164); *ma-ba-da-ra* (Krecher, "Schicht" [N 4]: 152); *mar-ʾ*a_x*-za* (Krebernik, "Syllabar 2" [N 6]: 20); *si-li-sa-a* (Fronzaroli, "Morfologia" [N 1]: 103; "The Eblaic Lexicon: Problems and Appraisal," *QuSem* 13 (1984): 123; Krebernik, "Syllabar 2" (N 6): 30); *za-la-sa* (Krebernik, "Syllabar 2" [N 6]: 10; *BFE*: 136; cf. F. Fales, "A Survey of Two-Word Eblaic Entries in the Bilingual Vocabulary," *QuSem* 13 (1984): 177). For *zu-zu-a* it will be noted that the logogram could also be a Semitic word; in list B it has the form of a dual (ti-gi-na, B v. V 28, without gloss) and the same form is found in the administrative texts.

8. The writings *a-na-a* and *i-da-a* have been consistently interpreted as duals: *dal-da-bù-um a-na-a* (Krebernik "Syllabar 2" [N 6]: 27; Hecker [N 7]: 217 n. 72;

When the writing -*Ca-a* appears in the attestations of the subgroup (a), the syllabogram -*a* serves to indicate the third consonant radical: *ga-ba-a* /qabl-ā(n)/ "the two hips"; *ma-ba-da-a* (variants of *ma-ba-da-*ʾ*à* /mabṭaḥ-ā(n)/ "trust"; cf. also *mar-ba-a*, *mu-ba-a*. Consequently the interpretation /širš-ā(n)/ previously proposed for *si-li-sa-a* is probably in error.[9] This gloss should instead be considered as a reduplicated form /šilšall-ā(n)/.[10]

The writing -*Ca-a*, however, in the attestations of the subgroup (b) constantly appears in words in which the syllabogram -*a* can indicate only the nominal termination: *a-na-a* "the two eyes" (cf. *dal-da-bù* 2 igi, B r. XIV′ 32; *ḫu-mu-zu* 2 igi, B r. XIV′ 28); *i-da-a* "the two hands" as opposed to the genitive singular *i-tim* (*bí-da-gi i-ti*[*m*], = šu-tar, A r. XV 3); cf. also *ga-na-a* as opposed to *ga-nu*. Since the syllabogram *a* can have the value /ya/ in the Ebla texts and considering that the closed syllable /CVC/ can be rendered as the writing *CVCV*, the writing -*Ca-a* ought to be interpreted as /Cay/.[11] In this fashion the scribe of.list A (and perhaps also that of list B) desired to distinguish graphically the termination of the genitive-accusative: /ᶜayn-ay(n)/, /yid-ay(n)/.[12]

In other bilingual lexical texts, the forms of the dual also end in -*Ca* when they are clearly in the genitive-accusative case:

Fales [N 7]: 182); *ḫu-ma-zu a-na-a* (Fronzaroli, "Morfologia" [N 1]: 103f.; Krebernik, "Syllabar 2" [N 6]: 27; M. Civil, "Bilingualism in Logographically Written Languages: Sumerian in Ebla," *BaE*: 88; Fales [N 7]: 181f.); *ma-wu i-da-a* (Fronzaroli, "Il verdetto per A'mur-Damu e sua madre (TM.75.G.1430)," *Studi Eblaiti* 3 (1980): 71 n. 27.); Krebernik, "Syllabar 2" [N 6]: 24; Krecher, "Schicht" [N 4]: 152; Fales [N 7]: 180); *na-si-ì a-na-a* (Krebernik, "Syllabar 2" [N 6]: 27f.; Fales [N 7]: 182); *šè-a-du ma-ḫa-rí a-na-a* (Krebernik "Syllabar 2" [N 6]: 28; Fales [N 7]: 181).

For the gloss *ga-ba-lu* ʾ*a*$_x$-*za-da* (= á-⌜gur⌝, B r. IX′ 32′f.), interpreted by Krebernik (*BFE*: 138) as containing a form of the dual, see Fronzaroli, "Eblaic Lexicon" (N 7): 124f., 140.

9. Cf. Fronzaroli, "Morfologia" (N 1): 103; Krebernik "Syllabar 2" (N 6): 30.

10. Perhaps from **šalšall-* (possibly also **šalšāl-*, /šilšāl-ā(n)/ with transition from *a* to *i* in pretonic position (cf. Krebernik "Syllabar 2" [N 6]: 22 n. 72). This word can be compared with the Semitic **šršr, šlšl* "chain; ring of chain" (cf. Akkadian *šeršerrum, šeršerratum*).

11. On the writing of the closed syllable, see Krebernik, "Syllabar 1" [N 4]: 224f.; on the value /ya/ of *a*, see Edzard, "Sumerisch 1 bis 10" (N 3): 123; Krebernik, "Syllabar 1" (N 4): 219f.; Krecher, "Schicht" (N 4): 158f.

12. The accurate writing -*Ca-a* for rendering the diphthong /-ay/ is also found in the gloss *gi-ti-ma-a* /qidmay/ "before" (= igi-me, TM.75.G.1445 r. I 1f.; Krecher (N 4): 163 n. 170; Steinkeller, "The Eblaite Preposition *qidimay*, 'before,'" *OA* 23 (1984): 33–37.

ga-ba-zi i-da-II (= á-ḫum, TM.75.G.1301 v. II 7f.)
ma-ḫa-zi i-da (= šu-šu-ra, TM.75.G.1301 v. II 5f.)
ma-u₉ i-da (= a-šu-luḫ, TM.75.G.1825 r. IV 12f.)[13]

This writing, even being less accurate than that of lists A and B, returns to the norm, given that at Ebla the diphthongs /aw/, /ay/ are usually expressed with the syllabograms of the type (*C*)*a*.[14] It will be noted, finally, that the documentation of the lexical texts does not allow us to establish whether the dual in Eblaic had nunation. In the interpretation given above (/-ā(n)/, /-ay(n)/) the nunation is suggested on comparative bases.

1.2. LITERARY TEXTS

Forms of the dual have also been indicated in literary texts. Since the difficulty of the interpretations is much greater, the attestations ought to be used with much caution. We limit ourselves here to examining those which are less uncertain:

(1) 2 ᵈ*Ba-li-ḫa* / *wa-ti-a* (*ARET* 5, 4 II 5f.)[15]
(2) én-é-nu-ru / ki / én-é-nu-ru / ᵈ*Ba-li-ḫa-a* (*ARET* 5, 16 I 1–4)
(3) *si-ba* / ki-ki / *si-ba* / 2 ᵈ*Ba-li-ḫa* (*ARET* 5, 5 VII 4–7)[16]

13. For *ga-ba-zi i-da*-II, see Krebernik "Syllabar 2" (N 6): 21; Hecker (N 7): 213 n. 52; Fales [N 7]: 180); for *ma-ḫa-zi i-da*, see Fronzaroli, "Morfologia" (N 1): 105 and n. 23; Krebernik, "Syllabar 2" (N 6): 20; Fales (N 7): 179; for *ma-u₉ i-da* (variants of *ma-wu i-da-a*), see above, n. 8.

14. Fronzaroli, "Un atto reale di donazione dagli Archivi di Ebla (TM.75.G.1766)," *Studi Eblaiti* 1 (1979): 8 and n. 12; Edzard, "Sumerisch 1 bis 10" (N 3): 126 and n. 31; Krebernik, "Syllabar 1" (N 4): 223.

15. The writing *wa-ti-a*, which can be a stative dual, is comparable to the gloss *wa-ti-um* (= zà-me, TM.75.G.10023 + r. VI 9f.). In the chancellery texts the sumerogram zà-me seems to have the meaning "it is available; it is present" (F. Pomponio, "Note su alcuni termini dei testi amministrativi di Ebla," *Vicino Oriente* 5 [1982]: 211ff.); the secondary form **wtw/y* of Semitic **ʾtw/y* "to come" (hypothesized by Pomponio, p. 213) is attested in Akkadian *watûm* "to discover; to find," in Old South Arabic *wtw* (*hwtw*, "to bring back," A. F. L. Beeston *et al.*, *Sabaic Dictionary* [Louvain-la-Neuve: Peeters, 1982]: 165; J. C. Biella, *Dictionary of Old South Arabic* [Chico: Scholars Press, 1982]: 153) and in the area of Modern South Arabic (W. W. Müller, *Die Wurzeln Mediae and Tertiae Y/W im Altsüdarabischen* [Tübingen: Huth, 1962]: 111; T. M. Johnstone, *Jibbāli Lexicon* [Oxford, 1981]: 294: íti "to come," útti "to find"). For a different interpretation of the gloss, cf. Krebernik, "Syllabar 2" (N 6): 41 ("gepriesen").

16. The possibility that *si-ba* was a noun is considered by Edzard, *ARET* 5: 27; Krebernik, *BFE*: 133f., thinks it is an imperative ("seid beschwören).

(4) *a-za-me-ga* / al_6 / *zi-na-ba-t*[*i*] / ^{d}ut[u] / al_6 / *su-lu-la-a* / 1 iti (*ARET* 5, 1 III 6–12), cf. *si-in* / *zi-ne-éb-ti* / ^{d}utu / *si-in* / 2 si / ^{d}*Sa-nu-ga-ru*$_{12}$ (*ARET* 5, 4 III 1–6)[17]

(5) GÁN-kéš / *bù* / *a-za-da-an* / *ù* / *bù* / *ḫa-la-mi-im* (*ARET* 5, 16 III 2–7)[18]

The name of the river Baliḫ, always indicated as a dual in the texts of Ebla, appears with the writing *-Ca* in (1) where presumably it is intended as a nominative. The form of the genitive-accusative, however, is rendered by the writing *-Ca-a* in (2), where ki and ^{d}*Ba-li-ḫa-a* could depend from én-é-nu-ru. It will be noted that in the text (3), perhaps the Eblaic interpretation of (2), the scribe uses the shorter writing *-Ca*.

One finds a more secure attestation of the writing *-Ca-a* for the form of genitive-accusative in *su-lu-la-a* (4), where this case is required by the preposition preceding. The parallel sentence of *ARET* 5, 4 occurs with the sumerogram 2 si. This allows proposing the interpretation /šurūr-ay(n)/ "the two rays" (cf. Akkadian *šarū-rum* "radiance"; Syriac *šrūrā* "sprout"), with reference to the two "horns" of the new moon. In the same text (*ARET* 5, 1 III 5) a form of the genitive-accusative dual has been indicated in *a-ma-na-a*, in a less comprehensible context.[19]

Finally, a form of the genitive-accusative with nunation is probably in *a-za-da-an* (5), even if the interpretation of the word remains uncertain. It is more difficult to decide if *tal-da-an* (*ARET* 5, 1 II 7) really represents /dalt-ayn/, as has been proposed.[20]

1.3 CHANCELLERY TEXTS

In the texts of the chancellery as well, the graphical distinction of the two cases of the dual is not always observed. Several attestations in the texts of the epistolary style will be examined first:

(6) 2 *ga-bí-ra* / *I-da*-NI / ÉxPAP / [ki] / [*du-b*]*a*-LUM (TM.75.G.2345 r. 1 1–5)[21]

17. For the interpretation, see Edzard, *ARET* 5: 20.
18. Cf. Krebernik, *BFE*: 133 and 137f.
19. Edzard, *ARET* 5: 19.
20. Edzard, *ARET* 5: 17.
21. For the interpretation of *ga-bí-ra* as a noun of function or title, see Fronzaroli, *SEL* 2 (1985): 28f. The sumerogram ÉxPAP could have in this context a

(7) *wa* šu ba_4-ti / ki / *ša-ti* / *En-na*-NI / *wa* / *Puzur$_4$-ra-ḫa-al$_6$* / *ga-bí-ra-a* (TM.75.G.2345 r. IV 6–12)[22]
(8) ki / *ga-bí-ra-a* (TM.75.G.2345 r. V 6f.; VI 4f.; v. I 7f.)
(9) *wa* / ì-na-sum-*kum* / é / *in* / *ba-da-a* / *ša* / 2 *li-im* (TM.75.G.1766 r. II 3–III 2)[23]
(10) *a-ti-ma* / zà-me / *sa-ba-da-su-ma* (TM.75.G.1672 v. IV 15–V 1; *sa-ba-da-su-ma,* also in v. V 9), cf. 2 *sa-ba-a-ti* (TM.75.G.1672 v. IV 11)[24]
(11) ⌜*a*⌝-*ʾà-wa-a* / 2 / *ba-da-ga* / *Áb-zu*^{ki} / *ša-a* / sag / *Bí-bí-Li-im* / *in* / *Ma-rí*^{ki} (TM.75.G.2290 v. IV 8–16)[25]
(12) *wa* / šu ba_4-ti / 2 gú-zi ì-giš / *a-ʾà-wa* / 30 sìla ì-giš (TM.75.G.2268 r. IV 19–V 2)

The scribe of TM.75.G.2345 employs the writing -*Ca* in (6) where the dual is presumably intended as a nominative, as opposed to the writing -*Ca-a* in (7) and (8), where *ga-bí-ra-a* is the *nomen rectum.* The writing of the genitive-accusative is found again in (9), where the case is required by the preceding preposition. In the text TM.75.G.1672 *sa-ba-da-su-ma* (10) can be interpreted as a dual genitive-accusative followed by a pronoun suffix; in the same text the plural of the same word is rendered by *sa-ba-a-tim* (r. V 12), *sa-ba-a-ti-su-ma* (v. I 6). A writing -*Ca* for the genitive-accusative followed by the pronoun suffix is found again in (11), where 2 / *ba-da-ga* can be interpreted as /bayt-ay-ka/ "your two houses." It is more difficult to decide if ⌜*a*⌝-*ʾà-wa-a* in (11) and *a-ʾà-wa* in (12) represent the same form; if so we had the more accurate writing in the first text and the more abbreviated in the second.

In conclusion, if one excepts the form attested in (12), the texts redacted in the epistolary style confirm the graphical distinction of the two cases of the dual. From the writings of (10) and (11),

verbal function; cf. the gloss *sa-ʾà-bu* (= é-pap, TM.75.G.10023+ v. VIII 21f.), for which Butz has mentioned the Akkadian *saʾābu* ("Bilingualismus als Catalysator," *BaE*: 128 n. 156). "They pour at the storehouse- ÉxPAP (what is due for) the field *d.*," can perhaps be proposed.

22. "And he received the field of PN_1 and PN_2, the two *g.*"; see Fronzaroli, "Le pronom déterminatif-relatif à Ebla," *MARI* 5 (1987): 271.

23. For the interpretation, cf. Fronzaroli, "Un atto reale" (N 14): 4; *Studi Eblaiti* 4 (1981): 171; Gelb (N 1): 31. On the basis of the material assembled in the present article I consider it now impossible that the writing *ba-da-a* would indicate a nominative dual (cf. "Morfologia" [N 1]: 103).

24. For the meaning of zà-me, see above, n. 15.

25. For the interpretation, see Fronzaroli, "Le pronom" (N 22): 272. "The two *a.* of your two houses in GN_1, those of s. of PN in GN_2," can perhaps be proposed.

however, it seems conclusive that where the form of genitive-accusative was followed by a pronoun suffix the accurate writing -*Ca-a* was not retained as necessary.

In administrative texts a logographic writing prevails which permits the invariable maintenance of the form of the noun even when the number is greater than "1" (for example 2 *gú-li-lum*, 3 *gú-li-lum*). Besides this there exist writings of the dual like the following:

(13) *gú-li*-II (*ARET* 2)
(14) *sa-ḫa-wa*-II (*ARET* 2; var. *sa-ḫa*-II, *ARET* 2)
(15) 2 *ti-gi-na* (*ARET* 2; var. 2 *ti-ki-na, ARET* 2)
(16) 2 *ti-sa-na* (*ARET* 4; var. *ti-sa-na-a*, *ARET* 3)
(17) 2 *ba-ga*-NE-*sa-a* (TM.75.G.1343 v. I 2 = *MEE* 2, 29; var. *ba-ga*-NE-*sa-sù*, TM.75.G.1292 r. VII 11 = *MEE* 2, 12)
(18) *a-na-a* / 2 dumu-nita-*a* / *Du-ḫal* (*ARET* 4)

The objects registered in the administrative texts, indicated always at the beginning of the paragraph, are rendered in the nominative case. Therefore, it is also probable that where forms of the dual are used, these ought to be considered in the nominative case. In (13) and (14) the abbreviated writings *gú-li*-II for /kulēl-ā(n)/ "two bracelets,"[26] *sa-ḫa*-II for /šaḫaw-ā(n)/ "two pendants"[27] will be noted. The variant *ti-sa-na-a* (16) could indicate a genitive-accusative subordinated from a preposition not registered in the text: 10 gín DILMUN bar_6:kù / 2 BU.DI / *ti-sa-na-a* "10 shekels of silver for two B. (and) two *t.*" (*ARET* 3, 440 v. V 1–3).[28] Less

26. The writing *gú-li-lum*, which has been compared with the Akkadian of Mari *kulīlum* (G. Pettinato, "Il commercio internazionale di Ebla: Economia statale e privata," *Orientalia Lovanensia Analecta* 5 [1979]: 188 n. 23; Edzard, *ARET* 2: 127), shows the contraction of the diphthong in the scheme of the diminutive 1*u*2*ay*3-. The same scheme is attested in Eblaic, with the diphthong preserved, in the gloss *ḫu-sa-b*[*ù*] (= giš-PA-mul-mul, TM.75,G.5653+ r. XV 10′f.; var. *ḫu-sa-bu_x*, TM.75.G.1426 r. II 4f.), and, with the diphthong contracted, in the variant *ḫu-si-bù* (A r. XIII 25f.; B r. VII′ 20f.), as has been noted by Krebernik, "Syllabar 2" (N 6): 17 and 23 n. 78.

27. The writing *sa-ḫa*-(*wa*-)II has been compared by Edzard (*ARET* 2: 137) with the gloss *sa-ḫa-wa-tum* (= $geštu_x$ (GIŠ.PI)-lá-KA, A r. XI 9f.). The two words can be derived from a verb **šḫw/y*, a form parallel to **šḫḫ* "to get loose, to lower oneself"; besides Hebrew and Judaic Aramaic, **šḫw/y* is preserved in the South Arabic area (Johnstone [N 15]: 264: *šúthi* "to be loose").

28. The same construction with writing of the genitive-accusative is found in the following text: 1 gín DILMUN kù-gi/*bù-ga-na-a* (TM.75.G.1299 r. V 4–v. I 1 = *MEE* 2, 16; *Studi Eblaiti* 4 [1981]: 138).

comprehensible is, however, the writing *ba-ga*-NE-*sa-a* (17), which is found at the beginning of the paragraph immediately after the registration of another object: 1 gír mar-tu kù-gi 2 *ba-ga*-NE-*sa-a* MAŠ kù-gi.

The writing *a-na-a* (18) forms part of the motivation of a consignment of clothes for services rendered on the occasion of a childbirth of the queen: *mu-ti-iš ma-a* / *ma-lik-tum* / dumu-nita / tu-da / *a-na-a* / 2 dumu-nita-*a* / *Du-ḫal* (*ARET* 4, 18 r. VII 15–21). If *mu-ti-iš ma-a* can be interpreted as /muddiš māy(ī)/ "the one who has renewed the water," *a-na-a* could have the meaning "the two springs" or "the two wells," but the syntax of the sentence of the sentence appears unusual: "the one who renewed the water (when) the queen had given birth to a son, (from the?) two wells of the two sons of PN."

2. INFLECTION OF THE PRONOUN

2.1 SUFFIX PRONOUN OF THE FIRST PERSON

A form of the suffix pronoun of the first person dual has been indicated in the writing *-na-a* (var. *-ne-a*), which recurs in two parallel texts of én-é-nu-ru:[29]

(18) *a*-LUM *sa-ba-du-na-a* (*ARET* 5, 19 XI 5), cf. *a*-LUM *sa-ba-sù* (*ARET* 5, 19 XI 4)
(19) *la si-ba-du-ne-a* (*ARET* 5, 8 IV 4)

The proposed interpretation ("Nicht unser beider Beschwörungen sind es") is probable but not absolutely certain.

In the chancellery texts appears a suffix *-na*, which has been interpreted as a dialectal variant of the suffix of the first personal plural *-nu*:[30]

(20) *áš-du-na* / ì-tìl (TM.75.G.1531 r. II 7f.)[31]

29. Krebernik, *BFE*: 114f.

30. Fronzaroli, "Morfologia" (N 1): 96f.; cf.Gelb (N 1): 26 (which supposes, however, *-ni* as a normal form of the genitive of the suffix pronoun of the first person plural).

31. For the interpretation of the sumerogram as ì-tìl, see Krecher, "The Preposition /min(u)/ 'from' and Ì.TI 'he was (present)'," *QuSem* 13 (1984): 78–83; therefore "with us it is available," or else "for our part it is available."

(21) *wa* / du-du / *a* / *na-ʾa*$_x$*-rí* / *a* / *wa-ki-lu-na* (TM.75.G.2366 r. V 14–VI 2)[32]

In both the attestations the context does not allow us to decide if the suffix pronoun can be interpreted as a dual. The hypothesis of a dialectal variant of the plural suffix seems, therefore, for the moment, more prudent.

2.2. SUFFIX PRONOUNS OF THE SECOND PERSON

A form of the suffix pronoun of the second person dual has been indicated in the writing *-gú-ma-a*:[33]

(22) *wa* / *a-da-ba-gú-ma-a* / *Íl-ba-Ma-lik* (TM.75.G.2094 r. II 6–8)
(23) *wa* / *a-da-ḫa-gú-ma-a* (TM.75.G.2094 r. II 9–III 1)[34]

The same suffix pronoun, but with a different ending, also appears joined to nominal forms:

(24) 1 *li-im* še *gú-bar* / ⌈é⌉ *-gú-*⌈*ma*⌉*-an* / *ù-ma* / 2 *li-im* še *gú-bar* / ⌈é⌉*-gú-ma-an* (TM.75.G.1531 v. II 6–III 1)[35]
(25) *wa* / du$_{11}$-ga / *si-in* / 2 maškim-*ga* / *a* / du-du-*gú-ma-an* / *áš-du-nu* / še / ì-na-sum (TM.75.G.2171 v. IV 11–V 5)[36]

In (25) it will be noted that the reference to two maškim confirms the interpretation of the suffix as a form of the dual.

32. For the inconsistency of the writing of the construct state in Eblaic, see Fronzaroli, "Morfologia" (N 1): 106; Edzard, "Zur Syntax der Ebla-Texte," *QuSem* 13 (1984): 105f. The writing *na-ʾa*$_x$*-rí* can be compared with *nʿr* "boy; servant," attested in Ugaritic, Phoenician, and Hebrew; for *wa-ki-lu-na*, see already Fronzaroli, "Il verdetto" (N 8): 37f. "and let him go, either my servant or our superintendent!" can perhaps be proposed.

33. von Soden (N 2): 360; Fronzaroli, "Morfologia" (N 1): 98.

34. In both the attestations the suffix pronoun is preceded by verbal forms; *a-da-ḫa* can be interpreted with sufficient certainty as belonging to the verb **ṭḫ*ʿ "to approach; to address oneself," also attested at Ebla in the form *i-da-ḫa-ú* (Gelb [N 1]: 36; Fronzaroli, "Morfologia" [N 1]: 109; Krebernik, *BFE*: 113).

35. "1000 *g.* of barley for the house of you two or else 2000 *g.* of barley for the house of you two"; for the employment of *ù-ma* in the Eblaic texts, see Fronzaroli, "Disposizioni reali per Tiṯaw-Liʾm (TM.75.G.2396, TM.75.G.1986+)," *Studi Eblaiti* 7 (1984): 10.

36. "And say to your two m.-functionaries: for the trip of you two, barley has been given by us."

2.3. SUFFIX PRONOUN OF THE THIRD PERSON

The writing *sa-ba-da-su-ma* (10), attested two times in the same text, could be interpreted as containing the prefix of the third person dual ("the two *s.* of their two"). The dual could refer to the king and to the queen which are the subject in both cases (or also to the two divinities who are offered the two *s.*). In the same text the writing *-su-ma* also appears after forms of the plural:

(26) *sa-ba-a-ti-su-ma* (TM.75.G.1672 v. I 6)
(27) *du-la-ti* / en / *ma-lik-tum* / kú / nag / *du-la-ti-su-ma* (TM.75.G.1672 v. III 4–9)[37]

The same writing also appears in *ARET* 2, 34 and in the parallel text TM.75.G.2320:

(28) *wa* / íl / 2 AN.AN.DU / *wa* / *ib-šè-a-ma* / *wa* / PAD-*su-ma* (TM.75.G.2320 r. IV 5–11; var. PAD-*sù*, *ARET* 2, 34 V 1); see also PAD-*su-ma* (TM.75.G.2320 r. V 7; var. PAD-*sù*, *ARET* 2, 34 V 8)
(29) *wa* / íl-*su-ma* (*ARET* 2, 34 V 3; var. íl, TM.75.G.2320 r. V 2); see also íl-*su-ma* (*ARET* 2, 34 VI 5; TM.75.2320 v. I 3)[38]

In these two attestations the dual suffix can refer to 2 AN.AN.DU; the presence of the verbal dual form *ib-šè-a-ma*[39] is also to be noted.

2.4. DETERMINATIVE-RELATIVE PRONOUN

The form of the genitive-accusative dual of the determinative-relative pronoun is securely attested in the writing *ša-a* (11), where it may refer to ⌈*a*⌉-*ʾà-wa-a*, or else to 2 / *ba-da-ga*.

37. "The king (and) the queen eat the *d.*, drink the *d.* of their two." The different writing of the second syllable does not allow the identification of *du-la-ti* with the gloss *du-lá-tum* (= nin-lú-uḫ, TM.75.G.11271 2′ f.), comparable with the Semitic **tawlaʿ-(at-)* "worm" (Fronzaroli, "Studi sul lessico comune semitico V," *ANLR* 23 [1968]: 297; in the South Arabic area this noun and its derivatives are attested as **twʿl*, Johnstone [N 15]: 272; also, Johnstone, *Ḥarsūsi Lexicon* [Oxford, 1977]: 128).

38. In "Morfologia" (N 1): 97 (i, m) I thought that *-su-ma* could be interpreted as a pronoun suffix of the third person singular followed by the enclitic *-ma*; nevertheless, the context renders more probable the interpretation as a dual suffix pronoun.

39. Cf. Edzard, *ARET* 2: 128. This verb is also attested in the gloss *ba-ša-um* (= al_6-gál, A v. XVI 24f.), comparable with the Akkadian *bašûm* "to be available" (Fronzaroli, "Il verdetto" [N 8]: 68; Pettinato, *MEE*: 325).

3. INFLECTION OF THE VERB

The verbal forms of the dual which can be identified with sufficient certainty are very rare. In the literary texts two forms of the dual imperative have been proposed in the following passage, where they may refer to the divine name ^{d}*Ba-li-ḫa*:

(30) ^{d}*Ba-li-ḫa* / *gi-ra-ba* / *wa li-da* (*ARET* 5, 18 II 2–4)[40]

A form of the dual of the stative is also probably in *wa-ti-a* (1), referring to 2 ^{d}*Ba-li-ḫa*.

In the texts of the chancellery a form of the dual is most probably in the writing *ib-šè-a-ma* (28), which can refer to 2 AN.AN.DU.

4. CONCLUDING OBSERVATIONS

The care with which the lexical list A distinguishes the form of the nominative dual from the form of the genitive-accusative proves that in the texts of Ebla the dual had a diptotic inflection. The literary texts and the texts of the chancellery follow, prevalently, the same accurate writing. As we have seen above (section 1.1), the writing -*Ca* sometimes used for the genitive-accusative does not pose problems as regards the norms of employment of the syllabary. A sole attestation of an administrative text (17) shows the writing -*Ca-a* where we would expect the form of the nominative.

In the forms of the absolute state the nunation occasionally seems indicated in literary texts; at least in one case (5), it is attested with sufficient certainty. The same alternation of a writing -*Ca-an* with -*Ca-a* for rendering /-ayn/ is found in the form of the suffix of the second person (section 2.2). Since there would not have been a reason to indicate nunation if it had not been made part of the morphological system of the language, these few attestations seem sufficient to prove its existence.

40. Krebernik, *BFE*: 192f., considers for the writing *li-da* the two possibilities permitted by the writing, **wld* "to give birth" and **wrd* "to descend." Taking account of the text (1), "the two Baliḫ are present," "O Baliḫ, approach and descend!" can be proposed here.

In conclusion, the sum of the attestations indicates that Eblaic knew the presupposed diptotic inflection, on comparative bases, from other Semitic languages:

	absolute state	construct state
nominative	/-ān/	/-ā/
genitive-accusative	/-ayn/	/-ay/

Unlike Old Akkadian, where the form of the genitive-accusative already appears with the contracted diphthong,[41] Eblaic preserved the original diphthong. Unlike Old South Arabic, where the lack of indication of *-y* in the orthography of the construct state before a suffix pronoun could be considered as an indication of a contraction of the diphthong,[42] the writing *-Ca* before suffix pronouns in Eblaic (10–11) indicates that the diphthong was also preserved in this case. Finally, unlike Ugaritic and Hebrew, where the dual shows mimation, Eblaic attests nunation, favoring the hypothesis that in Ugaritic and Hebrew the mimation of the dual was owed to the analogy on the forms of the singular.[43]

As regards the suffix pronouns, the first person, previously attested only in Ugaritic (*-ny*),[44] seems attested at Ebla in literary texts (*-na-a*, var. *-ne-a*). The Eblaic attestation, together with the fact that outside of the Semitic area a dual suffix pronoun *-ny* is found in Old Egyptian,[45] would favor the opinion that the existence

41. Gelb, *MAD* II^2: 139; for the contracted forms in the Northwest Semitic languages of the second millennium B.C.E., recently D. Sivan, "Dual Nouns in Ugaritic," *JSS* 28 (1983): 239 and n. 87.

42. According to an hypothesis of M. Höfner, *Altsüdarabische Grammatik* (Porta Linguarum Orientalium; Leipzig, 1943): 120; recently, cf. A. F. L. Beeston, *Sabaic Grammar* (JSS Monograph no. 6; Manchester: Univ. of Manchester, 1984): 28, §12:4.

43. For this proposal, see W. Diem, "Gedanken zur Frage der Mimation und Nunation in der semitischen Sprachen," *ZDMG* 125 (1975): 243; recently, W. Randall Garr, *Dialect Geography of Syria-Palestine, 1000-586 B.C.E.* (Philadelphia: Univ. of Pennsylvania, 1985): 91.

44. The interpretation of *-ny* as a dual suffix pronoun is generally admitted; recently, see S. Segert, *A Basic Grammar of the Ugaritic Language* (Berkeley: Univ. of California, 1984): 47; for a different opinion, cf. I. Š. Schiffmann, *Peredneaziatskiy Sbornik* 3 (1979): 229f., 277 (which was not accessible to me).

45. E. Edel, *Altägyptische Grammatik* I (Rome: PBI, 1955): 70, 72.

of the Ugaritic suffix pronoun constituted an archaism and not an innovation.[46]

The second person is attested with certainty in the orthography *-gú-ma-a* and *-gú-ma-an*, where the graphical alternation already noted of the inflection of the noun by rendering /-ayn/ appears anew. Nunation of the suffix pronoun was previously attested only in the two Old South Arabic languages, Minaean and Hadramitic. The form /-kumayn/ indicated by the two Eblaic writings is parallel to that attested, at least graphically, in some Hadramitic texts for the third person (*-*s^1*myn*) and presupposed by the Minaean writing and by the more frequent Hadramitic writing (*-*s^1*mn*).[47]

With respect to the writing *-su-ma*, which can be interpreted as the suffix pronoun /-šumay(n)/ of the third person dual, the variants of the type *-Ca-a* and *-Ca-an* are not known. The proposed interpretation seems very probable nonetheless because of the contexts in which the writing appears. In such cases *-Ca*, *-Ca-a*, *-Ca-an* ought to be considered, even in the pronoun, as three graphical approximations of the same ending /-ayn/:

first person	/-nay(n)/ (?)
second person	/-kumayn/
third person	/-šumay(n)/

It is to be noted that, while in the Eblaic forms of the plural *n* has prevailed over original *m* (for example, *-su-nu*, /-šunu/, developed from **-šumu*), in the dual where we do not have forms differentiated for masculine and feminine, *m* has been preserved.

In respect to the Semitic languages which have preserved the suffix pronouns of the second and third person dual, Eblaic shows the most affinity with Old South Arabic languages; besides Hadramitic and Minaean, already mentioned, Qatabanic (*-*s^1*my*) and Sabaean (*-hmy*) are comparable.[48] Arabic and Ugaritic, however,

46. The hypothesis that the Ugaritic *-ny* represents an innovation has been advanced by E. Wagner, "Die erste Person Dualis im Semitischen," *ZDMG* 102 (1952): 232.

47. For the attestations, see A. F. L. Beeston, *A Descriptive Grammar of Epigraphic South Arabian* (London: Luzac, 1962): 45f. The interpretation of the South Arabic writings with *y* (and with *w*) corresponding to etymological forms containing a diphthong is controversial; see, recently, the balanced position of Beeston, *Sabaic Grammar* (N 42): 7.

48. Beeston, *Epigraphic South Arabian* (N 47): 44f. Similar forms could have been in use in the pre-Islamic North Arabic area as well; in a Lihyan inscription

have not preserved either the diphthong or nunation (Arabic *-kumā*, *-humā*; Ugaritic *-km*, *-hm*). The forms proposed for Akkadian,[49] which are notably different from those attested in Eblaic and in the West Semitic languages, seem to largely depend upon an analogical remodelling on the forms of the plural.[50]

The writing *ša-a* (11) of the determinative-relative pronoun offers no difficulty. This pronoun came to be inflected at Ebla according to the gender, the number, and the case;[51] the context necessitates here a form of the genitive-accusative /ḏay/.[52]

As for the verbal inflection, the few forms recognizable with certainty (section 3) are all rendered with the writing *-Ca*.[53] This orthography, which agrees with the termination of the verbal dual in Akkadian, Ugaritic and Arabic (*-ā*),[54] would favor the hypothesis that the verbal dual was derived from the nominal dual (probably starting out from the forms of the stative).[55]

In conclusion, in the limits of the material discussed, Eblaic seems to have had a nominal diptotic inflection of the dual, whose termination of genitive-accusative is found in the personal pronoun suffixes while the termination of the nominative corresponds to that of the verbal forms.

-hmy is attested (W. Caskel, *Lihyan und Lihyanisch* [Cologne-Opladen, 1954]: 117, 82:3.

49. R. M. Whiting, "The Dual Personal Pronouns in Akkadian," *JNES* 31 (1972): 331–337.

50. As regards the first person, the suffix pronoun attested in Ugaritic (*-ny*) has been interpreted, still doubtfully, as /-naya/ (recently, Segert [N 44]: 47); if this proposal is correct, the form could be explained as due to analogy with the forms of the second and third person.

51. On the inflection of the determinative-relative pronoun in the Eblaic texts, see Fronzaroli, "Le pronom" (N 22): 267–274.

52. Comparable with the writing *ḏy* attested in the Old South Arabic area (Beeston, *Epigraphic South Arabian* [N 47]: 49; *Sabaic Grammar* [N 42]: 41, 63).

53. This is also valid for *da-za-a* (*ARET* 5, 16 I 6), if it could be interpreted as a form of the dual (Gelb [N 1]: 36: /taṣṣaʾā/); see therefore Krebernik, *BFE*: 134.

54. The Old South Arabic inscriptions, however, attests verbal forms of the dual with *-y, ty* (Beeston, *Epigraphic South Arabian* [N 47]: 23; *Sabaic Grammar* [N 42]: 14f.; C. Robin, *MAS-GELLAS* (1983): 173–184). According to Johnstone ("Dual Forms in Mehri and Ḥarsūsi," *BSOAS* 23 [1970]: 509f.), the diphthongal forms attested, or presupposed, in modern South Arabic languages would continue the forms attested in the ancient inscriptions.

55. The problems of the formation of the dual in Semitic languages, with ample discussion of the previous bibliography, have been examined by Ch. Fontinoy, *Le duel dans les langues sémitiques* (Paris: Société d'Édition "Les Belles Lettres," 1969); see also the critical examination of P. Marrassini, "A proposito del duale nelle lingue semitiche," *RSO* 49 (1975): 35–47.

MAARAV 5–6 (Spring, 1990): 127–143

PSALM 34 AND OTHER BIBLICAL ACROSTICS: EVIDENCE FROM THE ALEPPO CODEX

Paul W. Gaebelein, Jr.
FULLER THEOLOGICAL SEMINARY, PASADENA, CA

It is most gratifying to have been invited to contribute to this *Festschrift* honoring my teacher and friend, Professor Stanislav Segert. Since the publication of the first sections of his "Vorarbeiten zur hebräischen Metrik" (1953), Professor Segert has been in the vanguard of contributors to our understanding of poetry in Biblical Hebrew, Ugaritic, Ethiopic, and Greek translations.

In keeping with Prof. Segert's love of ancient poetry, the present essay deals with a particular genre of poem, the biblical acrostics, and will be focused on one example, Psalm 34. The division of the psalm into two parts, unequal in length and differing in content and style, has not generally been recognized in form-critical analyses. This feature is, however, confirmed by the way the psalm is written in a preserved portion of the first and best complete Masoretic codex of the Hebrew Bible. Moreover, the condition of this and other acrostics—some damaged, some intact—is not without interesting implications for the history of the biblical text during and after the trauma of the Babylonian exile.

THE ALEPPO CODEX

Three decades have passed since a dramatic announcement by President Ben-Zvi of Israel: כתר ארם צובא, "The Crown of Aram Zoba" (Aleppo), a codex zealously guarded for centuries by the

Sephardic community of Aleppo in their "Cave of Elijah," had not perished when the synagogue was burned during riots in 1948. "Though desecrated and pillaged, this venerable MS had been rescued from complete destruction and was hidden in a secret place. . . . The precious MS has been found and is now in safe keeping."[1] In the initial volume of *Textus* (1960), Ben-Zvi described what is known of the history of the MS: written by one Solomon ben Buyāᶜā and pointed by Aaron ben Asher in the first half of the 10th century, purchased and presented to the Karaite synagogue in Jerusalem, carried off to Cairo after the sack of Jerusalem by the Seljuks in 1071, redeemed and placed in the synagogue of the Jerusalemites and finally removed to Aleppo c. 1400.[2] In Cairo Maimonides used the codex as his authority for the correct Hebrew text. He wrote:

> Since I found great confusion in these matters in all the manuscripts I saw . . . I decided to write down here all the sections of the Law, both the open and the closed ones as well as the correct way of writing the poems, for the purpose of revising existing books by them and collating new ones. My authority in these matters was the well-known codex in Cairo which contains the twenty-four books and which was in Jerusalem several years ago. This book was referred to by all as an authority for the correct text, since it was collated by Ben Asher, who worked on it for many years and collated it many times.[3]

The authenticity of the Aleppo codex as the MS cited by Maimonides was accepted without question by Paul Kahle, who, in his foreword to *Biblia Hebraica*, noted with regret that the edition was not based on "the model codex of Ben Asher himself" since "the personal representations in Aleppo of Gotthold Weil and Hellmut Ritter" had "had no success."[4] It remained, however, for Prof. M. Goshen-Gottstein to prove the case rigorously by detective work in which the decisive clue was the layout of the Song of Moses (Deut 32) in 67 rather than 70 lines.[5]

1. I. Ben-Zvi, "The Codex of Ben Asher," *Textus* 1 (1960): 1.
2. *Ibid.:* 3–9.
3. *Code, Hilkhoth Sefer Torah*, quoted in Ben-Zvi (N 1): 7.
4. P. Kahle, "Prolegomena," in R. Kittel, ed., *Biblia Hebraica* (Stuttgart: Württembergische Bibelanstalt, 1937): xxix.
5. M. Goshen-Gottstein, "The Authenticity of the Aleppo Codex," *Textus* 1 (1960): 17–58; "The Aleppo Codex and the Rise of the Massoretic Biblical Text," *BA* 42/3 (1979): 145–163.

Further insight into exciting events was offered when an excellent photographic copy in color of the manuscript was published in 1976.[6] According to the English title page the codex was "rescued by Rabbi Moshe Tawil and transferred to Israel by Mr. Mordecai Fahham," but on the Hebrew title page the phrase rendered "transferred to Israel" is והועלה לישׂרעל בחרוף נפשׁ, literally, "brought up to Israel at the risk of his life." This beautiful facsimile of the preserved portion of the codex—beginning with Deut 28:16, continuing through Song of Songs 3:11 and including with lacunae all the Former and Latter Prophets, Chronicles, Psalms, Job, Proverbs, and Ruth—may be admired in libraries throughout the world. The original manuscript now serves as the basic exemplar for a remarkably complete critical edition of the text being produced with meticulous accuracy and all deliberate speed by the Hebrew University Bible Project.

A question remains, however, as to the way the facsimile may be put to practical use by scholars not involved with the Hebrew University Project. Masoretic manuscripts were copied with such amazing accuracy that with respect to its vowel points and accents the Aleppo Codex is almost identical with the Leningrad MS reproduced in *Biblia Hebraica* and the 16th century eclectic text of Ben Chayyim that appears in other printed editions of the Hebrew Bible. The Masora of the Aleppo Codex are superior to those of any other manuscript but the study of these notations is an esoteric field for the specialist. I would venture the suggestion that, just as Maimonides relied on ben Asher's codex for the "sections of the Law" (Torah) and "the correct way of writing the poems" (Ex 15 and Deut 32), so the modern reader may scrutinize the arrangement of poetry in the books of Job, Psalms, and Proverbs. Unlike the rest of the codex in which, with special exceptions, the entire text, prose and poetry, is written straight across each column, these three books display a clear distinction between poetry and prose. There is space after each colon of a poetic passage. This is not the case for prose. Contrary to the arrangement of several modern translations, the entire prologue to Job is written as prose, while the first six verses of Proverbs, printed as a prose introduction in *The Anchor Bible*,[7] are written as poetry.

6. M. Goshen-Gottstein, ed. *The Aleppo Codex* (Jerusalem: Magnes, 1979).

7. R. B. Y. Scott, *Proverbs, Ecclesiastes: Introduction, Translation, and Notes* (AB 18; Garden City: Doubleday, 1965): 33.

The acrostic poems are written in two different ways: (1) Each colon demarcated by an acrostic letter (*ʾalep, bet, gimel,* etc.) is systematically placed at the beginning of a line. (2) A colon demarcated by an acrostic letter is placed, after leaving a space, anywhere on a line, its place being determined by the length of the preceding lines—an arrangement no different from that of any other poem.

PSALM 34: A BIPARTITE ANALYSIS

The arrangement of the acrostic clearly distinguishes two sections: (1) The first section, *ʾalep-ḥet*, verses 2–8,[8] deals with incidents in the life of David cited in the superscription; the acrostic is defective, the letter *waw* being missing; no effort is made to place cola beginning with acrostic letters at the beginning of a line. (2) The second section, *ṭet-taw* plus a final line with initial *pe*, verses 9–23, is in wisdom style; the acrostic is complete; each acrostic letter is systematically placed at the beginning of a line.

This arrangement is not fortuitous, but before examining evidence that it conforms to the style and content of the psalm a brief review of other analyses is in order.

Writing at the turn of the century, C. A. Briggs[9] divided Psalm 34 into three equal 17-line strophes, verses 2–8, 9–15, 16–22. He did not account for the missing verse that should begin with *waw* and deleted the final *pe* verse as a "liturgical gloss." The result is an evenly-divided 21 line structure. In contrast, L. J. Liebreich[10] some fifty years later in a meticulous analysis based on "key words" concluded that "both the structure as well as the contents of this psalm point unmistakably to its logical division into four units"—verses 2–4, 5–11, 12–15, 16–23. In 1972, N. H. Ridderbos,[11] using a similar methodology, proposed a slightly different four-unit division: 2–4, 5–9, 10–15, 16–23. Finally P. Auffret[12] came full circle

8. Verse numbers *passim* are those of the printed Hebrew Bible.

9. C. A. Briggs, *A Critical and Exegetical Commentary on the Book of Psalms* (Edinburgh: Clark, 1906): 1.294–301.

10. L. J. Liebreich, "Psalms 34 and 145 in the Light of their Key Words," *HUCA* 27 (1956): 181–192.

11. N. H. Ridderbos, *Die Psalmen* (BZAW 117; Berlin: de Gruyter, 1972): 245–251.

12. P. Auffret, *Hymnes d'Égypt et d'Israel* (OBO 34; Göttingen: Vandenhoeck & Ruprecht, 1981): 76–91.

in 1981 and again recognized, as Briggs had done, a break at the end of verse 8, but then, in partial agreement with Liebreich and Ridderbos, decided on a four-part division: 2–4, 5–8, 9–15, 16–23.

All of the foregoing analyses have one thing in common: No mention is made of a qualitative difference between Briggs's "first strophe," verses 2–8, and the rest of the psalm; nor is such a difference hinted at in recent articles by Ceresko[13] and Kent.[14] It may well be that the indication of two sections by the writing of the acrostic is attested only in the Aleppo codex. The Psalm is not written thus in the Leningrad MS. The arrangement of the psalm in each of these early manuscripts is schematically represented in Figures 1 and 2. This unique feature of the Aleppo codex, however, seems hardly necessary to enable a sensitive reader to perceive a qualitative difference between the two sections. Such a difference should already have been perceptible. Three strands of evidence may be cited.

The first consideration is somewhat subjective but nonetheless important. The expression of thanksgiving, interspersed with exhortations, in the first section differs in no significant way from many similar passages in the Psalter. It is not wisdom literature *per se*. One wonders if it would ever have been classified as such if it had not been followed by the didactic instructions in the rest of the psalm.

The second consideration calls into question current opinion regarding the superscriptions of the Psalms which were omitted from *The New English Bible* as "almost certainly not original"[15]—a deletion with which I cannot agree. Indeed, two incidents described in 1 Sam 21:11–22:2 accord remarkably well with the first section of Psalm 34. As a student of mine observed, there is dry humor in the opening line, "I will bless the Lord *at all times*," even when feigning madness before the King of Gath, a nuance already noted in rabbinic literature.[16] A change in the vocalization of reflexive forms of the verbal root *h-l-l* was preserved for many centuries only in oral tradition. The unusual, but amply attested, *Hitpôʿēl* of 1 Sam 21:14 "feigned madness" is replaced by the

13. A. R. Cresko, "The ABC's of Wisdom in Psalm 34," *VT* 35 (1985): 99–104.

14. H. R. Kent, "Psalm 34," *Interpretation* 40/2 (1986): 175–180.

15. G. R. Driver, "Introduction," *The New English Bible* (Cambridge: University Press, 1961): xviii.

16. L. Ginzberg, *The Legends of the Jews* (New York: Jewish Publication Society of America, 1913): 4.90.

לְדָוִד   בְּשַׁנּוֹתוֹ אֶת־טַעְמוֹ לִפְנֵי אֲבִימֶלֶךְ
וַיְגָרְשֵׁהוּ וַיֵּלַךְ   אֲבָרְכָה אֶת־יְהוָה בְּכָל־
עֵת תָּמִיד תְּהִלָּתוֹ בְּפִי   בַּיהוָה תִּתְהַלֵּל נַפְשִׁי
יִשְׁמְעוּ עֲנָוִים וְיִשְׂמָחוּ   גַּדְּלוּ לַיהוָה אִתִּי
וּנְרוֹמְמָה שְׁמוֹ יַחְדָּו   דָּרַשְׁתִּי אֶת־יְהוָה
וְעָנָנִי וּמִכָּל־מְגוּרוֹתַי הִצִּילָנִי הִבִּיטוּ אֵלָיו
וְנָהָרוּ וּפְנֵיהֶם אַל־ יֶחְפָּרוּ   זֶה עָנִי קָרָא
וַיהוָה שָׁמֵעַ וּמִכָּל־צָרוֹתָיו הוֹשִׁיעוֹ   חֹנֶה
מַלְאַךְ־יְהוָה   סָבִיב לִירֵאָיו וַיְחַלְּצֵם
טַעֲמוּ וּרְאוּ כִּי־טוֹב יְהוָה אַשְׁרֵי הַגֶּבֶר יֶחֱסֶה־בּוֹ
יְראוּ אֶת־יְהוָה קְדֹשָׁיו   כִּי־אֵין מַחְסוֹר לִירֵאָיו
כְּפִירִים רָשׁוּ וְרָעֵבוּ וְדֹרְשֵׁי יְהוָה לֹא־ יַחְסְרוּ כָל־טוֹב (a)
לְכוּ־בָנִים שִׁמְעוּ־לִי יִרְאַת יְהוָה אֲלַמֶּדְכֶם
מִי־הָאִישׁ הֶחָפֵץ חַיִּים אֹהֵב יָמִים לִרְאוֹת טוֹב
נְצֹר לְשׁוֹנְךָ מֵרָע וּשְׂפָתֶיךָ מִדַּבֵּר מִרְמָה
סוּר מֵרָע וַעֲשֵׂה־טוֹב בַּקֵּשׁ שָׁלוֹם וְרָדְפֵהוּ
עֵינֵי יְהוָה אֶל־צַדִּיקִים וְאָזְנָיו אֶל־שַׁוְעָתָם
פְּנֵי יְהוָה בְּעֹשֵׂי רָע לְהַכְרִית מֵאֶרֶץ זִכְרָם
צָעֲקוּ וַיהוָה שָׁמֵעַ וּמִכָּל־צָרוֹתָם הִצִּילָם
קָרוֹב יְהוָה לְנִשְׁבְּרֵי־לֵב וְאֶת־דַּכְּאֵי־רוּחַ יוֹשִׁיעַ
רַבּוֹת רָעוֹת צַדִּיק וּמִכֻּלָּם יַצִּילֶנּוּ יְהוָה
שֹׁמֵר כָּל־עַצְמוֹתָיו אַחַת מֵהֵנָּה לֹא נִשְׁבָּרָה
תְּמוֹתֵת רָשָׁע רָעָה וְשֹׂנְאֵי צַדִּיק יֶאְשָׁמוּ
פּוֹדֶה יְהוָה נֶפֶשׁ עֲבָדָיו וְלֹא יֶאְשְׁמוּ כָּל־ הַחֹסִים בּוֹ (a)

(a) Writing compressed, closely but legibly, to fit on one line.

Fig. 1. Arrangement of Psalm 34 in the Aleppo Codex—a schematic representation.

לְדָוִד
בְּשַׁנּוֹתוֹ אֶת־טַעְמוֹ לִפְנֵי אֲבִימֶלֶךְ וַיְגָרְשֵׁהוּ
וַיֵּלַךְ אֲבָרֲכָה   אֶת־יְהוָה בְּכָל־עֵת תָּמִיד
תְּהִלָּתוֹ בְּפִי   בַּיהוָה תִּתְהַלֵּל נַפְשִׁי
יִשְׁמְעוּ עֲנָוִים וְיִשְׂמָחוּ גַּדְּלוּ לַיהוָה אִתִּי
וּנְרוֹמְמָה שְׁמוֹ יַחְדָּו   דָּרַשְׁתִּי אֶת־יְהוָה
וְעָנָנִי   וּמִכָּל־מְגוּרוֹתַי   הִצִּילָנִי הִבִּיטוּ
אֵלָיו וְנָהָרוּ וּפְנֵיהֶם אַל־ יֶחְפָּרוּ זֶה עָנִי קָרָא
וַיהוָה שָׁמֵעַ   וּמִכָּל־צָרוֹתָיו הוֹשִׁיעוֹ
חֹנֶה מַלְאַךְ־יְהוָה   סָבִיב לִירֵאָיו וַיְחַלְּצֵם
טַעֲמוּ וּרְאוּ כִּי־טוֹב יְהוָה אַשְׁרֵי הַגֶּבֶר יֶחֱסֶה־
בּוֹ יְראוּ אֶת־יְהוָה קְדֹשָׁיו כִּי־אֵין מַחְסוֹר
לִירֵאָיו כְּפִירִים רָשׁוּ וְרָעֵבוּ   וְדֹרְשֵׁי
יְהוָה לֹא־ יַחְסְרוּ כָל־טוֹב לְכוּ־בָנִים שִׁמְעוּ־לִי
יִרְאַת יְהוָה   אֲלַמֶּדְכֶם מִי־הָאִישׁ הֶחָפֵץ
חַיִּים   אֹהֵב יָמִים   לִרְאוֹת טוֹב נְצֹר
לְשׁוֹנְךָ מֵרָע וּשְׂפָתֶיךָ מִדַּבֵּר מִרְמָה סוּר
מֵרָע וַעֲשֵׂה־טוֹב   בַּקֵּשׁ שָׁלוֹם וְרָדְפֵהוּ
עֵינֵי יְהוָה   אֶל־צַדִּיקִים וְאָזְנָיו אֶל־
שַׁוְעָתָם פְּנֵי יְהוָה בְּעֹשֵׂי רָע לְהַכְרִית מֵאֶרֶץ
זִכְרָם צָעֲקוּ   וַיהוָה שָׁמֵעַ וּמִכָּל־צָרוֹתָם
הִצִּילָם   קָרוֹב יְהוָה לְנִשְׁבְּרֵי־לֵב וְאֶת־
דַּכְּאֵי־רוּחַ יוֹשִׁיעַ רַבּוֹת רָעוֹת צַדִּיק וּמִכֻּלָּם
יַצִּילֶנּוּ יְהוָה   שֹׁמֵר כָּל־עַצְמוֹתָיו אַחַת
מֵהֵנָּה לֹא נִשְׁבָּרָה   תְּמוֹתֵת רָשָׁע רָעָה
וְשֹׂנְאֵי צַדִּיק יֶאְשָׁמוּ   פּוֹדֶה יְהוָה נֶפֶשׁ
עֲבָדָיו וְלֹא יֶאְשְׁמוּ כָּל־הַחֹסִים בּוֹ

Fig. 2. Arrangement of Psalm 34 in the Leningrad Manuscript—a schematic representation.

ordinary *Hitpâ*ᶜ*ēl* in Psalm 34:3a which could be rendered, "It is in the Lord that I make my boast," since the position of the divine name at the beginning of the line is emphatic.

Based on the idea that David was praising God in his heart while apparently acting crazy, this subtle word-play can hardly be "a typically rabbinical touch" by which a scribe "gave the Psalm a davidic reference."[17] Correct vocalization of the verbs is essential to the original sense of each passage. In the text of 1 Samuel the king's cynical remark, "Am I so short of mademn that you bring this fellow here?" is immediately followed by David's escape to the cave of Adullam, where "all those who were in distress or in debt or discontented gathered around him and he became their leader" (1 Sam 22:2).[18] Might not this band of about 400 men be the ᶜ*nwym*, "the afflicted ones" of Psalm 34:3b who are to "hear and rejoice"? If such be the case, the psalmist has presented a kind of antiphonal structure of singular and plural clauses. That is, singular clauses referring to David occur in verses 2–3a, 5, 7, while allusions to the afflicted are plural in verses 3b–4, 6, 8. All this seems to link the defective acrostic in the first section of the psalm firmly to the text of 1 Samuel—regardless of whether or not the superscription is "original" or the date when it may have been added. The second section of the psalm differs from the first in both tone and content. It seems most unlikely that any poet would have envisioned David in his Robin Hood days giving a leisurely and polished wisdom lesson to his band of malcontents:

> Taste and see that the Lord is good
> . . . .
> Come, my children, listen to me;
> I will teach you the fear of the Lord.
> Whoever of you loves life
> and desires to see many good days
> Keep your tongue from evil
> and your lips from speaking lies.
> Turn from evil and do good;
> seek peace and pursue it.

The third consideration that sets verses 2–8 of Psalm 34 apart from the remaining lines is one for which no explanation is offered.

17. L. Sabourin, *The Psalms, their Origin and Meaning* (New York: Alba House, 1974): 285.

18. Translation here *et passim* from the New International Version.

It will merely be described. The initial colon of each verse differs in syntax from the second colon of the verse, and also from the initial colon of the next verse:

2a—1st sing. jussive verb
2b—verbless clause
3a—3rd fem. sing. imperfect verb
3b—3rd masc. pl. jussive verb
4a—pl. imperative verb
4b—1st pl. jussive verb
5a—1st sing. perfect verb
5b—3rd sing. perfect verb
6a—3rd pl. perfect verb
6b—nominal clause with 3rd pl. jussive verb
7a—3rd sing. perfect verb, subject *zh ᶜny*, "this poor man"
7b—3rd sing. perfect verb, subject YHWH
8a—sing. participle
8b—3rd sing. imperfect verb

Although there are 3rd s. pf. verbs in both halves of verse 7, the fact that the psalmist speaks of himself in the third person in the first colon, while the subject in the second colon is the Lord, may be considered tantamount to a change in syntax. Thus the first section of the Psalm is made up of seven consecutive verses containing fourteen cola with a change of syntax in each verse and colon. Obviously this feature is not present in the remainder of the psalm. There are plural imperative verbs in 9a and 10a; singular imperative verbs in 14a, 15a, and 15b; verbless clauses in 16 and 17. In general, Hebrew poetry is in this respect more like the second section on Psalm 34, though to demonstrate this proposition would go beyond the scope of this article.

Before moving on to a consideration of the other biblical acrostics, two further observations on Psalm 34 may be relevant. If the order of verses 16 and 17, beginning respectively with *ᶜayin* and *pe*, were reversed, as in chapters 2, 3, and 4 of the post-exilic book of Lamentations, the sense would be noticeably improved:

17 The face of the Lord is against those who do evil,
to cut off the memory of them from the earth;
16 The eyes of the Lord are upon the righteous
and his ears are attentive to their cry.
18 They cry out and the Lord hears them;
he delivers them from all their troubles.

There is an early precedent for such a reversal. A crudely written ostracon, recovered in Israel at Izbet Ṣarṭah and dating from the time of the judges, contains an abecedary in which the letter *pe* precedes *ᶜayin.*[19] In the acrostic poem about a virtuous wife, Prov 31:10–31, the Septuagint translator placed his Greek version of the *pe* verse, 31:26, ahead of verse 25 which begins in Hebrew with *ᶜayin*. This evidence is sufficient to establish the existence of a variant alphabetical tradition, *pe* before *ᶜayin*, attested archeologically at an early date, but reflected only in relatively late biblical texts: Lam, the Septuagint of Prov 31—and perhaps the wisdom section of Ps 34.

Finally, the last verse of Ps 34, which begins with the letter *pe* and was regarded by Briggs as a "liturgical gloss," seems instead to be an integral part of the poem since the redemption of the Lord's servants who take refuge in him forms a fine positive contrast to the fate of the wicked in the preceding *taw* verse. The same cannot be said of the final verse of the defective acrostic Ps 25. This verse also begins with *pe*, indeed the same verb, *pdh*, "redeem," but here the final exclamation, "Redeem Israel, O God, from all their troubles!" has no direct connection with a preceding very personal plea for deliverance. It may well be a liturgical gloss, possibly added under the influence of Ps 34. As P. Skehan acutely observed:

> In the word *aleph* are contained three consonants: the first in the alphabet; the twelfth, *lamed* . . . ; and the "extra" letter, *pe*. By going from *aleph* to *taw* and then adding *pe*, one makes *lamed* the exact middle of the series and sums up the whole alphabet in the name of its first letter.[20]

THE BIBLICAL ACROSTICS

For reference in the discussion that follows it is convenient to present here a catalogue of the biblical acrostics, citing briefly the subject matter of each poem, noting whether it is defective or complete and describing the way it is written in the Aleppo Codex:

19. A. Demsky, "A Proto-Canaanite Abecedary Dating from the Period of the Judges and its Implication for the History of the Alphabet," *Tel Aviv* 4 (1977): 14–27.

20. P. W. Skehan, *Studies in Israelite Poetry and Wisdom* (CBQMS 1; Washington: Catholic Biblical Association of America, 1971): 74, n.13.

Nahum 1
Incomplete, defective and perhaps uncertain.
Ps 4
Evening prayer
Acrostic: letters from bottom to top including the superscription spell *bnr zrwbbl*, "on the lamp of Zerubbabel."
Aleppo Codex: acrostic letters not systematically placed at the beginning of a line.
Pss 9 and 10
Deliverance from enemies
Acrostic: badly damaged; only *ʾ*, *b*, *g*, *w*, *z*, *ḥ*, *ṭ*, *y*, *k*, *l*, *q*, *r*, *š*, *t* are intact
Aleppo Codex: *ʾ*, *b*, *g*, *ḥ*, *y*, *k*, *l*, *q* at the beginning of a line
Ps 25
A personal prayer for deliverance with a wisdom strophe, verses 8–14, enclosed in it.
Acrostic: defective, *b*, *w*, *q* missing; a final verse begins with *pe*.
Aleppo Codex: *ʾalep* in *lacuna*, *g*, *d*, *h*, *l*, *m*, *n*, *s*, *ʿ*, *p*, *ṣ*, *r*, *š*, *p* at the beginning of a line.
Ps 34:2–8
Thanksgiving and exhortation
Acrostic: defective, *w* missing.
Aleppo Codex: No acrostic letter at the beginning of a line
Ps 34: 9–23
Wisdom instruction
Acrostic: complete; a final verse begins with *pe*
Aleppo Codex: Each acrostic letter at the beginning of a line
Ps 37
Wisdom instruction
Acrostic: defective, *ʿ*, *t* missing.[21]
Aleppo Codex: *b*, *y*, *k*, *n*, *p*, *ṣ*, *q*, *r*, *š* at the beginning of a line
Ps 111
Song of praise
Acrostic: complete; each colon begins with a letter of the alphabet.

21. Perhaps the letter *taw* should be considered part of the acrostic in Ps 37:39, since a word beginning with *taw* is preceded only by *šûreq* and when *waw* occurs elsewhere in acrostics it is regularly consonantal; however, the acrostic is still

Aleppo Codex: alternate letters at the beginning of a line, ᵓ, *g*, *h*, etc., but no systematic effort to maintain this scheme which is continued only through *k*.

Ps 112

Song of praise in wisdom style

Acrostic: complete; similar to Ps 111

Aleppo Codex: similar to Ps 111

Ps 119

Elaborately wrought poem extolling the Law

Acrostic: complete; eight verses begin with each letter.

Aleppo Codex: carefully written with a separate section for each letter which regularly stands at the beginning of a line.

Ps 145

Song of praise

Acrostic: defective, *n* missing

Aleppo Codex: Every letter except *b* and *g* at the beginning of a line.

Prov 31:10–31

A virtuous wife

Acrostic: complete; order of *ᶜayin* and *pe* reversed in Septuagint.

Aleppo Codex: Each letter at the beginning of a line.

Lam: chapters 1, 2, 3, and 4

The fall of Jerusalem

Acrostics: elaborate and complete; order of *ᶜayin* and *pe* reversed in chapters 2, 3, and 4.

Aleppo Codex: not preserved.

Contemplating this array of poems one is initially impressed by the variety of their content. Whether or not the acrostic functioned as a mnemonic device, it must surely have imposed upon each poet a constraint that may not only have improved the quality of his artistic output but also have given the reader an aesthetically satisfying sense of completeness. This is an old idea that finds expression at the end of a book often described by Prof. Segert as the most archaic in the New Testament, Revelation: "I am the Alpha and the Omega, the First and the Last, the Beginning and the End" (Rev 22:13). Such constraint seems equally appropriate

---

defective since the letter *ᶜayin* is missing. (An emendation to restore it in *BH*[3] seems quite unwarranted.)

when it is imposed upon a prayer for deliverance, a psalm of praise, a wisdom lesson or an acrostic dirge that might otherwise overflow into an outburst of uncontrolled weeping.

With regard to the preservation of the acrostics, attention will first be given to those that are complete. The letter *nun*, missing from Ps 145, is a classic case of the exception to prove a rule. It is one among 198 letters in nine acrostics written with repetitions on 396 lines. If this exception may be overlooked, an interesting proposition emerges. The complete acrostics of the Bible (Pss 111, 112, 119, 145; Prov 31:10–31; Lam 1–4) may be regarded as post-exilic. This is certainly the case with Lamentations. The poem in praise of a virtuous wife has some obvious late features. Four complete acrostics of the Psalter occur in the so-called fifth "book." Now it is well known that in the texts from Qumran the canonical order of the Psalms is fixed in Books I, II, and III of the Psalter, while it is fluid in Books IV and V with several apocryphal poems interspersed among the canonical psalms. The Qumran evidence confirms a long-standing general impression that, with some notable exceptions such as Ps 110, the psalms in the last third of the Psalter seem later than those in Books I–III. Many of these psalms, especially in Book V, may well be post-exilic, including the virtually complete acrostics Pss 111, 112, 119, 145.

On the other hand, the first three books of the Psalter are replete with archaic items, such as Pss 2, 18, 29, 68. It is noteworthy that four indubitably defective acrostics are in Book I. While the badly damaged acrostic in Pss 9 and 10 does contain the statement that the Lord will judge the world in righteousness (9:9) and the outcry "Why, Lord, do you stand afar off?" (10:1, cf. Ps 74:1), it need not necessarily, considering the style and the diction, be regarded as late. The personal prayer for deliverance in Ps 25 is interrupted by a wisdom strophe that is rather similar to Ps 37. The wording of these wisdom texts, especially Ps 37, has affinities with parts of the book of Prov often regarded by scholars as pre-exilic. Terse, single-line wisdom sentences, often followed in Ps 37 by a comment beginning with the conjunction *kî*, "for," have a quality of timeless verity. Ps 37:21 should remind a modern reader of people within his own circle of acquaintances:

> The wicked borrow and do not repay,
> but the righteous give generously.

This antithetical proverb is expressed by only seven Hebrew words, the last two of which are participles in hendiadys, *ḥônēn wənôtēn*. Discussion of the date of Ps 34, all or only part of which may be pre-exilic, will be deferred until some further evidence from the Aleppo Codex has been considered.

At first glance the writing of acrostics in the Codex may seem somewhat haphazard. Groups of verses occur with an acrostic letter at the beginning of each line while other parts of the same text do not display this feature. A sufficient explanation may be that, since Job, Psalms, and Proverbs are written with only two columns on a page, there is a natural tendency for the first word of a verse to stand at the beginning of a line. For example, 18 of the 28 verses of Ps 73 display this feature, including a series of nine consecutive verses, 7–15. The matter needs to be faced squarely. Was there a desire, conscious but incompletely realized, to write some of the poems, such as Ps 25, with each acrostic letter at the beginning of a line? This question may confidently be answered in the negative. The meticulous care exercised by the Tiberian masters militates against such an idea. Whatever their tradition required, they accomplished. One need only look at the *waw* and *šin* verses of the poem about a virtuous wife. Verses 15 and 30 of Prov 31, made up respectively of eight and nine words, are compressed closely but legibly onto one line since the tradition must have called for an acrostic letter at the beginning of each line. No such compression is generally apparent in the rest of the text of Job, Psalms, and Proverbs. In particular, it does not occur in Ps 25, nor does the sequence of nine verses with an acrostic letter at the beginning of each verse—*kap* through *šin* with *qop* missing—coincide at its beginning or end with any break in the sense of the poem.

With Ps 34 the situation is quite different. As already explained, the place where the practice of writing acrostic letters at the beginning of a line is started definitely coincides with a change in the sense of the poem. Moreover, in the long sequence of 15 verses, *ṭet* through *taw* with a final *pe* verse added, at least two verses, 34:11 and 34:23, each containing nine words, are compressed onto one line as closely as Prov 31:15 and 30. No such compression is apparent in the first section of the psalm, verses 2–8, in which it so happens that not a single acrostic letter stands at the beginning of a line.

CONCLUSION

It may be stated with assurance that among the acrostic texts of the Bible only the following were intentionally written with each acrostic letter at the beginning of a line in the Aleppo Codex:

Ps 34:9–23
Ps 119
Ps 145
Prov 31:10–31

No explanation for the rather odd displacement of *bet* and *gimel* in Ps 145 can be offered here. In the remaining acrostic texts no systematic effort was made to place acrostic letters at the beginning of a line:

Pss 9 and 10
Ps 25
Ps 34:2–8
Ps 37
Ps 111
Ps 112

The validity of this conclusion is confirmed by the fact that in Ps 34:9–23, Ps 145 and Prov 31:10–31 the writing of long verses was compressed to make them fit on one line—a practice not generally found elsewhere in the codex.[22]

When attention is turned to the defective acrostics, it is relevant to observe that portions of the Hebrew Bible committed to writing before the fall of Jerusalem may have suffered considerable damage during the exile. This damage may well account for a plethora of textual problems in pre-exilic texts, such as oracles of the seventh and eighth century prophets, that may not have been set in order by some putative deuteronomistic or priestly redactor. In the first part of the book of Isaiah the displacement to chapter 5 of a stanza from the terrible ode of judgment in chapters 9 and 10 is confirmed by the refrain in 5:25b, "Yet for all this his anger is not turned

22. In the *reš* stanza of Ps 119 an excessively long verse runs over on to the first part of the following line. This exception disturbs the scheme of placing the letter *reš* at the beginning of the next two lines, but aesthetically it does not disrupt the appearance of the layout since the psalm is beautifully written with a separate section for each letter of the alphabet.

away, his hand is still upraised." If, as Kaufmann[23] and Pope[24] suggest, the dialogues in the book of Job are pre-exilic, then dislocations in the third cycle of speeches may be the result of damage during the exile. The text of the pre-exilic psalms must also have been disturbed. Defective acrostics provide obvious evidence of damage, especially to the poem in Pss 9 and 10.

The division of Ps 34 into two parts is confirmed by a tradition reflected in the writing of the Aleppo Codex. It is inconceivable that the Tiberian masters should have analyzed Ps 34 *de novo* and reached a decision thus to divide it. They were not form critics. As the name Masorete implies, the task to which they dedicated their lives was to preserve and pass on received tradition.

How then may one explain this traditional division of Ps 34? It is possible that one poet, reflecting on the incidents recorded in 1 Sam 21:11–22:2, may have shaped, with quick changes of syntax, a terse poetical *réprise* of those incidents. He may then have developed from them a more leisurely and contemplative wisdom lesson, using the device of an acrostic to give unity to his two-part composition. A conscious awareness of those two parts—the *réprise* and the lesson—might have been sufficient to give rise to a long-standing tradition.

Another, far more speculative, hypothesis is that only the defective first section of Ps 34, verses 2–8, may be pre-exilic. That is, not only the *waw* verse but all the rest of the acrostic, *ṭet* through *taw*, was lost after the fall of Jerusalem. The wisdom section which we now have in the Bible seems later in style than, for example, Ps 37. Could it be that Psalm 34:9–23 was composed by another poet after the exile, and that some dim memory of two sources was preserved in the traditional layout of the psalm in the Aleppo Codex? This proposal complements rather than contravenes the perceptive form-critical studies of Liebreich, Ridderbos, and Auffret, since the second poet would very likely have tried to give a balanced structure to his reconstituted psalm.

This second hypothesis can be proposed only very tentatively in an essay presented to so careful a scholar as Prof. Segert. It is advanced here because, if it should turn out to be correct, a consistent pattern would emerge:

23. Y. Kaufmann, *The Religion of Israel* (tr. and abridged by M. Greenberg; Chicago: Univ. of Chicago, 1960): 338.

24. M. H. Pope, *Job: Introduction, Translation, and Notes* (AB 15; Garden City: Doubleday, 1965): xxx–xxxvii.

Defective pre-exilic acrostic texts:
- Pss 9 and 10
- Ps 25
- Ps 34:2–8
- Ps 37

Virtually complete post-exilic acrostic texts:
- Ps 34:9–23
- Ps 111
- Ps 112
- Ps 119
- Ps 145 (*n* missing)
- Prov 31:20–31
- Lam 1, 2, 3, 4

MAARAV 5–6 (Spring, 1990): 145–158

PHOENICIAN *WŠBRT MLṢM* AND JOB 33:23*

STANLEY GEVIRTZ ז"ל
HEBREW UNION COLLEGE-JEWISH INSTITUTE OF RELIGION
LOS ANGELES, CALIFORNIA

In the Phoenician inscription of Azitawadda that was discovered at Karatepe in eastern Turkey, there appears what has proved to be an enigmatic phrase, a veritable *crux interpretum*: *wšbrt mlṣm* (*KAI* 26 A i 8). In addition to the lexicographical uncertainties that are attendant on each of its component terms, its syntactical relationship is similarly unresolved. What is under debate here is whether the locution is to be construed with the series of nouns that precedes, or with the series of verbal clauses that follows. Indeed, the two issues of syntax and meaning, and the concomitant matter of morphological determination, are inextricably linked. That is to say, if *wšbrt mlṣm* is to be identified, as I believe it must, as a noun clause, a construct-chain that is dependent upon the preceding *bʿbr (bʿl wʾlm)* "thanks to (Baal and the gods)," then our phrase should signify something akin to "and the assembly (?) of the (divine) intermediaries," with uncertainty residing in the meaning of the *nomen regens*, *šbrt*. If, on the other hand, it is to be construed as a verbal clause, one that is independent of what comes before, it would mean, so its proponents assert, "And I broke (or: shattered) the evil-doers(?)," with uncertainty residing in the meaning of the direct object.

* This is a revised and expanded version of a paper that I read before the Northwest Semitic Epigraphy Forum of the Society of Biblical Literature and Exegesis during its annual convention held at the Anaheim Hilton Hotel in Anaheim, California, on Sunday, November 24, 1985. I am pleased to offer it as a token of friendship and esteem to our honoree, Professor Stanislav Segert.

Those who interpret *wšbrt mlṣm* as a verbal clause analyze *šbrt* as the first person common singular perfect of the root *šbr* "to break"—a verb not otherwise in evidence in Phoenician, though widely attested in cognate languages—and *mlṣm* as a noun in plural number that functions here as the direct object of the verb, and that is forced to bear the otherwise unattested meaning, "evil-doers," "thieves," "rebels," or the like. The principal objection to this interpretation, as has frequently been observed, is the fact that the regular syntactical pattern generally employed to express the historical narrative tense in Phoenician is the so-called "infinitive absolute" followed by its subject, in turn followed by the object, adverb(ial clause), or the like, as *wbn ʾnk ḥmyt* "And I built walls" (*KAI* 26 A i 17), or *wyšb ʾnk ʿl ksʾ ʾby* "And I sat on the throne of my father" (*KAI* 26 A i 11). It is the most frequently encountered syntactical construction in this inscription, occurring some twenty times.[1] On the other hand, one finds the first person common singular perfect form employed in this inscribed account only when the verb is preceded by its subject (here the independent personal pronoun and personal name) or by the direct object—a means, presumably, of providing special emphasis—as in: *wʾnk ʾztwd štnm tḥt pʿmy* "And/But I, Azatiwadda, set them beneath my feet" (*KAI* 26 A i 16–17), *wʾnk ʾztwd ʿntnm* "And/But I, Azatiwadda, humbled them" (*KAI* 26 A i 19–20), and *wdnnym yšbt šm* "And Danuneans I settled there" (*KAI* 26 A i 21–ii 1). Were *wšbrt mlṣm* a verbal clause, the construction would be unique in this inscription.

1. *yḥw ʾnk ʾyt dnnym* "I revitalized the Danuneans" (A i 3–4); *yrḥb ʾnk ʾrṣ ʿmq ʾdn* "I enlarged the territory of the Valley of Adana" (A i 4); *wmlʾ ʾnk ʿqrt pʿr* "And I filled the *storehouses*(?) of Paʿru" (A i 6); *wpʿl ʾnk ss ʿl ss* "And I acquired horse upon horse" (A i 6–7); *wtrq ʾnk kl hrʿ* "And I removed all the evil" (A i 9); *wyṭnʾ ʾnk bt ʾdny* "And I erected the house of Adanaya (?)" (A i 9–10); *wpʿl ʾnk lšrš ʾdny nʿm* "And I did (what was) good for *the root of Adanaya* (?)" (A i 10); *wyšb ʾnk ʿl ksʾ ʾby* "And I sat upon the throne of my father" (A i 11); *wšt ʾnk šlm* "And I established peace" (A i 11); *wbn ʾnk ḥmyt ʿzt* "And I built strong walls" (A i 13–14); *wbn ʾnk ḥmyt bmqmm hmt* "And I built walls in those places" (A i 17); *wʿn ʾnk ʾrṣt ʿzt* "And I subdued mighty lands" (A i 18); *wbn ʾnk hqrt z* "And I built this city" (A ii 9, 17); *wšt ʾnk šm ʾztwdy* "And I established its name, Azatiwaddiya" (A ii 9–10, 17–18); *yšb ʾnk bn bʿl krntryš* "I caused Baal K. to dwell in it" (A ii 18–19).

In the syntactical constructions, *yrdm ʾnk* "I caused them to go down" (A i 20), *yšbm ʾnk* "I caused them to dwell" (A i 20), and *wbny ʾnk* "And I built it" (A ii 11), the presence of a pronominal suffix, as has often been remarked, precludes identification of the verbal forms as infinitives *absolute*—at least in the traditional understanding of that designation.

Yet interpretation of *wšbrt mlṣm* as a noun clause, a construct-chain, dependent on *bʿbr* "thanks to," has been rejected by many because of the lack of any satisfactory explanation or etymology for the *nomen regens, šbrt*, and for the reason that advocates of this analysis have hitherto had to content themselves with translations based solely on the phrase's immediate context. Nevertheless, as I intend to show, a suitable etymology for *šbrt* is at hand. Before propounding it, however, it will prove helpful to examine the *nomen rectum, mlṣm*, and to fix its meaning.

Elsewhere in Phoenician (and Punic) inscriptions, *mlṣ*, the singular of *mlṣm*, appears as the title of an office, and has generally been rendered "interpreter,"[2] a definition that is based on that of Hebrew *mēlîṣ* as this term occurs in Gen. 42:23. Most often analyzed in Hebrew as a *hipʿîl* (in Phoenician as a *yipʿîl*) participle of the root *lyṣ* "to scorn"[3]—perhaps in origin signifying "to babble, prattle"[4]—Hebrew *mēlîṣ*, whatever its relationship to the verbal root *lyṣ* may yet prove to be, functions solely as a noun, and, in addition to its meaning "interpreter" in Gen. 42:23, exhibits the related meanings "intermediary" (Isa 43:27; Job 33:23) and "ambassador, envoy" (2 Chron 32:31). Never, it must be emphasized, does it convey pejorative sense. Those who would parse *šbrt* as a verb, "I broke," and render *mlṣm* by some term of disapprobation, "evil-doers," "rebels," "thieves," or the like, have been constrained to derive such conjectured translations from *lyṣ* "to scorn" or "to babble"—in *yipʿîl* stem: "to cause to scorn/babble" (?)—and to ignore the difficulty of tracing their semantic developments, or to resort to somewhat distant and strained Arabic etymologies.[5] But the two anomalies to which such an interpretation gives rise, namely, creation of an historical narrative tense construction not otherwise encountered in this inscription (in flagrant disregard for the usual patterns that find employment here—see above) and assignment of a meaning to *mlṣ(m)* which it displays neither elsewhere in Phoenician nor in Hebrew, serve to render the interpretation improbable.

2. *DISO*: 138.

3. *BDB*: 539; *DISO*: 138; *KB*³: 558 uncertainly.

4. H. N. Richardson, "Some Notes on *lîṣ* and Its Derivatives," *VT* 5 (1955): 163–179, 434–436.

5. E.g., F. Bron, *Recherches sur les inscriptions phéniciennes de Karatepe* (Hautes études orientales, 11; Genève et Paris, 1979): 53.

Those who would parse *wšbrt mlṣm* as a dependent noun clause have recognized that *mlṣm* must be a term for "(divine) intermediaries," and have referred, appropriately, to Job 33:23. This verse reads, *ʾim yēš ʿālāyw malʾāk mēlîṣ ʾeḥād minnî ʾālep ləhaggîd ləʾādām yošrô* "If there be beside him a messenger, an intermediary (*mēlîṣ*), one of (the) thousand, to proclaim (the) man's uprightness." Context indicates that, whether construed as being in apposition or in parallel, *malʾāk* "messenger," *mēlîṣ* "intermediary," and *ʾeḥād minnî ʾālep* "one of (the) thousand" here complement one another, and must have reference to a divine being of some sort.[6] And though the expression, "one of (the) thousand," has come in for a variety of interpretations,[7] it finds, I submit, its proper reflex in a locution that occurs with some frequency in documents dating from the late second millennium B.C.E., a reflex which tends to support the view that the reference is indeed to "lesser divinities," or, perhaps, to the pantheon in general.

The expression appears in letters, treaties, and edicts or grants that derive from the period of the Hittite New Kingdom, and that reflect its influence. Thus, e.g., a letter of the king of Amurru to the king of Ugarit contains the following greeting:

> May it be well with you! May (the) thousand gods (*li-im* DINGIR.MEŠ) keep [you]![8]

6. On *malʾāk* "(divine) messenger," see the references provided in *BDB*: 521*b*, sub meanings 2 and 3. Cf. A. Alt, "Die phönikischen Inschriften von Karatepe," *WO* I/4 (1949): 280f.; W. F. Albright *apud* R. T. O'Callaghan, "The Great Phoenician Portal Inscription from Karatepe," *Orientalia* N.S. 18 (1949): 185.

7. E.g., S. Terrien understands it to refer to "one of the thousand messengers of God's judgment and grace" (*Job* [IB, 3; New York and Nashville: Abingdon, 1954]: 1137); N. H. Tur Sinai is of the opinion that "one of the thousand" rather than having limitative meaning "stresses that God sends many such messengers and that man can easily listen to at least one of them" (*The Book of Job: A New Commentary* [rev. ed.; Jerusalem: Kiryat Sepher, 1967]: 473); R. Gordis thinks that the expression is merely "a hyperbolic phrase = 'however rare, difficult to find'" (*The Book of Job* [Moreshet Series II; New York, 1978]: 377); M. Pope, somewhat nearer the mark, suggests that "The heavenly court was a numerous body" (*Job* [AB, 15; Garden City, N.Y.: Doubleday, 1965]: 219; 3d ed., 1973: 251).

The feminine numeral, *ʾaḥat*, in the similar appearing but unrelated expression *ʾaḥat minnî-ʾālep* (Job 9:3), functions as an adverb, and the phrase signifies "once out of a thousand (times)."

8. RS 17.152:5. Text, transliteration, and translation: J. Nougayrol, *PRU* IV, Pl. XXI, and p. 214.

With greater deference, and more elaborately, does the ruler of Ušnatu, Ar(i)teššub, greet the ruler of Ugarit:

> With my father may it be very well! My father, may (the) thousand gods (*li-im* DINGIR.MEŠ) keep you in health![9]

Still more elaborately, a letter discovered at Ras ibn Hani includes the following greeting:

> May (the) thousand gods (*li-im* DINGIR.MEŠ), the gods of Biʾrutu, the gods of the queen of Ugarit, keep you in health![10]

The curse section of the treaty of alliance between Šuppiluliuma, ruler of Ḫatti, and Mattiwaza[11] of Mitanni, written in Akkadian, concludes:

> (If you . . . shall not keep the works of this treaty . . .) to (the) thousand gods (*li-im* DINGIR.MEŠ) be you enemies! May they pursue you![12]

Again, toward the end of an edict in which Šuppiluliuma acknowledges the loyalty of Niqmadu, ruler of Ugarit, and stipulates the tribute to be remitted by the latter, we find:

9. RS 17.143:5–8. Text, transliteration, and translation: J. Nougayrol, *PRU* IV, Pl. XVIII, and p. 217. Cf RS 17.83:5–7, *ibid.*, Pl. IX, and p. 216; and RS 17.288:4–6, *ibid.*, Pl. XXXV, and p. 215.

10. Hani 81/4:5–7. Text, transliteration, and translation: D. Arnaud, *Syria* 61 (1984): 15. So also, Arnaud informs us, in a letter of the king of Beirut to the prefect of Ugarit (RS 34.137:5), currently in press; cf. *ibid.*: 20 n. 19. I owe this reference to the courtesy of M. Tsevat.

11. For the reading of the first element in this name, KUR, as *šat*, and the name as *Šattiwaza*, see B. Landsberger, "Assyrische Königsliste und 'dunkles Zeitalter'," *JCS* 8 (1954): 130, sub V a. More recently, C. Zaccagnini, "Šattiwaza," *Oriens Antiquus* 13 (1974): 25–34, and G. Kestemont, *Diplomatique et droit internationale en Asie occidentale (1600–1200 av. J.C.)* (Publications de l'Institut Orientaliste de Louvain, 9 [Louvain-la-neuve, 1974]): 92 n. 15. For the reading of this name as *Kur-ti-wa-za* (= *Kṛti-vāja*) see H. G. Güterbock, "The Deeds of Suppiluliuma as Told by his Son Mursili II," *JCS* 10 (1956): 121f. n. 18, and, more recently, A. Kammenhüber, *Die Arier in Vorderen Orient* (Indogermanische Bibliothek; Heidelberg: C. Winter, 1968): 82–84.

12. *KBo* I, 1 rev. (59–60) . . . 68–69. Transliteration and translation: E. F. Weidner, *Politische Dokumente aus Kleinasien* (Boghazköi Studien, 8–9; Leipzig: Hinrichs, 1923): 37.

> As for the words that are inscribed on this tablet, (the) thousand gods (*li-im* DINGIR.MEŠ) do indeed know (them)![13]

And in a document in which the same Hittite monarch confers several towns and territories upon Niqmadu, the curse section begins:

> And he who shall alter the words of the tablet of this treaty, may (the) thousand gods (*li-im* DINGIR.MEŠ) know![14]

Somewhat later, at the start of the curse section of a text confirming the claim of Niqmepa of Ugarit to those same towns and territories that Šuppiluliuma had granted to Niqmadu and his successors, there is found:

> [And] whosoever shall alter the words of these tablets, may (the) thousand gods (*li-im* DINGIR.MEŠ) know it![15]

So also in treaties written in Hittite does the locution, here composed of Akkadograms, i.e., *LI-IM* DINGIR.MEŠ, occur. Thus, Šuppiluliuma's treaty with Ḫuqqana and the people of Ḫayaša relates that:

> I have put you under oath . . . and for this transaction we have called (the) thousand gods into council.[16]

In the treaty between Muwatalli, son and successor of Muršili II, with Alakšandu of Wiluša, following a list of curses we read:

> If, however, you keep these words, then may these thousand gods . . . keep you well![17]

13. RS 17.227:48–50. Text, transliteration, and translation: J. Nougayrol, *PRU* IV, Pl. XXV, and p. 43.

14. RS 17.340:16′–17′. Text, transliteration, and translation: J. Nougayrol, *PRU* IV, Pl. XLVIII, and p. 51.

15. RS 17.237:9′–10′. Text, transliteration, and translation: J. Nougayrol, *PRU* IV, Pl. XXX, and p. 65.

16. Transliteration and translation: J. Friedrich, "Staatsverträge des Ḫatti-Reiches in hethitischer Sprache II," *MVAG* 34/1 (1930): 110–111: ll. 38–40. Cf. the similar phraseology in the treaty of Muršili II with Targašnili of Ḫapalla. Transliteration and translation: J. Friedrich, "Staatsverträge des Ḫatti-Reiches in hethitischer Sprache I," *MVAG* 31/1 (1926): 68–69: l. 55. I owe this reference and the one following to the courtesy of M. Tsevat and J. Huehnergard.

17. Transliteration and translation: J. Friedrich, "Staatsverträge I" (N 16): 82–83: ll. 37–46.

And four times in the treaty of Tudḫaliya IV, the son and successor of Ḫattušili III, with Ulmiteššub of Dattašša,[18] appeal is made to "(the) thousand gods." Twice they are invoked as witnesses:

> To this word let . . . (several named deities) and (the) thousand gods of Ḫatti be witness![19]

> This is the tablet of the treaty that I have made for you. Now, then, (the) thousand gods have been called into council on behalf of this word. Let them attend to the tablet and be witness to it![20]

while twice they are invoked as agents of punishment for infraction of the treaty and agreement:

> If you, Ulmiteššub, do not keep the text of this tablet . . . then may these thousand gods utterly destroy you . . . ![21]

> Whoever makes trouble for him or takes away the country, or changes a single word of this tablet, may . . . (several named deities) and the thousand gods of this tablet utterly destroy that man's issue from Ḫatti![22]

And in the treaty between Ramses II, of Egypt, and Ḫattušili III, of Ḫatti, the curse, preserved only in Egyptian, but reflecting the presumed Hittite or Akkadian original, has been rendered:

> As for these words which are on this tablet of silver of the land of Hatti and of the land of Egypt—as for him who shall not keep them, a thousand gods of the land of Hatti, together with a thousand gods of the land of Egypt, shall destroy his house, his land, and his servants.[23]

The expression, "(the) thousand gods," seems thus far restricted to letters, treaties, and edicts or grants that stem from the Hittite sphere of influence of the late second millennium B.C.E., and is

18. *KBo* IV, 10. For an English translation of this text see D.J. McCarthy, *Treaty and Covenant* (Analecta Biblica, 21A; new. ed. Rome: Pontifical Biblical Institute, 1978): 305f.

19. *Ibid.*, ll. 48–49.

20. *Ibid.*, ll. 50ff.

21. *Ibid.*, rev. 5ff.

22. *Ibid.*, rev. 25ff.

23. The translation is that of J. A. Wilson in *ANET*: 201.

likely to have been of Hittite provenience.[24] One can only speculate, therefore, on the manner in which such a concept may have found its way into the terminology of Biblical Israel more than half a millennium later. Yet, it may be remarked, several second millennium B.C.E. Hittite political, legal, literary, religious, and cultic forms and procedures have been advanced in recent years as analogues to Israelite modes and practices.[25] However these, individually or severally, are to be evaluated, the sequence in Job 33:23, "a messenger, an intermediary, one of (the) thousand," together with the latter's reflection in documents of the late second millennium B.C.E., indicate that *mēlîṣ* in this verse has reference to a divine being, and that the conjectured meaning of Phoenician

24. The expression and the religious concept underlying it may antedate the Hittite New Kingdom inaugurated by Šuppiluliuma III. See A. Kempinski and S. Košak, "Der Išmeriga-Vertrag," *WO* 5 (1970): 201f., and the literature cited there. I owe this reference to the courtesy of G. Beckman.

25. For Israelite reflexes of second millennium B.C.E. Hittite:

Treaty Forms: V. Korošec, *Hethitische Staatsverträge* (Leipzig: Weicher, 1931); G. E. Mendenhall, "Covenant Forms in Israelite Tradition," *BA* 17 (1954): 50–76; K. Baltzer, *Das Bundesformular* (Neukirchen: Neukirchener-Verlag, 1960); English ed. *The Covenant Formulary* (Philadelphia: Fortress, 1971); W. Beyerlin, *Herkunft und Geschichte der ältesten Sinaitraditionen* (Tübingen: Mohr, 1961); D. J. McCarthy (N 18); M. G. Kline, *Treaty of the Great King: The Covenant Structure of Deuteronomy* (Grand Rapids: Eerdmans, 1963); F. C. Fensham, "Clauses of Protection in Hittite Vassal-Treaties and the Old Testament," *VT* 13 (1963): 133–143.

Vocabulary: C. Rabin, "Hittite Words in Hebrew," *Orientalia* N.S. 32 (1963): 113–139, but see the critical remarks of H. A. Hoffner, "The Hittites and Hurrians," in *Peoples of Old Testament Times* (ed. D. J. Wiseman; Oxford: Clarendon, 1973): 215.

Law: M. Lehmann, "Abraham's Purchase of Machpelah and Hittite Law," *BASOR* 129 (1953): 15–18, but see G. M. Tucker, "The Legal Background of Genesis 23," *JBL* 85 (1966): 77–84; F. C. Fensham, "Exodus xxi 18–19 in the light of Hittite Law §10," *VT* 10 (1960): 333-335.

Religious Practices and Terminology: S. Gevirtz, "Jericho and Shechem: A Religio-Literary Aspect of City Destruction," *VT* 13 (1963): 52–62; H. A: Hoffner, Jr., "Second Millennium Antecedents to the Hebrew *ʾÔḆ*," *JBL* 86 (1967): 385–401; *idem.*, "Hittite *Tarpiš* and Hebrew *Terāphîm*," *JNES* 27 (1968): 61–68, but see F. Josephson, "Anatolian Tarpa/i-," *Florilegium Anatolicum* (Paris: Éditions E. de Boccard, 1979): 177–184; J. Milgrom, "The Shared Custody of the Tabernacle and a Hittite Analogy," *JAOS* 90 (1970): 204–209; J. C. Moyer, "Hittite and Israelite Cultic Practices: A Selected Comparison" in *Scripture in Context II* (ed. W. W. Hallo, et al.: Winona Lake, Indiana: Eisenbrauns, 1983): 19–38.

Historiography: A. Malamat, "Doctrines of Causality in Hittite and Biblical Historiography: A Parallel," *VT* 5 (1955): 1–12.

Literature: H. A. Hoffner, Jr., "Some Contributions of Hittitology to Old Testament Study," *Tyndale Bulletin* 20 (1969): 52–53; M. Tsevat, "Two Old Testament Stories and their Hittite Analogues," *JAOS* 103 (1983): 321–326.

mlṣm in *KAI* 26 A i 8 as "(divine) intermediaries" has found confirmation.

We may turn now to a consideration of the *nomen regens*, *šbrt*. Context clearly requires a meaning "group, assembly"—that is to say, "thanks to Baal, and the gods, and the *assembly* of the (divine) intermediaries." I suggest, then, that graphemic *šbrt* here reflects phonemic /ś-b-r-t/, and that this, in turn, is an alternate form of *ṣbrt*.[26] The latter lexeme occurs in Ugaritic where it bears the desiderated meaning "band, company, assemblage," as in *UT* 49:I:11–13: . . . *tšmḫ ht* (12) *aṯrt* . *wbnh* . *ilt wṣb* (13) *rt* . *aryh* "Now let Athiratu rejoice, and her sons, Ilatu and the assemblage of her kin!"[27] This suggestion proceeds upon two assumptions: (1) that in Phoenician, as in Hebrew (and Ugaritic—see below), the grapheme *š* was polyphonous, reflecting phonemic /ś/ as well as /š/, and (2) that *ś* and *ṣ* alternate when, corresponding etymologically to Arabic *ḍ*, these derive from Proto-Semitic (PS) *ḏ̣—a fricative lateral.[28] From this perspective PS *ś was the voiceless unemphatic complement to PS *ḏ̣.[29] Let us examine these assumptions.

In the Phoenician "alphabet" etymological *š* and *ś* appear to have been written, for the most part, with the same sign. So also in the Ugaritic writing system does the grapheme *š* reflect etymological *š* and *ś*. This observation led earlier scholars to conclude that, by the time of the creation of these scripts, etymological *š* and *ś* had coalesced in Ugaritic and Phoenician—or, more precisely, perhaps, that these scripts originated among peoples in whose dialects PS /š/ and /ś/ had merged—and that the grapheme *š* whether in the Ugaritic or in the Phoenician script, represented but one speech sound, whose pronunciation was realized as [š].[30] And while the one, unequivocal, example that should serve to prove that Phoenician had indeed preserved phonemic /ś/, namely *ʿsr* "ten" (*KAI* 14:1) for the expected **ʿšr* (cf. Ugaritic *ʿšr, ʿšrt*, Phoenician *ʿšrt*,

26. W. F. Albright originally read *šbrt* as *ṣbrt*, but this was shown to be in error. See O'Callaghan (N 6): 185.

27. Cf. C. H. Gordon, *UT* §19.2142. Note Post-Biblical Hebrew *ṣibbûr* "congregation, community."

28. See the important study of R. C. Steiner, *The Case for Fricative-Laterals in Proto-Semitic* (AOS, No. 59; New Haven, Conn., 1977).

29. *Ibid.*: 121.

30. Z. S. Harris, *A Grammar of the Phoenician Language* (AOS, No. 8; New Haven, Conn., 1936): 22; *idem*, *Development of the Canaanite Dialects* (AOS, No. 16; New Haven, Conn., 1939): 33–35, 81. Cf. E. Y. Kutscher, "Contemporary Studies in North-western Semitic," *JSS* 10 (1965): 41.

and Hebrew *ᶜeśer, ᶜăśūrā, ᶜăśeret*, etc.) has been denigrated as an isolated case, and one that, moreover, may have been influenced by Aramaic,[31] this view has not met with general acceptance.[32] Note that in the very same inscription in which *ᶜsr* occurs, where one might have anticipated **ᶜšr*, we find *bšd* (= Hebrew *biśədē*) *šrn* "in the plain of Sharon" (*KAI* 14:19), quite in accord with historical spelling.

In addition, consideration should be given to the evidence provided by the isoglosses that are recorded in Deut 3:9. In this verse we are informed that "The Sidonians call (Mount) Ḥermôn Śiryôn, and the Amorites call it Śĕnîr." Inasmuch as both Śiryôn and Śĕnîr will have been considered foreign designations by the Biblical Hebrew speaking author and his audience, it would appear that we have been provided with transcriptions of the Sidonian (= Phoenician) and Amorite (= ?) pronunciations of their respective names for that mountain, which, in the author's own dialect was called Ḥermôn. The initial sound of the Phoenician and Amorite names must have been heard by him as [ś], and this indicates that speakers of those dialects in the author's day—just as he—distinguished /ś/ from /š/. For had they not, that is, had these dialects not preserved /ś/, had /ś/ and /š/ merged and been realized in pronunciation as [š], then what the author would have heard would have been [širyôn] and [šĕnîr], respectively, and he would have had no reason to transcribe them other than as **širyôn* and **šĕnîr*. Furthermore, to the example provided by Phoenician *ᶜsr*, may perhaps be added a few others from the lexica of Ugaritic and Phoenician.

Ugaritic attests to a quadriradical root *prsḥ* "to slump, collapse" (*UT* 68:22, 25) which has been compared with Arabic *faršaḥa* "to sit with legs apart," etc.[33] If these are indeed cognate, then the atypical correspondence Arabic *š* = Ugaritic *s*, may provide evidence for the preservation of /ś/ in Ugaritic.[34]

31. Harris, *Grammar* (N 30): 22. Cf. A. Murtonen, "The Semitic Sibilants," *JSS* 11 (1966): 146 n. 2.

32. E.g., J. Friedrich, *Phönizisch-punische Grammatik* (Analecta Orientalia, 32; Rome: Pontifical Biblical Institute, 1951; 2. Auflage, 1970): §§ 44, 46b.

33. C. H. Gordon, *UT*: 470f., §19.2112, hesitantly; S. Segert, *A Basic Grammar of the Ugaritic Language* (Berkeley: Univ. of California, 1984): 198. For the various nuances of Arabic *faršaḥa* see E. W. Lane, *An Arabic-English Lexicon*, Book I, Part 6: 2372. For the comparison of Ugaritic *prsḥ* with Akkadian *napalsuḫu* "to fall to the ground," see W. von Soden, *AHw.*: 733; Segert, *Grammar*: 198.

34. In RS 24.258 (*Ugaritica* V: 546ff.), ll. 3–4 there occurs the parallelism, *ᶜd šbᶜ* // *ᶜd škr* "to satiety" // "to drunkenness." The term *šbᶜ* "satiety," finds its cog-

Of interest, then, too, is it to consider the Ugaritic and Phoenician cognates of Hebrew *ḥśp*. Regularly assigned the definitions "to tear off, strip, lay bare" and "to draw (water, wine)," these two meanings are customarily viewed as being semantically related.[35] The two definitions, however, very likely reflect two distinct verbs that have fallen together graphemically in Hebrew. In its meaning "to draw (water, wine)"[36] Hebrew *ḥśp* is to be compared with Ugaritic *ḥsp* "to draw (water)" as in *tḥspn mh wtrḥṣ* "she draws water and washes" (*UT* ᶜ*nt* IV:86)[37]—note, too, that it appears as a qualifier of "wine" in *yn ḥsp* (*UT* 1084:24)—and with Akkadian *esēpu*.[38] In its meaning "to tear off, strip, lay bare (vegetation, clothing, etc.),"[39] on the other hand, Hebrew *ḥśp* is to be compared with Akkadian *ḫasāpu* "to tear out (hair, bricks),"[40] Phoenician *ḥsp* "to tear away (scepter)" (*KAI* 1:2),[41] and, in all probability, Ugaritic *ḫsp* (*UT* 1 Aqht 31).[42] The latter occurs in a broken context, but in view of the fact that it is immediately followed by *ib* "verdure"[43] in *yḫsp ib*[. . .], and that this phrase appears in association or parallel

---

nates in Hebrew *śōba*ᶜ and *śābā*ᶜ, Aramaic *su/ib*ᶜ*a*ᵓ, etc. In l. 16 of the same text the corresponding parallelism is transliterated similarly, ᶜ*d šb*ᶜ. . . ᶜ*d škr*. But the autograph copy of the text reads ᶜ*d sb*ᶜ. . . ᶜ*d škr*. Because there can be no doubt but that we are dealing with the very same vocable, were the spelling of the autograph correct, the self-evident explanation for this dual realization of the Ugaritic term for "satiety," *šb*ᶜ and *sb*ᶜ, would be that, in whatever dialect of Ugaritic this work may have been composed, etymological /š/ and /ś/ had not merged, and that the grapheme *š* was polyphonous, representing both /š/ and /ś/. His reading of a cast of this text, however, has convinced Loren Fisher that in l. 16 it is the autograph that is in error, and that the transliterated text is correct. Cf. "New Readings for the Ugaritic Texts in *Ugaritica V*," *UF* 3 (1971): 356.

35. E.g., *BDB*: 362; *KB*³: 345 sub *ḥśp* I. For a denial of any semantic relationship between the two meanings, see J. Blau, *On Pseudo-Corrections in Some Semitic Languages* (Jerusalem: Israel Academy of Sciences and Humanities, 1970): 124 n. 49. His tentative suggestion that a supposed Hebrew **ḥsp* "was absorbed by *ḥśp* because they were both formally and semantically similar" (p. 124), however, must be rejected.

36. Isa 30:14 (water); Hag 2:16 (wine).

37. U. Cassuto, *The Goddess Anath* (Jerusalem: Bialik Institute and Vaad ha-Lashon ha-Ivrit, 1951): 78 (English edition, 1971: 121).

38. *CAD* E: 331. Cf. M. Held in *Studies and Essays in Honor of Abraham A. Neuman* (eds. M. Ben-Horin, et al.; Leiden: Brill, 1962): 284 n. 2.

39. Vegetation: Joel 1:7; Ps 29:9; cf. Gen 30:37; Jer 49:10. Clothing, etc.: Isa 20:4; 47:2; 52:10; Jer 13:26; Ezek 4:7.

40. *CAD* Ḫ: 122; *AHw.*: 329.

41. Cf. Harris, *Grammar* (N 30): 103. Contrast Blau (N 35): 124.

42. Cf. H. Donner-W. Röllig, *KAI*, II: 4.

43. Cf. Hebrew ᵓ*ēb* "fresh shoots," ᵓ*ābîb* "fresh barley shoots," Arabic ᵓ*abbun* "herbage, pasture."

with *bgrn yḫrb* [. . .] "on the threshing-floor [. . .] is dried up," the meaning "to strip, lay bare (vegetation)" for Ugaritic *ḫsp*—in N-stem "to be stripped"—seems appropriate. Then, unless we are to assume that in each of these two verbs Hebrew has gone its own unique way in the selection of the sibilant *ś* as opposed to *s*, the appearance of *s* in these (rare!) cognates argues for the preservation of /ś/ in these dialects. There is no reason any longer, then, if ever there was, to deny the evidence of Phoenician *ʿsr* as indication of the polyphonous character of *š̌* and of the preservation in Phoenician of the phoneme /ś/. The paucity of examples of vacillation or confusion between the signs *š̌* and *s* in Phoenician documents from the mainland must be attributed to the conventional and highly conservative nature of historical spelling in Phoenicia proper.

If our proposal that Phoenician *šbrt* reflects /ś-b-r-t/ is correct, what remains is for us to provide a measure of verification for the phonological correspondence between Phoenician /ś-b-r-t/ and Ugaritic *ṣbrt*. Such alternation of *ś* and *ṣ* is not otherwise attested in Phoenician, but Biblical Hebrew provides one sure illustration and a few other more or less plausible instances of this phenomenon, while Akkadian and Ugaritic, too, I believe, may be enlisted in support of it.

The parade example in Biblical Hebrew is the pair of alternating roots meaning "to laugh," in Piʿel "to sport," *ṣḥq* and *śḥq* (Arabic *ḍaḥika*), and the name of the patriarch that presumably derives from them, *yiṣḥāq* and *yiśḥāq*. As is generally recognized, these roots are essential "doublets," constituting a virtually perfect synonymous pair. And arguments that have attempted to distinguish a geographical or chronological factor in the employment of them are not only inconclusive but disproved by the utilization of them both in one verse. Jdg 16:25 reads, "And when their hearts were merry they said, 'Summon Samson that he may sport (*wîśaḥeq-*) for us.' And they summoned Samson . . . and he sported (*wayəṣaḥēq*) before them. . . ." In view of the observation at one time that *ṣḥq* occurs in the older Biblical sources (but cf. Ezek 23:32), while *śḥq* occurs primarily in later sources (but cf. 1 Sam 18:7; 2 Sam 2:14; 6:21; Amos 7:9, 16), it has been suggested that the appearance of the two forms in the one verse, Jdg 16:25, represents "the kind of fluctuation of competing forms which is so common while sound-change is in progress."[44] If, on the other hand, as

44. Steiner (N 28): 119 n. 23.

seems more likely, *śḥq* was an early *dialectal* form that, for the most part, was excluded from early *literary* Hebrew, only to find acceptance at a later time,[45] then this might well account for the fact that, of the two forms employed in the one verse, *śḥq* and *ṣḥq*, the former, the presumed non-literary dialectal form, is set in the mouths of foreigners, the Philistines, while the latter, the literary form, is utilized by the narrator.

Other such synonymous or related pairs in Biblical Hebrew as *ṣpn* = *ś/spn* "to hide" (of uncertain etymology), and *ṣmḥ* = *śmḥ* "to grow, glow"[46] have been questioned,[47] while *ṣrb* = *śrp* "to burn, scorch" (cf. Arabic *ḍarama* "to be kindled, to blaze") is less certain because of the variation in the final root consonant.[48] Nevertheless, it is to be noted, in those pairs whose etymologies are not in dispute, whose cognates in Arabic exhibit *ḍ*, the sibilant, emphatic *ṣ* or unemphatic *ś*, derives from PS *ḏ̣.[49]

Akkadian, too, on occasion, evidences variation, vacillation, or what has been termed "confusion" between *š* and *ṣ* when the sibilant corresponds, in cognate forms, to Arabic *ḍ*, and may be said to derive, therefore, from PS *ḏ̣. Thus, alongside *miḫiṣtu* "wound" (from *maḫāṣu* "to hit, wound, strike"), as is well known, there occurs *miḫištu* with the same meaning,[50] while several forms of *napāṣu* "to thrust away, kick, crush" (cf. Arabic *nafaḍa* "to shake off") virtually interchange with forms of *napāšu* (A) "to breathe freely" as well as with forms of *napāšu* (B) "to card (wool)."[51]

45. Cf. J. Blau, "On Polyphony in Biblical Hebrew," *Proceedings of the Israel Academy of Sciences and Humanities* VI/2 (1982): 4 (= 108).

46. Cf. J. C. Greenfield, "Lexicographical Notes II," *HUCA* 30 (1959): 141–151.

47. Steiner (N 28): 118 n. 6.

48. Were Hebrew *ṣrb* a bi-form of *zrb* (thus *BDB*: 279, 863), it might prove a serious blow to the thesis here advocated, for the alternation of *ṣ* with *z* presupposes a derivation from PS *ṣ (cf. Z. Ben-Hayyim, *Torat HaHege* [ed. R. Rosenberg; Jerusalem, 1959]: 15). But *zrb*, a *hapax legomenon* in Job 6:17 (*yəzōrəbū*), on present evidence is best understood with Gesenius-Robinson (cited in *BDB*: 279) as cognate with Arabic *zariba* "to flow away," Aramaic *zrb* (*ʾitpeʿel* "to overflow"), *zərîbā* "overflow(ing)"—cf. J. Levy, *Wörterbuch über die Talmudim und Midraschim* I (2. Aufl., Berlin und Wien: B. Harz, 1924; Darmstadt, 1963): 551f.—and is probably a bi-form of *zrp*, in *hipʿîl* "to irrigate."

49. Cf. Ben-Hayyim (N 48): 15.

50. Cf. *CAD* M/2: 54; for this and other examples, see M. Held, "*mḫṣ*/**mḫš* in Ugaritic and Other Semitic Languages (A Study in Comparative Lexicography)," *JAOS* 79 (1959): 173.

51. Cf. *CAD* N/1: 285 (lex. section), 287 sub meaning 7b, 288 sub meanings 7b and 7c, 290 sub meaning 5b, and see the discussion, pp. 290f.

We may now consider the evidence provided by Ugaritic *mḫṣ* "to strike, to slay (by striking)." As its cognates (Akkadian *maḫāṣu*, Hebrew *mḥṣ*, Aramaic *mḥʾ*, and the phonologically related Arabic *maḫaḍa* "to churn") indicate, the root derives from PS *mḫḏ̣. Almost thirty years ago it was noted that first person common singular perfect forms of this verb in Ugaritic appear spelled not, as might be expected, **mḫṣt*, but as *mḫšt*.[52] If Ugaritic *š*, like its correspondents in Hebrew and Phoenician, as we have argued above, was polyphonous, representing both /š/ and /ś/, and as PS *ś was the voiceless unemphatic complement to PS *ḏ̣, a fricative-lateral, we may recognize in Ugaritic *mḫšt* the result of a conditioned shift: *ṣ* (< *ḏ̣) > /ś/ (= *š*) before unemphatic voiceless /t/.

In view of the generally accepted etymology of Ugaritic *ṣbrt* "band, company, assemblage," namely Hebrew *ṣbr* "to heap up," Arabic *ḍabara* "to collect, bind together," and the probable polyphonous character of Phoenician *š*, there is ample warrant to recognize in Phoenician *šbrt* a graphemic representation of phonemic /ś-b-r-t/ and a bi-form of (or, perhaps more accurately, a Phoenician counterpart to) Ugaritic *ṣbrt*. With this understanding, the meaning "group, assembly" for Phoenician *šbrt* proves to be not only contextually appropriate, but etymologically founded.

To summarize: Phoenician *wšbrt mlṣm* is a noun clause, dependent on *bʿbr bʿl wʾlm*. That *mlṣm* means "(divine) intermediaries" may be determined on the basis of Hebrew *mēlîṣ* "intermediary" as this term is employed in Gen 42:23 and especially Job 33:23. In the latter verse *mēlîṣ* appears immediately following *malʾāk* "messenger," and immediately preceding *ʾeḥād minnî ʾālep* "one of (the) thousand." Because elsewhere in Biblical Hebrew literature, as is well attested, *malʾāk* can refer to a "(divine) messenger" (e.g., 1 Kgs 13:18), and as the expression "one of (the) thousand" finds its reflex in the late second millennium B.C.E. Hittite locution, "(the) thousand gods," *mēlîṣ* "intermediary" in Job 33:23 may be understood to refer to one of these thousand. With respect to *šbrt*, insofar as Phoenician *š* was polyphonous, representing /ś/ as well as /š/, graphemic *šbrt* may be taken to reflect phonemic /ś-b-r-t/. Then, as *ś* and *ṣ* are found to interchange when, corresponding etymologically to Arabic *ḍ*, they derive from PS *ḏ̣, *šbrt* = /ś-b-r-t/ may be recognized as the Phoenician counterpart to Ugaritic *ṣbrt* "assembly," and the phrase, *wšbrt mlṣm*, immediately following *bʿbr bʿl wʾlm* "thanks to Baal and the gods," is to be rendered "and the assembly of the (divine) intermediaries."

52. M. Held (N 50): 169–176.

MAARAV 5–6 (Spring, 1990): 159–168

THE 'CLUSTER' IN BIBLICAL POETRY

JONAS C. GREENFIELD
THE HEBREW UNIVERSITY, JERUSALEM, ISRAEL

A great deal has been written in recent years concerning the rhetorical and poetic means available to the Canaanite poet.[1] The term "Canaanite" is used in its broadest sense to include the authors of the epic and other poetic texts from Ugarit, the writers of those Amarna letters in which "poetic" quotations have been found, and the composers of various Phoenician inscriptions in which rhetorical elements have been discerned.[2] Word pairs, parallelism, stress accentuation and other features have been much discussed in recent years and need no detailed reference here.[3] The relationship of Canaanite poetry to Biblical poetry has been a matter of ongoing interest for over fifty years and needs no defense at my hands, although there are some who at this late date are still fighting a sort of rear-guard battle and others who write about Biblical poetry as if it were created in a void.

This study will deal with a phenomenon in the relationship of Canaanite and Biblical poetry that has not received due attention; it is what I call a "cluster" for lack of a better name. In the

1. This paper assumes that the reader is *au courant* with Ugaritic studies and minimum bibliography will be offered.

2. I maintain the view, now become unpopular, that Ugaritic was not part of a vaguely undifferentiated "North-West Semitic" language current in the Middle and Late Bronze Ages, but that it was already clearly aligned with the Canaanite dialects, even though Ugarit was from the geographic point of view outside of Canaan proper. For the Amarna letters, see S. Gevirtz, "On Canaanite Rhetoric: The Evidence of the Amarna Letters from Tyre," *Orientalia* 42 (1973): 162–177.

3. D. Pardee has discussed the problem of meter in Ugaritic poetry in "Ugaritic and Hebrew Metrics," in *Ugarit in Retrospect* (ed. G. D. Young; Winona Lake, IN: Eisenbrauns, 1981): 113–130. The syllable counting prevalent in certain circles is a meaningless effort.

"cluster" the Biblical writer draws from the poetical resources available to him a number of word pairs and standard epithets and uses them to construct a complex poetic structure, or to set the background framework of the material that he is presenting. It is of minor consequence for this discussion if the resources were written or oral; indeed, a case can be made for the use of both types of material by the Biblical writers, but of that elsewhere.

First, two examples of the simple "cluster." The name of Baᶜal's holy mountain was *ṣpn*/*Ṣapunu*, which was also known as Hazi, the later Mons Casius (*kásιon óros*), the contemporary Jebel el-ᵓaqraᶜ. In the Ugaritic texts the name *ṣpn* is at times modified by *mrym* or by *ṣrrt*. There can be no doubt that *mrym* is the equivalent of Hebrew *mārôm*, the generally accepted translation being the "height" or "summit" of Zaphon, while *ṣrrt ṣpn* is understood as the remote parts of Zaphon and "summit of Zaphon" would do for it.[4] The collocation *ṣrrt ṣpn* as such is not found in Biblical poetry but *yarkᵊtê ṣāpôn* in the phrase *har-ṣiyyôn yarkᵊtê ṣāpôn* "Mount Zion, summit of Zaphon" (Ps 48: 3b) is in all likelihood a reflection of it.[5] As has been noted, use has been made of *ṣrrt ṣpn* in two Biblical passages, the first being Hosea 13:12:

> *ṣārûr ᶜăwôn ᵓeprayim* / *ṣᵊpûnā ḥaṭṭāᵓtô*
> "Ephraim's guilt is bound up, his sin stored away"

4. M. Astour, *RSP* II (Rome, 1975): 318–324, has discussed the use of *ṣpn* and its geographic location in detail. For a recent survey of the etymologies proposed for *ṣrrt* see M. Dietrich and O. Loretz, "*ṢRRT ṢPN*—Feste des Ṣapunu," *UF* 12 (1980): 394, none of which is satisfactory. As has been recognized, *mᵊrôm ṣiyyôn* (Jer 31:12) is calqued on *mrym ṣpn*.

5. The other passage in which *yarkᵊtê ṣāpôn* occurs is in Isa 14:13: *har môᶜēd yarkᵊtê ṣāpôn* "the mountain of the assembly, the summit of Zaphon" in a passage replete with mythological allusions. The use of *yarkᵊtê* for the summit of Zaphon is fitting, for besides referring to the recesses or remote parts of a cave, pit, or building, it is also used for the less accessible reaches of Mt. Ephraim in Jdg 19:1, 18 and of Mt. Lebanon in 2 Kgs 19:23 (= Isa 37:24). Note too that in the latter we also find *mārôm*//*yarkᵊtê*, surely a reflex of *mrym*//*ṣrrt*. Of interest is the transformation of Zaphon from a mythological to a geographical designation. Jer 1:14–15 uses *ṣāpôn* for the region from which the Babylonians came and also for the people of the North—Scythians, Cimmerians, Medes and Persians who threatened the tranquillity of the Fertile Crescent. In Jer 6:22; 25:32; 31:8, and 50:41 the term *yarkᵊtê ᵓāreṣ* refers to remote and distant parts of the earth. In three of these passages it is in parallelism with (*ᵓereṣ*) *ṣāpôn*, showing that this is a typical break-up of a sterotyped phrase.

It is clear that *ṣārûr*//*ṣᵊpûnā* is a reflex of *ṣrrt ṣpn*, even though the meaning of the two verbal forms (passive participles) in Hebrew is far removed from the Ugaritic phrase. The tone for this reminiscent use was set by verse 1c of this chapter, *wayyeʾšam babbaᶜal way-yāmot*, "he (Ephraim) incurred guilt through Baᶜal and died." There are other elements in this chapter that will be familiar to students of Ugaritic—(a) the comparison with four fleeting elements in verse 3 is reminiscent of the text from Ras Ibn Hani in which a similar comparison is made, including a reference to smoke from a lattice[6]; (b) the reference to Mot (*šᵊʾōl*/*māwet*) in verse 14; and others.

The second use of *ṣrrt ṣpn* is in Job 26:7–8:

> *nôṭeh ṣāpôn ᶜal-tôhû* / *tôleh ʾereṣ ᶜal bᵊlî-mā*
> *ṣôrēr mayim bᵊᶜābāw* / *wᵊlôʾ nibqaᶜ ᶜānān taḥtām*

> "He it is who stretched Zaphon over chaos,
> who suspended earth over emptiness.
> He who binds up the waters in his clouds;
> yet no cloud burst under their weight."

Zaphon is found here in a virtually unique use as "the heavens," demythologized as it were, followed by the verb *ṣôrēr* in the following line.[7] This chapter of Job has other Canaanite themes—the Rephaim are mentioned in verse 5, and in verses 12–13 the battle with the sea, and the defeat of the monsters Rahab and the *naḥaš bārīaḥ* (= Leviathan) is alluded to.[8] For the writer of Job *ṣrrt ṣpn* was a living phrase upon which he could draw and with which he could play, as he did with *mbk nhrt* elsewhere in the book.[9]

6. The text from Ras Ibn Hani was first published by A. Caquot in the *Annuaire du Collège de France, 79 année (1978–1979)* (Paris, 1979): 488–490; see too, *CRAIBL* (1979): 288–299. The text has been studied by J. C. de Moor, *UF* 12 (1980): 429–432 and Y. Avishur, *UF* 13 (1981): 13–25.

7. In Isa 14:13 *yarkᵊtê ṣāpōn* is in parallelism with *šāmayim*.

8. For this important theme in Ugaritic and Biblical literature, see now J. Day, *God's Conflict with the Dragon and the Sea* (Cambridge, 1985).

9. As in Job 28:11; cf. Marvin Pope, *Job: Introduction, Translation, and Notes* (AB 15; New York: Doubleday, 1965): 180–181 for the Ugaritic background.

Another example of a simple cluster may be found in Ps 24:3: *mî yaᶜăleh bᵊhar YHWH ûmî-yāqûm bimqôm qodšô*, "who shall ascend to the mountain of the Lord, and who can abide in his holy place?" We must turn to a well-known Ugaritic text (*CTA* 3 iii 26–28) where a series of terms used of Zaphon may be found:

26. *btk.ģry.il.ṣpn*	in my mountain, the godly Zaphon
27. *bqdš.bģr.nḥlty*	in (my) sanctuary, in the mountain of my inheritance

In 1.27 *qdš* is clearly equal to Heb. *qōdeš*, while *ģr* is the functional equivalent of Heb. *har*. They are used together for the place of divine residence. One may protest that *har* and *qōdeš* are common terms and it is therefore superfluous to look for a Canaanite antecedent, but verse 2 of the Psalm in praising God's might reminds us that "he founded it (*scil.* the world) upon the sea (*yam*) and established it upon the streams (*nᵊhārôt*)," that is, the creation of the world took place after the defeat of *zbl ym / ṯpṭ nhr*. In the Ugaritic texts it is only after that feat that Baᶜal merited a house of his own; but as is well known, the Ugaritic texts do not contain a creation story and there is no indication at Ugarit of creation after Baᶜal's having defeated Yam, there is simply the assumption of kingship. However, in a version that may have developed later, or in a different part of the Canaanite culture sphere, the three elements—victory, kingship, creation (i.e., the setting of the world in order)—were in all likelihood to be found, as in Enuma Elish. The Biblical recycling of the Canaanite mythic tradition reflects this, as was pointed out by M. D. Cassuto years ago. It is therefore not surprising that one finds in verses 7, 9 of this Psalm the line *śᵊʾû šᵊᶜārîm rāšêkem* "lift up, o gates, your heads," long since recognized as an echo of Baᶜal's call to his fellow gods cowering in fright of Yam's emissaries to raise their heads from their knees (*CTA* 2 i 27).[10] As if to round out the requisite elements noted above, God is hailed as the *melek hakkābôd* and is called a fierce warrior, *ᶜizzûz wᵊgibbōr.*[11] The Psalmist

10. This theme lived on and was adopted, like much else from the ancient world, by the Mandaeans. In a prayer, M. Lidzbarski, *Mandäische Liturgien* (Berlin, 1920): 212, No. XLVI, 1:2: *rišai nišqul min burkai unikapar ainai min dimihta* "he will raise my head from my knees and wipe the tears from my eyes."

11. For YHWH as hero, see J. C. Greenfield, "Baᶜal's Throne and Isa 6:1," in *Mélanges bibliques et orientaux en l'honneur de M. Mathias Delcor* (A. Caquot *et al.*, eds.; Neukirchen-Vluyn, 1985): 193–198.

has skillfully woven the simple "cluster" together with other Canaanite matters into his text.

The more complex "clusters" function in diverse manners in the various texts in which they are found. The examples presented below exemplify this. For the first example, Ps 18:38–41 will be examined:

ʾerdōp ʾôyᵊbay wᵊʾassîgēm / wᵊlôʾ ʾāšûb ʿad kallōtām
ʾemḥāṣēm wᵊlô yûkᵊlû qûm / yippᵊlû taḥat raglāy
watʾazzᵊrēnî ḥayil lammilḥāmā / takrîaʿ qâmay taḥtāy
wᵊʾôyᵊbay nātattā lî ʿōrep / ûmᵊśanᵊʾay ʾaṣmîtēm

"I pursued my enemies and overtook them; / I did not turn back till I destroyed them. I struck them down and they could rise no more; / they lay fallen at my feet. You have girded me with strength for battle, / brought my adversaries low before me, / made my enemies turn tail before me; / I wiped out my foes."

1. The words for enemy in Ugaritic which find their equivalent in this text are: *ib* = *ʾōyēb*, *qm* = *qâm*, and *śnu* = *mᵊśannēʾ*. They function variously as word pairs in Ugaritic—*ib* // *qm* (*CTA* 10 ii 25) and *ib* // *śnu* (*CTA* 4 vii 35–6).

2. The verbs used for "to smite, destroy" are *kly, mḫṣ*, and *ṣmt*, distributed in word pairs, *mḫṣ* // *ṣmt* (*CTA* 3 ii 7–8), *mḫṣ* // *kly* (*CTA* 5 i 1–2, 27–8).

3. The third pair that I would note, *krʿ* // *npl*, is not found in Ugaritic, but their functional equivalents *hbr* and *ql* are often found together (*CTA* 3 iii 6–7).[12] Neither *hbr* nor *ql* are found in Hebrew,[13] one may therefore surmise that in the version of these poems known to the Hebrew poet the more familiar *krʿ* // *npl* pair was used.

4. The verbs *kallôtām* (38b) and *ʾaṣmîtēm* (41b) form a sort of *inclusio*. If this analysis is correct, elements from three different word groups were used to form a "cluster."

Another "cluster" type may be found in Ps 21. The Canaanite referent in this Psalm has been noted by others. In speaking of the king, the Psalmist uses phraseology known to us from the tale of

12. But *tpl-tšthwy* (*CTA* 2 i 15) and *ykrʿ wyql* (*CTA* 5 vi 8) are known. The phrase *yippᵊlû taḥat raglay* is paralleled by Ugaritic *ql tḥt pʿn* "fall at the feet of" found frequently in 3 Aqhat.

13. Unless the enigmatic *hôbᵊrê šāmayim* of Isa 47:13 means simply "those who worship the heavens" rather than a specific divinatory act.

Aqhat (*CTA* 17–19). The young hunter Aqhat is offered silver and gold by the goddess Anat for his wondrous bow, saying, *irš ksp watnk / ḫrṣ wašlḥk* "ask for silver and I will give it to you, for gold and I will grant it to you" (*CTA* 17 vi 17–18); he rejected this proposal and she then offered him eternal life, *irš ḥym laqht ġzr / irš ḥym watnk / blmt wašlḥk* "ask for life, O hero Aqhat, ask for life and I will give it to you, for deathlessness and I will grant it to you" (*CTA* 17 vi 26–28). Aqhat rejected this too.[14] The elements to be noted are the verbs *ʾrš* "to ask for, desire," *ntn* "to give," *ḥym // blmt* "eternal life." In verse 3 of Psalm 21 we read *taʾăwat libbô nātattā lô waʾărešet śᵊpātāw bal-manaʿtā* and in verse 5 *ḥayyîm šāʾal mimmᵊkā nātattā lô ʾōrek yāmîm ʿôlām wāʿēd.* The context has changed; it is no longer the goddess offering but the king desiring, yet the borrowed elements in vocabulary are there—v.3 *nātattā* and *ʾărešet*, in v. 5 *ḥayyîm* and *šāʾal*, which is an equivalent of *ʾrš*. In the Ugaritic text the word parallel to *ḥym* is *blmt*, but in Psalm 21 this has been replaced by *ʾōrek yāmîm* "long life," a traditional wish for the king. In v. 3 of the Psalm the *ʿăṭeret paz* "golden diadem" which the king is promised may very well replace the original silver and gold offered Aqhat.

Psalm 27 is a composite psalm containing disparate elements. One of these is the unit contained in verses 4–6. In verse 4, the Psalmist does not ask for life as such but expresses his deeply felt desire with the words *šibtî bᵊbêt YHWH kol-yᵊmê ḥayyay / laḥzôt bᵊnōʿam YHWH / ûlᵊbaqqēr bᵊhêkālô* which may be translated "One thing I ask of the Lord, only that do I seek: to live in the house of the Lord all the days of my life, to gaze upon the beauty of the Lord, to frequent his temple."[15] If this verse is examined from a purely structural point of view, three terms are found in parallelism—*bêt YHWH / nōʿam YHWH / hêkal.* If this observation is correct then the translation proposed for *nōʿam* is wrong. In the passage from *CTA* 2 iii 26028 quoted above, *nʿm* is in appositive parallelism with *qdš* "sanctuary" and thus *nʿm*, the pleasant or goodly place, serves as an epithet for the sanctuary. Taking a hint from this use of *nʿm // qdš*, one could very well say that the Psalmist asks to spend his life not looking at the Lord's beauty but rather at the Lord's pleasant place. He desires to be on a sort of

14. As to what Anat really wanted, see, despite some recent demurrers, D. R. Hillers, "The Bow of Aqhat: The Meaning of a Mythological Theme," in *Orient and Occident* (H. A. Hoffner, ed.; Neukirchen-Vluyn, 1973): 71–80.

15. This, like most of the Biblical translations in this article, is based on *NJPS*.

perpetual pilgrimage. The numinous effect of the verse has been reduced, the meaning has been enhanced.

This verse is the introductory line to a series of "cluster" terms, for verse 5 continues with *kî yiṣpᵊnēnî bᵊsukkô bᵊyôm raʿā / yastîrēnî bᵊsēter ʾohŏlô / bᵊṣûr yᵊrômᵊmēnî*, which may be translated "He will shelter me in his pavilion on an evil day, grant me the protection of his tent, raise me high upon a rock." But we should note that *yiṣpᵊnēnî* echoes *Ṣapunu*, the mountain on which the *nʿm* of *CTA* 3 iii 28 was located, echoed in the previous line; that *Ṣapunu* was a *ǵr*, a mountain, a word whose etymological equivalent is Hebrew *ṣûr*, "rock, mountain," the next to last word in this verse;[16] while the last word *yᵊrômᵊmēnî* echoes *mārôm*, the Hebrew equivalent of *mrym*, which as noted above is found in *mrym ṣpn*, "the summit of Ṣapunu/Zaphon." Thus behind a straightforward line of Hebrew poetry, there are allusions drawn from the Canaanite repertory. This is also true of the following verse 6: (a) *wᵊʿattā yārûm rôšî ʿal ʾōyᵊbay*, which may contain a reference to the lifting of the head despite the presence of an enemy; (b) *wᵊʾezbᵊḥā bᵊʾohŏlô zibḥê tᵊrûʿā*: the sacrifice in the tent, possibly harking back to the *ʾōhel môʿēd*, but more likely to the fact that El's sanctuary was a tent; and (c) *ʾašîrā waʾăzammᵊrā lYHWH*, the first two words, admittedly widespread in Hebrew psalmody, are now known also as a Ugaritic collocation.[17]

The use of "clusters" is not limited to Psalms, as we have seen, and can be illustrated from other Biblical books. The sixth and seventh verses of Deut 32 present a good case; they may be characterized as closing one unit verses 5–6 and opening another, verses 7–9:

halYHWH tigmᵊlû-zôʾt / ʿam nābāl wᵊlôʾ ḥākām / hălôʾ-hûʾ
ʾābîkā qānekā / hûʾ ʿāśᵊkā wayᵊkônᵊnekā
zᵊkōr yᵊmôt ʿôlām / bînû šᵊnôt dôr-wādôr / šᵊʾal ʾābîkā
wᵊyaggēdkā / zᵊqēnêkā wᵊyôʾmᵊrû lāk

"Do you thus requite the Lord, O dull and witless people? Is not he the Father who created you, fashioned you and established you?

16. In the text from Ras Ibn Hani referred to above (N 6), we find in line 4 both *ẓr* and *sk* "mountain" and "thicket" together; can this bit of ambiguity add to the poetics of this verse?

17. See *Ugaritica* V, text 2 (p. 551): *dyšr wydmr* and J. C. Greenfield, "To Praise the Might of Hadad," in *La Vie de la Parole . . . Études offertes à Pierre Grelot* (H. Cazelles, ed.; Paris: Desclée, 1987): 3–12.

Remember the days of old, consider the years of ages past; ask your father, he will inform you, your elders, they will tell you."

The language used in these lines is based on the terminology used for the description of El. El is called *ḥym* (*CTA* 3 v 38; 4 iv 41, v 65), he is often called *ab* (*passim*) and the verbs *qny* (*CTA* 10 iii 6) and *knn* (*CTA* 4 iv 4; 10 iii 7) are used of him. El is called *ab šnm* "father of years" and is described as aged; *ᶜlm* and *drdr* constitute a well known pair but may also be epithets of El. Verse 8 mentions Elyon "the most high" and the reference to *bᵊnê ᵓādām* may serve to remind us that El was also *ab adm* "father of man."[18] The author of Deut 32 has woven into his covenant poem these and other elements of earlier literary traditions.

El and the language used of him also feature largely in the final example of a cluster to be presented here, this from Ezek 28:2–10, the third of the poems dealing with Tyre. The prophet derisively accuses the prince of Tyre (*nᵊgîd ṣōr*) of declaring that he is like El, and just as El's dwelling was in the midst of the waters (*CTA* 4 iv 21–22), so was that of the prince of Tyre. But the prophet reminds him that *wᵊᵓattā ᵓādām wᵊlôᵓ ᵓēl* "just a man and not a god." One of El's attributes, as noted above, is wisdom. The prophet goes on to upbraid the prince (v. 3) for considering himself wiser than Danel. Danel, who is known from the Ugaritic tale of Aqhat, and mentioned in Ezek 14:14, was a pious judge, and judgement, as the tale of Solomon shows, was the clearest sign of wisdom.[19] The prince's mortality is emphasized and his death is foretold by the prophet (v. 9) and this is a sign that he is just a man and the taunt *wᵊᵓattā ᵓādām wᵊlôᵓ ᵓēl* is repeated, another contrast with El, father of man, but himself deathless. When Anat promised Aqhat that he will "count years with Baᶜal and months with El's sons," Aqhat

18. Although much has been made of the use of the epithet *ᶜly* for Baᶜal in III KRT (= *CTA* 16) iii 5–8, there is no sign that he was called *ᶜlyn*, the equivalent of Hebrew or Phoenician Elyon/Elyun. In the Biblical tradition Elyon is often an appositive of El (Gen 14:18, 19, 20; Ps 78:35) or in parallelism with El (Num 24:16; Ps 73:11; 78:17–18; 107:11, etc.). Although Sanchouniathon *apud* Philo of Byblos sets Elioun two generations before El, there is no hint of a separate high god *ᶜlyn* in the Ugaritic texts, cf. the discussion in A. Baumgarten, *The Phoenician History of Philo of Byblos: A Commentary* (Leiden: Brill, 1981): 183–186. The pairing of *ᵓl wᶜlyn* in Sefire I A, 1.11 (*KAI* 222) shows that they were considered a unit as were *ṣmyn wᵓrq* "heaven and earth."

19. The challenge by H. H. P. Dressler to the identification of Danᵓel of Ezekiel (*VT* 29 [1979]: 152–161) with Ugaritic Dnil has been answered by J. Day (*VT* 30 [1980]: 174–184). Both the Biblical and Ugaritic names can be vocalized Daniel.

answered, [*w*]*mt.kl.amt.wan.mtm.amt* "I will die like everyone, indeed I will die" (*CTA* 17 vi 37). The prince of Tyre is rebuked with language taken from sources surely known to his Tyrian contemporaries.

The passages noted here are not unique and many other examples could be discussed. It is however equally important to reiterate that there are very many passages of a highly poetical nature in the Psalms, Job, and the Prophetic books that are totally free of Canaanite reference. Indeed, some Psalms contain, on the one hand, verses whose "pagan" ancestry is clearly discernible, and on the other, lines that are totally innocent of this. The "Canaanite element" was one component, and a very important one, of the broad spectrum of material available to the Hebrew poet, especially in the First Temple period. It is due to the accident of survival and discovery that the Canaanite heritage that has reached us comes from Ugarit; but there can be no doubt that similar myths, epics and tales, as well as hymns and prayers circulated in both oral and written form throughout Canaan proper not only in the Late Bronze Age but also in the Iron Age, that is from 1400–600 B.C.E., a period of a thousand years. They were a source of the folklore and the folk religion throughout the area, including monotheistic Judah and Israel. We may also assume that the various cities also had variant versions, using different words and phrases and on occasion crediting different gods with the same deeds.[20]

An additional assumption that must be stated clearly is that the Israelite contact with this tradition was not limited to a particular period, that of the conquest or the early period before the establishment of the kingdom, as some would like us to believe. This is a convenient assumption espoused by those who would like to force on us an early dating of Biblical texts with Canaanite overtones and mythological references. The contact was continual, and the prophets' inveighing against the influence of the Canaanite cult was

20. A good example would be the text published by C. F. Nims and R. C. Steiner as "A Paganized Version of Psalm 20:2–6 from the Aramaic Text in Demotic Script," *JAOS* 103 (1983): 261–274. There can be no doubt that the Biblical and the Aramaic text share a Canaanite *Vorlage*, however complex the transmission was. Note that the Demotic-Aramaic text has a reference to Ṣapunu and the Psalm to Zion; that in the Demotic text the god Ḥor has been inserted in the place of Baʾal or Hadad. In the fragment of this scroll published by R. A. Bowman, *JNES* 3 (1944): 227, we find *bʿl mn ṣpn*. By the way, the text published by Steiner and Nims have the word pairs, parallelism, and stress meter typical of Canaanite poetry.

based on daily experience. This danger is as deeply felt in Jeremiah as it is in his predecessors. It is in this light that the many references to the quelling of the sea in both Biblical poetic and prose works must be seen. This became a metaphor for the crossing of the Red Sea and at a later date for the return to Zion. Sheol's open mouth, another favorite metaphor, was a familiar development from the tales told of Mot. The irony of "death being swallowed up" (Isa 25:8) would be lost on an audience which did not know the referent.[21] From the practical point of view the use of parallelism, word pairs, and stress meter—the chief characteristics of Canaanite poetry—was not something that had to be learned at the feet of Ethan the Ezrachite, or Heman, Chalkol, and Darda, the sons of Mahol, by the Israelites. These elements were part and parcel of poetic writing and inherent in the use of the Hebrew language.

21. So too the mourning of Hadadrimmon in the valley of Megiddo (Zech 12:11) which must come from the mourning for Ba^{c}al during the period that he is dead, as known from the Ugaritic texts.

MAARAV 5-6 (Spring, 1990): 169-187

THE LANGUAGE OF THE SAMARIA PAPYRI: A PRELIMINARY STUDY

Douglas M. Gropp
THE CATHOLIC UNIVERSITY OF AMERICA, WASHINGTON, D.C.

The Samaria papyri are a group of fragmentary remains of legal documents once belonging to wealthy patricians of ancient Samaria. In 1962 Taᶜâmireh Bedouin recovered them from a cave in the Wâdi ed-Dâliyeh (about eight or nine miles north of Jericho, and on the western rim of the Jordan rift).[1] The earliest dated papyrus comes from sometime between the 30th and 39th year of Artaxerxes II (Mnemon), therefore between 375 and 365 B.C.E. (SPF 22:10).[2] The latest is from 335 B.C.E. (SP 1:1) in the reign of Darius III (Codomannus). Most of the papyri were probably written during the reign of Artaxerxes III (Ochus, 358–337 B.C.E.). Whenever the place of execution is extant on the papyri, it is always "Samaria."[3]

There are 18 fragments large enough for Prof. Frank Moore Cross to call them "papyri," and about nine further pieces of some

1. The cave is the Mughâret Abū Šinjeh.

2. "SP" will stand for "Samaria Papyrus." "SPF" will stand for "Samaria Papyrus Fragment." The fragments are numbered consecutively beginning with 19 after the eighteen papyri. Other abbreviations used herein: *AP* = A. E. Cowley, *Aramaic Papyri of the Fifth Century B.C.* (Oxford: Oxford Univ., 1923); *BMAP* = E. G. Kraeling, *The Brooklyn Museum Aramaic Papyri* (New Haven: Yale Univ., 1953).

3. For more introduction see F. M. Cross, "The Discovery of the Samaria Papyri," *BA* 26 (1963): 110–121; *idem.*, "Aspects of Samaritan and Jewish History in Late Persian and Hellenistic Times," *HTR* 59 (1966): 201–211; *idem.*, "Papyri of the Fourth Century B.C. from Dâliyeh," in D. N. Freedman and Jonas Greenfield, eds., *New Directions in Biblical Archaeology* (New York: Anchor, 1969): 41–62; figs. 34–39; *idem.*, "Samaria Papyrus 1: An Aramaic Slave Conveyance of 335 B.C.E. Found in the Wâdī ed-Dâliyeh," *Eretz-Israel* 18 (*Festschrift* N. Avigad; 1985): 7*–17*.

size. The first nine papyri are deeds of slave sale. There are a number of other slave sales among the remaining papyri and fragments. In spite of their fragmentary character it has proved possible to reconstruct these nine documents rather fully since they show striking conformity to a common formulary.[4] There is remarkably little variation in the verbal realization of each formula, and even less variation in the sequence of formulas. These reconstructions can then be tested against estimated line lengths.

Unfortunately, we have much less hope for success in reconstructing those papyri which fall into other generic categories. For instance, there are two documents which look like pledges of a slave in exchange for a loan. There is a sale of a house, a sale of living quarters/store-rooms in a house, and a sale (or antichretic pledge?) of a vineyard. There is one document of manumission or perhaps a release of a pledged slave, a receipt for a payment associated somehow with a pledge, and one small fragment that looks like a judicial settlement by oath. The first papyrus has been published by Cross (see note 3, above).

I only want here to highlight some of the distinctive features of the language of the Samaria papyri in its relation to other Aramaic, primarily of the Persian period. I will discuss these distinctive features under these categories: (1) orthography, (2) phonology, (3) morphology, (4) syntax, and (5) lexicon/foreign influences.

To anticipate my conclusion: The Samaria papyri are written not in the vernacular Aramaic of the fourth century inhabitants of Samaria, but in an *Official Aramaic* (OfA) virtually identical with that of the fifth century legal papyri from Elephantine.[5] This may

4. See my dissertation, "The Samaria Papyri from Wâdī ed-Dâliyeh: The Slave Sales" (Harvard University, 1986) for reconstructions of the texts of SP 1–9.

5. By Official Aramaic I mean the ideal standard dialect of the Persian period to which Aramaic scribes evidently aspired to conform when drafting documents of an official nature. Any given Aramaic text of the Persian period may adhere more or less to this standard dialect. It is noteworthy that genre is a considerably more significant factor in differentiating between those texts which deviate from the standard, than either geographical, chronological, or ethnic provenience. Thus the Aramaic of private letters deviates somewhat from the OfA of the legal and administrative documents. In my view, then, the Aramaic of the private letters from Hermopolis is a complex product of the interference between the standard OfA and the local vernacular Aramaic. The deviations from the standard give us the best clue as to the character of this vernacular. In fact, a systematic grammatical description of the Elephantine legal papyri, the Samaria papyri, and the Arsames correspondence (with due respect to the variation between these groups of texts) could constitute the nucleus for a more comprehensive grammar of OfA.

not come as a surprise, dealing as we are exclusively with formal legal documents of the chancellery of Samaria, still within the Persian period. It may, however, be disappointing for those who may have hoped to see an earlier stage of the Palestinian Aramaic that we know from later Samaritan, Christian Palestinian, and Galilean Aramaic, if only in scattered colloquialisms. The language of the Samaria papyri is, however, quite free of colloquialisms. I cannot, in fact, see in the little obvious variation between the two groups of legal papyri any real typological development from the fifth century to the fourth century texts.

1. ORTHOGRAPHY

It is important methodologically to distinguish between orthography and phonology in considering ancient documents, although we are utterly dependent on the orthography for discovering the phonology. Aside from the legitimate theoretical distinction, the relation between the two is often problematic. There is not always a one-to-one correspondence between the orthographic signs and the phonemes of the language. The correspondence may be broken by historical spelling, morphological writing, or some other convention. Some, not observing this distinction, have taken the vacillation in spelling etymological *ḏ (sometimes with *zayin*, sometimes with *dalet*) as evidence that the process of the merging of etymological *ḏ with *d* extended over a long period. Nevertheless, for obvious reasons orthography and phonology must be discussed in relation to each other. Phonologically speaking, the merger of *ḏ with *d* is a *fait accompli* by the Persian period. As evidence for this statement I would cite the hypercorrect *zyn wzbb* (*BMAP* 3:17, for *dyn wdbb*), which would not be possible on any other assumption. Outside of the small group of pronouns sharing the demonstrative formative element [ḏ-],most instances of etymological *ḏ are spelled with *dalet* in OfA. We cannot base our phonological inferences on the statistical predominance of one or another spelling. For me, the lapses often prove to be more revealing.[6]

6. See P. Leander, *Laut- und Formenlehre des Ägyptisch-aramäischen* (Göteborgs Högskolas Årsskrift 34; Göteborg: Univ. of Göteborg, 1928): 8–9, §2c–j.

In our papyri the pronominal forms *znh*, *zk*, and *zy*[7] are more consistently spelled with *zayin* than in the legal papyri from Elephantine.[8] The spelling with *zayin* is completely consistent in the Arsames correspondence. The only spelling with *dalet* in the Samaria papyri occurs in *dnh* in the first papyrus (SP 1:2).[9]

The masculine plural inflection [-īn] on nouns and adjectives is generally spelled without *yod* as *mater lectionis*. The only exceptions are *dynyn* twice in the same papyrus (SP 2:5, 9) and *dmyn* (SP 1:3; 6:3), always spelled with *yod*.[10]

There is only one instance where a *mater lectionis* is used to represent an etymologically short vowel—in *rwšm* "slave mark, tattoo" (SP 2:2). This is evidently the same word as *rušmā* "incision, mark, sign" in later Aramaic (Eastern and Western), *rṓšem* in Mishnaic and Rabbinic Hebrew.

2. PHONOLOGY

Everywhere where we would expect a diphthong historically, we find the place marked with a *yod* or *waw*.[11] There is only one exception. It occurs in a seemingly parenthetical clause which

7. Besides these pronominal forms, see *ʾdyn* (SP 10:4), *zkrn* (SP 7:7; cf also the element *-dkr* in the personal name *qwsdkr* [SP 9:1]), *ʾḥd* (SP 11:v:6).

8. The exceptions: *dnh* AP 16:9; BMAP 5:3, 10:3; *dk* BMAP 9:10; *dkʾ* (sic!) AP 14:6; *dky* AP 14:9; *dkm* BMAP 7:2 (= *zkm* "the same" AP 9:2, 20:4, 65:3; cf. Leander (N 6): 34, 35 (§14k, r); *dy* in BMAP 3:12, 12:30, 32 and *dylk* in BMAP 9:14; *dylky* AP 13:7, 11, 16.

9. Cross, "Samaria Papyrus I" (N 1).

10. This contrasts with the spelling *dmn* in the Elephantine legal papyri (BMAP 7:18; cf. AP 30:38).

11. (a) /ay/ *ʾdyn* (SP 10:4), *ʾḥry* construct (SP 4:6; 6:5; 13.v:1; 13.r:7), *ʾḥryk* (SP 1:6, 11), *bynyhm* (SP 1:5, 11; 12:2; 15:17; 16:7), *bytʾ* (SP 13.r:9; 15:5), *byt* construct (SPF 27:4), *bny* plural construct (SP 3:10), *bnyn*, if with 1st pl. suffix (SP 8:5), *bnyk* (SP 1:6), *dmy* plural construct (SP 7:15), *mhymnn* (SP 1:12; 4:13), *ʿlymʾ* (?; SP 13.r:5), *qdmyk* (SPF 23.r:2), *qdmyn* (SP 9:11), *rby* plural construct (SP 7:7); note the consistent spelling of *šmryn* in contrast with the Hebrew spelling *šmrn*, and the Assyrian transcription *ša-me-re-na*, but in agreement with the Babylonian transcription of the name *ša-ma!-ra-ʾ-in*.

(b) /aw/ *ʾw* (SP 2:6; 5:7; 6:6, 7; 8:7; 14:13, 16; 15:13), *ʾḥrwhy* (SP 1:4), *bnwhy* (SP 1:4; 4:7, 11; 6:4; 14:18; 15:12, 13; 16:8; SPF 26:6), *dmwhy* (SP 3:8), *hww* (SP 5:5), *hmw* (?; SP 1:12; 4:13), *ḥwbn* (SP 1:10), *hwdt* (SP 2:11), *ywmn* (SP 10.v:6), *ywmʾ* (SP 11.v:5), *ywmy* (SP 13.r:10), *qdmwhy* (SP 3:4). It should be observed that the diphthong is not always the syllable with primary stress in these examples.

awkwardly interrupts the list of witnesses to the sale at the end of the document. This clause is attested twice in our papyri. The first time it is spelled with *waw*: *whwdt dynʾ* "and I acknowledge the obligation (?)/penalty stipulation (?)" (SP 2:11). The second time it is spelled without a *waw*: *whdt d*[*yn*]*ʾ* (SP 3:10), apparently in the same hand as the rest of the document. I am very hesitant to posit a scribal error here. Perhaps it is a rare scribal lapse from OfA in our papyri.

Diphthongs are apparently also preserved consistently in the Arsames correspondence and in the Elephantine legal papyri.[12] This stands in striking contrast to the situation in the Hermopolis papyri where diphthongs are regularly contracted in unstressed positions, if not everywhere.

The non-assimilation/dissimilation of /nC/ is absolutely consistent in the Samaria papyri. Note especially the second masculine singular independent pronoun *ʾnt*, and the various forms of the imperfect of the root *ntn*.[13] This agrees with the picture we get of the OfA reflected in the Elephantine legal papyri[14] and the Arsames

12. Exceptions: *ʾdn* BMAP 9:17; *ymyn* BMAP 9:17; *rškm* AP 25:12; *bnyhm* AP 13:14, 25:7; BMAP 4:10, 11 may be a special case due to the immediate succession of two syllables with the same diphthong. The same explanation probably holds for the same lexical item in Old Aramaic. In fact, its occurrence in Elephantine, in contrast to *bynyhm* in the Samaria papyri may be an inheritance from a more "western" tradition of Old Aramaic preserved in legal contexts. The word *znyhwm* AP 31:8 (letter) (cf. *zynʾ* RES 1300:9, cp. Avestan *zaēna* and Syriac *zaynā*) is nonstandard in several respects.

13. *ʾnt* (SP 1:7, 9; 13.r:11; 16:2), *mdyntʾ* (?; sP 4:1; 5:1; SPF 26:1), *mn* preposition (*passim*), *hnṭlt* (?; SPF 21:9), *yntn* (SP 2:6; 3:6; 10.v:4; 12:7; 13.r:5; 18:5), *ʾntn* (SP 1:9; SPF 21:10, 12; 24:9), *yntnwn* (SPF 27:5), *nntn* (SP 4:8, 10, 11; 7:13, 14; 11.r:10; 14:17).

14. Out of many examples, the few exceptions: *mdʿm* AP 49:3, 4 (J. Naveh, *The Development of the Aramaic Script* [Jerusalem: Israel Academy of Sciences, 1970]: 34, describes the hand of AP 49 as "extreme-vulgar of the beginning of the fifth century B.C.E."; Cowley [N 2]: 153, notes that "the writing is very unusual, probably by an unpracticed hand." He also notes (p. 154) that *mkl* stands for *mʾkl* in line 4. See further on *ḥṭn* below); *kkrn* AP 50:9 (contrast *knkrn* AP 30:28, 31:27; note also *knkr* in AP 26:17, which is part of the Arsames correspondence); *mdšh* BMAP 9:14 (if from the root *ndš*; but cf. E. Y. Kutscher, "New Aramaic Texts," *JAOS* 74 [1954]: 237). The doubled /ṭ/ in *ḥṭh* "wheat" appears only once in a legal text of the Persian period (but also in the fragment AP 67:13? Cowley [N 2]: 175 describes the *ḥet* and *ṭet* as having "unusual forms"), and there it lacks nasalization: *ḥṭn* AP 49:2 (but see above about this text). Elsewhere this word appears nasalized (Ahiqar 129; AP 81:2, 3, 4, 28; F. Vattioni, "Epigrafici aramaici," *Augustinianum* 10 [1970]: 510, no. 83:1); we might also expect *ngrnky* and *yršnkm* instead of the *ngrky* and *yrškm* that we have in AP 1:4 and 25:15 respectively, unless we explain these as jussive

correspondence.[15] The Proverbs of Ahiqar are also quite consistent in preserving /nC/.[16] I believe this to be a genuinely phonological, rather than merely orthographic, feature of OfA.[17]

The evidence bearing on the question of the origins and diffusion of this feature presents a very complicated picture. I can only sketch it here in outline. Unassimilated /nC/ never appears in Old Aramaic inscriptions—that is, apart from the recently published Aramaic-Akkadian bilingual inscription from Tell Fakhariyah. There the form *mhnḥt* (line 2) appears.[18] There are no counter examples, and the case for non-assimilation of /nC/ in the dialect of this inscription can be further supported by appealing to the parallel phenomenon of the non-assimilation of /l/ in forms of the root *lqḥ*: *mlqḥ* (line 10), *ylqḥ* (line 17), *tlqḥ* (line 18).[19]

---

forms serving as modals; the form *kʿt* occurring frequently in the Elephantine papyri and the Arsames correspondence, stands out as a special case, and is perhaps to be explained as dialect borrowing. (It occurs already in Old Aramaic at Sefire III:24.). Cf. Leander (N 6): 13–14 (§3m–o); 17–18 (§6i–j); 56–57 (§35).

15. The Arsames correspondence is completely consistent on this point. The only possible counter-examples are *kʿt*, which has been discussed above, and *spytkn* AP 26:9, 22, which J. D. Whitehead, "Some Distinctive Features of the Language of the Aramaic Arsames Correspondence," *JNES* 37 (1978): 131, n. 75 explains as a place name + *-kn* suffix.

16. See J. M. Lindenberger, *The Aramaic Proverbs of Ahiqar* (Baltimore: Johns Hopkins Univ., 1983): 282–283.

17. A. Spitaler, "Zur Frage der Geminatendissimilation im Semitischen: zugleich ein Beitrag zur Kenntnis der Orthographie des Reichsaramäischen," *Zeitschrift für indogermanische Forschungen* 61 (1952–54): 257–266, has argued that the orthographic presence of the *nun* in these forms is merely graphic. It is either etymological spelling or an extension of this convention to mark consonantal gemination. Spitaler's thesis has been adequately refuted by R. Macuch, *Handbook of Classical and Modern Mandaic* (Berlin: de Gruyter, 1965): xlvii–liii, and E. Y. Kutscher, "Aramaic," in T. A. Sebeok, ed., *Current Trends in Linguistics* 6: *Linguistics in South West Asia and North Africa* (The Hague and Paris: Mouton, 1971): 374–375.

18. K. Beyer, *Die aramäischen Texten vom Toten Meer* (Göttingen: Vandenhoeck & Ruprecht, 1984): 89, is the first, to my knowledge, to point out the possible significance of this form.

19. In addition to (1) the non-assimilation of /nC/ in *mhnḥt* and (2) the non-assimilation of /lC/ in various forms of *lqḥ*, the Aramaic of the Tell Fakhariyah inscription shares several other isoglosses with OfA in contrast to Old Aramaic (the language described by R. Degen in his *Altaramäische Grammatik der Inschriften des 10.-8. Jh. v. Chr.* [Abhandlungen für die Kunde des Morgenlandes 38/3; Wiesbaden: Deutsche Morgenländische Gesellschaft, 1969]), namely, (3) G-stem infinitives with *mem*-preformative (*lmʾrk*, lines 7, 14; *lmld*, line 9; *lmšmʿ*, line 9; *lmlqḥ*, line 10, (4) the use of *yhb* for the perfect (line 10), and (5) the use of *zy* + Noun as a periphrase of the construct relationship (lines 1, 16–17, 23).

The evidence from Aramaic inscriptions of the seventh and sixth centuries B.C.E. is messy, with assimilated and unassimilated forms appearing side-by-side in the same inscription.[20] I will not try to account for this mixture here.

As I have already stressed, /nC/ is consistently preserved in the Elephantine legal papyri, the Arsames correspondence, and the Samaria papyri. By contrast, assimilation is regular in the Hermopolis letters.[21]

I consider the appearance of *nun* in these environments in the Aramaic epigraphic material after the Persian period to be a purely graphic convention inherited from OfA. Nabatean, with its Arabic-speaking background, may be an exception.[22] On the other hand, the non-assimilation of /nC/ seems to be a living phenomenon in Mandaic and in dialects of Modern Syriac.[23]

The independent pronouns *ʾnt, ʾnty, ʾntm*, and forms like *ʾnttʾ* "wife" cannot be understood except as genuinely preserving a proto-Northwest Semitic (and proto-Semitic!) situation.[24] Aramaic dialects which did not assimilate /nC/ must have maintained their existence over a long period. Once a prestigious non-assimilating dialect came into contact with speakers of assimilating dialects, this originally phonological feature could have spread morphonemically—that is, speakers of assimilating dialects could now pronounce /n/ in certain verb forms which had already fallen into the I-*nun* class in certain phases of their derivation and inflection. This is how I would understand forms like *yndʿ* and *hnʿl* from the roots

20. So, for example, in the Nerab inscriptions (seventh century B.C.E.): *tnṣr* KAI 225:12; *ynṣr* KAI 225:13; but also *ysḥw* KAI 225:9; *ʾt* KAI 225:5; 226:8, and in the Meissner papyrus (515 B.C.E.): 1st comm. sing. *ntnt* (line 11), 2nd masc. sing. *ntnt* (12); *ʾntn* (10); but also *ʾtnnhy* (11) *tšʾ* (13), *ʾṣl* (14).

21. The only exceptions are surely graphic: *mndʿm* 5:4 (in contrast to *mdʿm* 1:10; 4:10; 5:2); *ʾnšth* "wife" 3:3; 4:14 (a conflation of OfA and Old Aramaic spelling conventions).

22. Cf. E. Y. Kutscher, "The Language of the Genesis Apocryphon," *Scripta Hierosolymitana* 4 (1958): 19–20.

23. Cf. Macuch, *Handbook* (N 17): xlix–li, liii.

24. Amorite personal names frequently show unassimilated forms, particularly in the verb *ntn* (cf. W. F. Albright, "An Archaic Hebrew Proverb in an Amarna Letter from Central Palestine," *BASOR* 89 (1943): 31, n. 17; I. J. Gelb, "La lingua degli Amoriti," *ANLR* (Serie 8, vol. 13, fasc. 3–4, 1958): 151 (§2.8.1–4), 162 (§3.3.8.4); H. B. Huffmon, *Amorite Personal Names in the Mari Texts* [Baltimore: Johns Hopkins Univ., 1965]: 301). At present I see Middle Bronze Age Amorite as close to proto-Northwest Semitic, and therefore ancestral to both the Aramaic and Canaanite groups of languages.

*yd*ᶜ and ᶜ*ll* respectively. At a later stage, this morphophonemic extension of a phonological situation could again approach a phonological rule by applying to the resolution of consonantal gemination (/CC/ > /nC/) without an etymological or analogical basis.

The non-assimilation of /nC/ in OfA cannot be disassociated from the nasalization in Babylonian Akkadian.[25] It is too simplistic, however, to posit an Akkadian origin for the phenomenon.[26] It is better with S. A. Kaufman to speak of a geographical phenomenon.[27]

3. MORPHOLOGY

The formative element [-ha-] consistently appears in causative stem verb forms, prefixed in the perfect and infixed in the imperfect and participle.[28] In this respect, too, the Elephantine legal papyri[29]

25. Cf. W. von Soden, *Grundriss der akkadischen Grammatik* (Analecta Orientalia 33/47; Rome: PBI, 1969): 33 (§32b, c), 34 (§33f), 125 (§96j, k), 137 (§102d); J. Aro, *Studien zur mittelbabylonischen Grammatik* (Studia orientalia 20; Helsinki, 1955): 37.

26. As Kutscher does, "Contemporary Studies in North-Western Semitic," *JSS* 10 (1965): 38; *idem.*, "The Hermopolis Papyri," *IOS* 1 (1971): 106; "Aramaic" (N 17): 374. Besides the problem of leaving the second person independent pronouns unexplained, the conditions of nasalization in Akkadian are not exactly the same as for OfA: "Nasalierung vor stimmlosen Konsonanten ist selten und begegnet nur j/spB" (*GAG* [N 25]: 33 [§32c]).

27. *The Akkadian Influences on Aramaic* (Assyriological Studies 19; Chicago: Univ. of Chicago, 1974): 120–121. Whitehead (N 15): 125, draws Old Persian into the discussion. Akkadian, Elamite, and Greek transcriptions of Persian words shows that /n/ and /m/ were pronounced before consonants, even though these nasals were for the most part omitted in the writing before consonants. Cf. R. G. Kent, *Old Persian: Grammar, Texts, Lexicon* (New Haven: American Oriental Society, 1953): 17–18 (§39), 38–39 (§108–§111); A. Meillet and E. Benveniste, *Grammaire du vieux-perse*² (Paris: Champion, 1931): 43–44 (§81), 82–83 (§136), 88 (§144).

28. *hḥsn* (SP 3:4; 15:8), *thḥs⟨n⟩n* (SP 2:9), *mhḥsn* (SP 7:9), *hwdt* (SP 2:11), *hdt* (SP 3:10), *hnṭlt* or *hnsbt* (SPF 21:9), *hqymw* (SP 1:5, 11; 3:9; 8:5; 9:6; 15:17, SPF 27:5), ʾ*htyb* (SP 15:15; SPF 21:12), *nhtyb* (SP 4:10; 7:13). I would parse *mhymnn* as from the quadriliteral root *hymn* (from a synchronic point of view).

29. There are a more few exceptions in the Brooklyn Museum papyri than in the papyri republished in Cowley. The few exceptions are strangely limited in this corpus to verbs that are I-*nun* or are treated as such in the causative stem: *ynpq* AP 13:12 (but *yhnpq* AP 13:11!); *ynpqwn* BMAP 9:21; 10:15; ʾ*nṣl* BMAP 2:13; *tn*ᶜ*l* BMAP 12:22. Kraeling (N 2): 243, considers the difficult form *ykhylwn* BMAP 9:21

and the Arsames correspondence[30] agree with the Samaria papyri. The Hermopolis letters deviate from OfA on this point, too. In spite of some orthographic inconsistency, several forms make clear that the Hermopolis dialect prefixed [-ʾa-] to the perfect and imperative, and infixed simply [-a-] in the imperfect, infinitive, and participle.[31]

In the Samaria papyri third masculine plural suffix is always *-hm*, presumably with a double phonemic contrast with the feminine form.[32] This agrees with the Elephantine legal papyri[33] and the Arsames correspondence, but contrasts with the Hermopolis letters, which regularly have *-hn* and *-kn* as masculine plural suffixes.

4. SYNTAX

Most discussions of "word order" in early Aramaic try to determine whether the order is "fixed" or "free," basing their conclusions on the statistical predominance of one or another order. Such studies rarely take into account either (1) the transformational

---

to be a causative. J. T. Milik (*RB* 61 [1954]: 251) and Kutscher (who dissents more vigorously: "New Texts" [N 14]: 237) treat it as a G stem. Perhaps it is a scribal error. (Or could the root *khl*/*ykl* have still a third variant *kyl* not attested elsewhere, but which may have infected the spelling of this form?) The forms *tškḥ* AP 10:9, 10, 17 and *tškḥwn* AP 37:10 (letter) (compare *thškḥ* BMAP 11:11b, *yhškḥwn* AP 38:7 [letter], and perfect regularly formed with *ha-*) should be considered in connection with the problematic formal history of this verb (cf. J. L. Malone, "The Development of the Anomalous Syriac Verb ʾeškáḥ 'to find,'" *Afroasiatic Linguistics* 1/2 [1974]: 1–10).

30. Again, the Arsames correspondence is completely consistent in maintaining this feature.

31. Note the forms *ʾth* C imperfect 1st sing., 4:10; *ytwnh* C imperfect 3rd masc. pl. + 3rd fem. or masc. suffix, 6:10; *ytw* C jussive 3rd masc. pl., 3:12; 4:7; 5:5!; 8:6a; *ʾtyh* C imperative 2nd fem. sing., 1:10; *lmtyh* and *lmytyt*, both C infinitives (in the same construction!) in the same line: 3:11; *ʾwšrty* C perfect 2nd fem. sing., 4:4; *twšr* C jussive 3rd fem. sing., 2:7; *tšry* C jussive 2nd fem. sing., 1:10; *mwšrthm* C infinitive, 2:13; *ʾtrtn* C perfect 2nd masc. pl., 4:5; *mns* C participle, 2:3; *mḥth* C infinitive, 5:6; *ʾpqny* C perfect 3rd masc. sing. + 1st sing. suffix, 6:4; *mpqn* C participle, 5:3. In addition, note the forms of the verb *ʾškḥ*. The various forms of the root *ybl* are probably better parsed as G stem.

32. *bynyhm* (SP 1:5, 11; 3:5; 8:5; 12:2; 15:17; 16:7), *lhm* (SP 4:8; 7:2). The 3rd masc. pl. independent pronoun is *hmw* (SP 1:12; 4:13).

33. Note, however, *bynyhn* BMAP 12:19, 21 (and compare the anomalous *bynym* in a parallel passage BMAP 10:5). Otherwise the 3rd masc. pl. suffix *-hn* only occurs in letters: *bhn* AP 34:6; *lhn* AP 34:6; 37:4, 14.

history of each sentence in question, or (2) the functional distribution of each sentence in the larger discourse. Apart from these two last considerations I do not believe that firm conclusions can be drawn. The normal (unmarked) order of clause constituents is difficult to assess in the Samaria papyri. The material is extremely fragmentary. Seldom is a whole sentence visible on the papyrus. Moreover, the sale formulary of the Samaria papyri is rather closely modeled on cuneiform antecedents—at times following the Akkadian word order artificially. I will therefore confine this discussion of syntax in the Samaria papyri to the following isolated features.

The definite article normally seems to express "definiteness," by which I mean it refers either to an item previously mentioned in the text, or to something conspicuous in the situational context.[34] I know of only one clear and one other possible exception to this general rule. The form *lʿlmʾ* "in perpetuity" occurs at least eight times in the Samaria papyri. In such an adverbial expression in the Persian period we would rather have expected *lʿlm.*[35] The other problematic case occurs in a clause which is pivotal in the sale documents: *wrʿyw ḥd mn ḥd ʾsrʾ bynyhm* "they were mutually satisfied with the bond between them."[36] In the legal formulary this clause marks the transition from the "operative clauses" to the "*Schlussklauseln*," it often also marks a shift from a third person to a first-second person style of discourse. The word *ʾsrʾ* "the bond" or "obligation" has not been previously mentioned in the operative clauses. It may, however, refer immediately in the situational context to the very document being drawn up.

The preposition [*l*-] marks direct objects in the Samaria papryi. In all cases but one it governs a proper name. Once it occurs instead with a second masculine singular pronominal suffix;[37] *l*- also marks the direct object a number of times in the Elephantine legal papyri.[38] Of course, an historical account of *l*- introducing a

34. A contrast between definite and indefinite is clear, for example, in the predictable alternation of *ksp* and *kspʾ*.

35. The normal form in the Elephantine legal papyri is *ʿd ʿlm*; *lʿlmʾ* is, however, attested in Nabatean and Palmyrene, and in the slave sale from Dura-Europas (line 11). Cf. also *mn ʿlmʾ wʿd ʿlmʾ* in Dan 2:20.

36. The form in question seems to appear clearly in SP 2:4. It probably also occurs in SP 16:7.

37. *šbq ʾnh lk* "I release you" SP 13:v.1.

38. AP 7:5; 13:2, 5; 15:[3], 27; BMAP 2:3, 9, 14; 5:4; 7:3, 21, 24. It also occurs in the Ahiqar narrative (line 76) and in the Behistun inscription (line 3). In Biblical

direct object must also track the parallel development of the accusative particle *yāt*. I will not discuss it fully here, but the general outline of the development seems to be as follows: Old Aramaic (Sfire and Zakkur) uses *ʾyt* sporadically to mark the direct object. The use of *l-* for this same function must have been introduced by OfA. Some of the western dialects like Christian Palestinian and Galilean Aramaic, which accepted the use of *l-* as a direct object marker, retained the use of the *yāt-* with suffixes.[39]

The syntax of personal pronouns is interesting. Whenever a pronoun combines with a participle or verbal adjective, it follows the verbal form.[40] A typical form runs as follows: *lʾ šlyṭ ʾnh l-*PN *zk* "I will (no longer) have authority over the said slave." In the corresponding *šallīṭ*-clause in the Elephantine legal papyri, the pronoun more commonly precedes than follows the predicate adjective. (Note, too, that in the Elephantine legal papyri *šallīṭ* governs its object by *b-* rather than *l-*. I have only been able to find a single instance of *šlyṭ* construed with *l-*[noun] outside the Samaria papyri.[41] On the other hand, if the pronoun is associated with a fientic verb (perfect or imperfect)—in which case it is not constitutive to the construction—the pronoun always precedes the verb.[42] Observing this pattern has proved helpful to me in reconstructing the papyri.

A striking feature of the sale formulary is the asyndetically connected verbs with no intervening words that form a single

Aramaic it is quite frequent. Within this larger corpus it is used predominantly (though not exclusively) with personal objects.

39. T. Nöldeke, "Beiträge zur Kenntniss der aramäischen Dialecte. II. Über den christlich-palästinischen Dialect," *ZDMG* 22 (1868): 511 (§42); G. Dalman, *Grammatik des jüdisch-palästinischen Aramäisch*[2] (Leipzig: Hinrichs, 1905): 110–111 (§16c). The syntactic distribution in Neofiti is more complicated and less regular. Cf. D. M. Golomb, *A Grammar of Targum Neofiti* (HSM 34; Chico, Ca.: Scholars Press, 1985): 26, 65, 208–211. The range of usage of *l-* and *yāt* in Neofiti has evidently been extended by a series of analogies between the usage of the two particles and between the usage of these two particles and that of the various Hebrew particles they customarily translate.

40. E.g., SP 1:8, 9; 2:7, 8; 3:8; 4:13; 6:9; 7:12, 13, 16; 13.v:1; 18:7; SPF 25:2. The pronoun *hmw* in the clause [*šhdyʾ zy*] *yḥtmwn hmw mhymnn* "[The witnesses who] affix their seals are trustworthy," may precede the passive participle because it was felt to be resumptive. However, the pronoun follows the more general rule in the identical clause in SP 4:13.

41. That is in 4QAmram[d] Frg.1:2: *wʾnh šlyṭ lʾn*[. . .]. Text published by J. T. Milik, "4Q Visions de ʾAmram et une citation d'Origène," *RB* 79 (1972): 84.

42. E.g, SP 1:5, 6; 2:6; 3:6, 7; 4:8; 5:6, 8; 9:9. SP 11.v:6 may be an only apparent exception.

clause structure. So we find *ʾšlm ʾntn* "I will pay in recompense" in the clause concerning the payment of a fine,[43] *ʾmrq ʾntn* "I will clear (the slave of all adverse claims) and return (him to you)" in the defension clause,[44] and *ʾhtyb ʾntn* in the clause concerning the return of the sale price.[45] There are several other examples of this phenomenon in the receipt-quittance clause and in the hypothetical denial of receipt of the sale price.[46] Similar verb combinations do occur in Elephantine, but outside of frequent constructions with the quasi-auxiliary verb *khl*, they are almost always connected by the conjunction *w-*.[47] This feature may be due to Akkadian influence. I have found parallels for almost all of these phrases in late Neo-Babylonian legal texts.[48]

In a number of instances in the Samaria papyri *kzy*[49] and *zy*[50] signal the onset of direct discourse. This usage is found in the book of Daniel (2:25; 5:7; 6:6, 14) and becomes common in several of the later dialects, such as Christian Palestinian Aramaic, Syriac, and Mandaic.[51] In view of its use to signal direct discourse in the

43. SP 1:9; 4:11; 5:11; 12:7; 14:17.

44. SP 2:6; 3:6; 18:5; SPF 21:10.

45. SP 4:10; 7:13; SPF 21:12.

46. *ʾṭyr mkyr* "(the sale price is) paid (and) received" (SP 3:3); *lʾ mqbl ʾnh mkyr* "I have not taken in, received (the sale price)" (SP 3:8; SPF 25:2).

47. E.g., *zbn wyhb* BMAP 3:3, 10, 13; 12:3, 6–7, 9, 15, 17, 25, 29; *ʾšlm wʾntn* BMAP 11:4, 7; *šlmt wyhbt* BMAP 11:5, 8; cf. AP 35:5, 7; *nqwm wnpṣl wnntn* BMAP 3:20; *ʾḥwb wʾntn* BMAP 4:14–15; 10:10; 11:6; *yḥwb wyntn* BMAP 10:13. Note, however, the occurrence of *[š]lmt yhbt lk* . . . in AP 29:6.

48. This is obviously the case with *ʾṭyr mkyr* and *mqbl ʾnh mkyr* (see below under "5. Lexicon/Foreign influences"). *ʾmrq ʾntn* and *ʾhtyb ʾntn* are derived from the parallel late Neo-Babylonian legal formulas *umarraqamma ana* PN *inamdin* and *utarramma ana* PN *inamdin*. It is also possible that *ʾšlm ʾntn* is a reflection of the late Neo-Babylonian *uṭṭaramma ana* PN *inamdin*. But it is more likely that the latter Aramaic hendiadys derives from a native Aramaic tradition, coming ultimately, perhaps, through Neo-Assyrian channels. See the preceding note for the Aramaic evidence. For the construction in Neo-Assyrian legal texts, cf. e.g. J. N. Postgate, *Fifty Neo-Assyrian Legal Documents* (Warminster: Aris & Phillips, 1976): nos. 40.A:10; 47: [13(?)]; J. Kohler and A. Ungnad, *Assyrische Rechtsurkunden* (Leipzig: Pfeiffer, 1913): no. 237:5; and VAS 1 97:8.

49. SP 3:8; 5:9; 8:7; 14:15.

50. SP 1:5; 11.v:4, 5, 6, 7; 16:7; 18:3; SPF 22:5.

51. Cf. F. Schulthess, *Grammatik des christlichen-palästinischen Aramäisch* (Tübingen: Mohr, 1924): 97 (§193); T. Nöldeke, *Compendious Syriac Grammar* (tr. J. A. Crichton; London: Williams & Norgate, 1904): 300 (§367); Nöldeke, *Mandäische Grammatik* (Halle: Waisenhaus, 1875): 469 (§309); also Dalman, *Grammatik* (N 39): 239 (§54).

Samaria papyri, perhaps it can be proposed elsewhere with this function in OfA.[52]

5. LEXICON/FOREIGN INFLUENCES

The Samaria papyri differ somewhat from the Elephantine legal papyri and Arsames correspondence in vocabulary. This is due primarily to the difference in legal terminology evidenced in the Samaria papryi.

The Samaria papyri share with these fifth-century documents some Akkadian loan words like *byrtʾ*[53] "fortress," *knt*[54] "colleague," *pḥt*[55] "governor," and *sgnʾ*[56] "prefect." They also contain several loans from Neo-Babylonian not found in the fifth-century documents. For instance, the Samaria papyri provide the earliest attestations for *gṭʾ* in Aramaic.[57] It is a loan from late Neo-Babylonian, probably with the general meaning "document."[58] It seems to be used interchangeably with *šṭr*, which occurs more frequently in the papyri.[59] Interestingly, the Samaria papyri use the Neo-Babylonian terms for documents, rather than the Neo-Assyrian terms,[60] and so align themselves with the Aramaic dockets from Babylonia[61] and the deeds from Murabbaʿat and the Naḥal Ḥever[62] over against

52. Cf. e.g. AP 6:7; 45:4; 18:2 (compared with BMAP 7:41). Note also the use of *kdy* at the beginning of the Nabatean contract from the Naḥal Ḥever published by J. Starcky, "Un contrat nabatéen sur papyrus," *RB* 61 (1954): 163, frag. A, line 2.

53. Partially reconstructed in SP 4:1.

54. SP 5:7.

55. SP 7:17; 8:10.

56. SP 8:12; 10.v:10; 11.r:13.

57. SP 3:12; 10.v:10.

58. Cf. Kaufman (N 27): 52–53.

59. SP 6:6; 7:9, 14; 8:12; 9:16; 11.r:14; 12:9, 11.

60. For a discussion of these Neo-Assyrian terms, especially *ṭuppu, dannutu, egirtu*, and *nizbu*, see Postgate (N 48): 3.

61. All the Aramaic dockets published prior to 1972 have been conveniently gathered by F. Vattioni, "Epigrafia aramaica," *Augustinianum* 10 (1970): 493–532. The term *šṭr* appears very frequently in the dockets from Nippur (Vattioni nos. 49–54, 56–92, 97, 98, 127, 128, 135, 142). The term *gṭ* never occurs among the dockets.

62. Cf. J. T. Milik in *DJD* II (Oxford: Clarendon, 1969): no. 19:8, 21, p. 105, pl. 30, where *gṭ šbqyn* means "deed of divorce." In the Givʿat ha-Mivṭar inscription, *gṭ* means simply a "deed (of sale)," E. S. Rosenthal, "The Givʿat ha-Mivṭar Inscription," *IEJ* 23 (1973): 72-81, pl. 19. The term *šṭr* is common: For Murabbaʿat, see Milik, no. 19:11, 24, 105; no. 20:14, p. 110; no. 21:19, pl. 115; no. 26:7, p. 137; no.

the Aramaic dockets from Assyria[63] and the Elephantine legal papyri.[64]

Note also the phrase *šḫrṣ dmyn gmyrn*[65] "the stipulated price, the full price." *Šḫrṣ* is a direct loan from Neo-Babylonian *šīm ḫarīṣ*.[66] It shows the regular correspondence of Babylonian *š* and Aramaic *š* (as opposed to the Assyrian *š* = Aramaic *s*), and the late Neo-Babylonian development of intervocalic (here possibly post-vocalic!) *m* > *w*.[67] In this interpretation it should probably be

---

28.r:10, p. 140; in the Nabatean contract published by Starcky (N 52): 163–165, frag. A, lines 2, 3, 8, 9, 10, 11; frag. C, lines 4, 6. The Syriac slave sale from Dura-Europas is called a *šṭrʾ*, cf. lines 15, 18, 30, and verso, line 2.

63. The dockets from the Assyrian sphere use the terms *ʾgrt* (Vattioni nos. 19 and 20, both on debt-notes from Nineveh) and *dnt* (Vattioni nos. 8–18, all on deeds of conveyance from Nineveh). It also occurs on a clay tablet from Assur (Vattioni no. 146:4). The form *dnyt* appears on a clay tablet from Tell Halaf, E. Lipinski, *Studies in Aramaic Inscriptions and Onomastics* (Louvain: Leuven Univ., 1975): 140. The term *spr* appears on a single docket on an Assyrian tablet of unknown provenience republished by A. R. Millard, "Some Aramaic Epigraphs," *Iraq* 34 (1972): 134–137. On the other hand, there is one occurrence of *šṭr* at Nineveh (Vattioni no. 31:1).

64. The normal term for document at Elephantine is *spr*. The term *spr* is used once at Murabbaʿat, Milik (N 62): no. 19:7, p. 105. See Y. Muffs, *Studies in the Aramaic Legal Papyri from Elephantine* (Leiden: Brill, 1969) for a discussion of the terms *nbz* in AP 11:6 (p. 186) and *dnh* in AP 10:23 (pp. 187–189). The term *ʾgrt/h* occurs at Elephantine, but only with the meaning "letter." Cf. Kaufman (N 27): 48, for discussion on the origins of *egirtu/ʾgrt* with references to previous discussions; on *nizbu*, see p. 77.

65. The most complete example is in SP 1:3. J. C. Greenfield, "Babylonian-Aramaic Relationships" in Hans-Jörg Nissen and Johannes Renger, eds., *XXV Rencontre Assyriologique Internationale Berlin July 3–7, 1978* 1/2 (Berlin: Dietrich Reimer, 1982): 478, cites the parallel *šḫrṣ dmyn gmyryn* in an unpublished Nabatean document from the Babata archive found in caves of the Naḥal Ḥever. The phrase *dmyn gmyryn* appears alone in a clause very similar to the "declaration of sale" in the Samaria papyri in an Aramaic house sale from the Naḥal Ḥever, published by J. T. Milik ("Un contrat juif de l'an 134 après J.-C.," *RB* 61 [1954]: 183, pl. 4). Lines 5–6 read: *zbnt lk bksp zwzyn dy hmwn tmn*[*y*]*ʾ wslʿyn trtn dmyn gmryn lʿlm*. In a Nabatean tomb inscription (CIS II 199:8) *dmy mgmr slʿyn ʾlp ḥrty* constitutes the fine that the one who profanes the tomb by using it in some other way than is stipulated in the inscription must pay.

66. First deciphered by Cross and noted in "Samaria Papyrus" (N 1): 11*.

67. Cf. Kaufman (N 27): 140–142, 143–144; *GAG*: 31 (§31a). All the references cited in the *CAD* s.v. *ḫarīṣu* (6:103) are written ŠÁM *ḫarīṣ*. Perhaps, then, it was pronounced *šīwḫarīṣ* in late Neo-Babylonian. In the light of this possibility, the evidence of the Babylonian loans in Aramaic showing post-vocalic *m* > *w* listed by Kaufman (N 27): 144, n. 24 should be reconsidered.

pronounced [šūḥərīṣ]. W. L. Moran, however, has suggested[68] that the *m* was assimilated,[69] and therefore may have been pronounced [šiḥḥərīṣ].

The phrase *dmyn gmyrn* is calqued on Neo-Babylonian *šīmi gamrūti.*[70] To my knowledge, *šīm ḫarīṣ* and *šīmī gamrūti* existed only as alternatives in the antecedent cuneiform legal formularies; they were never combined. Perhaps, then, it was Aramaic scribes who first combined the phrases in their own adapted sale formulary.

The phrase *ʾṭyr mkyr* "(the money) is paid and received" also occurs in the slave sales.[71] It corresponds to the common late Neo-Babylonian receipt-quittance formula *maḫir eṭir*, which replaced the earlier formula *maḫir/nadin zaku.*[72] The word *ʾṭyr* is a direct Neo-Babylonian loan, albeit shaped into an Aramaic passive participle.[73] Similarly, it is hard to disassociate *mkyr* from Akkadian *maḫir.*[74] Although the normal Neo-Babylonian sequence is *maḫir*

68. In private communication.

69. Cf. *GAG* §31f–g; K. Deller, "*iḫḫaṣ = imḫaṣ auch altbabylonisch?," *Or* 35 (1966): 33-35.

70. Cf. M. San Nicolò and A. Ungnad, *Neubabylonische Rechts- und Verwaltungsurkunden. Beiheft zu Band I: Glossar* (A. Ungnad) (Leipzig: J. C. Hinrichs, 1937): 55; H. Petschow, *Die neubabylonischen Kaufformulare* (Leipziger rechswissenschaftliche Studien 118; Leipzig: Theodor Weicher, 1939): 49–53; K. Tallqvist, *Die Sprache der Contracte Nabû-Nâʾids* (Helsingfors: Frenckell & Sohn, 1890): 61. Ungnad treated *šīmī* in this phrase as a *plurale tantum.* This recalls the plural form of *šīmu* in Old Akkadian deeds, and Middle Babylonian conveyances from Alalakh. Cf. Muffs (N 64): 200.

71. The clearest example is SP 3:3.

72. See Petschow (N 70): 53–55; and Muffs (N 64): 125–126. Compare also *apil zaku* in Middle Assyrian slave sales. Cf. E. Ebeling, *Urkunden des Archivs von Assur aus mittelassyrischer Zeit*, Part III: "Assyrische Kauf-, Zessions-, und Schenkungsurkunden" (= *Mitteilungen der altorientalischen Gesellschaft* 7; Leipzig: Harrassowitz, 1933): 82, 83.

73. Cf. *CAD* 4:411b-412a, s.v. *eṭru.* Note that the Talmudic slave sale cited in *B. Bab. Bat.* 29b and *B. Bab. Meṣ.* 39b is called *ʿyṭrʾ*. Cf. Muffs (N 64): 126, n. 2, Kaufman (N 27): 50–51. The Munich manuscript has *ʾyṭrʾ* in the latter text (M. Jastrow, *A Dictionary of the Targumim, the Talmud Babli and Yerushalmi, and the Midrashic Literature* [New York: Traditional, 1903]: 1068b) making a closer parallel to *ʾṭyr* in the Samaria papyri.

74. The root *mkr* is rare in Aramaic. It does, however, appear in Syriac, with the restricted meaning "to acquire a wife (by paying the *mohar*)" (cf. the Peshitta of 2 Sam 3:14), "to betroth," or "to be betrothed." J. Levy, *Chaldäisches Wörterbuch über die Targumim und einen grossen Theil des rabbinischen Schriftums* (Leipzig: Baumgärtner and London: David Nutt, 1868): 2.36, cites one example of the Aramaic verb *mkr*; it occurs in the Dt stem, and has the same meaning as the verb

eṭir, the sequence found in the Samaria papyri is also attested.[75] The correspondence Akkadian *ḫ* = Aramaic *k* may seem a bit irregular. But if we assume (1) that post-vocalic /k/ was spirantized in Aramaic of the Persian period, and (2) that Aramaic /ḥ/ was pronounced as a pharyngeal (as in Arabic), rather than as a velar fricative, then the correspondence would make good phonetic sense.[76] In any case, the existence of the root *mkr* in Aramaic (or Hebrew) with a commercial usage may have contributed to this irregular transcription.

We find the construction *zy lʾ* in the formula *zy lʾ dynn wlʾ ḥwbn* "without (further) litigation or liabilities."[77] Kaufman argues (rightly) that *d(y) lʾ* with the meaning "without" in later Aramaic (including Biblical) is a loan from the late Neo-Babylonian[78] usage of *ša lā* "without."[79] Compare the similar late Neo-Babylonian phrases *ša lā dīnu u ragāmu, ša lā dīni u dabībi*, and *ša lā dīnu u lā ḫarāru.*[80]

The Samaria papyri evidence the earliest use of the verb *marreq* in an Aramaic defension clause. Although the root *mrq* is not attested in Aramaic earlier than the Samaria papyri, it is evidently an Aramaic loan word in late Neo-Babylonian.[81] It is used in the defension clause of late Neo-Babylonian deeds of sale from the

---

in Syriac. The range of use of *mkr* in Aramaic does not fit the context in the Samaria papyri, where the subject of *mkyr* is *kspʾ*.

75. E.g., *eṭir nadin maḫir* in V. Schell, *RA* 24 (1927) 39:19; *eṭirtu maḫīti* in BE 10 73:6.

76. This runs counter to Kaufman's rule: Akkadian *ḫ* = Aramaic *ḥ*. The rule may hold only for some cases, whereas my rule could apply to the messy counter-examples he tries to explain on pp. 142–143 of his *Akkadian Influences* (N 27). We might say that Aramaic scribes sometimes hesitated between their normal phonemic transcription for Akkadian *ḫ* in *ḥ*, and a phonetic transcription (in postvocalic transcription) in *k*. Moran suggests, alternatively, that *mkyr* is borrowed from a phonetically variant form of *maḫir*, namely **makir*. Cf. *GAG* §25d; *AHw* s.v. *makāru* II, 588b; M. Held, *JCS* 15 (1961): 12; W. G. Lambert, *Iraq* 31 (1969): 38; E. Salonen, "Über den Laut H im Akkadischen," *Studia Orientalia* 46 (1975): 292, 297, 299.

77. E.g., SP 1:10; 2:9; 6:10.

78. Cf. *GAG*: 169 (§115s); but cf. the *Ergänzungsheft*: 25**.

79. *Influences* (N 27): 98. W. Baumgartner, in L. Koehler and Baumgartner, eds., *Lexicon in Veteris Testamenti Libros* (Leiden: Brill, 1953): 1065a, presumes influence in the opposite direction.

80. Cf. *CAD* 3:153b–154a s.v. *dīnu*.

81. As first suggested by A. T. Clay, *Legal and Commercial Transactions, Dated in the Assyrian, Neo-Babylonian and Persian Periods, Chiefly from Nippur* (The Babylonian Expedition of the University of Pennsylvania 8/1; Philadelphia: Univ. of Pennsylvania, 1908): 22n, and then followed by many others.

reign of Darius I. But the use of the root is broader in Aramaic.[82] In any case, it has its *Sitz-im-Leben* in the Babylonian-Aramaic symbiosis of the Persian period. It reappears in a clause guaranteeing defension in deeds of sale from the Naḥal Ḥever[83] and Murabbaᶜat,[84] and then later in a defension clause in the slave sale from Dura-Europas of 243 C.E. (lines 12–15).[85]

Perhaps the most arresting Akkadian loan word in the Samaria papyri is *nyšᵓ* with the meaning "slaves" or "slave-group."[86] It occurs four times in the papyri.[87] In most, if not all, of these instances, the material reading presents difficulties, but not always the same difficulties. It is treated syntactically as a feminine plural.[88] It is probably to be pronounced [nīšē], though it could conceivably have been treated as a collective [nīš] plus determinative suffix [-ā]. The phrase *nšy byt* with the meaning "domestic servants" or the like appears a number of times in the Arsames correspondence.[89] The phrase in the Arsames correspondence looks like an Aramaicized reflex of the Akkadian *nišē bīti*, so we cannot infer much from the sibilant. The form *nyšᵓ* of the Samaria papyri, however, has not been Aramaicized and therefore can be treated as a direct loan from Neo-Babylonian in view of the sibilant correspondence. The phrase *nīš bīti* is quite common at Nuzi and in late Neo-Babylonian texts.[90] The absolute use of *nyšᵓ*, however, actually fits the Neo-Assyrian usage of *nišē* better.

The starkest contrast between the language of the Samaria papyri and that of the Elephantine papyri and the Arsames correspondence[91] is the virtual absence of Persian influence in the Samaria

82. See for example its use in 11QtgJob 29:1; cf. also Jastrow (N 73): 846b–847; C. Brockelmann, *Lexicon Syriacum* (Halle: Max Niemeyer, 1928): 405b.

83. J. T. Milik, "Deux documents inédits du désert de Juda," *Biblica* 38 (1957): 259, pl. II.

84. Milik (N 62): 137, no. 26:3–6, pl. 39; cf. also no. 30 (a Hebrew deed of sale). lines 23–25, p. 145, pl. 42.

85. The apodosis of a defension quoted by Rava (ca. 300 C.E.) in *B. Bab. Meṣ* 51a; 15a also contains the verb *mrq*.

86. F. M. Cross first deciphered this form.

87. SP 5:4, 9; 7:16; 12:1.

88. It is followed by the demonstrative *ᵓlk* (SP 5:4; 7:16). In SP 12:1 *nyšᵓ* is followed by the numeral *ᵓrbᶜ*.

89. G. R. Driver, *Aramaic Documents of the Fifth Century B.C.*^{2} (Oxford: Clarendon, 1957 [hereinafter AD]): no. 8:2; 9:2; frag. 3.2:2; frag. 3.13:2, 3; frag. 3:14.

90. Cf. the spelling LÚ *ni-iš* É-*šu* in Dar 340:3.

91. Cf. especially the studies of E. Benveniste, "Terms et noms achéménides en araméen," *JA* 225 (1934): 177–193 and "Éléments perses en araméen d'égypte," *JA* 242 (1954): 297–310. The thirteen letters of the Arsames correspondence contain

papyri. Two personal names with Persian elements are attested: *bgbrt* and *yhwbgh*. The first is purely Persian.[92] The second combines the Yahwistic name element with the Persian element *baga* "god"!

Some have sought Persian influence in the use of *šmh* introducing personal names. This usage is common in the slave sales among the Samaria papyri when the slave who is sold is first introduced. The construction is not attested in Aramaic before the Persian period, but can be found also in the Elephantine legal papryi, the Arsames correspondence, the Ahiqar narrative, the Behistun inscription, the Aramaic papyri from North Saqqara, and in Ezra 5:14. This is a common feature of Old Persian style, and could be Persian in origin. But Roland Kent in his grammar of Old Persian tentatively suggests an Aramaic origin for the construction![93] In the Behistun inscription the construction occurs in the Aramaic, Akkadian, Old Persian, and Elamite versions. Which is original? "PN *šumšu*" of the Akkadian version is the most precise equivalent to the Aramaic *šmh*. The construction in the Old Persian and Elamite versions lacks the pronominal element. Further, the Akkadian construction is known from Old Babylonian documents dealing with slaves.[94] Interestingly, the construction is used especially of slaves in the Elephantine legal papyri,[95] the Samaria papyri,[96] and the Aramaic papyri from North Saqqara.[97] The frequent use of the same construction in the Arsames correspondence

---

more Persian words than all of the Elephantine papyri combined. Persian influence has evidently penetrated deeply into the syntax of the Arsames correspondence as well. Cf. Whitehead (N 15): 127–136.

92. Probably *bagā-bṛta* "lifted up/esteemed by god." Compare the name *ba-ga-bar-ta* in a Late Babylonian document from the time of Alexander III (*CT* 49, no. 5, line 2). The reference and etymology is from a note of R. Zadok written to F. M. Cross.

93. Kent (N 27): 98 (§312).

94. See the note in M. S. Schorr, *Urkunden des altbabylonischen Zivil- und Prozessrechts* (VAB 5; Leipzig: Hinrichs, 1913): 47. Kaufman (N 27): 40 discounts this Old Babylonian evidence (presumably because of the historical distance between Old Babylonian contracts and the use of *šmh* in OfA). Instead, he claims "that precisely this construction (NN *rn-f*) is the regular one in all stages of Egyptian." Note, however, PN *šumšu* of a slave in Late Babylonian (VAB 3 35 §29:53).

95. AP 28:4, 5, 9, 13; BMAP 2:3; 5:2, 4; 6:3; 7:3; 8:3.

96. SP 1:2; 3:1; 4:2; 5:2; 6:2; 7:1, 2; 9:1; 10.v:2; SPF 19:2.

97. J. B. Segal (with contributions by H. S. Smith), *Aramaic Texts from North Saqqara* (London: Egypt Exploration Society, 1983): nos. 5:1; 9:3; 10a:4; 17:1; 29:3, 6; 55a:4; 60:4; 63:2, 3.

could be seen as designating subordinates (i.e., *ʿbdn*) in the adminstrative hierarchy.[98] Kutscher offers the fullest and most balanced discussion of the question of the original source of this expression, and finally leaves the matter undecided.[99]

The Samaria papyri constitute a conservative instance of OfA—more conservative, in fact, than is provided by the Elephantine legal papyri of the fifth century. In contrast to the Arsames correspondence, the Samaria papyri reflect little or no Persian influence in vocabulary or syntax—a rather interesting conclusion for papyri datable toward the end of the Persian period. On the other hand, the Samaria papyri show a greater proportion of specifically late Neo-Babylonian loans. This last feature is clearly due to the dependence of the sale formulary of the Samaria papyri on the late Neo-Babylonian formulary for the sale of movables (from the reign of Darius I). There are a number of features that we would consider to be characteristic of OfA not represented in the Samaria papyri, but the language of the Samaria papyri should provide one complementary base for any future definition of Official Aramaic.

98. See especially AD 5:2–6 (and compare AP 33:1–5). Cf. also AD 3:1, 3; 6:2; 8:1, 2; 9:1; 10:3. Note also an occurrence in Job 1:1; *ʾyš hyh bʾrṣ ʿwṣ ʾywb šmw* "there was a man in the land of Uz, Job by name." The Lord later comments to the Satan: "Have you noticed *my servant* Job?" (1:8) (I do not want to press this last connection of *šmw* with *ʿbd* too much.)

99. "Two 'Passive' Constructions in Aramaic in the Light of Persian," *Proceedings of the International Conference of Semitic Studies held in Jerusalem, 19–23 July 1965* (Jerusalem: The Israel Academy of Sciences and Humanities, 1969): 133. Cf. H. Bauer and P. Leander, *Grammatik des Biblisch-Aramäischen* (Tübingen: Max Niemeyer, 1927): 358–359 (§108p–q).

MAARAV 5-6 (Spring, 1990): 189-205

PROTO-SEMITIC: IS THE CONCEPT NO LONGER VALID?*

WILLIAM SANFORD LASOR
FULLER THEOLOGICAL SEMINARY, PASADENA, CALIFORNIA

In the early stages of Comparative Semitics, it was commonly accepted that the Semitic languages—and the Semitic peoples—came from a common source. The original habitat was believed to be the Arabian peninsula, and the original language was given the name Proto-Semitic (*Ursemitische*).[1] For the development of the various languages, the figure of a tree was sometimes used.[2] From the original "trunk" (Proto-Semitic) developed the "limbs" (the groups of languages) and the "branches" (the subgroups and individual languages).

More recent studies have challenged this view. This has resulted from modern discoveries and methodologies. One of the most recent challenges has come from Professor Mario Liverani.[3] He writes,

> The study of the connections between the many Semitic languages in the historical period (for which we have much evidence) disproves

* Dedicated to my friend and colleague of many years, Professor Stanislav Segert, with cordial greetings and best wishes.

1. Cf. C. Brockelmann, *Grundriss der vergleichenden Grammatik der semitischen Sprachen* (Berlin: Reuther & Richard, 1908): 1.2. Brockelmann rejected the idea that it was possible to reconstruct a Proto-Semitic people or language, pp. 4-5. Cf. also G. Bergsträsser, *Einführung in die semitischen Sprachen* (Munich: Max Hueber, 1928): 1.

2. Cf. the "Stammbaumtheorie" put forth by A. A. Schleicher, *Compendium der vergleichenden Grammatik der indogermanischen Sprachen* (1866).

3. M. Liverani, "Semites," in G. W. Bromiley *et al.*, eds., *International Standard Bible Encyclopedia,* (Grand Rapids: Zondervan, 1988): 4.388-392.

> the rectilinear development (of the genealogical-tree type) which has been theorized for the period previous to the use of writing. Instead, we are faced with more complex superimpositions, interconnections, extinction of some branches which, however, have left elements in the branches by which they were overcome, etc.[4]

He asserts, "Going backward in time, one cannot imagine the many Semitic languages as having been increasingly similar to one another and finally unified in origins. . . . Rather, they must be imagined as having been in a perpetually unstable relationship among themselves."[5] He considers "the reconstruction of 'Proto-Semitic'" a convention, more than a historical truth.[6]

One cannot argue with the material which Professor Liverani has presented. It is certainly true that the historical development of the individual Semitic languages has been complex, and that a simple linear development should be rejected. The theory that the Arabian peninsula was the original home of the Semitic peoples may be challenged, as Professor Liverani has pointed out, by the fact that there is no common Semitic word for "mountain" (of which Arabia has plenty), whereas there is a common word for "river" (of which Arabia has none). It might also be pointed out that Arabia has numerous seasonal river-beds, to which the Arabs have given the name *wâdī*; however, this word is not commonly found in other Semitic languages. More reasonable would be the theory that the Semites originated in an agricultural valley region, as proposed by I. Guidi more than a century ago.[7]

However, the theory of "proto-Semitic" cannot so easily be set aside. Professor Liverani almost admits as much when he writes that in a time before the "urban revolution," "the complex of the Semitic peoples [could] have been more homogeneous, more tight-knit."[8] The thesis of this paper is to demonstrate the reasonability of an *Ursprache*, a common linguistic origin of the most basic elements of the Semitic languages. This will be based on the

4. Liverani (N 3): 389. J. Schmidt, facing objections that had been raised against Schleicher's genealogical-tree theory, put forth a similar idea in his "wave theory," *Die Verwandtschaftsverhältnisse der indogermanischen Sprachen* (1872).

5. Liverani (N 3): 389.

6. *Ibid.* Brockelmann (N 1): 1.4, already called it "erst recht eine Fiktion."

7. *Della sede primitiva dei popoli semitici* (Reale Accademia dei Lincei, CCLXXVI, Memorie, Rome, 1879). Another suggestion was East Africa (Brockelmann [N 1]: 1.2).

8. Liverani (N 3): 391.

common grammatical elements of the Semitic languages, the common vocabulary for domestic and cultural elements, and above all, the phonemic development of the most basic and common words in all Semitic languages.

Grammatical elements that are common to Semitic languages, but not common in languages of contiguous peoples include the following. The prevailing tendency to form words from three consonants (although I readily admit that there are biconsonantals, quadriconsonantals, and even monoconsonantals that appear to be elementary). In substantives, the use of the "construct" to express the genitival relationship; elements of noun morphology, such as gemination of the middle radical, the use of preformative elements *m-*, *t-*, and of sufformative elements such as *-ân* (> *-ôn*), and *-îs*. In verbs, the "stems" or "buildings" such as the H-/Š-/A-causative, the N-reflexive, the D-intensive or forensic, and stems with prefixed or infixed *-t-*;[9] and the two-aspect system rather than a three-tense system.[10] Other evidence could be presented, but that there are common morphological and syntactical elements of Semitic languages is beyond dispute.[11] This statement, however, should not be oversimplified.

There are, indeed, elements that have penetrated from other languages: reduplication perhaps from Libico-berber; many elements in Ethiopic from Cushitic or other neighboring peoples; Sumerian elements in Akkadian, possibly the *waw*-conversive from Egyptian into Hebrew, etc. But the common elements far outnumber the anomalies.

9. The most regular—almost artificially so, it would seem—is Ethiopic with the following forms:

faᶜala	*faᶜᶜala*	*fâᶜala*
ᵓafᶜala	*ᵓafᶜᶜala*	*ᵓafâᶜala*
tafaᶜala	*tafaᶜᶜala*	*tafâᶜala*
ᵓastafᶜala	*ᵓastafaᶜᶜala*	*ᵓastafâᶜala*

Some of these forms are found in every Semitic language. I have use the verb *fᶜl* rather than the more commonly used *qṭl* because the latter obscures the infixed-*t* found in some Semitic languages, e.g., Akkadian and Ugaritic.

10. This last point has been disputed by some Akkadiologists, who see the infixed-*t* as a perfect tense, cf. W. von Soden, *Grundriss der akkadischen Grammatik* (Rome: PBI, 1969): 104 (§80a). But in early Assyrian and Babylonian this theory collapses; there is no evidence of a three-tense system in the Laws of Eshnunna or in the Code of Hammurabi.

11. Bergsträsser summarizes the evidence in an excellent way (N 1): 2–19.

Common prepositions and adverbs, as well as common nouns and verbs, are found, with regular phonemic and phonetic developments. I shall not labor this point, for the next part of my paper will cover much of the same ground from the phonemic point of view.

A large number of the words that are basic in any vocabulary are completely cognate in the Semitic languages. By cognate, I mean that they are composed of the same consonantal phonemes. They are not formed of translational elements, such as Ger. *unterschreiben*, Eng. *subscribe*, or Ger. *umgestalten*, Eng. *transform*. Rather, they are composed of phonemes that follow exact rules of phonetic shift from language to language and are in almost every class predictable.

These are in the following categories: the numerals; words for members of the family or clan and closely related words; words for familial activities; words for parts of the body; common pronouns and pronominal suffixes; common prepositions, conjunctions, and adverbs; words for periods of time; words for various physical phenomena; words for common activities; names for certain animals and animal husbandry; agricultural terms; and words for religion, the cult, and government.

To the list which I have presented in this article, I could add many more words. Specifically, I have omitted most of the cognates which are found in only part of the Semitic world, for example, cognates found in Arabic, Ethiopic, and Hebrew, or cognates found in Akkadian, Aramaic, Ugaritic, and Hebrew. It is my opinion that research in such groups of words could provide valuable material for economic, sociological, and ethnographic studies. I have omitted words which apparently were loan words, although those that came in at an early date, so that the regular phonetic shifts occurred, cannot always be identified as borrowings from another language group.

But I think there is more than enough to support my main thesis: it would be difficult to conceive of a group of unrelated languages which had so many basic words that are cognate. In fact, there would be little communication in any individual Semitic language if these basic words were not present. It is my opinion that the Semitic languages that have such an extensive basic vocabulary must have developed from a parent language, which for convenience' sake we may call Proto-Semitic.

As for the *Urheimat*, the original home of the Semites, I shall leave that for another study and another scholar.

COGNATE WORDS SHOWING PHONEMIC RELATIONSHIPS[12]

Meaning[13]	*OSA*	*Arabic*	*Ethiopic*	*Hebrew*	*Aramaic*	*Ugar*	*Akkadian*	*P-S*
Numerals								
One	ʾḥd	ʾḥadu	ʾeḥadᵉ	ʾeḥād	ḥad	aḥd	êdu	ʾḥd
Two	t̲ny	it̲nan		šnáyim	tinyānā	t̲n		t̲ny
Two	try			tartān	trein		tartennu	try
Both, two	klʾ	kilâ	kelʾᵉ	kiláyim		klat	kilatan	klʾ
Three	t̲lt̲	t̲alât̲i	salâša	šālôš	tᵉlâtê	t̲lt̲	šalaštu	s̀lt̲[12]
Three	s̀lt̲		salas?					
Four	ʾrbʿt	ʾarbaʿu	ʾarbaʿ	ʾarbaʿ	ʾarbaʿ	ʾrbʿ	arbaʾu	ʾrbʿ
Five	ḫms̀	ḫamsu	ḫamsatu	ḥa̱mēš	ḥămēš	ḫmš	ḫamšu	ḫms̀
Six	s̀dt̲	sâdišu	sedestᵉ	šiššä	šittā	t̲dt̲	sudušu	s̀dt̲
Seven	s̀bʿ	sabʿu	sebaʿ	šébaʿ	šᵉbaʿ	šbʿ	šibi	s̀bʿ

12. In the following lists, I have used a common system of transliteration with some modification. The pure-long vowel, as distinct from the stress-lengthened vowel, I indicate wherever certain with circumflex (*â, ô*). Arab. words ending in *ʾâlif maqṣûra* I have indicated by *à*; Heb. nouns ending in *qāmāṣ-hê* by *ä*; Aram. nouns ending in *qāmāṣ-ʾālep* by *ā*. Arab *t̲â* and *d̲âl* are transliterated by *t̲* and *d̲*; to avoid confusion I have omitted the underbar from the *raphe* forms of Heb. *bgkdpt*, since these are allophones and not phonemic. For OSA sibilants, to avoid prejudging the phonemic relationship, I use the following: *s* = 𐩯, Arab. *s*, Heb. *s*; *s̀* = 𐩦, Arab, *s*, Heb. *š*; *ś* = 𐩪, Arab. *š*, Heb. *ś*; cf. W. S. LaSor, "The Sibilants in Old South Arabic," *JQR* 48 (1957–58): 161–173. Owing to the uncertainty about pronunciation of Geʿez, I have represented the sixth form of the letters as a short *e*, a vocal shewa, or a silent shewa, as seemed to me to be appropriate; my apologies to Ethiopic scholars.

13. For "meaning," wherever applicable, I have attempted to give a term whose semantic range will include the meanings in the several languages. To attempt to give specific meanings for each language would make the table unmanageable.

COGNATE WORDS SHOWING PHONEMIC RELATIONSHIPS—*continued*

Meaning	*OSA*	*Arabic*	*Ethiopic*	*Hebrew*	*Aramaic*	*Ugar*	*Akkadian*	*P-S*
Eight	ṯmn	ṯamân	samânt^{e}	š^{e}mônê	t^{e}mânyā	ṯmny	šamâni	ṯmny
Nine	tś̀ʿt	tisʿu	tesʿa	tēšaʿ	t^{e}šaʿ	tšʿ	tišit	tś̀ʿ
Ten	ʿśr	ʿašru	ʿašrū	ʿéśer	ʿăsar	ʿšr	ešru	ʿśr
Twenty	ʿśry	ʿašrîn	ʿešrū	ʿeśrîm	ʿesrîn	ʿšrm	ešru	ʿśrû
Thirty	ṯlṯy	ṯalâṯîn	salâšâ	š^{e}lôšîm	t^{e}lâtîn	ṯlṯm	šalâša	ś̀lṯy[14]
100	mʾt	miʾâtu	mâʾet^{e}	mēʾä	m^{e}ʾâ	mit	mê	mʾ
1000	ʾlf	ʾalfu	ʾalfu	ʾélep	ʾlep	alp	lipu	ʾlp
Members of family								
Family, tent	ʾhl	ʾahlu		ʾōhel		ahl	âlu	ʾhl
Father	ʾb	ʾabu	ʾabu	ʾāb	ʾabbā	ab	abu	ʾb
Mother	ʾm	ʾummu	ʾemm^{e}	ʾēm	ʾimmâ	um	ummu	ʾmm
Son	bn	ibnu		bēn	b^{e}nîn	bn	binu	bn
Daughter	bnt	bintu		bat		bt	bintu	bnt
Brother	ʾḫ	ʾaḫu	ʾeḫwĕ	ʾaḥ	ʾaḥ	ʾḫ	aḫu	ʾḫ
Sister	ʾḫt	ʾuḫtu	ʾeḫat^{e}	ʾāḥôt	ʾaḥatā	aḫt	aḫâtu	ʾḫt
Husband			mōt^{e}	m^{e}tîm	mt	mt	mutu	mt
Husband, owner	bʿl	baʿlu	bâʿal^{e}	báʿal	baʿlā	bʿl	bêlu	bʿl
Husband's father		ḥamu	ḥam^{e}	ḥām	ḥămā		amu	ḥm
Husband's mother		ḥamâtu	ḥamât^{e}	ḥamôt	ḥămatā			ḥmt
Bride	kll			kallä	kalltā	klt	kallatu	kll
Wife	ʾnṯ	ʾunṯà	ʾanest^{e}	ʾiššä	ʾint^{e}tā	anṯ	aššatu	ʾnṯ
Rival wife	ḍr	ḍarratu	ḍarara	ṣara	ʿartā	ṣrt	ṣirritu	ḍrr
Handmaid	ʾmt	ʾamä	ʾamat^{e}	ʾâmä	ʾamtā	amt	amtu	ʾmt
House	byt	baytu	bêt^{e}	báyit	baytā	byt	bîtu	byt

Firstborn	bkr	bikr	bakwer	b^{e}kôr	bukrā	bkr	bukru	bkr
Man (male)	ʾnś	ʾunâsu		ʾĕnôš	ʾĕnâš	ʾnš	nišu	ʾnś
Young man	ǵlm	ǵulâmu		ʿélem	ʿulaymā	ǵlm		ǵlm
Old man	śyb	šâba	śêba	śêbä	sîb	šyb	šêbu	śyb
Give birth	wld	walada	walada	yālad	y^{e}lîd	yld	alâdu	wld
Suckle		ǵâla	ʿĕwāl^e	ʿûl	ʿûlā			ǵwl
To clothe	lbś	labisa	lab^{e}sa	lābaš	l^{e}baš	lbš	labâsu	lbś
Marry	ḫtn	ḫutûnä		ḥātān	ḥatnā	ḫtn	ḫatnu	ḫtn
Name	śm	ismu	sem^e	šēm	š^{e}mā	šm	šumu	śm
Mention, remember	ḏkr	ḏakara	zakara	zākar	d^{e}kar		zikâru	ḏkr
Inherit	wrṯ	wariṯa	warasa	yāraš	y^{e}rêt			wrṯ
Live	ḥyw	ḥayya	ḥay^{e}wa	ḥāyā	ḥăyā	ḥwy		ḥyy
Die	mt	mâta	mōta	mût	mût	mt	mâtu	m(w)t
Weep		bakà	bakaya	bākā	b^{e}kā	bky	bakû	bky
Bury	qbr	qabara	qabara	qābar	q^{e}bar	qbr	qibîru	qbr
Parts of the Body								
Head	rʾś	raʾsu	reʾ^{e}se	rôʾš	rēšā	riš	rêšu	rʾś
Eye	ʿyn	ʿaynu	ʿay^{e}ne	ʿáyin	ʿaynā	ʿn	ênu	ʿyn
Ear	ʾḏn	ʾuḏnu	ʾezn^e	ʾōzen	ʾudnā	udn	uznu	ʾḏn
Nose, face	ʾnf	ʾanfu	ʾanf^e	ʾap	ʾanpîn	ap	appu	ʾnp
Mouth	f	fuhu	ʾef^e	pê	pûmā	p	pû	p
Lip		šafatu		śāpä	septā	špt	šaptu	śpy
Tongue	lśn	lisânu	lesân^e	lāšôn	liššân	lšn	lišânu	lśn
Tooth		sinnu	senn^e	šēn	šinnā		šinnu	śnn

14. This form, along with varying assimilation, will account for all the cognate forms.

COGNATE WORDS SHOWING PHONEMIC RELATIONSHIPS—*continued*

Meaning	*OSA*	*Arabic*	*Ethiopic*	*Hebrew*	*Aramaic*	*Ugar*	*Akkadian*	*P-S*
Shoulder	ṯkm			šékem		ṯkn		ṯkn
Arm		ḏiraʿu	mazraʿet^{e}	zerôaʿ	d^{e}raʿa	ḏrʿ	zurû	ḏrʿ
Hand	yd	yadu	ʾed^{e}	yād	y^{e}dā	yd	îdu	yd
Left	śʾml	šimâlu		ś^{e}môʾl	semmâlā	šmal	šumêlu	śmʾl
Right	ymn	yamînu	yemân^{e}	yāmîn	yammînā	ymn	imnu	ymn
Hollow of hand	ḥfn	ḥufnatu	ḥepn^{e}	ḥōpen	ḥupnā	ḥpn	upnu	ḥpn
Finger	ʾṣbʿ	ʾiṣbaʿu	ʾeṣbâʿt^{e}	ʾeṣbaʿ	ʾeṣb^{e}ʿā	uṣbʿt	ṣibû	ʾṣbʿ
(Finger)-nail		ẓufru	ṣepr^{e}	ṣippōren	ṭuprā		ṣupru	ẓpr
Self, soul	nš̀	nafsu	naps^{e}	népeš	napšā	npš		npš̀
Flesh	bśr	bašaru		bāśār	besrā	bšr	bišru	bśr
Bone		ʿaẓmu	ʿaḍm^{e}	ʿéṣem	ʿiṭmā	ʿẓm		ʿẓm
Bosom		ḥiḍnu	ḥeḍn^{e}	ḥōṣen	ḥannā			ḥḍn
Belly		baṭnu		béṭen				bṭn
Wrinkled Stomach		karišu	karśe	kārēś	karsā		karšu	krś
Foot	rgl	riǧlu		régel	reglā			rgl
Heart	lb	lubbu	lebb^{e}	lēbāb	libbā	lb	libbu	lbb
Liver		kabidu	kabd^{e}	kābēd	kabdā	kbd	kabittu	kbd
Kidney			kwalit	kilyä	kûlyā		kalitû	kly
Blood	dm	damu	dam^{e}	dām	dəmā	dm	damu	dm
Voice, sound		qawlu	qal^{e}	qôl	qâlā	ql	qûlu	qwl
Pronouns								
I	ʾny	ʾanâ	ʾana	ʾănî	ʾănā	ʾn		ʾn
I				ʾânôkî		ʾnk	anâku	ʾnk
We		naḥnu	neḥna	ʾănaḥnû	ʾănaḥnā		nîni	ʾnḫ

You m.s.	ʾt	ʾanta·	ʾanta	ʾattā	ʾant^{e}	at	atta	ʾnt
You m.p.		ʾantum	ʾant^{e}mu	ʾattem	ʾantûn	atm	attunu	ʾntm
You f.s.		ʾantî	ʾantî	ʾatt^{e}	ʾanty	at	atti	ʾnty
You f.p.		ʾantunna	ʾanten^{e}	ʾatten	ʾanten			ʾntn
He	hw/ŝw[15]	huwa	weʾ^{e}etu	hûʾ	hûʾ	hw	šû	hw/ŝw
She	hy/ŝy	hiya	yeʾ^{e}tī	hîʾ	hîʾ	hy	šî	hy/ŝy
They m.	hm/ŝm	hum	ʾĕmuntū	hēm	himmô	hm	šunu	hm/ŝm
They f.	hn/ŝn	hunna		hēnnā	hinnîn		šinma	hn/ŝn
Who/what		ma	ment^{e}	mā	mā		minû	m
Who?	mn	man	mannū		man	mn	mannu	mn
That	ḏ	ḏû	zâ	zè	dî	ḏ	šû	ḏ
Prepositions, Conjunctions, Adverbs								
In	b	bi	ba	b-	b-	b		b
In	wŝṭ	wasṭa	westa					wŝṭ
To	l	li	la	la	l	l		l
As, like	k	ka	ka	ki	k	k	ki(mâ)	k
From	bn	min	ʾemna	min	min			mn
Upon	ʿly	ʿalà		ʿăl(î)	ʿal	ʿl		ʿly
With	ʿm	maʿ		ʿim	ʿim	ʿm		ʿm
Not	lʾ	lâ		lôʾ	lâ	l		l
Not	ʾl		ʾalbō	ʾal	ʾal		ʾl	ʾl
And	w	wa	wa	w	w	w	u	w
If	hn	ʾin	ʾemma	ʾim	ʾen	hm		hm
Or	ʾw	ʾaw	ʾaw	ʾô	ʾaw	u		ʾw

15. In dialects other than Sabean, *ŝ* regularly occurs instead of *h* in pronominal forms and in the causative stem (H/Ŝ) of the verb; cf. M. Höfner, *Altsüdarabische Grammatik* (Leipzig, 1943): 30–35, 84.

COGNATE WORDS SHOWING PHONEMIC RELATIONSHIPS—*continued*

Meaning	*OSA*	*Arabic*	*Ethiopic*	*Hebrew*	*Aramaic*	*Ugar*	*Akkadian*	*P-S*
Lo!	hn	ʾinna	ʾen	hēn		hn		ʾn
Then	ʾḏ	ʾiḏ		ʾāz	ʾĕdáyin			ʾḏ
After	bʿd	baʿda	baʿd^{e}	báʿad		bʿd		bʿd
Between	byn	bayna	bayna	bên	bên	byn		byn
Until	ʿdy	ʿadà		ʿădê	ʿd	ʿd	adi	ʿdy
Where?		ʾayyu	ʾayy^{e}	ʾay		iy		ʾy
Where?		ʾayna		ʾáyin			ainu	ʾyn
There, thither	ṯmm	ṯamma		šāmmā	tammân	ṯm		ṯmm
Under	tḥt	taḥtu	tāḥt^{e}	táḥat	t^{e}ḥût	tḥt		tḥt
All	kll	kullu	kwell^{e}	kōl	kūl	kl	kullatu	kll
Time periods								
Day	ywm	yawmu	yōm^{e}	yôm	yawmā	ym	ûmu	ywm
Night	lyl	laylu	lēlit^{e}	láyil	lêlā		lîlâtu	lyl
Yesterday		tamâli	temâlm^{e}	ʾetmôl	ʾitt^{e}malê		timâli	tmly
Year, change	s̀n	sanatu		šānä	š^{e}nā	šnt	šattu	s̀n(y)
Summer	qyẓ	qayẓu		qáyiṣ	qayṭā	qyẓ		qyẓ
Winter, harvest	ḫrf	ḫarîfu	ḫarîf^{e}	ḥōrep			ḫarpu	ḫrp
Saeculum	ʿlm	ʿalâmu	ʿâlam^{e}	ʿôlām	ʿâl^{e}mā	ʿlm		ʿlm
Generation	dr	dawru		dôr	dâr	dr	dâru	dwr
Old		ḏiqnu		zāqēn	d^{e}qan	dqn	ziqnu	ḏqn
New	ḥdṯ	ḥadaṯa	ḥadasa	ḥādāš	ḥadat	ḥdṯ	eššu	ḥdṯ
Physical phenomena								
Heaven	s̀my	samâʾu	samây^{e}	šāmáyim	š^{e}mayyā	šmm	šamû	s̀my
Sun	śms̀	šamsu		šémeš	šimšā	špš	šamšu	śms̀

Moon, month	wrḫ		warḫ^e	yārēaḥ	yarḥā	yrḫ	warḫu	wrḫ
Star	kwkb	kawkabu	kōkab^e	kôkāb	kawk^{e}bā	kbkb	kakkabu	kbkb
Flash, lightning rod	brq	baraqa	baraqa	bāraq	b^{e}raq	brq	barâqu	brq
Flame		lahiba	lahaba	láhab	lahăba		laʾabu	lhb
Light		ʾawwara		ʾôr	ʾôrā	ar	urru	ʾwr
Shine			nagĕha	nāgah	n^{e}gah	ngh	nagû	ngh
Shadow	ẓll	ẓillu	ṣalala	ṣēl	ṭ^{e}lâlā	ẓl	ṣillu	ẓll
Rain	mṭr	maṭaru		māṭār	miṭrā	mṭr	meṭru	mṭr
Hail, cold	brdm	baradu		bārād	bardā			brd
Snow		ṯalǧu		šéleg	talgā		šalgu	ṯlg
Water	mw	mâʾu	mây^e	máyim	mayyā	my	mû	mw
River, stream	nhr	nahru		nāhār	nahărā	nhr	nâru	nhr
Wadi				náḥal	naḥlā	nḫlm	naḫlu	nḫl
Sea		yammu		yām	yammā	ym	iâmu	ymm
Earth	ʾrḍ	ʾarḍu		ʾéreṣ	ʾarqā[16]	arṣ	irṣitu	ʾrḍ
Valley		buqʿatu		biqʿä	b^{e}qaʿ	bqʿ	baqat(?)	bqʿ
Dust	ʿfr(?)	ʿafru		ʿāpār	ʿaprā	ʿpr	epru	ʿpr
Lowland	ŝpl	safula		š^{e}pēlä	š^{e}pal	špl	šapâlu	ŝpl
Wet, moist		raṭuba	raṭeba	rāṭōb	r^{e}ṭab		raṭâbu	rṭb
Dry, waste		ḫariba		ḥārēb	ḥărab	ḫrb	ḫarâbu	ḫrb
Common activities								
Breathe		nafaḥa	nafeḥa	nāpaḥ	n^{e}paḥ			npḥ
Blow	nfḫ	nafaḫa	nafeḫa	nāpaḥ	n^{e}paḥ	mpḫm	nappâḫu	npḫ
Sit, dwell	wṯb		ʾawsaba	yāšab	y^{e}tēb	yṯb	wašâbu	wṯb

16. In Old Aramaic, P–S *$ḍ$ has become *q* or ʿ; later it is exclusively ʿ. Both forms are found in Jer 10:11 and in Aramaic papyrus No. 6, lines 15–16, A. Cowley, *Aramaic Papyri of the Fifth Century B.C.* (Oxford, 1923): 16, 18.

COGNATE WORDS SHOWING PHONEMIC RELATIONSHIPS—*continued*

Meaning	*OSA*	*Arabic*	*Ethiopic*	*Hebrew*	*Aramaic*	*Ugar*	*Akkadian*	*P-S*
Rise	mqm	qâma	qōma	qûm	qûm	mqm	kumu	qwm
Walk				hālak	hallēk	hlk	alâku	hlk
Gird	mḫgrt	ḥağara		ḥāgar	ḥ^{e}gar	ḥgr	agâru	ḥgr
Mount, ride	rkb	rakiba	rakaba	rākab	r^{e}keb	rkb	rakâbu	rkb
Say, see	ʾmr	ʾamara	ʾamara	ʾāmar	ʾămar	ʾmr	amâru	ʾmr
Ask, request	mś̀ʾl	saʾala	saʾela	šāʾal	š^{e}ʾel	šʾl	šaʾâlu	ś̀ʾl
Tell, count		sifru	safara	sôpēr	saprā	spr	sipru	spr
Hear	ś̀mʿ	samiʿa	sameʿa	šāmaʿ	š^{e}maʿ	šmʿ	šemu	ś̀mʿ
Call, invite	qrʾ	qaraʾa		qārāʾ	q^{e}rā	qrʾ	qarû	qrʾ
Give	whb	wahaba	wahaba	yāhab	y^{e}hab			whb
Take, seize	lqḥ	laqiḥa	laqeḥa	lāqaḥ	lqḥ	lqḥ	liqû	lqḥ
Seize, grasp	ʾḫḏ	ʾaḫaḏa	ʾaḫaza	ʾāḥaz	ʾĕḥad	ʾḫd	aḫâzu	ʾḫḏ
Bellow, cry	gʿr	ğaʿara	gaʿara	gāʿar	g^{e}ʿar	gʿr	gêru	gʿr
Be small, few		ṣaǵura		ṣaʿîr	ṣ^{e}ʿar	ṣǵr	ṣeḫru	ṣǵr
Be great, many	rb	rabba	rababa	rābab	rab	rb	rabbu	rbb
Be full	mlʾ	malaʾa	maleʾa	mālēʾ	m^{e}lā	mlʾ	malû	mlʾ
Be empty		râqa		rîq	rîq		rêqu	ryq
Be strong	ʿztm	ʿazza	ʿazaza	ʿaz	ʿaz	ʿz	ezêzu	ʿzz
Be before, east	qdm	qadama	qadema	qédem	q^{e}dam	qdm	qudmu	qdm
Gap, opening	ṯʿr(?)	ṯaǵru	saʿara	šáʿar	trʿ	ṯǵr		ṯǵr
Open	ftḥ	fataḥa	fateḥa	pātaḥ	p^{e}taḥ	ptḥ	patû	ptḥ
Close, shut			śagart^{e}	sāgar	s^{e}gar	sgr		sgr
Go in	bwʾ	bâʾa	bōʾ^{e}	bôʾ		bwʾ	bâʾu	bwʾ
Enter, west	ǵrb	ǵarbu	ʿarebu	ʿéreb	ʿărab	ʿrb(!)	erêbu	ǵrb
Go out	wḍʾ		waḍeʾa	yāṣāʾ	y^{e}ā	yṣa	âṣû	wḍʾ

Depart, leave		ʿazaba		ʿāzab			ezêbu	ʿzb
Arrive	mẓʾ		maṣeʾa	māṣāʾ	m^{e}ṭā	mṣʾ	maṣû	mẓʾ / mṣʾ
Bring tidings	bśr	boširа	ʾabsara	bāśar		bšr	bussur	bśr
Return	ṯwb	ṯâba		šûb	tûb	ṯwb		ṯwb
Draw near	qrb	qariba	qareba	qārēb	qrb	qrb	qarâbu	qrb
Be distant	rḥq		reḥeqa	rāḥaq	r^{e}ḥêq	rḥq	rûqu	rḥq
Pass over, by	ʿbr	ʿabara		ʿābar	ʿăbar		ebêru	ʿbr
Pass, succeed	ḫlf	ḫalafa	ḫalafa	ḥālap	ḥălap			ḫlp
Be thirsty	ẓmʾ	ẓamiʾa	ṣameʾa	ṣāmēʾ		ẓmʾ(?)	ṣûmu	ẓmʾ
Draw water		dalâ	dalawa	dālä	d^{e}lā		dalû	dlw
Spring (water)	ʿyn	ʾaynu	ʿayn^{e}	ʿáyin	ʿaynā	ʿn	ênu	ʿyn
Drink	šty		sateya	šātä	š^{e}tā	šty	šatû	šty
Spill		safaka	sabaka	šāpak	š^{e}pak	špk	sapâku	špk
Wine	wyn	waynu	wayn^{e}	yáyin		yyn	îno(?)	wyn
Milk	ḥlb	ḥalibu	ḥalib^{e}	ḥālab	ḥalbā	ḥlb	alibu	ḥlb
Butter, curds	ḫmʾt	ḫamâ?		ḥemʾä		ḫmat		ḫmʾ
Lift, carry	nśʾ	našaʾa	našeʾa	nāśāʾ	n^{e}sā	nšʾ	našû	nśʾ
Be sound, well	šlm	salâmu	salâm^{e}	šālēm	š^{e}lem	šlm	šalâmu	šlm
Be ill		dawiya	dawaya	dāwā	d^{e}wî	dw	diʾû	dwy
Be sick	mrḍ	mariḍa		māraṣ	m^{e}raʿ	mrṣ	marâṣu	mrḍ
Be sweet		maṭqatu	mĕtuq^{e}	mātōq	m^{e}taq	mtq	mataqu	mtq[17]
Be bitter		murru	marara	mārar	m^{e}rar		marâru	mrr
Be hungry		raǵuba	reḫeba	raʿab		rǵb	rûbatu	rǵb
Be satisfied	śbʿ	šabʿa		śābēaʿ	s^{e}baʿ	šbʿ	šebû	śbʿ
Be drunken		sakira	sakera	šākar	šikrā	škr	šikaru	škr

17. Despite the discussions of dissimilation of *ṭ* > *t* under influence of *q*, the evidence is inconclusive, cf. Arab. qtl, qṭn, qṭf, qtr.

COGNATE WORDS SHOWING PHONEMIC RELATIONSHIPS—*continued*

Meaning	*OSA*	*Arabic*	*Ethiopic*	*Hebrew*	*Aramaic*	*Ugar*	*Akkadian*	*P-S*
Urine, urinate		maṯânatu	śēna	šáyin	tân	ṯyn	istîn	šyn
Bite, nip		qaraṣa	qaraṣa	qāraṣ	q^{e}riṣā	qrṣ	qarasu	qrṣ
Taste	ṭʿm	ṭaʿima	ṭeʿ^{e}ma	ʿṭāʿam	ṭ^{e}em		ṭêmu	ṭʿm
Swallow		baliʿa	bal^{e}ʿa	bālaʿ	b^{e}laʿ		belû	blʿ
Hunt, game	ṣyd	ṣâda		ṣáyid	ṣîd	ṣd	ṣâdu	ṣyd
Seize, hold		ḍabaṭa	ḍabaṭa	ṣābaṭ	ʿăbaṭ	msbṭm	ṣabâtu	ḍbṭ
Smite, slay	mḫḍ	maḫaḍa	maḥaṣa	māhaṣ		mḫṣ	maḫâṣu	mḫḍ
Plunder	ṯll	ṯallatu		šālal			šalâlu	ṯll
Slaughter, cook	ṭbḫ	ṭabaḫa	ṭab^{e}ḫa	ṭābaḥ	t^{e}baḥ	ṭbḫ	ṭabâḫu	ṭbḫ
Divide		falağa	falag^{e}	pālag	p^{e}leg		palgu	plg
Cut off		qaṣṣa		qāṣaṣ	q^{e}ṣaṣ	qṣ	qaṣâṣu	qṣṣ
Roast		qalà	qalaya	qālä	q^{e}lā		qalû	qly
Flame		lahhaba	lahaba	láhab	lahăbā		laʾabu	lhb
Coal		faḥmu	feḥm^{e}	peḥām	p^{e}ḥam	pḥm	pêntu	pḥm
Grind	ṭḥn	ṭaḥana	ṭeḥ^{e}ne	ṭāḥan	t^{e}ḥan	ṭḥn		ṭḥn
Crush, pulverize	dqq	daqqa	daqaqa	dāqaq	daqqēq	dq	daqâqu?	dqq
Flour		qamḥu	qamḥ^{e}	qémaḥ	qimḥā	qmḥ	qêmu?	qmḥ
Pit, well		biʾru		b^{e}ʾēr	b^{e}ʾērā	bir	bêru	bʾr
Bathe		raḥaḍa	reḥ^{e}ḍa	rāḥaṣ		rḥṣ	raḫâṣu?	rḥḍ
Dip, dye		ṣabaǵa		ṣébaʿ	ṣ^{e}baʿ		ṣubâtu	ṣbǵ
Form, create		waṣru		yāṣar	yaṣṣ^{e}rā	yṣr	eṣêru	wṣr
Build	bny	banà		bānä	b^{e}nā	bny	banû	bny
Set up, erect	nṣb	naṣaba		hiṣṣîb	n^{e}ṣab	nṣb	naṣâbu	nṣb
Watch	nṣr?	naẓara	naṣara	nāṣar	n^{e}ṭar	nẓr?	naṣâru	nẓr
Put	śym	šâma	śēma	śîm	sâm		šâmu	śym
Pierce	nqb	naqaba		nāqab	n^{e}qab		naqbu	nqb

Bind, confine	ʾśr	ʾasara	ʾasara	ʾāsar	ʾăsar	ʾsr	asâru	ʾśr
Bind up	ḥbs	ḥabbasa		ḥābaš	ḥ^{e}baš	ḥbš?	abâšu	ḥbs
Bind, pledge	ḥbl	ḥabala	ḥabala	ḥābal	ḥăbal	ḥbl		ḥbl
Strike, beat	ḫbṭ	ḫabaṭa		ḥābaṭ	ḥăbaṭ		ḫabâtu?	ḫbṭ
Cease, futile		baṭala	baṭala	bāṭal	b^{e}ṭel		baṭâlu	bṭl
Seek, inquire		baǵà		bāʿä	b^{e}ʿā	bǵy	baʾu	bǵy
Dam up		sakara		sākar	s^{e}kar		sikêru	skr
Search, collect	ḥfś	ḥafaša	ḥafaśa	ḥāpaś	ḥăpas	ḥpšt		ḫpś
Hire, workman	ʾgr	ʾağara		ʾāgûr	ʾăgîrā	agr	agâru	ʾgr
Animals								
Beast, cattle	bʿr	baʿîru	baʿ^{e}rawī	b^{e}ʿîr	b^{e}ʿîrā			bʿr
Bull	ṯwr	ṯawru	sōr^{e}	šôr	tôrā	ṯwr	šuru	ṯwr
Calf	ʿgl	ʿiğlu	egwīl^{e}	ʿégel	ʿiglā	ʿgl	agalê	ʿgl
Large cattle	bqr	baqaru		bāqār	baqrā			bqr
Small cattle	ḍʾn	ḍâʾnu		ṣôʾn	ʿânā	ṣin	ṣênî	ḍʿn
Ram				ʾáyil	ʾáyil	ayl	ailu	ʾyl
Lamb	śhw	šâʾu		śē		š	šuʾu	š?
He-ass	ḥmr	ḥimâru		ḥămôr	ḥămârā	ḥmr	imêru	ḥmr
She-ass		ʾatânu		ʾātôn	ʾattânā	atn	atânu	ʾtn
Kid		ğadyu		g^{e}dî	gadyā	gdy	gadiya	gdy
Camel	gml	ğamalu	gamal^{e}	gāmal	gamlā		gammalu	gml
Gazelle	ẓbyt	ẓabyu		ṣ^{e}bî	ṭabyā	ẓby	ṣabîtu	ẓby
Hart		ʾayyalu	hayal^{e}?	ʾayyāl	ʾayy^{e}lā	ʾyl	ayalu	ʾyyl
Dog		kalbu	kalb^{e}	kéleb	kalbā	klb	kalbu	klb
Wolf, jackal	ḏʾb	ḏiʾbu	zeʾeb^{e}	z^{e}ʾēb	dîbā		zîbu	ḏʾb
Lion	ʾry	ʾarwa	ʾarwē	ʾărî	ʾaryā		aria	ʾrw
Leopard, panther	nmr	namiru	namr^{e}	nāmēr	nimrā		nimru	nmr
Griffin vulture	nśr	nasru	nesr^{e}	néšer	nišrā	nšr	našru	nśr
Shear, fleece	gzz	ğazza		gēz	g^{e}zaz	gzz	gizzu	gzz

COGNATE WORDS SHOWING PHONEMIC RELATIONSHIPS—*continued*

Meaning	*OSA*	*Arabic*	*Ethiopic*	*Hebrew*	*Aramaic*	*Ugar*	*Akkadian*	*P-S*
Pluck		qaṭafa		qāṭap	q^{e}ṭap		qaṭâpu	qṭp
Graze	rʿy	raʿà	reʿ^{e}ya	rāʿä	r^{e}ʿā	rʿy	rêʾû	rʿy
Wing, extremity	knf	kanafu	kenf^{e}	kānap	kanpā	knp	kappu	knp
Tail	qrn	qarnu	qarn^{e}	qéren	qarnā	qrn	qarnu	qrn
Fly		ʿâfa	ʿōf^{e}	ʿûp	ʿûpā	ʿwp		ʿwp
Manger, stall		ʾâriyyu		ʾûryä	ʾûryā	aryy?	urû	ʾry
Agriculture								
Tree, wood	ʿḍm	ʿiḍatu	ʿeḍ^{e}	ʿēṣ	ʾaʿ	ʿṣ	iṣṣu	ʿḍ
Cedar		ʾarzu	ʾarz^{e}	ʾérez	ʾarzā	arz		ʾrz
Cyprus				b^{e}rôš	b^{e}rûtā		burašu	brṯ
Olive tree/oil		zaytûn	zayt^{e}	záyit	zêtā	zt		zyt
Oil, fat		samina		šémen	š^{e}men	šmn	šamnu	s̀mn
Vine	gfn	ǧafnu		gépen	gupnē	gpn	gapnu	gpn
Grape	ʿnb	ʿinabu		ʿēnāb	ʿinn^{e}bā		inbu?	ʿnb
Fig		tînu		t^{eʾ}ēnä	tên^{e}tā		tittu	tyn
Wheat		ḥinṭatu		ḥittä	ḥinṭîn	ḥṭṭ		ḥnṭ
Barley	śʿrm	šaʿiru		ś^{eʿ}ōrä	s^{eʿ}ârtā	šʿr		śʿr
Groats	bql	baqlu	baqwel^{e}		bûqâlā	bql	buqlu	bql
Garden	gnn	ǧannatu	gannat^{e}	gan	ginnā	gn	gannatu	gnn
Garlic		tûmu		šûm	tûmā		šûmu	ṯwm
Onion	tṣl	baṣalu	baṣal^{e}	bāṣāl	bûṣlā			bṣl
Beans		fûlu	fâl^{e}	pôl	pôlā			pwl
Cummin		kammûnu	kammin^{e}	kammôn	kammônā	kmn		kmn?
Balsam		bašâmu		bōśem	busmā			bśm
Honey	dbs̀	dibsu		d^{e}baš	dubšā			dbs̀

Eggs		bayḍatu		bêṣä	bîʿătā			byḍ?
Nuts		ğûzu	gawz^{e}	ʾĕgôz	gawz			gwz?
Pistachio		buṭmu		boṭ^{e}nîm	beṭm^{e}tā		buṭnu	bṭm/n?
Till, plow	ḥrṯ	ḥaraṯa	ḥarasa	ḥāraš	ḥărat	ḥrṯ		ḥrṯ
Sow		zaraʿa	zar^{e}ʿa	zāraʿ	z^{e}raʿ		zirû	dzrʿ
Scatter, winnow	ḏrʾ	ḏarrà	zarawa	zārā	d^{e}rā	drʿ	zirû	ḏrw/y
Water, irrigate	šqy	saqà	sakaya	šāqā	š^{e}qā	šqy	šaqû	šqy
Tread	dwš?	dâsa		dûš	dâš		dâšu	dwš
Root	šrś	šarsu	śerw^{e}?	šōreš	šuršā	šrš	šuršu	šrś
Religion, cult terms, government								
God	ʾl			ʾēl		il	ilu	ʾl
God	ʾlh	ʾilâhu		ʾĕlôah	ʾalâhā			ʾlh
Praise, shout		halla	tamāh^{e}lala	hallēl	hallēl	hll?	alâlu	hll
Kneel, bless	brk	baraka	baraka	bārak	b^{e}rek	brk	birku	brk
Bow down		sağada	sagada	sāgad	s^{e}ged			sgd
Dedicate, vow	nḏr	naḏara		nēzer	n^{e}dar	ndr	nazâru	nḏr
Make pilgrimage	ḥgg	ḥağğa		ḥāgag	ḥaggî			ḥgg
Be sacred, devote	ḥrm	ḥaruma	ḥarama	heḥĕrîm	ʾaḥrem			ḥrm
Sacrifice	ḏbḥ	ḏabaḥa	zabeḥa	zạbaḥ	d^{e}baḥ	dbḥ	zibû	ḏbḥ
Sin, miss mark	ḫṭʾ	ḫaṭiʾa	ḫateʾa	ḥāṭāʾ	ḥăṭāʾ	ḫṭʾ	ḫaṭû	ḫṭʾ
Holy, set apart	qdš	qudsu	qadasa	qādôš	qaddîš	qdš	qadâšu	qdš
Messenger, send	lʾk	malʾaku	malʾak^{e}	malʾāk	malʾăkā	lak		lʾk
Priest		kâhinu	kâhen^{e}	kôhēn	kâhănā	khn		khn
Incense	mqṭr	qutru	qetâr^{e}	q^{e}ṭōret	qîṭrā	qṭr	qutru	qṭr?
Cover, expiate	kfr	kafara		kippēr	k^{e}par			kpr
Peace	šlm	salâmu	salâm^{e}	šālôm	s^{e}lâmā	šlm	šalâmu	šlm
Rule, ruler		sulṭân	śalaṭa	šālaṭ	s^{e}laṭ	šlyṭ?	šalaṭu	šlṭ
Judge	dyn	dâna		dîn	dîn	dyn	dânu	dyn
Straight, just	ṣdq	ṣadqu	ṣadeqa	ṣaddîq	ṣ^{e}deq	ṣdq	ṣaduq	ṣdq
Set up, erect	mṣb	naṣaba		maṣṣēbä	n^{e}ṣab	nṣb	naṣâbu	nṣb

MAARAV 5–6 (Spring, 1990): 207–220

FROM UGARIT TO GADES: MEDITERRANEAN VETERINARY MEDICINE*

LOREN R. MACK-FISHER

For several years I have been interested in veterinary medicine.[1] The geographical area of this interest is the Mediterranean and the time period covers almost three thousand years—from the Ugaritic hippiatric texts to the *Hippiatrica* of Ruellius in 1530 C.E.[2] We start at Ugarit.

* During my Claremont years I had the pleasure of occasional contacts with Professor Stanislav Segert. I am pleased to contribute to his *Festschrift*. His heritage abounds with greatness in so many ways—from Kepler to Kafka, and his own contributions have enhanced the gift of Prague.

1. This interest has had its practical side for "works and days" on our ranch (in Round Valley, Mendocino County, CA) and now it is being intensified, daily, by Barbara, my wife, who is a student in the School of Veterinary Medicine at UC Davis. Also Professor Calvin Schwabe of UC Davis has been very helpful. He has been interested in my work on the Ugaritic hippiatric texts, and he has urged me to look at the possibility of a Semitic background for the Latin *veterinarius*. His own work can be seen in Calvin W. Schwabe, *Cattle, Priests and Progress in Medicine* (Minneapolis: Univ. of Minnesota, 1978): 144–153.

My work is still unfinished, but I have given two papers on the subject recently. The first ("The Ugaritic Hippiatric Texts") was read at the "All-UC Conference on the History and Pre-History of Man-Animal Relationships" at UC Davis, April 25–27, 1986, and the second ("Mediterranean Veterinary Medicine: From Ugarit to Columella") was read at the fall, 1986, session of the University Association of Research Scholars, California State University, Sacramento. The work of Chaim Cohen and Daniel Sivan, *The Ugaritic Hippiatric Texts: A Critical Edition* (American Oriental Series 9; New Haven: American Oriental Society, 1983) has been very helpful for my studies, but I will wait to see Dennis Pardee's work on these texts before I finish my translation with notes and commentary. And who knows? Perhaps Pardee's work will mean that mine is not needed.

2. The *Hippiatrica* is known in both a Latin text: Iohanne Ruellio Suessionensi, *Veterinariae Medicinae*, Liber Primus, 1530, and a Greek text: *Veterinariae Medicinae*, Liber Duo, 1537.

It is well known that in 1933 fragments of two hippiatric texts were found "in a building standing at some distance from the library"[3] in ancient Ugarit. These texts did not cause much excitement; other texts were more important. Later, during the seventeenth season at Ugarit, another text was found (RS 17.120) which was almost complete. Then in 1960, the twenty-third season, another hippiatric fragment was discovered. As of now, we have a total of four texts. These four texts have been published in a critical edition by Chaim Cohen and Daniel Sivan.[4] This edition has been helpful, but we still do not really know very much about these texts. In other words, we do not really know anything about that building where the first two texts were found. The fourth fragment was copied on a text containing some "bilingual Sumerian-Akkadian wisdom,"[5] and this will be discussed later in this essay.

At this point, I am mainly interested in the larger text (RS 17.120) which was found in the "library" of Rašapabu, the *akil kâri* (i.e., the official over the port/merchant quarter) of Ugarit. I assume that this text was used by Rašapabu and by those who worked under his supervision. Rašapabu's "library" did not contain religious texts or any ancient Near Eastern classical literature. In fact, it was not a library at all, but rather a collection of twenty texts (fifteen Akkadian texts and five Ugaritic) dealing with family affairs, real estate, court judgments, economics, and veterinary medicine.[6] These texts helped Rašapabu in his activities and recorded those activities. It is clear that he dealt with merchants and other officials[7] from many places on behalf of Ugarit. He bought livestock and commodities; he made trade agreements, collected some tax, and I think that he was responsible for veterinary service.

He probably took care of animals belonging to the state, and he may have cared for pack animals belonging to the foreign mer-

3. Claude F. A. Schaeffer, *The Cuneiform Texts of Ras Shamra-Ugarit* (The Schweich Lectures, 1936; London: Oxford, 1939): 41.

4. See N 1. For a discussion of the fourth text (RS 23.484), see p. 58.

5. Cohen and Sivan (N 1): 58 and see Jean Nougayrol, "Sagesses en Dictions," in Claude F. A. Schaeffer, ed., *Ugaritica V* (Mission de Ras Shamra XVI; Paris: Imprimerie Nationale, 1968): 291–300, and note text 165 on p. 297.

6. Jean Nougayrol, "Textes Suméro-Accadiens des archives et bibliothèques privées d'Ugarit," *Ugaritica V* (N 5):1–21 and Claude F. A. Schaeffer, "Commentaires sur les lettres et documents trouvés dans les bibliothèques privées d'Ugarit," *Ugaritica V* (N 5): 609–629.

7. E.g., the *rbṣ*, an Ugaritic word which we know in Akkadian (*râbiṣu*).

chants. Rašapabu's *spr. nʿm. ššwm*, "A Manual: The Health of Horses" (a 1250 B.C.E. edition), was no doubt useful for him and even more so for the veterinarians who worked under his direction. Such a hypothesis may be supported in part by the following text:

. . . *y.bṭr.bd.mlkt*	" . . . a veterinarian under the supervision of the queen."
. . . *bṭr. bd. mlkt*	" . . . a veterinarian under the supervision of the queen."[8]

In this professional list we have veterinarians who worked for the queen, and I suppose that there could have been others who worked for Rašapabu. I translate *bṭr* "veterinarian." It should be vocalized *bâṭiru*. This helps to understand the antiquity of the Arabic root *bṭr*, "to incise," or the form *baiṭār*, "veterinary surgeon." It is no longer possible to imagine that the Arabic root and word for "veterinary surgeon" came from the Greek *hippiatros*. Even if we did not have the Ugaritic word to argue for the Arabic root, I would expect that the Greek would have entered Syriac and Arabic as it did into Rabbinic literature, namely, *ʾippyayṭrōs*.[9] Obviously, it would be helpful to see Ugaritic *bâṭiru* in something other than a list, but for now I would translate "veterinarian" with just a hint of anachronism. I will want to pursue this point later, but now it is important to look at the formal characteristics of the "Manual."

In order to comment on the structure, I will quote from section IV of the "Manual." I will not comment on the translation at this time, except to say that the following translation is very similar to Cohen and Sivan:[10]

9. *[w].k.l.yḫrʾu.w.l.yṯtn.ššw*
10. *[mss].št.qlql.w.št.ʿrgz*
11. *[yd]k.ʾaḥdh.w.yṣq.b.ʾaph*

8. Text 2015 in Cyrus H. Gordon's *Ugaritic Textbook* (Analecta Orientalia 58; Rome: PBI, 1965): 7* or see Charles Virolleaud, *Le Palais Royal d'Ugarit* V (Mission de Ras Shamra XI; Paris: Imprimerie Nationale, 1965): 28–29, Text 15–18.106.

9. See Siegmund Frankel, *Die Aramäischen Fremdwörter im Arabischen* (1886; reprint, Hildesheim: Olms, 1962): 265f. He claimed that the Arabic came from the Greek. I think that such a theory is not a live option today.

10. Cohen and Sivan (N 1): 14, 48–51.

9. [or], if the horse does not defecate and does not urinate,
10. [the juice] of a measure of Cassia and a measure of the *ʿrgz*-plant
11. [should be com]pounded together, and it should be administered through his (the animal's) nose.

Although Cohen and Sivan have dealt with this structure in detail,[11] it should, in a brief way, be repeated here. The structure of each entry is very simple. First, the problem or symptom is given. Second, the prescription is stated along with the method of preparation. Third, there is the method of administration. It is interesting to compare this structure with the structure of a much later text which I consider a late edition of our Ugaritic text. I am referring to the 1530 C.E. edition of the *Hippiatrica*.[12] In this late collection of quotes, there are quotes from Mago of Carthage. It may be that these two quotes are from the translation of Mago's works from Punic to Latin in about 140 B.C.E. by order of the Roman Senate.[13] The second of these passages was noted years ago by A. M. Honeyman, and he related the third part of it to the Ugaritic tradition.[14] The Latin text reads:

1. *asserit autem, cum urinae difficultate torqueatur equus,*
2. *si priorum pedum ex infimis unguibus delimata scobis in hemina vini,*
3. *per nares infundatur, cieri urinam.*

I have set this out in three parts to make clear the structural elements. Just as in the Ugaritic text we have: (1) symptoms, (2) prescription and preparation, and (3) administration. The prescription has changed, but that is about it. This manual tradition had a long life. I should mention that it is misleading for Cohen and Sivan to discuss this Latin translation of Mago as if it was "a Latin inscription from Carthage."[15]

But all of this is only introduction. There are so many questions. How do traditions last so long? How did this manual get to Mago? Who is Mago? And what was the nature of his work?

11. *Ibid.:* 48–51.
12. See N 2.
13. *Ibid.* See the Latin text, p. 37, 44f.
14. A. M. Honeyman, "Varia Punica," *American Journal of Philology* 68 (1947): 77–82.
15. Cohen and Sivan (N 1): 17, 23.

The manual tradition moved west. I would like to say that we can trace this westward movement, but that is not the case. It is as if it went underground in Ugarit and came up in Carthage. We do not even have the word *bṭr* in any extant Phoenician or Punic texts.[16] We do not have veterinary manuals in either language. In fact, to get in touch once more with East Mediterranean veterinary traditions, it is necessary to go to Rome. In so doing, I have spent most of my time with Marcus Terentius Varro (116–27 B.C.E.) and with Lucius Columella (4 B.C.E.–65 C.E.).

It is important to note that both Varro and Columella have a lot of respect for the "ancients," and it is in the works of Varro and Columella that we find a lot of ancient traditions. Varro, after praising more than fifty authors who wrote on agriculture, says, "All these are surpassed in reputation by Mago of Carthage, who gathered into twenty-eight books, written in the Punic tongue, the subjects they had dealt with separately."[17] This praise of Mago of Carthage was more than a formal word of politeness. Varro says, "On the subject of health there are many rules; these have been copied down from Mago's treatise, and I see to it that my head herdsman is reading some of them repeatedly."[18] In fact, I think that only Columella surpasses Varro's praise and use of Mago.

Columella (writing after Varro) was a native of Gades (Cadiz, Spain). He was undoubtedly surrounded by Punic tradition, and at many points he shows a knowledge of such. He praises the "ancients" in general and Punic traditions in particular.[19] After writing about the Greeks and the Romans who wrote on agriculture, he says, " . . . still paying greatest reverence to the Carthaginian Mago as the father of husbandry (*rusticationis parentem*), inasmuch as his twenty-eight memorable volumes were translated into the Latin tongue by senatorial decree."[20] Varro is aware of a Greek transla-

16. Even though, as we will discuss later, there is reason to suggest that it was used in Punic.

17. Marcus Terentius Varro, *On Agriculture* (tr. Harrison Boyd Ash, LCL; Cambridge: Harvard Univ., 1936): 165f. (I, i, 10).

18. Varro (N 17): 377 (II, v, 18). It should be noted that Varro stresses that the head herdsman should be able to read and write in many other places (pp. 227, 327f., 343, 349, 391, 411). This is important.

19. Lucius Junius Moderatus Columella, *On Agriculture* (tr. Harrison Boyd Ash; 3 vols.; LCL; Cambridge: Harvard Univ., 1942): I.31–33 (I, i, 5–12).

20. Columella (N 19): I.35 (I, i, 13). On the Latin translation of Mago also see Pline l'Ancien, *Histoire Naturelle* (tr. Henri Le Bonniec with André Le Boeuffle;

tion of Mago,[21] but it is odd that he does not mention the Latin translation since he must have used it with his herdsmen.

They liked Mago, but who is Mago? The name Mago was very common in the Mediterranean world; this was true for centuries. The root *mgn* is known in Hebrew, Syriac, Arabic, Phoenician, Akkadian, and Ugaritic. It means "to beseech (with gifts)" or "gift." At Ugarit, we have the name *bn.mgn*,[22] and in its Akkadian form (from the Rašapabu collection) we have *^{m}ṣi-id-qa-na mâr ma-ga-ni amîl ^{al}ilu*[*-ištanˁi* . . .].[23] The name occurs in fourteen Phoenician texts,[24] but most of these instances refer to different persons in various times and places. I do think that from now on we should use the spelling Magon (except in quotes from others) in our work, but that does not help very much. The name is common, but who is the Magon of Carthage, the great husbandman and the author of 28 books? For now I am going along with a very old view (Justin, XVIII, 2–7) which was affirmed anew by J. P. Mahaffy in 1889.

Magon could have been the famous general who was the youngest brother of Hannibal and the son of Hamilcar Barca. This would put him in the late third century B.C.E., but Mahaffy argues persuasively as follows:

> Mago to whom it [the 28 books on agriculture] was attributed was the first and greatest of the name, who founded the might of Carthage (says Justin), by his military and political reforms, and whose house inherited his power and ruled the state for 150 years. But if this be indeed the alleged author who lived earlier than 500 B.C., I suspect that the attribution of the work to him is but another instance of the attributing a great and popular work to an old and popular name.[25]

Paris: Société d'Édition "Les Belles Lettres," 1972): 65 (Boox XVIII, ch. V). According to Pliny this translation was made just after the fall of Carthage, i.e., after 146 B.C.E.

21. Varro (N 17): 167 (I, i, 10).

22. Virolleaud (N 8): 117:6.

23. Nougayrol (N 6): 16–20, text 12:4.

24. *KAI* 49:36; 52:2; 60:2; 65:8, 10; 77:2; 81:6; 93:2; 95:2; 96:5; 97:3; 101:3, 4; 103:3; 104:2; and 113:A2, B3. Also note *KAI* II: 67 and the reference to Greek *Magōn* and Latin *Magonus*.

25. J. P. Mahaffy, "The Work of Mago on Agriculture," *Hermathena* 7 (1889): 29–35.

Mahaffy notes that Columella (*R.R.*, Vol. III, Book XII, iv, 2) refers to both Magon and Hamilcar as being part of the Carthaginian tradition. Then Mahaffy says:

> But if this statement implies a belief that the greatest Punic generals were the men who knew most about farming, it seems to me a sort of mythical tradition that made Mago the author. And, if so, it is likely enough that the 28 books were not all in the original work, but that it was gradually enlarged in the days of Hamilcar (either the son of Mago I or the Barcide) and others, so that it came to represent the accumulated wisdom of centuries.[26]

At this point it is easy enough to point out that Mahaffy was on the right track, but he was not critical enough. Even the "original work" was full of traditional material and some of it going back even to Ugarit and beyond.

What Mahaffy says concerning "wisdom" collections is very true. Because of this, we should note the "wisdom" character of this material. Columella acknowledges this character when he points to the sources of their "wisdom." He says:

> To the other injunctions we add one which one of the Seven Sages delivered to posterity for all time: that measure and proportion be applied to all things, and that this be understood as spoken not only to those who are to embark on some other enterprise, but also to those who are to acquire land—not to want to buy more than a regard for their reckoning allows. For this is the meaning of that famous maxim of our own poet: "Admire large farms, but yet a small one till." This precept, which a most learned man has expressed in verse, is, in my opinion, a heritage from antiquity, inasmuch as it is agreed that the Carthaginians, a very shrewd people, had the saying that the farm should be weaker than the farmer; for, as he must wrestle with it, if the land prove the stronger, the master is crushed.[27]

26. *Ibid.:* 32. Also note Cyrus H. Gordon, *The Ancient Near East*[3] (New York: Norton, 1965): 126, where he suggests that a story about Isaac's farming (Gen 26:12) is "a statement worth recording because in the heroic age the aristocratic leaders are landowners, who personally excel in agriculture between military campaigns."

27. Columella (N 19): I.47–49 (I, iii, 8, 9).

So, at a glance, we see that Columella's sources for "wisdom" include the Seven Sages,[28] Virgil,[29] and Magon (his usual source for the Carthaginians).[30] And, all of this sounds a lot like *The Instruction of Amen-em-opet*, VII, 14–15, "Do not strain to seek an excess, when thy needs are safe for thee."[31] It seems that Magon's work must have contained proverbs, mythology,[32] professional instructions, and just a lot of good sense on many subjects. It is now becoming clear what is happening. We are talking about international wisdom or didactic literature. Now, it seems that it could be very important that the fourth Ugaritic hippiatric text was copied on the back of a wisdom text (this means three languages on this text). That professional training could provide the focus for the work of wisdom schools in the Mediterranean world is well known. Such instruction in Egypt was used in the training

28. *Ibid.*: 33, note a, "The Seven Sages of Greece, all belonging to the period from 620 to 550 B.C. The names are variously given, but those usually mentioned are: Cleobulus, Periander, Pittacus, Bias, Thales, Chilon, and Solon."

29. Virgil, *Georgics*, II, 412–413.

30. Columella (N 19): I. 36–39 (I, i, 18), at the beginning of his work, says that the farmer needs to be on the farm and to be focused on farm problems (in addition to having a farm of the right size): "And I believe that Mago the Carthaginian was pointing this out most particularly when he began his writings with such sentiments as these: 'One who has bought land should sell his town house, so that he will have no desire to worship the household gods of the city rather than those of the country; the man who takes greater delight in his city residence will have no need of a country estate.'"

31. *ANET*^{2}: 422.

32. By mythology, I am suggesting that one should look for all types, but etiological stories make up a large part of the myth. One interesting example has to do with bees. Note Columella (N 19): II.485 (IX, xiv, 6), "Now Democritus, Mago and likewise Virgil have recorded that bees can be generated at this same time of the year from a slain bullock. Mago indeed also asserts that the same thing may be done from the bellies of oxen." But Columella agrees with Celsus that this method of obtaining bees is not necessary. I wish that I knew all of what Magon said on this subject. Virgil really mythologizes this subject in Georgic 4 (see Gary B. Miles, *Virgil's Georgics* [Berkeley: Univ. of California, 1980]: 253–289, for a very interesting discussion of the *bugonia*). Most think that Virgil got some of his information on this from Varro, who says "It is from the putrefied body of this animal that there spring the sweetest bees, those honey-mothers from which the Greeks therefore call bees 'the ox-sprung' (*bougeneis*)" (Varro [N 17]: 369 [II, v, 5]), and Varro also says, "In the first place, bees are produced partly from bees, and partly from the rotted carcass of a bullock. And so Archelaus, in an epigram, says that they are 'the roaming children of a dead cow'" (Varro [N 16]: 501 [III, xvi, 4]). After all this, Samson's riddle (Judg 14:14) does not sound quite so strange: a carcass with bees and honey!

of scribes and councilors; this may be the case for Prov 22:17–24:34. Wisdom schools could produce a manual for veterinarians (like Rašapabu's), but they could also relate such manuals to other types of wisdom. A. Leo Oppenheim said, concerning manuals, or, as he called them, "procedural instructions":

> Under unknown circumstances, the technical lore of certain artisans which cater to the need of the court was fixed in writing, presumably upon a royal order. Once admitted to and incorporated into the corpus of traditional writings, these texts continued to be copied by tradition-conscious scribes and kept in private or royal libraries.[33]

We will probably never know in what form Magon received this material, i.e, in manual form or combined with other manual traditions and wisdom from perhaps the court school at Ugarit. But I am willing to guess that Magon's 28 books formed a work that we could call (along with Samuel Noah Kramer) a *Farmer's Almanac*. In other words, it belongs to a long succession of works which begin at Sumer. Kramer says in his discussion of the *Farmer's Almanac* from Nippur that:

> Before the Nippur discovery, two similar farmer's "handbooks" were known from ancient days: Virgil's far-famed and highly poetic *Georgics* and Hesiod's *Works and Days*. The latter, which is by far the earlier of the two, was probably written in the eighth century B.C. On the other hand, the newly restored Sumerian clay document was actually inscribed about 1700 B.C., and thus antedates Hesiod's work by approximately a millennium.[34]

In his interesting book, *Hesiod and the Near East*, P. Walcot has a chapter on "Didactic Literature in Greece and the Near East." He has a very nice discussion of ancient almanac literature. Yet he is concerned about the "geographical and chronological" gap from Sumer to Hesiod. At this point, he brings up the subject of Magon. He says that Magon provides only an "elusive" clue as to how to bridge the gap. He would like to bridge the gap via Magon and the Phoenicians, but where are the texts? In order to make a start

33. A. Leo Oppenheim, "Introduction," in Oppenheim et al., *Glass and Glassmaking in Ancient Mesopotamia* (Corning, NY: The Corning Museum of Glass, 1970): 6.

34. Samuel Noah Kramer, *From the Tablets of Sumer* (Indian Hills, CO: Falcon's Wing, 1956): 61f. This "handbook" begins, "In the days of yore a farmer gave (these) instructions to his son."

towards an answer to this question, he refers to the only evidence that he has from the general Phoenician area, namely, the tenth century B.C.E. Gezer calendar.[35] The Gezer Calendar is important, but I think that we now have additional evidence in light of the manual tradition from Ugarit. Walcot makes another interesting comment concerning the importance of the calendar in all of these works.[36] This is true for the Nippur text, Hesiod, and Virgil. I would like to add that it is also true for Varro,[37] Columella,[38] and Pliny.[39] It is very likely that if we had a text of Magon, we would also have another calendar.[40] If Magon's work was a large almanac, this would explain why Varro would have only copied parts of it, i.e., those parts pertaining to veterinary medicine, and to this subject I would like to return.

Both Varro and Columella use the veterinary material from Magon. Columella usually mentions his source, but sometimes Varro forgets to do this.[41] Also Columella is a better source for Magon's work in other ways. For one thing, he knew more about Punic tradition, and even though he expanded and narrated some of the manual traditions that he received from Magon, the manual form can still be seen. Columella, *R.R.*, Vol. II, Book VI is devoted to the care of cows and horses. Some of Columella's instructions show clearly the simple form of the Magon quote that we have seen in the *Hippiatrica*. For example, in Book VI, v, 3 there is (1) the description of the symptoms, (2) the prescription, and (3) the administration. I will give parts (2) and (3):

> Sometimes a potion consisting of equal weights of cinnamon, myrrh and frankincense and a like quantity of the blood of a sea-tortoise is

35. P. Walcot, *Hesiod and the Near East* (Cardiff: Univ. of Wales, 1966): 96, 97.

36. *Ibid.* There is even a calendar, as he notes, "on the back of our papyrus text of the Instruction of Amen-em-Opet" (101).

37. Varro (N 17): I, xxviii, 1-xxxvii, 5.

38. Columella (N 19): III: XI, ii.

39. *Natural History*, XVIII, 56-74.

40. See Columella (N 19): III.385 (XVII, i), "On Trees": "Mago is of the opinion that the olive-tree should be planted in dry ground during the autumn after the equinox before mid-winter."

41. This can be seen by comparing the text of Columella (N 19): II.125 (VI, i, 1-3) where Columella gives Magon's description of a good ox, with a "near" parallel in Varro (N 17): 371f. (II, v, 7-9), but Varro does not mention Magon. On this example note Miles (N 32): 182-184, where he gives Virgil's description of a good cow. He says that Virgil got this from Varro. The Virgil passage (*Georgic* 3:51-59) and Varro's are very close, but the real source may still be Magon. I doubt if Virgil would use Magon except unknowingly, but this remains a question for me.

> mixed with three *sextarii* of old wine and poured through the animal's nostrils (*per nares infunditur*).[42]

It is clear that Columella gives us a lot of tradition from Magon which goes back to Ugarit and to the Near East in general.[43] If this is true, I wonder if Columella could help us with a difficult line in RS 17.120? In line 30 we have the symptom given:

k.yraš.w.ykhp.mi[*d.ššw*].

Cohen and Sivan leave the two verbs untranslated ("If a horse *yraš* and *ykhp* incessantly . . .").[44] Cyrus Gordon translates: "When a horse *tosses* his head and *whinnies* much . . ."[45] Gordon sees the first verb as a denominative from *riš* "head." Cohen and Sivan reject this route and then they say that it is "difficult to understand how such *natural* head-movement could represent a symptom of the horse's malady."[46] This is not difficult to understand for anyone who has been around horses and has worked with them.[47] Cohen and Sivan also get off on the wrong foot (or hoof!) when they discuss *ykhp*.[48] They think that *yraš* has something to do with "mange," so they like K. Aartun's suggestion that *ykhp* means "(mit dem Huf) scharren." The problem is that they take "scharren" to mean "scratch" (but with horses it means "to paw"), and then they mildly scold Aartun for suggesting that horses scratch themselves with their hooves. Obviously, Aartun is talking about a

42. Columella (N 19): II.140 (VI, v, 3). This formula in part three occurs many times in Columella and is identical with the Magon quote in the *Hippiatrica*.

43. Some treatments and methods of treatment can be paralleled in other medical texts. Columella (N 19): II.173 (VI, xvii, 7), in dealing with "maladies of the eyes" says, "if there is a white film on the eye, . . . the shell of a cuttle-fish ground up and blown into the eye three times a day through a pipe . . ." Compare this with "'resin-of-copper' and the 'white-drug' you pulverize, by means of a tube (?) of bronze you blow (it) into his eyes" (*CAD* 6 [Ḫ]: 189.

44. Cohen and Sivan (N 1): 10.

45. Cyrus H. Gordon, *Ugaritic Literature* (Rome: PBI, 1949): 129, see text 55:28 or 56:21 and 32. But see Gordon, *Textbook* (N 8): 418, no. 1210, "*khp*: verb describing a certain action of a horse."

46. Cohen and Sivan (N 1): 33.

47. By the way, there are some funny observations and some real mistakes in the Latin texts, but these people really knew a lot about animals. They were even concerned about the sounds that animals make. Varro (N 17): 315 (II, i, 6–7) says, in discussing sheep, "the Greeks call these *mēla* from the sound of their bleating" but he goes on to say that the bleating does not give the sound *me* but rather *be* (hence in Latin there is *balare*). However, on this question, the Greeks are correct.

48. Cohen and Sivan (N 1): 39 and also see K. Aartun, *Die Partikeln des Ugaritischen* II (AOAT 21, 2; Neukirchen-Vluyn: Neukirchener, 1978): 94, n. 940.

horse pawing the ground. I have come to the same position by relating *ykhp* to the Arabic root *khp* "cave" (the verbal form could mean "to dig"). I have not found in Columella any exact parallel to this symptom phrase, but there are some good examples of parallel structure within the symptom clause. The first example has to do with internal pain and indigestion in cattle. It is the pain that makes the animal bellow and among other things "toss its head and lash its tail continually" (*et agitare caput, caudamque crebrius agere cogit*).[49] A better example is where Columella is dealing with worms in horses. He says:

> It is a sign of their presence when horses roll about on the ground in internal pain or bring heads near their bellies or frequently flick their tails (*si admovent caput utero, si caudam saepius iactant*).[50]

These examples may not help us in any exact way (even if they go back to Magon), but I think that they point us in the right direction and they are full of very astute observations. In any case, I will suggest that "when [a horse] lowers its head and paws the ground incessantly," you have on your hands a horse in severe pain—a horse with colic. And this is the way I understand line 30.

Columella is the first Latin author to use the word *veterinarius*, "veterinarian."[51] After looking at all of the places where he uses this word, I would say that he sees the veterinarian as a very knowledgeable person—skilled in surgery and in all aspects of animal care. The word can refer to the skill of the farrier (as is also the case in Arabic), but I would not translate *veterinarius* in Book XI, i, 12, as "farrier."[52] Varro does not use this term, nor does he comment on it in his book *De Lingua Latina*. He does know the Greek term *hippiatros*.[53] Professor Calvin Schwabe of the School of Veterinary Medicine, University of California at Davis, has collected a lot of material on the etymology of the word "veterinary." There have been many etymological suggestions. Some have thought that it comes from *vetus* and others say that it is from *veho* by way of the form *veterinus*, "beast of burden."

49. Columella (N 19): II.149 (VI, vi, 3).
50. *Ibid.*: 207 (VI, xxx, 9).
51. *Ibid.*: 153 (VI, viii, 1), 249 (VII, iii, 16), 271 (v, 14).
52. *Ibid.*: 57. Here the veterinarian is a teacher.
53. Varro (N 17): 391 (II, vii, 14).

One of the most interesting references that Prof. Schwabe gave to me was by R. H. A. Merlen, a veterinarian at the Royal Veterinary College, London.[54] Merlen has some very interesting suggestions, and I think that he is on the right track. He suggests that the word *veterinarius* is from a Semitic root. The problem is that he mixes together *btr* (in Hebrew, Arabic, and Akkadian)[55] with *bṭr* (in Ugaritic and Arabic) which has the emphatic *ṭ*. Both roots can mean "to cut," but they should not be confused. Merlen makes some interesting points concerning how *bṭr* (my clarification) came into Latin in the translation of Magon. This is probably not the case because the translation was before the time of Varro and he did not use such a term. Merlen also suggests, as an alternative to his first suggestion, that Columella could have picked up the Punic word *bṭr* in Gades. This, I think, is much closer to a possible explanation.

But I would also change the direction just a bit. Columella and others did use Punic terms. It is possible that *bṭr* first came into Latin as *veterinus*, "beast of burden" or perhaps "castrated one."[56] In this case it would not be from *veho*. We know that *veterinus* was used by others before the time of Columella, but Columella was in the right place to know that the term *veterinus* was derived from the Punic *bṭr* which was a professional term designating the skilled surgeon. So, if Columella wanted a professional term in Latin it would be very natural to take *veterinus* plus *-arius* equaling *veterinarius* (analogous to *ferrarius* and *vinarius*), i.e., one who deals with such animals.[57] In other words, the Punic vet gave his name first to the pack animal and only later to the professionals.

I think it is an interesting theory, and we should remember that Columella has detailed information from Magon on all aspects of castration.[58] This does not mean that Columella used *veterinarius* only in this narrow sense. It became a very broad term, in part

54. R. H. A. Merlen, "A Note on the Word 'Veterinary,'" *The Veterinary Record* 89 (July 31, 1971): 136–138. (This is the journal of the British Veterinary Association.)

55. Akkadian is a problem. See *AHW*: 144, for *butturu* meaning "to cut" and a "Pferdename." This could be important, but both von Soden and *CAD* 2 (B): 356 read it this way and von Soden relates it to Hebrew *btr*. My question would be can we read this *buṭṭuru*?

56. Merlen (N 54) also makes a similar suggestion. You do not need a stud horse in a pack-train.

57. This is comparable to the use of Greek *temnō*.

58. Columella (N 19): II.187–189 (VI, xxvi, 1–4).

because Latin had its own terms for castration and beasts of burden (*castro* and *jumentum*). Obviously, I like the theory, because I want to see *bṭr* at Gades. But I too must wait for a text, and I wait in the Hebrew sense: I hope! It is very interesting to note that the second chapter of this story can be told as fact. At a much later time, the Semitic root *bṭr* in its Arabic form came into Spanish as *albeiteria* and into Portuguese as *alveiteria*.[59]

This essay is just that; it is an attempt, an attempt to test the waters. And at times I felt that I was at the wrong end of the Mediterranean. This feeling must be overcome. Fernand Braudel says that one of the great truths that remains unchallenged in his work on the Mediterranean is "the unity and coherence of the Mediterranean region."[60] For our studies we need more texts and a lot more work, but it is also important to give more than an academic nod to "unity and coherence." We do know some interesting things concerning the westward journey of veterinary traditions from Ugarit to Gades. This does not mean that the direction of other journeys of other traditions was always westward. But if we want to trace these journeys, we will need to prepare ourselves and set sail. In fact, after reading Professor Segert's *Grammar of Phoenician and Punic*, I would like to know a lot more about Plautus and his *Poenulus*. But first I think that I will try to reconstruct Magon's *Almanac*. We need to be like Braudel who says, "I have loved the Mediterranean with passion," but he also makes the land which surrounds the sea important—the task also needs those who "praise the sea and stay on land."[61]

59. Again, I thank Prof. Schwabe for this point.

60. Fernand Braudel, *The Mediterranean* I (tr. Sian Reynolds; New York: Harper & Row, 1972): 14.

61. *Ibid.*: 17.

MAARAV 5–6 (Spring, 1990): 221–237

SOME ORTHOGRAPHICO-PHONETIC PROBLEMS OF ANCIENT ARAMAIC AND THE LIVING ARAMAIC PRONUNCIATIONS

RUDOLF MACUCH
BERLIN

Stanislav Segert presented in his standard work, *Altaramäische Grammatik* (Leipzig 1975, 2nd ed. 1983), a complete formal treatment of all typical linguistic phenomena of three related literary periods of Ancient Aramaic (AA): Early, Imperial, and Biblical Aramaic (EA, RA [*Reichsaramäisch*], and BA respectively). In spite of some archaic traits of EA, which may be merely orthographic or really phonetic, the parallel description of these three periods of AA proved to be successful because of many problems common to both EA and RA and external uniformity of RA lasting for several centuries until the appearance of national Aramaic languages in writing (1.8),[1] by which the artificial compactness of Ancient Aramaic was broken.

Professor Segert's grammar is not only a useful tool for the understanding of ancient Aramaic documents (which was the author's main purpose, 0.1.9) but also a welcome introduction to all kinds of historical, orthographico-phonetic and other linguistic and grammatical problems of Aramaic in general. However, many open problems could only have been mentioned, because they are so complicated that their detailed discussion would burst the frame of a grammar destined for practical rather than merely theoretical

1. Numbers in parentheses refer to paragraphs of S. Segert, *Altaramäische Grammatik*.

purposes. Moreover, attempts to solve problems of ancient languages through later traditions or modern dialects are often problematical and can hardly be undertaken without reserve. It is difficult to impute later pronunciations to an ancient language, even if they correspond exactly to its orthographical forms, and it is still more difficult if the pronunciation has changed and no longer corresponds to the ancient orthography which already at that time might have been merely historical. Nevertheless, this hypothetical method of comparison of ancient languages with their late descendants is the only possible method in dealing with some vexing problems of AA orthography and phonetics, and Segert rightly recognized this comparative method as proper and helpful (3.1.4. *Heranziehung von anderen semitischen Sprachüberlieferungen*). As a sign of respect and tribute of honor to this outstanding colleague in Semitic studies may I present some of these problems on the margin of his Ancient Aramaic grammar by simply following the sequence in which he mentioned them.

I

The problem of AA pronunciation is complicated by the fact that the Aramaeans not only took over the Canaanite alphabet but also preserved a large number of Canaanite scribal practices, grammatical forms, and loan-words which they might have borrowed simultaneously with the script. Such simultaneous borrowings of foreign lexical and grammatical forms were not at all unusual in the Ancient Near East and are attested not only through Sumerian logograms in Akkadian long before the invention of the alphabet but also through Aramaic ideograms in the Middle Persian script, Pahlavi, a long time after it. A supposition of ideographical Canaanisms in Ancient Aramaic would be the easiest solution of the complicated problem of why AA scribes replaced the Proto-Semitic interdentals *ḏ* and *ṯ* by the Canaanite sibilants *z* and *š* (3.2.5.3.1) and not by simple Aramaic dentals *d* and *t* known from all living pronunciations of Aramaic, as the scribes themselves occasionally wrote them when they forgot the artificial rule and were writing as they spoke; conversely, they changed even an etymological *d* to *z* or *š* to *t* when they wanted to keep to a rule of historical orthography which they did not properly understand. This situation, as reflected in EA and RA, could obviously not have existed in a spoken language.

In spite of this statement it is not easy to consider the Canaanite elements in EA as mere ideograms. They are too numerous and not only of orthographical and lexical but also of syntactic nature, so much so that a prominent German Semitist, J. Friedrich, ventured to postulate a specific position for the language of the EA inscriptions of Ya'udī in the family of Northwest-Semitic languages.[2] He thought they contain too little Aramaic and too many peculiarities and archaisms for being simply considered as primitive Aramaic with Canaanite admixtures.[3] Friedrich's opinion called forth a lively discussion[4] which is not yet closed. Its outcome will probably be as Segert stated: "There are certain lexical and grammatical phenomena common to both Canaanite languages and the inscriptions of Ya'udī, but the character of the latter is predominantly Aramaic in both grammatical and lexical respects, although some typical traits of Aramaic, maybe even the determinate state, are missing" (1.4.2.2).

In Ya'udi inscriptions we still have to do with a *Vorstufe* of Aramaic, with an Aramaic-to-be, an archaic local dialect, in which underdeveloped Aramaic forms without literary tradition cannot be separated from orthographical, lexical, and even syntactical Canaanisms which already had a literary tradition of several centuries. But these and similar non-Aramaic elements are also attested in the inscriptions from Sfīre (1.4.3.5) not far away from Zencirli (Ya'udi) and written approximately at the same time as well as in some other EA inscriptions. Although these inscriptions manifest a certain progress of genuine Aramaic forms, they are still full of orthographical, lexical and even syntactical Canaanisms[5] and may even surpass Ya'udi inscriptions in this respect, cf. the Aramaic spelling of the ending of the imperfect of verbs III *y* in Ya'udi: *yrqy* H 22, *yršy* H 27 f., etc., against the Canaanite spelling

2. J. Friedrich, *Phönizisch-punische Grammatik* (Analecta Orientalia 32; Rome: PBI, 1951): 153ff., and "Zur Stellung des Jaudischen in der nordwestsemitischen Sprachgeschichte," *Studies in Honor of Benno Landsberger* (Assyriological Studies 16; Chicago: University of Chicago, 1965): 425–429.

3. "Zur Stellung des Jaudischen" (N 2): Assyriological Studies 16; Chicago: University of Chicago, 428.

4. See bibliography to the problem of Ya'udi in *KAI* II: 214.

5. See Ruth Stiehl, *Kanaanäisch und Aramäisch*, in F. Altheim-R. Stiehl, *Die Araber in der alten Welt* I (Berlin: de Gruyter): 213–236; J. C. Greenfield, *Qawwīm diyaleqṭiyyīm bā-ārāmīt ha-qədūmā*, in *Lešōnēnū*, 32 (1968): 359–369; R. Macuch, "Gesprochenes Aramäisch und aramäische Schriftsprache," in F. Altheim-R. Stiehl, *Christentum am Roten Meer* I (Berlin: de Gruyter): 537–557.

in Sfīre: *yhwh* A II 4, *ybʿh* B II 8, etc., whereas feminine forms are already spelled in an Aramaic way as in Ya'udī: *thry* A I, *thwy* A I 25, 32, etc.[6] There can hardly be a doubt that the forms ending in *-h* and in *-y* could have been pronounced differently and that the difference was not merely orthographical.

The greatest problem, however, consists in syntactical Canaanisms which can hardly be depreciated as merely orthographical phenomena. The most surprising is the double use of the typically non-Aramaic *waw consecutivum imperfecti* in a short phrase in the inscription of the king *Zkr: wʾśʾ ydy ʾl bʿlš*[*my*]*n wyʿnny bʿlšmy*[*n*] A 11 "and I raised my hands to B., and B. answered me."[7]

This construction is known only from an earlier period of Hebrew, from which it was later also driven out under Aramaic influence. An explanation of its occurrence in an EA inscription is extremely difficult, but it is easier to explain it as a literary cliché than as a specimen of spoken AA. In this sense I have to rectify a concession I made to Friedrich nineteen years ago.[8] Written forms had greater vigor than spoken language. Writing in the Ancient Near East was an exclusive business of official scribes who kept to literary traditions more than to the language spoken by themselves. The inscriptions they made were not destined for the masses, who did not know how to read. If they wanted to understand the inscriptions they needed interpreters as for a foreign language. And if the scribe of the *Zkr* inscription had to interpret his *waw consecutiva imperfecti* quoted above, he could hardly have done it without using the normal Aramaic construction with the perfect in both cases.

Nevertheless, this strange syntactical example clearly proves how far EA scribes could have gone in imitating foreign models of a language written long before they started to write. Taking over a script meant much more than learning the alphabet. It meant to adapt oneself completely to the literary culture of a foreign language, not only in its orthography but also in its vocabulary and phraseology. The ancient scribes were bilingual, and it was sometimes easier for them to write as they were used to reading a foreign language rather than adapting its script to their own speech, as it may be sufficiently proved by the borrowing of

6. Macuch, "Gesprochenes Aramäisch" (N 5): 545.

7. Stiehl, (N 5): 232; Macuch, "Gesprochenes Aramäisch" (N 5): 545f.

8. Macuch, Ibid., 546.

Aramaic ideograms into Middle Persian Pahlavi script about a thousand years later.

The inventor has a higher position than an imitator. People who invented scripts for their own languages debarred themselves from foreign influence and took a leading role in the cultural history of mankind. People who thoughtlessly imitated them entered a spiritual dependence from which they were unable to free themselves for long centuries to come. That we find too little Aramaic in EA inscriptions uselessly overloaded by Canaanite elements may exactly be due to the fact that the Aramaeans adopted the Canaanite alphabetical script without properly adapting it to their own language, and their scribes were more comfortable writing in Canaanite than in Aramaic.

These superfluous Canaanisms were successively eliminated in later Aramaic inscriptions, which imitated a new artificial language, RA, introduced by official Assyrian and Iranian scribes. But even this new scribal tradition was unable to get rid of orthographical Canaanite inheritance completely. The Proto-Semitic interdentals *ḏ* and *ṯ* continued to be written *z* and *š*, as in Canaanite and Akkadian, and were only occasionally and rarely replaced by *d* and *t*, as they were really spoken, and their rendering through *z* and *š* became so popular that the scribes saw no inconvenience in replacing even an etymological *d* and *t* through *z* and *š*.

Much scholarly effort has gone into attempts at a historico-phonetical explanation of this merely orthographical and phonetically irrelevant phenomenon. Scholarly opinions have been comprehensively summarized by Ruth Stiehl in her chapter *Kanaanäisch und Aramäisch*,[9] where she adduced all pertinent material and added conclusive solutions. Whereas she is right as to the strange spelling of the frequent technical juridical term of the Jewish papyri of Elephantine *dyn wdbb* "suit and process" as *zyn wzbb* Kraeling 3:17, which she considers as a "mistake due to excessive archaizing"[10] (just as Joshua Blau later designated it as a "hyper-archaic form,"[11] her conclusion that similar allophonic spellings in Mandaic, even *zyqlʾ* "palm" and *zmʾ* "blood," ought to

9. See note 5.

10. "Fehler infolge übereifriger Archaisierung," p. 233.

11. J. Blau, *On Pseudo-Corrections in Some Semitic Languages* (Jerusalem: Israel Academy of Sciences and Humanities, 1970): 47.

represent actual pronunciation[12] is valid only of the traditional, not of the living colloquial pronunciation.

The occurrence of the doublets *zahḇā/dahḇā* "gold," *ziqnā/deqnā* "beard," *ZḴR-DḴR* "to remember" and some others, the initial *z-d* of which goes back to Proto-Semitic *ḏ*, in Mandaic[13] is indeed surprising. It is against all expectation that particularly the Mandaeans who more than other Aramaeans broke with the traditional orthography would have preserved such a typical historico-orthographical phenomenon of AA, and yet it is not the only one (see II). The fact that the Mandaeans in spite of all the freedoms of their otherwise largely phonetic spelling could not get rid of this heritage of historical orthography of AA may be considered as one of the strongest proofs of its vigor. It is less surprising that after having accepted the double spelling with *z-d* in words going back to Proto-Semitic *ḏ*, the Mandaeans extended it by false analogy also to *zeqlā-deqlā* and *zəma-dəmā*, in which *d* is etymological. They were unable to distinguish between right and wrong, and their traditional pronunciation inclines to read all these words literally as they are written. Fortunately, all these words remained in colloquial Mandaic and are pronounced exclusively with *d*: *dahḇa*, *deqnā*, *edḵar* as well as *deqlā* and *dəmā*. Accordingly, there was no double pronunciation of literary doublets in the living language, and traditional readings attributing phonetic value to historical orthography are based on ignorance of historico-orthographical rules. Double spellings and especially hyperarchaizing pseudo-corrections in AA prove that this ignorance is almost as ancient as the historical orthography itself.

A supposition that the replacing of Proto-Semitic interdentals through dentals started in the East of the Aramaic speaking world and might only later have reached the Western Aramaeans who could originally have used the sibilants in their stead (3.2.6.3) need not be excluded. But such a possibility could hardly account for the Mandaean historical orthography which could not have been fixed before the third Christian century. The problem seems to be merely orthographical.

12. Ibid.; Blau rightly considers these forms as hyper-archaic.

13. Th. Nöldeke, *Mandäische Grammatik* (Darmstadt: Wissenschafliche Buchgesellschaft, 1964 [1875]): 43f. (§46). R. Macuch, *Handbook of Classical and Modern Mandaic* (Berlin: de Gruyter, 1965): 66–69 (§38).

II

A similar problem of AA is the rendering of the Proto-Semitic voiced emphatic lateral spirant *ḍ* through the postvelar occlusive *q* and later through the fricative pharyngeal ᶜ, through which it was replaced in Aramaic dialects. The most frequent and typical examples are *ᵓrqᵓ*, later *ᵓrᶜᵓ* (< *ᵓrḍ*) "earth" and *qmrᵓ*, later *ᶜmrᵓ* (< *ḍmr*) "wool"; both the older and the younger form of the former occur in an Aramaic gloss in Jer 10:11 (3.2.7.6). Whereas the replacing of Proto-Semitic interdentals *ḏ* and *ṯ* through Canaanite-Akkadian sibilants *z* and *š* instead of the dentals *d* and *t* of the actual Aramaic pronunciation (see above) is merely orthographic, the writing of Proto-Semitic *ḍ* with *q* might have had a phonetic reason for which the scribes did not dare to designate it simply with *ṣ*, by which it was replaced in Canaanite and Akkadian. The *q* < *ḍ* must have had some phonetic value, which differed from both the Canaanite-Akkadian *ṣ* and the ᶜ of the later Aramaic pronunciation, although a later scribe of Jer 10:11 could no more distinguish between the ancient historico-orthographical *ᵓarqā* and the later phonetical *ᵓarᶜā* and wrote both almost side by side. But in spite of this carelessness and lack of distinction of the later Aramaeans themselves, it is a problem which still may cause scholars many sleepless nights.

The main difficulty of this problem consists in the fact that neither the original pronunciation of the Proto-Semitic *ḍ* nor that of the ancient Aramaic *q* which replaced it is known to us, and we can only postulate both according to our imagination. According to C. Brockelmann,[14] the Proto-Semitic *ḍ* > *q* ought to be conceived as "a sounding velar explosive," which later passed to "the spirant *ǵ* parallel to the change of the Proto-Semitic *ǵ* to ᶜ." According to H. H. Schaeder,[15] it was "an emphatic, probably velar spirant" with a tendency "to pass into a laryngeal through the pushing back of the place of articulation (*durch Rückverlegung der Artikulationsstelle*)." Similarly Segert defined it as a postvelar spirant (3.2.6.5). This is the standard explanation of the phenomenon, and due to the mentioned difficulty, we shall hardly

14. *Grundriß der vergleichenden Grammatik der semitischen Sprachen* I (Hildesheim, 1961): 134.

15. *Iranische Beiträge*, I, p. 246f.

learn much more about it. In a dissertation *The Case for Fricative-Laterals in Proto-Semitic* by Richard C. Steiner,[16] dedicated to the fate of Proto-Semitic *ḍ* and *š*, this problem was neglected. Although the author presented the following correct paradigmatic development (p. 115)

	alveolar lateral		velar		pharyngeal
emphatic	*ḍ*	⟶	q_2	⟶	ʕ
	↓		↓		↓
unemphatic	*s′* (>s)		*g*		ʔ (>∅)

and treated at large the fate of Proto-Semitic *ś* in different Semitic languages (pp. 111–120) or *ḍ* > *ṣ* in pre-Aramaic (pp. 149–154) etc., the problem of *ḍ* > *q* in AA escaped his attention.

At any rate, this secondary *q*—we may designate it with Steiner as q_2 in order to distinguish it from the etymological *q*—seems to have been only an approximate sign for a sound for which the Canaanite-Aramaic alphabet had no proper letter. But we have to assume that it did not yet completely collapse with ᶜ as it did later. Under these circumstances, its pronunciation as a velar *ǵ* (supposed also by Segert 3.2.6.5) is the only possible assumption. It did not, however, enjoy a long life and its voice-shift to the pharyngeal ᶜ known from later Aramaic dialects except South-Babylonian already took place in the period of RA.

It is, therefore, most surprising that exactly the South-Babylonian Mandaeans, in whose language all laryngeals (except *h*) vanished and who divested themselves of the ballast of historical orthography to a high degree, preserved this ancient orthographical phenomenon in three words, *arqa* "earth," *aqna* "sheep," and *aqamra* "wool" (all three going back to Proto-Semitic *ḍ*), to which they "pseudo-correctly" added even *aqapra* (:*-frā*) "dust," the *q* of which stands in the place of the Proto-Semitic ᶜ.

The orthographico-phonetic problem caused by the *q* in these four words in Mandaic is as complicated as that of the replacing of the Proto-Semitic *ḍ* through *q* in AA. At the time when Mandaic orthography was fixed, all Aramaeans wrote and pronounced these words with ᶜ and there was absolutely no trace of its pronunciation as a postvelar fricative which may be postulated for an earlier

16. New Haven, Conn., 1977.

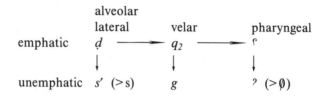

period of AA. It would be still more senseless to suppose that especially the Mandaeans, who had no ᶜ in their language before the invention of their alphabet would have preserved an ancient West-Aramaic pronunciation of q_2, ǵ, or however it might have sounded.

Nevertheless, it might have been exactly the circumstance that they had no ᶜ which forced the inventors of the Mandaean script to keep to the archaic AA orthography.

H. H. Schaeder[17] proposed a theory of inverse writing of the words *aqamra* and *aqna*: The Mandaeans probably took them over from some ancient scribal tradition and adapted them to their own pronunciation (*amrā* and *ānā*) by putting an *a* before *q*. He meant: "Es paßt zu dem 'Geist', wie er aus den Schriften der Mandäer weht, daß sie sich solche Mittel ausdachten, um ihrer Sprache Patina zu verleihen." This theory appears ingenious and seems to have been generally accepted, although the suspicion it implies can hardly be justified. The Mandaeans were certainly not looking for special means in order to give their scriptures an appearance of antiquity. They simply accepted the AA spelling of these words without deliberation, since they were unable to replace their *q* by ᶜ, because this had no consonantal but vocal value in their alphabet. Moreover, the superfluous prosthetic vowel is so frequent in Mandaic[18] that it is difficult to suppose that in these two cases it could exceptionally have been supposed to annul the following consonant. If the ancient scribes had really intended this annulment, they reached exactly the contrary of what they wanted, as is proved by the traditional pronunciation: *aqamra*, *aqna* and *aqafra*. The only word in which the *q* is recognized neither by the traditional nor by the colloquial pronunciation is *arqa*, pronounced *ara*, although it contains no prosthetic vowel. Words beginning with *aq*- are not rare in Mandaic[19] and several of them are provided with a superfluous prosthetic vowel which in no way indicates the annulment of the following *q*. How should later readers of Mandaic have realized that in *aqammī* "before him," *aqārī* "near him," etc., there is q_1 which ought to be pronounced, but *aqamra*, etc., contain q_2 which is to be omitted in pronunciation?

17. Ibid., 247 n. 2.

18. Macuch, *Handbook* (N 13): §77, pp. 124f., cf. Id., *Zur Sprache und Literatur der Mandäer* (*Studia Mandaica* I) (Berlin: de Gruyter, 1976): pp. 144ff.

19. See E. S. Drower and R. Macuch, *A Mandaic Dictionary* (Oxford: Clarendon, 1963): 35f.

For the hyper-archaic *aqapra* there is also a variant *agapra* (= *aǵafra*) proving that a literal reading of this word must have a longer tradition. This is all the more surprising as a shorter form of this word *apra* (= *afra*) occurs several times in both the classical and the postclassical literature and is the only form of the word used in modern Mandaic.

Similarly there are shorter variants of the other words: *amra* (MD 23 b) and *ana* (cf. *anai*, Johannesbuch 41:8, with secondary traditional pronunciation *anne* "my sheep"). The latter word is attested also in a metathesized form *anqia* (Gs 20:21) but in this case it is easier to assume a merely graphical metathesis of a silent letter than a real phonetic phenomenon. It was easier to change the place of a silent letter than of a sound which would really have been bound to the preceding vowel in pronunciation.[20]

The crucial word of this group is *arqa* pronounced *ara* in both the traditional and the colloquial pronunciation, although it is consistently written with *q*. Only in some modern corruptions of *arqa bigal* "dust on the feet" (a humble self-designation of copyists in colophons): *arbigal/r*, *arabigar*, *rbigar*, etc.[21] is its *q*, as a rule, omitted. But even these corrupt forms as well as the modern construct state *ar-tīḇel*[22] (< classical *arqa* [*d-*] *tibil*[23]) "earthly world" sufficiently prove that *arqa* could hardly ever have been pronounced with *q*, with which it is written. Similarly modern *afra* "dust" proves that the orthographical variants *aq/gafra* are artificial forms which never existed in the living language. As to the other two words (*aqamra* and *aqna*), there can hardly be a doubt that their living pronunciation could have corresponded only to their shorter doublets without *q*, whereas a mechanical literal reading of their ancient orthographical variants with *q* could have started only after these words died out. Unlike *arqa* = *ara*, their traditional pronunciation has no historical continuity.

III

A noteworthy peculiarity of EA is the spelling of *QTL* with a non-emphatic *t* which was replaced by *QṬL* only in RA (3.7.2.2.3).

20. See similar merely graphical metatheses of silent laryngeal letters in Samaritan Aramaic, R. Macuch, *Grammatik des Samaritanischen Aramäisch* (Berlin: de Gruyter, 1982): 19ff. (§6b).

21. Th. Nöldeke, *Mandäische Grammatik* (N 13): 79 with n. 2; Macuch, *Handbook* (N 13): 53f.

22. *Handbook* (N 13): 485a.

23. Drower and Macuch (N 19): 485a.

Apart from EA, Arabic and Ethiopic, the emphatic *ṭ* in this root is a common Semitic phenomenon and in Aramaic its emphasis became so strong that it occasionally caused regressive dissimilations of the preceding emphatic, as in *ykṭlwk* in the stele of Nerab (N I 11); in Mandaic there is not only a dissimilated *GṬL* but also a whole series of dissimilations *g* < *q* before *ṭ*.[24] It seems, however, that this *ṭ* which might have been progressively emphasized committed patricide and deprived the preceding sound—which caused its emphaticization—of its own emphatic character.

In EA, *QTL* might have been as natural as *qatala* in Arabic and Ethiopic, because its non-emphatic *t* was preserved from contamination with the preceding emphatic *q* by a full vowel in the basic form of the verb. A pronunciation *qāṭal* was possible without emphatic *t*, whereas a pronunciation *qṭal* was absolutely impossible without it. Once the language was used to this standard pronunciation it might have resisted the assimilation in the imperfect in which both sounds (*q* and *t*) came into immediate contact.

The reduction of a short vowel in open unstressed syllables did not develop in all Aramaic dialects equally and simultaneously. Some early West Aramaic dialects have even saved the vowel in this position through prolongation. In spite of all the doubts that may be raised against the traditional pronunciation of Samaritan Aramaic one must admit that its reading *šābaxtāni* Sam. Targ. Deut 28:20 admirably corresponds to the μεταγραφή of the same word said by Jesus on the cross, σαβαχθανεί (Matt 27:46, Mark 15:34) and both exhibit the same vocal structure.[25] It would be, therefore, quite natural to suppose a pronunciation *qāṭal* in Zencirli and Sfīre in the eighth century B.C.E.

IV

The AA pronunciation of *nḇš(h)* "soul" with a voiced *b* instead of the unvoiced *p* (3.7.2.4.1) is explicable by regressive dissimilation of sonority. It can still be observed in the frequent Neo-Mandaic reflexive pronoun *nāḇš-*[26] and it is also proved by Neo-Syriac *nōš(a)*[27] (< **naḇš-*). Living West Aramaic dialects re-

24. *Handbook* (N 13): 74:6–20.

25. Macuch, *Grammatik* (N 20): 61–63 (§14 ea).

26. Macuch, *Handbook* (N 13): LXI. Several examples of this reflexive pronoun occur in my *Neumandäische Chrestomathie* (in "Porta Linguarum Orientalium," O. Harrassowitz, Wiesbaden).

27. R. Macuch and E. Panoussi, *Neusyrische Chrestomathie* (Wiesbaden: Harrassowitz, 1974): 94a.

placed this original Aramaic reflexive pronoun with other expressions borrowed from Arabic.

V

The dissimilatory as well as analogical infix *n* (less often *l* or *r*) is very typical for RA, although it has numerous parallels not only in Semitic but also in Indo-European languages. It mostly results from dissimilation of geminated consonants (3.7.5.3.1), but it may also repose on analogy (*Systemzwang*, 3.7.5.1.4) or other reasons.

Since in RA there are some cases of etymological spelling *n* + consonant on one hand and of the non-etymological infix *n* + consonant on the other, both kinds of spelling being inconsistent, different conceptions and quite contradictory solutions of the problem are logically possible. The etymological *n* was either not yet assimilated, which could contradict its assimilation in EA (cf. *ʾt* "thou" against *ʾnt* of the later RA and BA) as well as in later Aramaic dialects, which is improbable, or it might have resulted from redissimilation of the formerly assimilated *n*, which is still less possible. Less problematical may appear the non-etymological *n* resulting from dissimilation of geminated consonants or analogical nasalization confirmed through traditional pronunciation of BA as well as in different living Aramaic dialects and other Semitic languages.

An original solution of the problem was proposed by Anton Spitaler in his article "Zur Frage der Geminatendissimilation im Semitischen—Zugleich ein Beitrag zur Orthographie des Reichsaramäischen," *Indogermanische Forschungen*, LXI (1954): 257–266. The etymological *n* which was totally assimilated in EA and retained this status in later Aramaic dialects could certainly not have been secondarily redissimilated in the period of RA; its use in the script simply meant the reduplication of the following consonant. The non-etymological *n* was simply a graphical analogy of the former and could never have had real phonetic value. This is one extreme position.

A second extreme position was taken by me in the introduction to my *Handbook of Classical and Modern Mandaic*, pp. XLVII–LIII, where in a uselessly sharp polemic tone, which I regret, I pretended that this secondary graphical *n* must have absolutely had phonetic value in all cases. Since I included my hard attack on Spitaler's theory in my introduction to a language the name of which would not be possible without an infixed *n*, a superficial reader might have got an impression that I feared that Spitaler's merely logical and theoretical proposal would endanger the pronunciation of the name of this language and religion. In fact, J. Blau[28] pronounced this opinion: "Macuch was, it seems, upset by the fact that Spitaler's theory allegedly affected the pronunciation of the word, 'Mandaic', and he therefore included his attack on his Mandaic *Handbook* (!)," as if a discussion of this problem were there out of place!

In order to avoid future misunderstandings a reconsideration of the above mentioned extreme positions is necessary.

Spitaler's point of view is strictly logical. Its fault is that it is *only* logical, concentrated exclusively on an inconsistent scribal practice and consciously excluding the possibilities of different pronunciations in the living language recognized by the author himself.[29] Another defect of his short article about this complicated problem is that it was written in haste and the author did not sufficiently develop all plausible ideas he must have had in mind and could therefore easily be misunderstood.

My mentioned rejoinder suffers from essential misunderstanding of this exclusively logical theory. RA was a literary language the pronunciation of which will always remain unknown and might even have been artificial to a high degree. We are not authorized to impute to it any of the later traditional and living pronunciations of Aramaic, although on the other hand we are not allowed to ignore them. But the value of both the written and the spoken forms remains merely relative. This statement does not, of course, bring us closer to the knowledge of the pronunciation of RA but it saves us from hasty conclusions.

The masoretes of classical Syriac, a similarly literary language spread over a greater part of the former Achaemenid Empire, introduced a *linea occultans* over each etymological or non-etymological *n* which ought not to be pronounced and was merely meant to designate the gemination of the following consonant. This practice might have reposed on an orthographical heritage of RA notwithstanding the diffusion of the secondary *n* in different

28. Blau (N 11): 126 n. 2.

29. "Es ist natürlich nicht zu leugnen, daß in der lebenden Sprache Formen mit und ohne Dissimilation nebeneinander denkbar sind und auch wirklich vorkommen," Spitaler (see above, p. 232): 263.

Syriac dialects. A similar practice might have been transmitted orally in RA long before the invention of the *linea occultans* of the Syriac masoretes since RA was a normalized literary, not a spoken, language.

Nevertheless, a merely oral tradition has no great chance to outlive the spoken language if it consistently contradicts its most popular forms. Who can guarantee that mediocre readers will always read the language according to its ancient artificial rules and not as they are used to speak it? The situation of the South-Babylonian Jews and Mandaeans was quite different from that of the North-Mesopotamian Christians of Syriac language living in the greater part of the former Achaemenid empire from northern Iran up to Turkey and Lebanon. Whereas the latter continued to suppress the popular infix *n* appearing in the script in the sense of the ancient tradition of Official Aramaic, the former must have been glad to be finally able to break with this superfluous traditional ballast and to write as they spoke and to read as they wrote.

Under these circumstances neither the abundance of the infix *n*'s in the South-Babylonian Aramaic of the Jews and Mandaeans nor their recognizing of its phonetic value in their traditional reading of these languages is surprising. In this corner of the Aramaic-speaking world this infix was a living phenomenon. The speakers had already gotten used to it through numerous Sumero-Akkadian and ancient Iranian loan-words. In the orthography of the latter this infix did not even appear in the script but must have been pronounced according to the Avestan, Middle Persian and Modern Persian testimonies.[30] Accordingly, the infix *n* (before labials spelled phonetically *m*) might even have been more frequent in pronunciation than it appears in writing; compare *K^e^t̲īb̲: sypnyh* (Dan 3:10) against *Q^e^rê: sumponyāh* (Dan 3:5, 15) corresponding better to the original Greek συμφωνία.

This single example from BA would, of course, not suffice to combat Spitaler's theory of inverse spelling in RA and BA. Why should the Aramaeans have pronounced a Greek loan-word exactly as the Greeks did? In Syriac the same Greek loan-word was written as *ṣepponyā*, and the understanding of Greek phonetics in the South of Mesopotamia was hardly better than in the North where not only numerous Greek loan-words but also syntactical elements invaded the language. The mentioned *K^e^t̲īb̲*, Dan 3:10 (expected

30. Macuch, *Mandäer* (N 18): 5f.

pronunciation **si/upponyā*) could even confirm Spitaler's theory: The totally assimilated form would be better Aramaic according to the Syriac model. But on the other hand why should *sumponyāh* have been written phonetically with *m* and not with *n*? The indication of a phonetic reality (regressive labialization of *n*) could hardly have belonged to the conditions of inverse writing of the presumed historical orthography.[31]

The phonetic taste of Syriac scribal practices was quite different from South-Mesopotamian Aramaic. The former totally assimilated etymological *n* to the dentals and labials and did not recognize the phonetic value of the secondary *n* when it appeared in the script, which was possible in a normalized literary language. The latter, as a rule, recognized the phonetic value of the infix they used in daily speech. But as to the etymological *n* totally assimilated to the following dental in North-Mesopotamian and Western Aramaic dialects, the South-Babylonians not only retained it in the script, but also their later traditional pronunciations recognized its phonetic value, whereas originally it might have represented only an inverse writing, as Spitaler rightly assumed. This may be sufficiently proved by some examples from modern Mandaic which contradict the classical spelling as well as its literal traditional pronunciation.

The most frequent word of this kind is the pronoun of the 2nd person sg. and pl. *att* and *atton*, written *ant* Q (Kt. *'nth*) and *antūn* in BA. Classical Mandaic exhibits strange forms *anat*, pl. *anatun* (read *anatton*), for which spoken Mandaic knows only *at* and *atton*. The insertion of *a* in the classical forms is hardly explicable through natural phonetic development which ought to have preserved the etymological *n* from total regressive assimilation. It is still less appropriate to have given way to the simple Neo-Mandaic forms in which not only this assimilation took place but which also may with full right be considered as originally Aramaic and even more ancient than the classical spelling which ought to represent an inverse writing according to Spitaler's theory or that of Schaeder *à propos* of *aqamra*, etc. (see above).

Further examples: Neo-Mandaic *eṯṯā* = classical *ʿnta* (traditional pronunciation *enṯā*) "woman"; *appā* = cl. *anpia* (: *anp/fī*), and so on. At least in such cases, in which modern Mandaic exhibits total regressive assimilation of etymological *n*, its classical spelling ought

31. Ibid.

to be considered as merely orthographical in spite of the popularity of the infix *n* in this language.[32]

Despite the fact that Spitaler's theory of inverse writing in RA has been rehabilitated, there still remains the question of how far the recognition of the phonetic value of the secondary *n* in BA is justified. Spitaler's statement about the reliability of the traditional reading of the Jewish masoretes was negative.[33] It obviously could not have met with general agreement. After my attempt to refute his theory on the basis of the traditional pronunciation of Mandaic and parallel developments in other Semitic languages,[34] J. Blau tried to disprove it on similar grounds by adducing some examples from Arabic (mostly known already from Aramaic) and a μεταγραφή of a Palmyrenian proper name.[35] Both refutations remain ineffective, because these and similar examples were known to Spitaler and he purposely pronounced his theory against them. An orthographical practice of an ancient language can be disproved neither by examples from later languages nor by problematic traditional pronunciations or inconsistent transliterations. It has to be treated exclusively as an inner concern of people who used to write and read it.

We have seen (I–II) that Mandaic stood very close to the historical orthography of RA in spite of all its orthographical freedoms with which it surpassed all other Aramaic dialects. In the case of the infix *n* it was also closely connected with RA, although it surpassed it in the free use of this infix. I am forced to declare that especially the word "ma*n*da"—in which some scholars, among them also J. Blau, inclined to seek my main argument against Spitaler's theory—has absolutely no importance for this problem, because it was coined by the founders of the Mandaean religion, not by its believers. It is noteworthy that as opposed to BA (*inda*^{c}, *tinda*^{c}, *yind*$^{e c}$*ûn*, *manda*^{c}) Mandaic knows only non-dissimilated forms of the verb *YDA* (< *yd*^{c}): *nidda*, *tidda*, etc., and for profane wisdom it uses *madda*, not *manda*, which remained reserved to the highest religious notions "gnosis" and "gnostic Saviour" which were certainly not invented by common people. The founders of the Mandaean religion found this word in a written, most probably

32. For further examples, including some "hyper-correct" writings of the infix *n*, see *Einführung, Anhang* 1, to my *Neumandäische Chrestomathie* (N 26).

33. Spitaler (see above, p. 232): 263.

34. *Handbook* (N 13): XLVIIff.

35. Blau (N 11): 127–129.

Jewish source. The people could easily learn and understand it, because they were used to the infix *n* from their common language reposing on a Babylonian substratum. But this is the only word in which this infix has become prominently phonemic. However, because its distinctive value was merely artificial, it never entered into any other form of the verb *YDA*.

As a result, Ma*n*daic as a language and religion of the infix *n* *par excellence* proves in no way that the BA verbal forms *ʾindaʿ* and so forth must have been pronounced with the secondary *n* with which they are written. If the Mandaeans, in whose language this infix is so popular and in whose religion it plays such a prominent role were satisfied with the consistent pronunciation *nidda*, etc., a similar pronunciation might have accounted for RA and BA as well. It is, therefore, possible and probable that in the second century B.C.E. when the book of Daniel was written this orthographical *n* might not have been consistently pronounced. But it must have already been pronounced at the beginning of our era when the founders of the Mandaean religion took over the word *manda*(ʿ) from a Jewish or a related source. Therefore, the Jewish masoretes by their sanctioning of the phonetic value of this secondary *n* might have preserved not an original but rather an ancient traditional pronunciation going back to the beginning of our era.

MAARAV 5-6 (Spring, 1990): 239-280

STRUCTURE AND MEANING IN HEBREW POETRY: THE EXAMPLE OF PSALM 23

DENNIS PARDEE
THE UNIVERSITY OF CHICAGO

To understand how a poem is constructed is to begin to understand what it expresses.[1]

In my previous studies of Ugaritic and Hebrew poetry I have chosen examples of poems of which the structure was relatively regular.[2] It now appears high time to try out the interpretative tools explored in *Hebrew and Ugaritic Poetic Parallelism* on a somewhat more recalcitrant example. A poem of which the structure fits poorly into the now traditional analysis according to *parallelismus membrorum* will also provide the opportunity to deal directly with the problem of the dividing line between poetry and prose.[3]

1. A. Berlin, "The Rhetoric of Psalm 145," *Biblical and Related Studies Presented to Samuel Iwry* (eds. A. Kort, S. Morschauser; Winona Lake, IN: Eisenbrauns, 1985): 17-22, quotation from p. 18.

2. Psalm 89 ("The Semantic Parallelism of Psalm 89," *In the Shelter of Elyon: Essays on Ancient Palestinian Life and Literature in Honor of G. W. Ahlström* [JSOT , Supplement Series, vol. 31, 1984] 121-37); *ʿnt* III 37′-IV 51′ ("Will the Dragon Never Be Muzzled?", *UF* 16 [1984] 251-55); *ʿnt* I and Proverbs 2 (*Ugaritic and Hebrew Poetic Parallelism: A Trial Cut (ʿnt I and Proverbs 2)* [Leiden: Brill, 1988]).

3. J. Kugel, *The Idea of Biblical Poetry* (New Haven: Yale University Press, 1981). See especially his comments on this psalm on pp. 49-51.

Psalm 23 appears particularly appropriate for such a study for several reasons: (1) The text is relatively sure and one can concentrate for the most part on interpretation rather than on textual criticism; (2) The psalm is extremely well known and its cadences roll off of many of our lips, either in Hebrew or in translation, and it is of interest to take a new look to see to what extent these cadences reflect poetic structure; (3) Though this psalm has often been studied, often indeed from one or the other of the perspectives utilized below,[4] I know of no study that attempts a global analysis in which all forms of parallelism/repetition are sought out in their principal distributions. This study attempts, therefore, to answer the following questions: Does Psalm 23 fit the broad definitions that have been given of poetry in general and, more particularly, does it fit those that have been devised for Hebrew poetry?[5] Should the answer to that double question be positive, does Psalm 23 nevertheless require changes in our description of Hebrew poetry?

Text and Translation

1) A psalm of the David-cycle.	מזמור לדוד
YHWH is my shepherd, I shall lack nothing:	יהוה רעי לא אחסר
2) In grassy pastures he has me lie,	בנאות דשא ירביצני
Beside restful waters he leads me;	על מי מנחות ינהלני
3) He gives me new life,	נפשי ישובב
He leads me in the right ways	ינחני במעגלי צדק
For his own name's sake.	למען שמו
4) Even when I go	גם כי אלך
Through the darkest valley	בגיא צלמות
I do not fear any evil;	לא אירא רע

4. T. J. Meek, "The Metrical Structure of Psalm 23," *JBL* 67 (1948): 233–235; G. Schramm, "Poetic Patterning in Biblical Hebrew," *Michigan Oriental Studies in Honor of George C. Cameron* (ed. L. L. Orlin; Ann Arbor: Univ. of Michigan, 1976): 167–191, esp. 187–191; S. Mittmann, "Aufbau und Einheit des Danklieds Psalm 23," *ZTK* 77 (1980): 1–23.

5. For bibliography, see Pardee, "Ugaritic and Hebrew Metrics," *Ugarit in Retrospect: Fifty Years of Ugarit and Ugaritic* (ed. G. D. Young; Winona Lake, IN: Eisenbrauns, 1981): 113–130, and "Ugaritic and Hebrew Poetry: Parallelism," Appendix I in *Ugaritic and Hebrew Poetic Parallelism* (N 2).

When you are with me,	כי אתה עמדי
Your rod and your staff,	שבטך ומשענתך
They are what comfort me.	המה ינחמני
5) You spread a table in front of me,	תערך לפני שלחן
Over against my adversaries;	נגד צררי
You anoint my head with oil,	דשנת בשמן ראשי
My cup is full.	כוסי רויה
6) Yes, goodness and kindness will stay by me	אך טוב וחסד ירדפוני
As long as I live:	כל ימי חיי
I will return to the house of YHWH	ושבתי בבית יהוה
As long as I live.	לארך ימים

Vocalized Text

1) *ʾmizmôr l^{ə}dāwīd*

yahwe^{h} rōʿi^{y} lōʾ ʾeḥsār
2) *binʾō^{w}t dešeʾ yarbī^{y}ṣēnī^{y}*
ʿal-mē^{y} m^{ə}nūḥō^{w}t y^{ə}naḥălēnī^{y}

3) *napšī^{y} y^{ə}šō^{w}bēb*
yanḥēnī^{y} b^{ə}maʿg^{ə}lē^{y}-ṣedeq
l^{ə}maʿan š^{ə}mō^{w}

4) *gam kī^{y}-ʾēlēk*
b^{ə}gēʾ ṣalmāwet
lōʾ-ʾī^{y}rāʾ rāʿ

kī^{y}-ʾattā^{h} ʿimmādī^{y}
šibṭ^{ə}kā ū^{w}mišʿantekā
hēmmā^{h} y^{ə}naḥămūnī^{y}

5) *taʿărōk l^{ə}pānay šulḥān*
neged ṣōr^{ə}rāy

diššantā baššemen rōʾšī^{y}
kō^{w}sī^{y} r^{ə}wāyā^{h}

6) *ᵓak ṭōʷb wāḥesed yirdᵊpūʷnīʸ*
kol-yᵊmēʸ ḥayyāy

wᵊšabtīʸ bᵊbēʸt-yahweʰ
lᵊᵓōrek yāmīʸm

Quantitative Analysis

	Word Count[6]	Syllable Count	Consonant Count[7]	Vocable Count[8]	Verse-unit Count[9]
1–2)	3//3//3	7//9//10[10]	13//15//15	22//25//27	3//3//3
3)	2//3//2	5//9//5	9//14//7	15//24//12	2//3//1[11]
4a)	2//2//2	4//5//4	7//9//8	13//14//13	2//2//2
4b)	2//2//2	6//8//7	9//11//9	18//21//19	2//2//2
5a)	3//2	8//6	12//7	23//14	3//1
5b)	3//2	8//5	12//8	23//14	3//2
6a)	3//2	9//5	16//8	26//15	3//2
6b)	3//2	7//5	13//8	20//15	2//1

REMARKS:

Since the structure of a Ugaritic or Hebrew poem often centers around semantic parallelism and the semantic parallelism is what is most obviously missing in this work, the quantitative divisions are

6. Single particles are not counted as "words" but compound particles, such as *l mᶜn* in vs. 3, are.

7. Consonant count is the quantification device utilized by O. Loretz: "Die Analyse der ugaritischen und hebräischen Poesie mittels Stichometrie und Konsonantenzählung," *UF* 7 (1975): 265–269 (see assessment in *Ugaritic and Hebrew Poetic Parallelism* [N 2]: n. 8); idem, "Kolometrie ugaritischer und hebräischer Poesie: Grundlagen, informationstheoretische und literaturwissenschaftliche Aspekte," *ZAW* 98 (1986): 249–266.

8. A system of analysis devised by D. N. Freedman: "Strophe and Meter in Exodus 15," *A Light Unto My Path: Old Testament Studies in Honor of Jacob M. Myers* (eds. H. N. Bream et al., Philadelphia: Temple Univ., 1974): 163–203, esp. 169 (see my *Ugaritic and Hebrew Poetic Parallelism* [N 2]: n. 9).

9. B. Margalit's term for his metrical units: "Studia Ugaritica I: 'Introduction to Ugaritic Prosody'," *UF* 7 (1975): 289–313 (see *Ugaritic and Hebrew Poetic Parallelism* [N 2]: n. 10).

10. "Medial" shewa is not vocalized above but will be counted as a syllable because it represents a historical vowel (the Massoretic vocalization is generally followed for syllable and vocable counting; for the pros and cons of analyzing the "historical" versus the Massoretic text, see my *Ugaritic and Hebrew Poetic Parallelism* [N 2]: § 2.8.1).

11. See Margalit (N 9): 295–296.

not at all obvious. The divisions just indicated are the result of extensive cogitation and discussion[12] and are tied in with many considerations regarding both the micro-structure and the macro-structure of the text.[13] These aspects will be alluded to in the course of the following analyses and the question of divisions will be discussed again in the conclusions.

It might be observed at this point, however, that taking verses 5 and 6 as two long-member bicola would produce lines considerably longer than those lines that are characterized by reasonably good parallelism, especially the last two line-segments of vss. 1–2 and the first two of vs. 3. The counts would be:

5)	5//5	14//13	19//20	37//37	4//5
6)	5//5	14//12	24//21	41//35	5//3

It can further be observed that if the division of vss. 5 and 6 proposed here is correct, these four bicola give little comfort to the theory that the 3//2 meter is properly denoted *qinah* "lamentation," for these lines contain the portion of this text which refers to the victory celebration.

12. I wish to thank the members of classes in Hebrew poetry in which this psalm was taught for their many probing questions and enlightening comments.

13. For bibliography on recent studies of Hebrew "metrics" see *JNES* 42 (1983): 299, n. 3. For a conspectus of divisions of Psalm 23, see O. Loretz, "Psalmenstudien III," *UF* 6 (1974): 174–210, esp. 187–191 (to which one may add T. J. Meek, "The Metrical Structure of Psalm 23," *JBL* 67 [1948]: 233–235, with previous literature). Loretz' own division (p. 190) is a radical rejection of about two-thirds of the work as secondary. Such an analysis assumes that a "poem" could not be created in the present form—a hypothesis that has yet to be proven (see my review of Loretz' *Der Prolog des Jesaja Buches (1,1-2, 5). Ugaritologische und kolometrische Studien zum Jesaja-Buch I* [Ugaritisch-Biblische Literatur 1; Altenberge: Akademische Bibliotek, 1984], *JAOS* 107 [1987]:143–144). D. N. Freedman's division of this poem ("The Twenty-third Psalm," *Michigan Oriental Studies in Honor of George G. Cameron* [ed. L. L. Orlin: Ann Arbor: Univ. of Michigan, 1976]: 139–166 [reprinted unchanged in *Poetry, Poetry, and Prophecy: Studies in Early Hebrew Poetry* (Winona Lake, IN: Eisenbrauns, 1980): 275–302]) seems to reflect his search for "strophes" and "stanzas" rather than the poetic structure. I cannot account otherwise for his assignment of vs. 4a to the preceding unit; none of the authors cited by Loretz adopt such a division and it appears to me to be out of the question. This approach is a form of metricism and must be rejected on that account. A more recent and more overtly metrical analysis is that of Mittmann (N 4), who finds in Ps 23 lines of five accents (2 + 3 or 3 + 2). If the recent repudiations of Hebrew metricism alluded to at the head of this note were not convincing enough, Mittmann's divisions would do the trick: the first two words are taken to be extra-metrical and the entire second half of vs. 4, from *kī*^{y} *ʾattā*^{h} on, is labled a "Zusatz" (p. 2).

Parallelism: Repetitive Parallelism

1–2)	yhwh rʿy lʾ ʾḥsr	yhwh lʾ						
	b nʾwt dšʾ yrbyṣny		b					
	ʿl-my mnḥwt ynhlny							
3)	npšy yšwbb			yšwbb				
	ynḥny b mʿgly-ṣdq		b					
	l mʿn šmw				l			
4a)	gm ky-ʾlk					ky		
	b gyʾ ṣlmwt		b					
	lʾ-ʾyrʾ rʿ	lʾ						
4b)	ky-ʾth ʿmdy					ky		
	šbṭk w mšʿntk						w	
	hmh ynḥmny							
5a)	tʿrk l pny šlḥn				l			
	ngd ṣrry							
5b)	dšnt b šmn rʾšy		b					
	kwsy rwyh							
6a)	ʾk ṭwb w ḥsd yrdpwny						w	
	kl-ymy ḥyy							ymy
6b)	w šbty b byt-yhwh	yhwh	b	šbty			w	
	l ʾrk ymym				l			ymym

REMARKS:

In comparison with other poems I have analyzed, this psalm has a low incidence of repetitive parallelism. The only certain cases of repetition of major elements are *ym* "day" and the proper noun *yhwh*. There is, of course, versional evidence for taking *šbty* from *yšb* rather than from *šb*, with emendation to **w*^{ə}*yāšabtî*^{y}, with revocalization to *w*^{ə}*šibtī*^{y}, or with various fashions of taking the form as it stands as from a root meaning "to sit."[14] Thus the burden of verbatim repetition is borne by minor elements (parti-

taken to be extra-metrical and the entire second half of vs. 4, from *kī*^{y} *ʾattā*^{h} on, is labled a "Zusatz" (p. 2).

14. E. Power, "The Shepherd's Two Rods in Modern Palestine and in some Passages of the Old Testament (Ps 23, 4; Zach. 11, 7 ss.; 1 Sam. 17, 43)," *Biblica* 9 (1928): 434–442, esp. 442; J. Morgenstern, "Psalm 23," *JBL* 65 (1946): 13–24, esp. 19; Meek (N 13): 235; Tournay, "En marge d'une traduction des Psaumes," *RB* 63 (1956): 496–512, esp. 504; L. Koehler, "Psalm 23," *ZAW* 68 (1957): 227–234, esp. 233; M. Dahood, "Ugaritic Lexicography," *Mélanges Eugène Tisserant, Vol. I, Ecriture Saint-Ancien Orient* (Città del Vaticano, 1964): 81–104, esp. 91; idem,

cles), none of which occurs frequently enough to invite special attention and only rarely in phrases in which the poetic function of the repetition of the particle is clearly definable (see various remarks below on *b m*ᶜ*gly-šdq* || *b gy*ᵓ *ṣlmwt*, vss. 3, 4a). It must be concluded that repetitive parallelism was not a primary structural device in this particular work.

The small number of repetitive parallelisms makes the charting of distributions easy: there are two distant parallelisms (*yhwh* and *šb*) and one in near distribution (*ym*—the distribution is "regular" if vs. 6 is considered a single bicolon).[15] *yhwh* functions as a quasi-*inclusio*, occurring as the first word of the first verse and as the third-last word in the last verse.[16] The repetition of *šb* emphasizes

---

Psalms I. 1-50. Introduction, Translation, and Notes (AB 16; Garden City, NY: Doubleday: 1965): 148; idem, Review, *Orientalia* n.s. 48 (1979): 449; L. H. Brockington, "The Use of the Hebrew Verb ישב to Describe an Act of Religious Observance," *Essays in Honour of Griffithes Wheeler Thatcher 1863-1950* (ed. E. C. B. MacLaurin; Sydney: Sydney Univ., 1967): 119-125; O. Eissfeldt, "Bleiben im Hause Jahwes," *Beiträge zur Alten Geschichte und deren Nachleben: Festschrift für Franz Altheim zum 6.10.68* (eds. R. Stiehl, H. E. Stier; Berlin: de Gruyter, 1969): 76-81; F. I. Andersen, "Biconsontantal Byforms of Weak Hebrew Roots," *ZAW* 82 (1970): 270-275, esp. 273; A. R. Johnson, "Psalm 23 and the Household of Faith," *Proclamation and Presence: Old Testament Essays in Honour of Gwynne Henton Davies* (eds., J. I. Durham, J. R. Porter; Richmond: John Knox, 1970): 255-271, esp. 261-262; A. Ammassari, "Il Salmo 23," *Bibbia e Oriente* 16 (1974): 257-262, esp. 258; P. Milne, "Psalm 23: Echoes of the Exodus," *Sciences Religieuses/Studies in Religion* 4 (1974-75): 237-247, esp. 238, 245 (one must object to Milne's description of the "form" as "ambiguous"—there is nothing ambiguous about the Hebrew form; the question is whether the Massoretic form is to be interpreted prima facie as from *šb*, reanalyzed as a new form of another root, or emended); Y. Avishur, "Word Pairs Common to Phoenician and Biblical Hebrew," *UF* 7 (1975): 13-47, esp. 36, n. 56; Freedman, "Psalm" (N 13): 162-164; Schramm, (N 4): 190; Mittmann (N 4): 3, 14-16; M. L. Barré and J. S. Kselman, "New Exodus, Covenant, and Restoration in Psalm 23," *The Word of the Lord Shall Go Forth: Essays in Honor of David Noel Freedman in Celebration of his Sixtieth Birthday* (eds. C. L. Meyers, M. O'Connor; American Schools of Oriental Research, Special Volume Series, 1; Winona Lake, IN: Eisenbrauns, 1983): 97-127, esp. 98, 110-114. Of authors whom I have consulted only the following have demurred from this consensus: H. Schmidt, *Die Psalmen* (Handbuch zum Alten Testament 15; Tübingen: Mohr, 1934): 40; E. Vogt, "The 'Place in Life' of Ps 23," *Biblica* 34 (1953): 195-211, esp. 209; A. L. Merrill, rather hesitantly, "Psalm xxiii and the Jerusalem Tradition," *VT* 15 (1965): 354-360.

15. For the definition of my terms for distributions of parallelisms, see *Ugaritic and Hebrew Poetic Parallelism* (N 2): n. 12 and appendix I, and *JNES* 42 (1983): 301.

16. Milne (N 14): 238; Freedman, "Psalm" (N 13): 147, 148.

YHWH's restorative powers.[17] The repetition of *ym* in the last two verses certifies that the "days" of the protagonist will be long ones ("my days" // "length of days").

One of the more important of the particle parallelisms is that of *ky* in vs. 4a and b, for it sets up parallelistically the conditions for deliverance: when in straits and when YHWH is present, one need fear no evil and one is comforted. Whatever the correct translation of the two *ky*'s may be,[18] the word is the same in the Hebrew and can be seen correlating the two lines.

Parallelism: Semantic Parallelism[19]

(1–2)	*yhwh rʿy lʾ ʾḥsr*	A	a b c	1^1	2	3^1	4
	b nʾwt dšʾ yrbyṣny	B	d^2 e	5^1	6 I	7	8 I
	ʿl-my mnḥwt ynhlny	B′	d'^2 e′	9	10	11	8 II
(3)	*npšy yšwbb*	A	a b	12	13 I^1		
	ynḥny b mʿgly-ṣdq	A′	b(+ a) c^2	8 III	5^2	6 II	14 I
	l mʿn šmw	B	d^2	15^1	16	17	
(4a)	*gm ky-ʾlk*	A	a^2	18	19^1	13 II	
	b gyʾ ṣlmwt	B	b^2	5^3	6 III	20 I	
	lʾ-ʾyrʾ rʿ	B′	c b′	3^2	21	20 II	
(4b)	*ky-ʾth ʿmdy*	A	a b	19^2	22 I	23	
	šbṭk w mšʿntk	B	c c′ [c,c′ ~ a]	24 I	25^1	24 II	
	hmh ynḥmny	B′	(c+c′) d	22 II	26		
(5a)	*tʿrk l pny šlḥn*	A	a b c	27	15^2	28 I	29
	ngd ṣrry	B	b′ d	28 II	30		

17. If *wəšabtīʸ* is emended as a form of the verb *yšb* then the parallelism is primarily a phonetic one (not even a semantic parallelism of primary verbs of movement, for *yšb* is only a quasi-verb of movement).

18. The lack of *w*- before the second *ky* may be seen as indicating for that word its explanatory nuance ("for") rather than its circumstantial one ("when, as"), but the absence of *w*- in poetry cannot be used as a firm syntactic indicator.

19. This notation is done in three columns, the first for the macro-parallelism of the line, the second for the micro-parallelism of the line (particles still excluded, however), and the third for the micro-parallelism of the entire work. The system used in the third column was described in my "Psalm 89" (N 2). In brief, the first number indicates a word or a parallel set, the Roman numeral indicates the parallelism where one exists, and the superscript number indicates the number of occurrences of a given word (e.g., 1^1 = 1st word of the text, the absence of a Roman numeral means that there is no other word in this text parallel to this one, the superscript "1" indicates that this is the first occurrence of this word and that at least one other occurrence is to be found below; 13 I^1 = 13th word or set of parallelisms, 1st word of this set of parallelisms, 1st occurrence of this word).

(5b)	*dšnt b šmn rʾšy*	A	a a′b	31 I	5^4	31 II	32	
	kwsy rwyh	A′	c (a+a′)′	33	34			
(6a)	*ʾk ṭwb w ḥsd yrdpwny*	A	a a′b	35	14 II		26^2	36
	kl-ymy ḥyy	B	c^2	37	38^1	39		
(6b)	*w šbty b byt-yhwh*	A	a b^2	25^3	13 I^2	5^5	40	1^2
	l ʾrk ymym	B	c^2	15^3	41	38^2		

List of words as semantic parallels:

1		*yhwh* (vss. 1–2, 6b)
2		*RʿH* (vs. 1–2)
3		*lʾ* (vss. 1–2, 4a)
4		*ḤSR* (vs. 1–2)
5		*b* (vss. 1–2, 3, 4a, 5b, 6b)
6	I	*NWH* (vs. 1–2)
	II	*ʿGL* (vs. 3)
	III	*GYʾ* (vs. 4a)
7		*DŠʾ* (vs. 1–2)
8	I	*RBṢ* (vs. 1–2)
	II	*NHL* (vs. 1–2)
	III	*NḤH* (vs. 3)
9		*ʿl* (vs. 2)
10		*MY* (vs. 2)
11		*NḤ* (vs. 2)
12		*NPŠ* (vs. 3)
13	I	*ŠB* (vss. 3, 6b)
	II	*HLK* (vs. 4a)
14	I	*ṢDQ* (vs. 3)
	II	*ṬB* (vs. 6a) [note antithetic parallel with Rʿʿ, vs. 4a]
	III	*ḤSD* (vs. 6a)
15		*l* (vss. 3, 5a, 6b)
16		*mʿn* (vs. 3)
17		*ŠM* (vs. 3)
18		*gm* (vs. 4a)
19		*ky* (vss. 3, 4b)
20	I	*ṣlmwt* (vs. 4a) [note antithetic parallel with *ḤYH*, vs. 6a]
	II	*Rʿʿ* (vs. 4a) [note antithetic parallel with *ṬB*, vs. 6a]
21		*YRʾ* (vs. 4a)
22	I	*ʾth* (vs. 4b)
	II	*hmh* (vs. 4b)
23		*ʿmd* (vs. 4b)

24	I	*ŠBṬ* (vs. 4b)
	II	*ŠᶜN* (vs. 4b)
25		*w* (vss. 4b, 6a, 6b)
26		*NḤM* (vs. 4b)
27		*ᶜRK* (vs. 5a)
28	I	*pn* (vs. 5a)
	II	*ngd* (vs. 5a)
29		*šlḥn* (vs. 5a)
30		*ṢRR* (vs. 5a)
31	I	*DŠN* (vs. 5b)
	II	*ŠMN* (vs. 5b)
32		*Rᵓ Š* (vs. 5b)
33		*KS* (vs. 5b)
34		*RWH* (vs. 5b)
35		*ᵓk* (vs. 6a)
36		*RDP* (vs. 6a)
37		*KLL* (vs. 6a)
38		*YM* (vss. 6a, 6b)
39		*ḤYH* (vs. 6a) [note antithetic parallel with *ṣlmwt*, vs. 4a]
40		*BT* (vs. 6b)
41		*ᵓRK* (vs. 6b)

REMARKS:

The macro-analysis forces one to choose among the several elements of a line-segment in applying an overall valence. One sees, for example, a problem in vs. 3, for the macro-analysis does not show the grammatical and semantic split in the middle of the second line-segment, with *ynḥny* corresponding to the preceding line-segment and *b mᶜgly-ṣdq* having no semantic or grammatical correspondence with what follows (AA′B reflects the preference in this portion of the analysis for semantics over grammar). The insistence on semantic analysis forces the analysis ABB′ in vs. 4a, for here the semantic proximity of *gyᵓ ṣlmwt* // *rᶜ* must have precedence over the grammatical parallelism *ᵓlk* // *ᵓyrᵓ*. Vs. 5a is classified as AB whereas 5b is AA′ because the only semantic parallel in 5a is that of the nominal-prepositional phrases and the overall parallelism is thus "synthetic," whereas in 5b the dissimilar grammatical parallelism *dṣnt b šmn* // *rwyh* produces a semantic parallelism that denotes abundance of liquids.

In the second and third columns, numbers do not always correspond to letters in equivalent ways because the numbers are applied only to individual words, whereas compounds were considered for the attributions of letters, e.g., *bnʾwt dšʾ* // *ʿl-my mnḥwt* were considered parallels as compounds but none of the individual pairs lines up as a good parallel ("pasture" and "water" can be said to belong to the broadly defined category "where one leads sheep" but each would have its own set of narrowly defined parallels, none of which occurs in this work; ditto for "grass" and "water").

The low incidence of repetitive parallelism shows up again in this notation, for very few words other than particles have superscript numbers as part of the identification number. Moreover, there is only one weak tie-in to a parallel set among the few repetitive parallels: *šb* and *hlk*, classified as a semantic parallelism of primary verbs of movement. With regard to the other two repetitive parallelisms, there is no other divine name to serve as parallel to *yhwh* and no primary time word to serve as parallel to *ym*. This is another significant difference from Ps 89, Prov 2, and *ʿnt* I.

The sets of semantic parallels are: ##6 (geographical terms for where flocks are led), 8 (verbs for leading flocks), 13 (primary verbs of movement), 14 (virtues), 20 (an evil and evil), 22 (independent pronouns), 24 (words for "staff"), 28 (nouns which in their role as prepositions denote position "in front of"), and 31 (words denoting "fat"). Of all these sets, only one word is repeated (#6 I *šb*) and that repetition is in different verbal stems (*polel-qal*) and the second occurrence is textually dubious. Most sets have only two terms; three sets have three members each (#6 [nouns for where flocks are led], #8 [verbs for leading flocks], and #14 [nouns denoting the virtues of being led by YHWH]). These few parallelisms and clusters of parallel terms demonstrate well that what we intimated at the beginning of this study, viz. that semantic parallelism as traditionally viewed and analyzed does not characterize this work to the extent of other biblical Hebrew poems, is indeed the case. The semantic parallelisms indicated above by letters had extensive recourse, moreover, to the parallelism of compounds and these deserve their own analysis.

Without defending the concept at length, I referred occasionally in *Ugaritic and Hebrew Poetic Parallelism*[20] to "sequential" or "functional" parallelism. By these terms were meant words or

20. E.g., §1.3.5 on section VIII; 2.3.1.0 on verse 18; note 113.

phrases that are grammatically or positionally parallel but of which the semantic proximity is so tenuous that only the context indicates a form of synonymity. Obvious examples are noun // pronoun (Prov 2:1 *bny* // *ᵓtk* "my son // with you") or name // body part (Prov 2:6 *yhwh* // *pyw* "YHWH // his mouth"). Less obvious examples are *lqḥ* // *msk* "take // mix" (*ᶜnt* I 16–17), two actions necessarily sequential in the process of mixing a drink, and *byt* // *mᶜgl* "house // path" (Prov 2:18), two parts of the "strange woman's" domicile. Such "functional" parallels, especially as formed by compound phrases, appear to play a relatively more important role in the structure of Ps 23 than in any of the works that I have analyzed to date. They are:

—*b nᵓwt dšᵓ* // *ᶜl-my mnḥwt* (vss. 1–2): the grammatical structure is tight (prepositional phrases; construct chains) but the synonymity of the individual terms is very weak (already discussed above at the head of these remarks). On the other hand, the combination of "grassy fields" and "quiet waters" is functionally appropriate for flocks.

—*npšy yšwbb* // *ynḥny* (vs. 3): It is generally recognized that *npš* can function in biblical Hebrew as a strong form of personal pronoun (compare Eng. "my*self*"). In this particular verse the word undoubtedly has a stronger meaning as well: the "gullet" that needs wetting in order to maintain the "vital life force." Nonetheless, the parallelism *npšy* // *-ny*, where one finds both *npš* and *-y* in parallel with the verbal pronominal suffix *-ny*, appears to reflect a purposeful repetition on the part of the author. To this aspect of the parallelism is added the grammatical parallelism (two transitive verbs + objects) and the weak semantic parallelism of the verbs (transitive forms indicating movement).

—*šbṭk w mšᶜntk* // *hmh* (vs. 4b): an example of the noun // pronoun[21] parallelism mentioned above.

—*dšnt bšmn* (vs. 5b): not an example of parallelism of compounds but one of "sequential" parallelism produced by the grammatical structure: *dešen* // *šemen* would be a stand-

21. Dahood's analysis of *hmh* as an interjection "Behold" (*Psalms I* (N 14): 145, 147; taken up again in idem, "Stichometry and Destiny in Psalm 23,4," *Biblica* 60 [1979]: 417–419, esp. 417; followed by Milne (N 14): 238–239; Freedman, "Psalm" (N 13): 142, 157–58) is gratuitous. The syntactic structure is clear and commonly attested ("cleft sentence") while the semantic ("emphasis") and quasi-metrical (filling out the third line-segment) functions of the word are relatively clear.

ard parallel pair; *diššēn bəšemen* contains the same two basic notions in a grammatical sequence denoting action + material.

—*dšnt bšmn* // *rwyh* (vs. 5b): the structure just discussed is in turn paralleled by a nominal predicate that denotes liquidity in another form.

Those sets of parallelisms that do appear in this work are for the most part in "regular" distribution, i.e., between the members of a verse. All of the other distributions are attested, however. Of "internal" or "half-line" parallelism there are three clear examples: *šbṭk w mšʿntk* (vs. 4b), *dšnt b šmn* (vs. 5b, discussed in preceding paragraph), *ṭwb w ḥsd* (vs. 6a). By comparison, there were two examples of this distribution in *ʿnt* I and five in Prov 2.[22] The first three tricola are characterized by the sets which denote leading flocks and where they are led, as well as the two primary verbs of movement, in "near" distribution (##6, 8, 13—the latter, in the repetitive parallelism of *šb*, also contains a "distant" distribution). The terms for good and evil are in "near," "regular," and "distant" distribution (##14, 20).

In addition, the use of antonymic parallelism must be mentioned. Though there are no instances of antonymic parallelism in "regular" distribution, there are two antonymic pairs distributed distantly: "evil // good" and "death"[23] // life" (both sets in vss. 4a, 6a). These parallelisms of individual terms furnish a basis for the analysis of the macrostructure of the work, in which vs. 4a constitutes the negative aspect and 6a the lexically specific positive antithesis. Another antithetic structure, more complicated than the ones just mentioned, is *b mʿgly-ṣdq* // *b gyʾ ṣlmwt* (vss. 3, 4a),

22. *Ugaritic and Hebrew Poetic Parallelism* (N 2): §§1.3.2 and 2.3.2, respectively.

23. If *ṣlmwt* consists of *ṣl* + *mwt*; if not, there is nevertheless a punning parallelism, for the last part of *ṣalmāwet* is, according to the Massoretic tradition, vocalized like *māwet* "death" (see especially D. Winton Thomas, "צַלְמָוֶת in the Old Testament," *JSS* 7 [1962]: 191–200; J. Barr, "Philology and Exegesis: Some General Remarks, with Illustrations from Job," *Questions disputées de l'Ancien Testament* [Journées Bibliques de Louvain 23; Bibliotheca Ephemeridum Theologicarum Lovaniensium 33; Gembloux: Duculot, 1974]: 40–61, esp. 50–55; M. Dahood, "Stichometry" (N 21): 417–419, esp. 417, n. 3; S. Ribichini, P. Xella, "'La valle dei passanti' (Ezechiele 39:11)," *UF* 12 [1980]: 434–437, esp. 436; W. L. Michel, "ṢLMWT, 'Deep Darkness' or 'Shadow of Death'?" *Biblical Research* 29 [1984]: 5–20). The possible compound nature of this noun has led me to consider it a parallel to *Rʿʿ* "evil" while not classifying *ṬB* "good" and *ḤYH* "live" as belonging to a parallel set (the fact that *ṬB* belongs to its own lexically cohesive set was also dissuasive).

which includes repetitive (*b* // *b*), phonetic (*b-g-ṣ* // *b-g-ṣ*, with *m* and *l* in each but out of sequence, as well as -*ē*- vowel and a "segholate" structure in each), syntactic (prepositional three-member phrases), and antithetic semantic parallelism in "near" distribution. The antonymy of these phrases is provided, of course, by the final element (*mʿgly* ~ *gyʾ*; *ṣdq* ≠ *ṣlmwt*). Of these three lexically expressed contrasts,[24] "evil/good" are true antonyms in J. Lyons'[25] terminology (gradable opposites) and "death/life" are "complements" (ungradable opposites).[26] *ṣdq*/*ṣlmwt* is more difficult to pin down because of the etymological problem of the second element, but it is probable that, viewed from the perspective of the rustic imagery being used, they are considered "gradable opposites" (some paths and some valleys are more safe/dangerous than others).

Grammatical parallelism will be discussed below but it is of use to indicate at this point the grammatical structures into which the semantic parallelisms fall. The emphasis in recent years on grammatical aspects of parallelism has permitted a refinement of semantic-parallelism analysis, refinement that extends in two directions. The analysis of grammatical parallelism in its own right has permitted the analyst (1) to avoid classifying parallels as semantic for grammatical reasons alone (e.g., from this work *dšʾ* and *mnḥwt*, vss. 1–2, discussed above this section)[27] and, (2) conversely, to avoid rejecting a semantic parallelism on the basis of grammatical dissimilarity (e.g., from this work *dšnt b šmn*, vs. 5b, discussed above, this section).

—In the first line (vss. 1–2), the grammatical parallelism is very tight and one might have been induced thereby to find

24. There are, of course, other "antonymic" relationships in the text which are not expressed by discrete lexical items, such as, especially, *ṣrry* and "I" in vs. 5. Since the "I" in that opposition is expressed only pronominally and prepositionally (*lpny*) and since the word *ṣrry* itself bears the 1c.s. suffix, resulting in a very complex distribution of the antonymic elements, this example is not listed in the main discussion.

25. *Semantics* (Cambridge: Cambridge Univ., 1977): I.279.

26. This categorization is not totally adequate because of the metaphorical usage in Hebrew of "death" for a "mortally dangerous situation" but in general "life" and "death" may be said to be ungradable opposites.

27. A prime example from *ʿnt* I was *lqḥ* // *msk* (ll. 16–17), referred to here above as an example of "sequential" parallelism: the grammatical fit between the two verbs in that text is precise, but the semantic proximity is provided by the context alone.

semantic parallelism in each of the elements. The verbs provide the best parallelism, in that both actions denote duties of the shepherd. As regards the nominal phrases, however, we have allowed ourselves to see parallelism only in the head nouns and in the compound phrases, reasoning that the *nomina recta* were semantically distant (*dšʾ* // *mnḥwt*).

—Dahood[28] tried to make a case for the semantic parallelism of *b nʾwt dšʾ yrbyṣny* (vs. 2a) and *ynḥny b mʿgly-ṣdq* (vs. 3b) and was criticized for this by M. Held[29] on the grounds that the terms are not elsewhere attested as parallels. We can give Dahood a measure of right here, for there is no denying the extensive grammatical parallelism, the broad semantic parallelism of the verbs and of the head nouns of the prepositional phrases,[30] and the morpho-phonetic parallelism of the suffixes on the verbs. If my division of the text be granted, all these are "near" parallelisms and at least one of their functions is to bind the "weak" structure of vs. 3 into the larger structure of the work.

—The complex grammatical and semantic parallelism of the first two segments of the second line (vs. 3) has already been discussed. We did not allow ourselves to be led by the close grammatical parallelism of the verbs and of the objects of the verbs into calling *yšwbb* and *ynḥny* semantic pairs because of the different nature of these two verbs (*šb* is a primary verb of movement, transitivized here by stem usage, not a common verb for tending flocks, whereas *nḥh* is a common verb for leading). Nor did we allow the fact that *b mʿgly-ṣdq* and *l mʿn šmw* are prepositional phrases to induce us into calling them semantic parallels.

—The grammatical dissimilarity of *dšnt* and *bšmn* has just been mentioned. That of *dšnt b šmn* and *rwyh* (verb + prepositional phrase of material // predicate noun) is another

28. Psalms I (N 14): 146.

29. "Hebrew *maʿgāl*: A Study in Lexical Parallelism," *JANES* 6 (1974): 107–116, esp. 112; cf. E. L. Greenstein, "How Does Parallelism Mean?" *A Sense of Text: The Art of Language and the Study of Biblical Literature* (JQR Supplement; Winona Lake, IN: Eisenbrauns, 1983): 41–70, esp. 65.

30. For a discussion of parallelism as a principle of poetic formation, rather than as a set thesaurus of parallel pairs (Held's principal argument against Dahood is that the terms are not elsewhere used as parallels), see my remarks, with bibliography, in "Ugaritic and Hebrew Poetry: Parallelism," Appendix I in *Ugaritic and Hebrew Poetic Parallelism* (N 2).

good example of not allowing such grammatical dissimilarity to blind us to semantic similarity.

One can conclude from this discussion of the various aspects of semantic parallelism that, though Ps 23 is not characterized by a single form of semantic parallelism, attention to the combination of forms and distributions has uncovered more instances of semantic patterning than one might have expected from a superficial reading or from a translation.

Grammatical Parallelism

Micro-analysis:

1–2)	yhwh rʿy lʾ ʾḥsr	pr.**n.m.s.abs./n.m.s.+1c.s.pr.**/neg./ **1c.s.impf.**Qal
	b nʾwt dšʾ yrbyṣny	**prep./n.f.pl.const./n.m.s.abs./ 3m.s.impf.**Hi.+**1c.s.pr.**
	ʿl-my mnḥwt ynhlny	**prep./n.m.?const./n.f.pl.abs./ 3m.s.impf.**Pi.+**1c.s.pr.**
3)	npšy yšwbb	**n.**f.s.+**1c.s.pr./3m.s.impf.**Pol.
	ynḥny b mʿgly-ṣdq	**3m.s.impf.**Hi.+**1c.s.pr./prep./ n.m.**pl.**const./n.m.s.**abs.
	l mʿn šmw	**/prep./n.m.**s.const./**n.m.s.**+3m.s.pr.
4a)	gm ky-ʾlk	adv./conj./**1c.s.impf.Qal**
	b gyʾ ṣlmwt	prep./**n.m.s.**constr./**n.m.s.abs.**
	lʾ-ʾyrʾrʿ	neg./**1c.s.impf.Qal/n.m.s.abs.**
4b)	ky-ʾth ʿmdy	**conj.**/2m.s.**indep.pr.**/prep.+1c.s.pr.
	šbṭk w mšʿntk	**n.m.s.+2m.s.pr./conj./n.f.s.+2m.s.pr.**
	hmh ynḥmny	**3m.pl.indep.pr./3m.pl.**impf.Pi.
5a)	tʿrk l pny šlḥn	2m.s.impf.Qal/**prep./ n.m.pl.+1c.s.pr./n.m.s.**abs.
	ngd ṣrry	**n.m.s.const.**(functioning as **prep.)/n.m.pl.+1c.s.pr.**
5b)	dšnt b šmn rʾšy	2m.s.pf.Pi./prep./**n.m.s.abs./ n.m.s.+1c.s.pr.**
	kwsy rwyh	**n.f.s.+1c.s.pr./n.f.s.abs.**

6a)	ʾk ṭwb w ḥsd	adv./**n.m.s.abs.**/conj./**n.m.s.abs.**/
	yrdpwny	3m.pl.impf.Qal+**1c.s.pr.**
	kl-ymy ḥyy	**n.m.s.constr./n.m.pl.const./**
		n.m.pl.const.+1c.s.pr.
6b)	w šbty b byt-yhwh	conj./1c.s.pf.Qal/**prep./n.m.s.const.**/
		pr.**n.m.s.abs.**
	l ʾrk ymym	**prep./n.m.s.constr./n.m.**pl.**abs.**

REMARKS:

I have neither found nor been able to devise a totally satisfying system of notation for grammatical micro-analysis.[31] As an experiment, I have here simply parsed the text arranged as poetic lines, indicating parallelisms by bold-face type. This is not the perfect system, for the grammatical parallelisms are not always *positionally* parallel or they may have different syntactic distributions in adjacent line-segments.

These problems are well represented in vs. 1, where the distribution of analyzed features is different from one line-segment to another but where most features are repeated at one point or another in the line, producing the result of virtually total bold-face representation. It would be more useful to analyze this tricolon according to its ABB macrostructure and according to the positionally parallel elements, for thus the small differences between the second and third line-segments, as opposed to the major differences between those two line-segments and the first would show up more clearly:

A pr.n.m.s.abs./n.m.s.+1c.s.pr./neg./1c.s.impf.Qal
B **prep./n.f.**pl.**const./n.**m.s.**abs./3m.s.impf.**Hi.+**1c.s.pr.**
B′ **prep./n.**m.?**const./n.**f.pl.**abs./3m.s.impf.**Pi.+**1c.s.pr.**

On the other hand, the good grammatical parallelism of the second and third line-segments of vs. 3, in the absence of semantic

31. The only system of which I am aware that attempts micro-analysis is S. A. Geller's (*Parallelism in Early Biblical Poetry* [Harvard Semitic Monographs, 20; Missoula: Scholars Press, 1979]). I have analyzed his system in detail in *Ugaritic and Hebrew Poetic Parallelism* (N 2). My primary criticism there was that the notation bears too much information in that Geller devised it to denote morphology, syntax, meter, and parallelism; it is thus so dense as to be virtually impenetrable for dense-minded ones such as myself.

parallelism, shows up clearly in this notation, especially when space permits the placement of the notation of the two prepositional clauses in vertical alignment.

One could have overlooked the precise grammatical parallelism of the two verbs in vs. 4a without this notation (this is the only case in this psalm where the verbs of one line are in the same stem-formation), while the precise grammatical parallelism of the last word in the second and third line-segments makes one check to see if they might be semantically parallel as well—which they are.

In vs. 4b the bold-facing of "3m.pl.indep.pr." in the third line-segment indicates the grammatically pivotal nature of *hmh*: it is of the same general category as the 2d person independent pronoun[32] in the first line-segment while sharing the person and number only with the following verb.

The plethora of nouns and of nouns serving as prepositions in vs. 5a means that virtually all features analysed are repeated at one point or another (only the 2m.s.impf. Qal verb and the "abs." feature of *šlḥn* are excepted).

Again in vs. 5b the plethora of nouns has produced repetition of features (only the verb and preposition are not repeated). The verb in 5b is the only simple perfect verbal form in the psalm. If *w^ə^šabtî^y^* in vs. 6b is indeed *waw*-consecutive + pf., as I tend to believe, the verbal syntax of this work is significantly prosaic and one may wish to explain the pf. *dšnt* as a subordination of this form to *tᶜrk*[33] rather than in more narrowly poetic poetic terms (*qtl/yqtl* alternation[34]).

Vs. 6a is similar to the surrounding lines in that the verb is not repeated. Otherwise,only the particles *ᵓk* and *w* are not repeated.

One sees a less precise parallelism of the nouns in vs. 6b; this is owing to the presence of a proper noun and to the fact that the singular/plural ratio is 3/1.

Syntactic analysis:

(1–2)	yhwh rᶜy lᵓ ᵓḥsr	S P V	3/2/2
	b nᵓwt dšᵓ yrbyṣny	M V^{+O}	3/2/1
	ᶜl-my mnḥwt ynhlny	M V^{+O}	3/2/1

32. This is not a "pseudo-parallélisme" (Tournay [N 14]: 505) but a common form of parallelism and a distinct sub-type, as Geller (N 31) has shown.

33. Mittmann (N 4: 12) places the perfect *diššantā* and the nominal predicate *rəwāyā^h^* on a similar footing and explains them both as explicating the preceding line.

34. Kugel (N 3): 50.

(3)	npšy yšwbb	O V	2/2/1
	ynḥny b mʿgly-ṣdq	V^{+O} M	3/2/1
	l mʿn šmw	M	2/1/0
(4a)	gm ky-ʾlk	V	2/1/1
	b gyʾ ṣlmwt	M	2/1/0
	lʾ-ʾyrʾ rʿ	V O	2/2/1
(4b)	ky-ʾth ʿmdy	S P	2/2/1
	šbṭk w mšʿntk	S S	2/1/0
	hmh ynḥmny	S V^{+O}	2/2/1
(5a)	tʿrk l pny šlḥn	V M O	3/3/1
	ngd ṣrry	M	2/1/0
(5b)	dšnt b šmn rʾšy	V M O	3/3/1
	kwsy rwyh	S P	2/2/1
(6a)	ʾk ṭwb w ḥsd yrdpwny	S S V^{+O}	3/2/1
	kl-ymy ḥyy	M	2/1/0
(6b)	w šbty b byt-yhwh	V M	3/2/1
	l ʾrk ymym	M	2/1/0

REMARKS:

The two columns given here represent my reformulation of T. E. Collins' notation[35] and the basic hierarchical analysis of syntactic units devised by M. O'Connor.[36] The only significant change that I have made to Collins' notation is the introduction of "P" to represent the predicate of a nominal sentence (in the main body of his book, Collins analyzed only verbal sentences). This first column represents the macro-grammatical parallelism and reveals in a

35. *Line-Forms in Hebrew Poetry* (Studia Pohl: Series Maior 7; Rome: Biblical Institute, 1978). This represents, of course, simply the notation used for the analysis of "line-forms," not the analysis itself. In my notation, M = modifier phrase, O = direct object of a verb (superscripted when affixed to the verb), P = predicate of a nominal sentence, S = subject of a nominal or verbal sentence, V = verb.

36. *Hebrew Verse Structure* (Winona Lake, IN: Eisenbrauns, 1980). The first number represents "units" (individual verbs and nouns, along with dependent particles), the second "constituents" (each verb and nominal phrase, along with dependent particles), the third "clause predicators" (a verbal clause of which the verb is the predicator or a nominal clause with no express predicator).

more readily perceptible fashion than does the chart of microparallelisms the parallelism of larger units. The grammatical ABB structure of the first tricolon stands out more clearly in this chart than it did in the preceding chart as does the pivotal split in the second line-segment of the second tricolon (see remarks above to vss. 1–2 and vs. 3).

All line-segments meet O'Connor's "constraint" rules.[37] The only questionable line-segment is the first one of vs. 4a, which consists of two particles and a verb. It appears to me from O'Connor's discussions and examples that an adverb, even if so short a one as *gm*,[38] can be counted as a "unit." In the quantitative analysis above, it was assumed that the concentration of two particles functioned as a "word" or as a "verse-unit."

If vss. 5–6 are taken as forming two long bicola, rather than four short ones as I have done, the results will be the following:

5a)	tᶜrk l pny šlḥn ngd ṣrry	V	M	O	M		5/4/1
5b)	dšnt b šmn r⊃šy kwsy rwyh	V	M	O	S	P	5/5/2
6a)	⊃k ṭwb w ḥsd yrdpwny kl-ymy ḥyy	S	S	V+o		M	5/4/1
6b)	w šbty b byt-yhwh l ⊃rk ymym	V	M	M			5/3/1

With this lineation, two constraints are broken, both in vs. 5b, which has five constituents and one nominal phrase for each of the clause predicators.[39] Serious syntactic reasons do exist, therefore, for not taking these verses as long-member bicola—as indeed the quantitative analysis has already indicated.

Phonetic Parallelism

Consonants:

(1–2)	yhwh rᶜy l⊃ ⊃ḥsr	y,y	r,r	⊃,⊃		
	b n⊃wt dš⊃ yrbyṣny	y,y	r	⊃,⊃	b,b	n,n
	ᶜl-my mnḥwt ynhlny	y,y,y			n,n,n	m,m

37. No "line" (my line-segment) contains (1) fewer than two "units" or more than five, (2) fewer than one constituent or more than four, (3) more than three clause predicators (p. 87—there are three more rules regarding higher-level associations, none of which is broken in in this lineation of Ps 23).

38. Ibid., pp. 299, 300–303, 338 (on the last page *šm* is listed as a constituent—and hence is a unit).

39. Constraint no. 5, not given in note 37, says that in lines with two clause predicators, only one has dependent nominal phrases.

(3)	npšy yšwbb	n	š,š	y,y	b,b			
	ynḥny b mᶜgly-ṣdq	n,n		y,y,y	b	m	ᶜ	l
	l mᶜn šmw	n	š			m,m	ᶜ	l
(4a)	gm ky-ʾlk	g	m	k,k	y	ʾ	l	
	b gyʾ ṣlmwt	g	m		y	ʾ	l	
	lʾ-ʾyrʾ rᶜ				y	ʾ,ʾ,ʾ	l	r,r
(4b)	ky-ʾth[40] ᶜmdy	k	y,y	t	ᶜ	m		
	šbṭk w mšᶜntk	k,k		t	ᶜ	m	š,š	n
	hmh ynḥmny		y,y			m,m		n,n
(5a)	tᶜrk l pny šlḥn	r	l,l	n,n	y			
	ngd ṣrry	r,r		n	y			
(5b)	dšnt b šmn rʾšy	š,š	n,n	r	y			
	kwsy rwyh			r	y,y			
(6a)	ʾk ṭwb w ḥsd yrdpwny	k	ḥ	d,d	y			
	kl-ymy ḥyy	k	ḥ		y,y,y			
(6b)	w šbty b byt-yhwh	w,w	b,b,b	t,t	y,y,y			
	l ʾrk ymym				y,y	m,m		

Vowels:

(1–2)	*yahwe^{h} rōᶜī^{y} lōʾ ʾeḥsār*	a	e,e	ō,ō	ī	
	binʾō^{w}t dešeʾ yarbī^{y}ṣēnī^{y}	a	e,e	ō	ī,ī	ē
	ᶜal-mē^{y} m^{ə}nūḥō^{w}t y^{ə}naḥălēnī^{y}	a,a		ō	ī	ē,ē
(3)	*napšī^{y} y^{ə}šō^{w}bēb*	a	ī	ō	ē	
	yanḥēnī^{y} b^{ə}maᶜg^{ə}lē^{y}-ṣedeq	a,a	ī		ē,ē	e,e
	l^{ə}maᶜan š^{ə}mō^{w}	a,a		ō		
(4a)	*gam kī^{y}-ʾēlēk*	a	ī	ē,ē		
	b^{ə}gē^{y}ʾ ṣalmāwet	a		ē	ā	
	lōʾ-ʾī^{y}rāʾ rāᶜ		ī		ā,ā	
(4b)	*kī^{y}-ʾattā^{h} ᶜimmādī^{y}*	ī,ī	a	ā,ā	i	
	šibṭ^{ə}kā ū^{w}mišᶜantekā		a	ā,ā	i,i	ū
	hēmmā^{h} y^{ə}naḥămūnī^{y}	ī	a	ā		ū
(5a)	*taᶜărōk l^{ə}pānāy šulḥān*	ō	ā,ā,ā			
	neged ṣōr^{ə}rāy	ō	ā	e,e		
(5b)	*diššantā baššemen rōʾšī^{y}*	a,a	ā	e,e	ō	ī
	kō^{w}sī^{y} r^{ə}wāyā^{h}		ā,ā		ō	ī
(6a)	*ʾak ṭō^{w}b wāḥesed yird^{ə}pū^{w}nī^{y}*	a	ā	e,e		
	kol-y^{ə}mē^{y} ḥayyāy	a	ā			
(6b)	*w^{ə}šabtī^{y} b^{ə}bē^{y}t-yahwe^{h}*		a,a	ī	e	
	l^{ə}ʾōrek yāmī^{y}m			ī	e	

40. The *h*'s in this verse are not listed because in two cases the *h* is *mater lectionis* for a historically pure long vowel. Ditto in vss. 5bb and 6aa (*w*).

The only recurring sounds that might provide a phonetic pattern for the work as a whole are those of the 1 c. s. suffixal pronoun—a combination, therefore, of morpheme parallelism and of phonetic parallelism. If one includes all of the 1 c. s. suffixal morphemes along with *-ī-* in other formations (including one that is part of a 1 c. s. prefixal morpheme, the *-ī-* of *ʾīʸrāʾ* in vs. 4a) one finds these elements in virtually every line-segment: either a 1 c. s. morpheme or the sound *-ī-* is found in all but three line-segments of a total of twenty. There is only one case of "regular" parallelism consisting only of 1 c. s. morphemes containing different vowels (vs. 6a). The distribution is as follows:

1–2) *-ī*// *-ī-*, *-(ēn)ī*// *-(ēn)ī*
3) *-ī*// *-(ēn)ī* // -
4a) *-ī*// - // *-ī-*
4b) *-ī*, *-ī*// - // *-ī*
5a) *-āy*// *-āy*
5b) *-ī*// *-ī*
6a) *-ī*// *-āy*
6b) *-ī*// *-ī-*

This pattern of repetition fits with what I have observed in my previous—very limited—studies of phonetic patterning: large structures tend to be linked with morpheme repetition.

Some of the more obvious smaller structures: the particular 1 c. s. suffixal morpheme *-ēnī* (vss. 1–2, 3); *-šīʸ yəš-* (vs. 3);[41] several sound linkages between the semantically antithetic phrases *bəmaᶜgəlēʸ ṣedeq* and *bəgēʸʾ ṣalmāwet* (vss. 3, 4a—see above at "Semantic Parallelism"); the tip-to-tip triangles of *ē* and *ā* in vs. 4a; three *alep*'s and the sequential repetition of the syllable *-rā-* in vs. 4aγ; four *-ā-*'s as part of three different pronouns in vs. 4b (with another *-ā-* in the preposition); *šī-*/*-iš-* and *-kā* in each of the words for "rod" in vs. 4b; *-š-* in each word of the first line-segment of vs. 5b joined to a partial phonetic parallelism (*-s-*) in regular distribution. Note that in vs. 3 all but one (*-ōʷ*) of the phonetic elements of the grammatically and semantically non parallel third line-segment repeat phonetic elements of the previous two line-segments. The same is true of the third line-segment of vs. 4a (only

41. Schramm ([N 4]: 191) observes the presence of labials here and with /š/ in several other places in this work.

/ ʾ / is not repeated), though there the grammatical and semantic structure is a bit tighter.

I am dubious that consonant parallelism is sufficient to produce a sound parallelism between *rō*^{c}*ī*^{y} (vs. 1) and *rā*^{c} in vs. 4 or between *dešeʾ* in vs. 2 and *diššantā* in vs. 5[42] because of the distances involved.[43]

Deletion/Compensation

This phrase is Geller's term for the common phenomenon otherwise known as "gapping" and the quasi-metrical "compensation" in a parallel line-segment for the "deleted" word. For example, *ʿnt* I 10–11 *ks ytn b dh // krpn b klʾat ydh* "a cup he puts in his hand, a goblet in his two hands." The verb is "deleted" from the second half-line and the prepositional phrase is expanded from one word to two.[44] It was necessary to cite an example from a text other than Ps 23, for there are no simple examples of deletion-compensation in this work. Already in Prov 2, though there were many complicated examples of deletion-compensation,[45] there were no clear instances of a single major syntactic constituent being deleted in the second half-line and its absence being compensated for by the expansion of a syntactic unit already present in the first half-line.[46]

For deletion-compensation to function, there must be clear syntactic parallelism. Where such parallelism is present in Ps 23, deletion is virtually absent:

—In the first tricolon the syntactic structures of the first line-segment as compared with the second and third are quite different, while the similarity of the second to the third is unbroken by deletion.

42. Schramm (N 4): 190–191; Dahood, "Stichometry" (N 21): 417, on *rō*^{c}*ī*^{y} / *ra*^{c}.

43. See my remarks on how the various types of parallelism function at various distances in *Ugaritic and Hebrew Poetic Parallelism* (N 2).

44. See Geller (N 31), *passim* and my *Ugaritic and Hebrew Poetic Parallelism* (N 2) §1.8 on this particular example.

45. See ibid. §2.8.

46. For relatively complicated examples of deletion-compensation, see Prov 2:3, where a compound conjunction is deleted from the second half-line and a new object phrase is inserted (without a parallel object phrase in the first half-line); vs.9, where a conjunction and a verb are deleted and the object phrase is expanded; vs. 19, where a subject phrase is deleted from the second half-line and a new object phrase is inserted.

—In the second tricolon both major syntactic constituents of the first line-segment are present in the second but the object phrase (*npšy*) is pronominalized and suffixed (*-ny*). One can say that this "abbreviation" of the object phrase is compensated for by the insertion of the modifier phrase *b mᶜgly-ṣdq*, but there is no syntactic "deletion."

—If vs. 4a is correctly analysed as a tricolon the "synthetic" form of the line precludes deletion-compensation analysis. The same is true, *mutatis mutandis*, of vss. 5a, 6a, and 6b.

—The first two line-segments of vs. 4b show a form of deletion-compensation similar to that found in Prov 2: the conjunction *ky* and the prepositional predicate phrase *ᶜmdy* are deleted from the second half-line and the subject phrase *ᵓth* is expanded to *šbṭk w mšᶜntk*. In the third line-segment, the subject phrase is reduced back to one word, *hmh*, and a verbal phrase is inserted.

—In vs. 5b the prepositional phrase of the first half-line is deleted from the second, but there is no compensation for this deletion and the "metrical" structure is 3//2.

Ps 23 contains, therefore, either semantic parallelism distributed very regularly (vs. 2) or semantic and other types of parallelism in various distributions; but it contains very few lines characterized by gapping in one segment with syntactic replacement in a corresponding segment. This aspect of the structure of Ps 23 is significantly different from both *ᶜnt* I and Prov 2, though Prov 2 already showed less "deletion-compensation" of major elements than did *ᶜnt* I.

Distributions of Parallelisms

Half-line:

1) *šbṭk* + *mšᶜntk* (vs. 4b)
2) *dšnt* + *šmn* (vs. 5b)
3) *ṭwb* + *ḥsd* (vs. 6a)

"Regular":

1) *nᵓwt dšᵓ* // *my mnḥwt* (vss. 1–2)
2) *yrbyṣny* // *ynhlny* (vss. 1–2) [verbs and suffixed pronouns]
3) There is "regular" parallelism of 1 c. s. morphemes in all lines except vs. 6b, all suffix morphemes except in vs. 4a.
4) *yšwbb* + *npšy* // *ynḥny* (vs. 3) [pronoun parallelism contributing to a rather weak semantic parallelism of the verbs]
5) *ṣlmwt* // *rᶜ* (vs. 4a)

6) *ʾth* // *šbṭk* + *mšʿntk* (vs. 4b) [pronoun parallelism as well as a sort of "whole-part" parallelism of YHWH and his rod and staff]
7) *šbṭk* + *mšʿntk* // *hmh* (vs. 4b) [noun-pronoun]
8) *lpny* // *ngd* (vs. 5a) [semantic and grammatical]
9) *dšnt* + *šmn* // *rwyh* (vs. 5b)

Near:

1) *b* . . . *b* . . . *b* (vss. 1–4a)
2) *nʾwt* . . . *mʿgly* . . . *gyʾ* (vss. 1–4a)
3) *yrbyṣyny* // *ynhlny* . . . *ynḥny* (vss. 1–3)
4) There is at least one 1 c. s. morpheme in every verse and at least two in all but vs. 6b.
5) *yšwbb* . . . *ʾlk* (vss. 3–4a)
6) *ky* . . . *ky* (vss. 4a–4b)
7) *pny* . . . *rʾšy* (vss. 5a–5b) [body parts, though *l pny* is strongly prepositionalized]
8) *šlḥn* . . . *kwsy* (vss. 5a–5b) [a weak semantic parallel: each would have its own closer parallels]
9) *w* . . . *w* (vss. 6a–6b)
10 *ymy* . . . *ymym* (vss. 6a–6b)

Distant:

1) *yhwh* (repetitive, vss. 1, 6b)
2) *lʾ* (repetitive, vss. 1–2, 4a)
3) *b* (repetitive, vss. 1–2, 3, 4a, 5b, 6b)
4) *nʾwt* . . . *mʿgly* . . . *gyʾ* (vss. 1–4a) [continuous near and distant]
5) *yrbyṣyny* // *ynhlny* . . . *ynḥny* (vss. 1–3) [continuous near and distant]
6) There is at least one 1 c. s. morpheme in every verse and at least two in all but vs. 6b. [continuous near and distant]
7) *yšwbb* . . . *ʾlk*; *šbty* (vss. 3, 4a, 6b) [near and distant; semantic and repetitive]
8) *ṣdq*; *ṭwb* + *ḥsd* (vss. 3, 6a) + antithetic parallels noted in the list of words as semantic parallels at ##14, 20.
9) *l* (repetitive, vss. 3, 5a, 6b)

REMARKS:

There are two sets of "minor elements" that play major roles in the structure of this work: the 1 c. s. suffixal and prefixal pronouns that permeate the work and the play of independent and suffixal pronouns in vs. 4a. The latter produces a particularly complicated structure: *ʾth* corresponds grammatically to the suffixed pronouns *-k*, while the nouns bearing these pronouns are in some sense surrogates for YHWH himself (hence the term "whole-part" above, borrowed from Geller). The pronoun *hmh* in the third line-segment, on the other hand, is resumptive of the two nouns in the middle segment. All of these relationships are bonded together yet more strongly by the phonetic parallelism of the *-ā-*.

"Regular" parallelism does not play as important a role in this text as compared with the two texts analyzed in *Ugaritic and Hebrew Poetic Parallelism*: the ratios of "regular" to "near" in *ʿnt* I and Prov 2 were, respectively, 24:9 and 60:19 as compared with 9:10 here; regular:distant = 24:10 and 60:27 as compared with 9:9 here); regular:internal = 24:4 and 60:12 as compared with 9:3 here. Comparing the absolute numbers just cited with the numbers of line-segments, one sees:

	line-segments	internal	regular	near	distant
ʿnt I	22	4 (1:0.18)	24 (1:1.09)	9 (1:0.41)	10 (1:0.45)
Prov 2	44	12 (1:0.27)	60 (1:1.34)	19 (1:0.43)	27 (1:0.61)
Ps 23	20	3 (1:0.15)	9 (1:0.45)	10 (1:0.50)	9 (1:0.45)

Thus Ps 23 has approximately the same number of "internal" parallelisms per number of line-segments as does *ʿnt* I but only about half as many as Prov 2; fewer than half as many "regular" parallelisms as *ʿnt* I and a third as many as Prov 2; about 15% more "near" parallelisms than either of the other two texts; and exactly the same number of "distant" parallelisms as *ʿnt* I but about a third fewer than Prov 2. On the basis of this analysis, therefore, Ps 23 is about as "parallelistic" as *ʿnt* I in all respects except "regular" parallelism but considerably less "parallelistic" than Prov 2 in all respects except "near" parallelism.

We may now proceed to a summary of the distributions in terms of the types of parallelism (especially repetitive, grammatical, and phonetic; only parallelisms which include a semantic component are listed in the preceding chart). There is no **repetitive** parallelism in internal distribution. This distribution differs from *ʿnt* I (one instance of internal repetitive parallelism) and from Prov 2 (two instances of internal parallelism of minor elements). There is only one example out of three of **grammatical** *dissimilarity* joined to semantic parallelism (*dšnt* + *šmn*, vs. 5b). *ʿnt* I has one example (from a total of four internal parallelisms) of grammatical dissimilarity, but in that case the type of parallelism is repetitive (*ymsk bmskh*, l. 17). Prov 2 also shows one example (of a total of 12) but the dissimilarity is not so abrupt (participle // finite verb in vs. 11). The other cases of internal semantic parallelism involve synonyms in the same grammatical form (*šbṭk* + *mšʿntk* [vs. 4b], *ṭwb* + *ḥsd* [vs. 6a]). There is one very striking case in Ps 23 of internal **phonetic** parallelism (*ʾīʾrāʾ rāʿ*, vs. 4a) and several less striking ones; I have found nothing so obvious in *ʿnt* I or Prov 2.

Repetitive parallelism does not occur in regular distribution in Ps 23, only in the near and distant distributions. This is quite a different situation from *ʿnt* I, where there were six repetitive parallelisms in regular distribution, three of nouns and three of particles. In Prov 2, on the other hand, this distribution of repetitive parallelism is frequent but largely limited to particles (eleven cases of particles, only two of substantives). As for **grammatical** parallelism in regular distribution, though there is some semantico-grammatical parallelism (esp. the second and third line-segments of the first verse), it may be said that Ps 23 is characterized by "non-parallel" lines. The lack of parallelism in these lines may or may not extend to both semantic and grammatical features. In vs. 3 the grammatical parallelism of the prepositional phrases includes no semantic element; in vs. 5a the prepositions themselves are semantically parallel but the nouns of these phrases are not; in vs. 6a there is neither grammatical nor semantic parallelism except for that of the 1 c. s. pronouns. Both of the other texts here being compared had a higher proportion of tightly structured lines; though the gradations of semantic and grammatical parallelism in regular distribution in Ps 23 may be found in these two texts, there is not so high a proportion of lines seriously lacking in semantic and even grammatical parallelism. One does find in *ʿnt* I, however, three verses that show similarities to the "non-parallelistic" verses of Ps 23: the bicolon in ll. 12–13 is a form of list which includes some grammatical disparity (nouns of different gender, number, and case); ll. 18–19 have a complex structure of verbs in the first line-segment and a noun with a prepositional phrase in the second, but the noun is semantically related to the verbs (verbs of making music // instrument; comparable to Ps 23:4ab,γ, where *ṣlmwt* and *rʿ* are in very different syntactic structures); ll. 20–21 has a modifier clause as the second line-segment (like vss. 3c, 4ab, 5ab, 6ab, and 6bb in Ps 23) with no obvious semantic parallelism between the line-segments. It is not without interest that the poem that shares these "irregular" features with Ps 23 is the Ugaritic one, viz., the more archaic one. In Prov 2 there was a fairly large number of synonymous parallelisms in regular distribution that lacked grammatical parallelism (seven in twenty-two verses) and an even greater number of parallels that were grammatical but not semantic (nine) but only two that lacked important elements of both grammar and semantic proximity (*hᶜzbym* // *llkt* in vs. 13 and *lᶜśwt* // *bthpkwt* in vs. 14). There was no case in Prov 2 where the entire structure of a verse was characterized by lack of semantic or grammatical parallelism (nothing like *ᶜnt* I 20–21 or Ps 23:6a and 6b). *ᶜnt* I and Ps 23 share, therefore, the feature of "non-parallel" line-segments, with varying degrees of semantic and grammatical non-parallelism. In both works the lack of regular parallelism may be compensated for by near parallelism (e.g., *yšr . . . yšr* // *bᶜl . . . bᶜl* in the three bicola in *ᶜnt* I 18–24; *ymy . . . ymym* in Ps 23:6a and 6b). As we saw above, however, the incidence of near distributions of semantic parallelisms is just as high in Prov 2 as in *ᶜnt* I and one cannot, therefore, speak of near parallelism as only operating when regular distributions are absent. The **phonetic** parallelism in regular distribution of Ps 23 does not seem to differ in any remarkable way from that of the other two texts: the tendency to concentrate a few consonants and vowels (contrast vss. 1–3) where there is no parallelism of *ā*, with vss. 4–5 where *ā* is repeated) within a given verse is clear but the passage from structure to meaning in phonetic parallelism is particularly difficult.[47] It can in any case be said regarding Ps 23 that the incidence of consonant repetition ("consonantism" or "alliteration") is at as high a level as in the two poems here being compared and that certain vowel patterns are visible as well. Since semantic and grammatical parallelism are not consistently strong, one might argue that phonetic parallelism plays a particularly important role in this work.

There are as many instances of near distribution of **repetitive** parallelism as in *ᶜnt* I (five) but more of these are particles (three substantives in *ᶜnt* I as opposed to only one in Ps 23). In Prov 2 repetitive parallelism in near distribution played an important role (fourteen instances of which seven were substantives). This comparatively less important role of repetitive parallelism in this particular distribution in Ps 23 is only a function of the comparatively less important role of repetitive parallelism throughout

47. See R. Jakobson and L. R. Waugh, *The Sound Shape of Language* (Bloomington: Indiana Univ., 1979).

the work, however, for the near distribution of the various combinations of types of parallelism is the one area in which Ps 23 outshines the other two texts (see the tabulation above, this section). This strength in near parallelism is achieved, however, by particle repetition at the expense of substantives, for in Ps 23 a full half the near parallels are particles, while in *ˁnt* I only two of nine are particles. Prov 2 approaches the ratio of Ps 23, with seven of nineteen near parallelisms consisting of particles. This repetition of particles does seem to contribute to near structures (witness the *b*- in the first three tricola, perhaps the *ky* in vss. 4a and 4b and the *w*- in vss. 6a and 6b). Let us remember that particle repetition did not play a role in either internal or regular parallelism in Ps 23 (in contrast with the other two poems being compared) and the same will be seen to be true in the distant distribution. **Semantic** parallelism *per se* is not especially well represented in near distribution in Ps 23: the only strong cases are the "leading to pasture" nouns and verbs in vss. 1–4a. The other examples are weaker (primary verbs of movement; body parts of which one is prepositionalized; "table // cup"). In contrast, six of nine near parallels in *ˁnt* I are semantically strong and about half of those in Prov 2 may be so characterized. It was concluded regarding **grammatical** parallelism in *ˁnt* I and Prov 2 that it only played a role in supralinear structures when it was part of a larger structure, repetitive or semantic, the reasoning being that the relatively few features of grammar do not permit the infinite shadings of lexicon. In Ps 23 there is the quasi-metrical problem of the proper division of vss. 5 and 6, already discussed above (at quantitative analysis and at grammatical parallelism). Both "meter" and "syntactic constraints" seem to indicate that vss. 5 and 6 are to be divided into two bicola each, but from the perspective of semantic and grammatical parallelism each verse could be an individual bicolon. The recognition of the near distribution as a proper forum for parallelism allows us to resolve the problem. The "author" produced four bicola (and gave sufficient indication of that structure, primarily the syntactic independence of the two segments of vs. 5a, so that the listener would not be totally disoriented) but arranged the grammatical parallelisms primarily in "near" distribution: *tˁrk . . . dšnt* (the only two 2m.s.verbal forms in the work), *l pny šlḥn . . . b šmn rʾšy* (vss. 5a and 5b), *kl-ymy ḥyy . . . b byt-yhwh // l ʾrk ymym* (vss. 6a and 6b; in this case the somewhat weak grammatical parallelism of unmarked adverbial with prepositional phrases is strengthened by *ymy . . . ymym*, the one near repetitive parallelism of a substantive).

This grammatical parallelism is linked with repetitive parallelism (1 c. s. suffixes and *ymy* // *ymym*) but there is not a uniquely semantic parallelism. It might be argued, therefore, that grammatical similarity plays a greater structural role in these four bicola than anywhere else in the poems here being compared. This might be said to constitute a further argument in favor of looking for grammatical similarity before looking for grammatical dissimilarity.[48] An argument could be made for **phonetic** parallelism contributing significantly to the near structure in vs. 5 (there is significant repetition of three consonants in the verse as well as many repetitions of vowels) but the same degree of phonetic repetition cannot be seen in vs. 6. As in my previous study the same conclusion was reached regarding phonetic repetition as regarding grammatical, viz., that they do not usually operate beyond the line level, it is not surprising that there are no other phonetic structures to point out in near distribution (other than the all-pervasive vowels and consonants of the 1 c. s. suffixes).

Parallelisms in distant structures were found in my previous studies to be primarily of the repetitive and semantic types and semantic parallelism is usually mixed with repetitive parallelism in distant structures. There is nothing in Ps 23 that changes this picture, though the relatively reduced role of repetitive parallelism in the work as a whole is reflected in the low overall incidence of distant parallelism in this work. The *inclusio* formed by the divine name is the clearest example of **repetitive** distant parallelism but as no other divine names appear in this work, there is no semantic parallelism linked with this repetition. The primary verbs of movement form a combination of repetitive and **semantic** parallels which includes the distant structure *yšwbb . . . šbty* but the second element of this particular example is, as has already been pointed out, textually dubious. All other distant repetitive parallels are of particles and none of these is linked with another clear structure in such a way as to make the contribution of the particle clear. This is a negative reflection of results obtained in the analysis of *ʿnt* I and Prov 2, for in those works particles were seen to *participate* in clearly definable ways in distant structures but not to *constitute* in and of themselves clearly recognizable distant structures. Because of their relatively limited repertories of features, **grammatical** and **phonetic** parallelism are not expected to constitute independent

48. See my *Ugaritic and Hebrew Poetic Parallelism* (N 2), Appendix II.

distant structures and they do not do so in Ps 23—except in the ubiquity of the 1 c. s. pronominal forms (which occur, of course, in all distributions). But neither do grammatical and phonetic parallelisms *participate* in distant structures as they did in both *ʿnt* I and Prov 2.

These results may be added to those extracted from the analysis of *ʿnt* I and Prov 2, viz., that certain Hebrew "wisdom" poetry was more tightly organized than was some Ugaritic narrative poetry: certain Hebrew lyric poetry will make even greater demands on non-"regular" structural devices than do either of the other genres. Need it be added that detailed analyses of many other works (including some prose works to see how they compare) are needed before anything approaching a description according to genres is possible?[49] What I have considered to be one of the most basic conclusions regarding the types and distributions of parallelism in Ugaritic and Hebrew poetry, viz., that the lack of "regular" semantic parallelism may be made up for by other types of parallelism in other distributions, is corroborated by the analysis of Ps 23. The ABB structure of the first tricolon is a standard structure of Ugaritic and Hebrew poetry (whether it be analyzed as a tricolon or as a monocolon plus a bicolon); viewed as a tricolon, the extreme regularity of the parallelism of the second and third line-segments can be seen as compensating for the lack of semantic parallelism between the first line-segment and the other two. In the second tricolon, grammatical and phonetic parallelism provide the cohesion within the line, while near parallelism on both sides, both semantic and grammatical (especially *b nʾwt dšʾ . . . b mʿgly-ṣdq . . . b gyʾ ṣlmwt*) provide a surrounding structure. The third tricolon is syntactically continuous but contains regular semantic parallelism (*ṣlmwt* // *rʿ*) and the strongest half-line phonetic parallelism of the work (*ʾīʸrāʾ rāʿ*). There is also the strong grammatical, semantic (antonymic), and phonetic near parallelism of *b gyʾ ṣlmwt* with *b mʿgly-ṣdq* in vs. 3. Vs. 4b has both the strong internal parallelism *šbṭk* + *mšʿntk* and the strong functional parallelism of *ʾth* // *šbṭk* + *mšʿntk* // *hmh*; the semantic and grammatical parallelisms of the second and third half-lines are strengthened by phonetic parallelism. It has already been pointed out above that the primary structural feature of vss. 5–6 is near grammatical parallelism,

49. For semi-popular analyses according to genre, see Robert Alter, *The Art of Biblical Poetry* (New York: Basic Books, 1985).

strengthened by near (*ymy . . . ymym*; *w- . . . w-*) and distant (*yhwh*) repetitive parallelism and by phonetic parallelism in the case of vs. 5.

A valid conclusion to the formal part of this inquiry appears to be that Ps 23 does constitute a piece of poetry. The basic reason for this conclusion may be stated from two perspectives: (1) There are too many poetic features for the work to be characterized as simple prose; (2) All sections which are heavily characterized by prose syntax contain or are surrounded by poetic features and the work cannot be characterized as elevated prose or as poetry with prosaic intrusions.[50] Whoever created this work was aware of how what we characterize as "regular" Hebrew poetry worked but he chose for whatever reason (because he was an individualist? because he belonged to a poetic school which produced a poetry with the formal characteristics that we see in Ps 23?) to produce a form of poetry in which the poetic devices would be distributed less regularly than, say, in Prov 2.

I would argue, adopting in a rather naive and philological way the methodology and terminology of E. Schauber and E. Spolsky (the "preference model" of interpretation),[51] that the indicators of poetry are set conspicuously at the head of this work (the second and third segments of the first line) and that regular semantic parallelism and the other types and distributions of parallelism[52]

50. An example of the latter: I cannot agree with R. Althann (*A Philological Analysis of Jeremiah 4–6 in the Light of Northwest Semitic* [Biblica et Orientalia 38; Rome: Pontifical Biblical Institute, 1983]: 166–170, 303–307) that all of Jer 5:18–19 constitutes poetry. Not until the last part of vs. 19 (*kʾšr . . .*) does one find anything even approaching parallelism (the features adduced on p. 304 are either created by the author [*lōʾ* > *lēʾ*] or are simply prose repetitions [*tʾmrw . . . wʾmrt*; *lnw . . . ʾlyhm*]). To me it appears necessary to argue that the stretch of prose in Jer 5:18–19a is simply too long to be assimilated into a poetic structure and that this prose section is clearly set off by narrative discourse markers that serve also to introduce the poetry of vs. 19b. I do not mean to imply that the distinction between prose and poetry in Jeremiah will always be so clear, for that is a work characterized by admixtures of prose and poetry, probably in all degrees (poetry, prosaicized poetry, elevated prose, prose), and only a very careful analysis which would include some responsible text criticism could begin to describe the formal characteristics of the work.

51. *The Bounds of Interpretation: Linguistic Theory and Literary Text* (Stanford: Stanford Univ., 1986).

52. It is the failure to look at types and distributions of parallelism other than "regular" semantic parallelism that have led Kugel to give an even more pessimistic assessment of the parallelistic structure of this poem than it merits (*Idea* [N 3]: 50–51). F. Landy, in assessing Kugel's work ("Poetics and Parallelism: Some

are then used frequently enough throughout the rest of the work that the listener can be in no doubt that it is poetry that he is hearing. These features are strong enough that the listener will give preference to them in his registering of what the formal structure of this work is and will reject the "non-poetic" structures as indicators of prose.[53]

Macrostructure

The microstructures with which we have been working to this point indicate fairly clearly the larger structure of the work. The *inclusio* formed by the repetitive parallelism indicates the wish to integrate the first statement regarding YHWH as the shepherd with the final statement regarding dwelling in YHWH's house. In between, however, there has been a radical shift in the parallelistic structure and in the imagery. This shift took place in two steps. The first step is the shift from "herding" verbs in vss. 1–3 (semantic parallel group #6); the second is the complete shift from herding imagery to festal imagery and is coupled with the "metric" structure of the text, the shift from tricola to bicola between vss. 4 and 5.

Comments on James Kugel's *The Idea of Biblical Poetry*," *JSOT* 28 [1984]: 61–87, esp. 76–78), has taken an approach very similar to the one I advocate in this paragraph but also underevaluates the presence of genuine parallelism by failing to consider all the types and distributions.

53. For my reaction to Kugel's *Idea* (N 3), see my "Types and Distributions of Parallelism in Ugaritic and Hebrew Poetry" (communication to the Society of Biblical Literature in 1981; published as Appendix II in *Ugaritic and Hebrew Poetic Parallelism* [N 2]). With regard to the classification of poetry as compared with prose, to date Kugel has, in my estimation, done little more than point out that a gray area exists between the two. He is surely at least partially correct, however, in his suggestion (*JSOT* 28 [1984] 110) that one must evoke syntactic criteria to describe the difference and that what is necessary now is a rigorous comparison between prose and poetic syntax, not just a description of poetic syntax. By overemphasizing the gray area and by giving more weight to the general "seconding" function of parallelism than to a description of its details, however (what I referred to in my paper cited earlier in this note as refusing to classify the trees because one has perceived how the forest works), Kugel has apparently led some to extreme conclusions regarding the overt manifestations of parallelism. It is patent nonsense to say in general that parallelism "is found just as frequently in biblical prose as in biblical poetry" (B. Vawter, *Biblica* 66 [1985]: 208, n. 4). Though given pieces of either prose or poetry may exhibit features of the other, to say that II Kings 17, for example, contains an equivalent number of parallelistic structures, defined lexically or grammatically, as Prov 2 makes no sense to me.

The main characteristic of the first section is the passivity of the "speaker" as he is "herded" by YHWH. In the second section the sheep-herding terminology continues but the "speaker" acts (*ʾlk*, *ʾyrʾ*) and YHWH, by means of his surrogates (*šbṭk wmšʿntk*), reacts. This reaction is expressed by a term which, though it has phonetic features in common with the verbs of herding in vss. 1–3, is more properly used for a human object (*nḥm*). In vss. 5–6 the herding imagery is dropped completely: there are no semantic parallels with any of the specifically rustic terms (nouns and verbs) used above, the parallels being either with more general words (*yhwh*; *yšwbb . . . šbty*) or antonymic (*ṭwb* + *ḥsd*, vs. 6a, with *rʿ*, vs. 4a; *ḥyy*, vs. 6a, with *ṣlmwt*, vs. 4a).

The three main sections depict, therefore, (1) the happy state of being herded by YHWH, (2) the dangers in that state and the continued guidance of YHWH the shepherd, (3) a new state of felicity expressed in purely human terms. This structure is the classic one of felicity, crisis, and victory, felicity. But this classic structure is given a novel twist by the shift from non-human to human imagery in vs. 5—imagery which if the shift is not observed puts sheep and goats at the table. The rhetorical progression of this twist is from bucolic imagery to ambiguous terms to the depiction of human prosperity: *šbṭ* is ambiguous; *nḥm* is at best ambiguous; *šlḥn* leaves no doubt that a switch in imagery has been made. The rhetorical progression is matched by a "metrical" one, the shift from tricola to bicola in the banqueting scene. It will be suggested in the commentary that this combination of bucolic and royal imagery is only comprehensible in the context of royal ideology. The first-person expression[54] of the piece and the rather muted national/royal motifs have, however, made it immediately self-applicable to Everyman. The combination of bucolic imagery and the prevalence of first-person indicators, with the ultimate triumph of *ego*,[55] are sufficient to account for the long-term popularity of this work.

54. Mittmann's concentration on the "Du-Teil" and the "Er-Teil" of this psalm (N 4): 18–20) is so complete that he overlooks the ubiquitous and hardly incidental "Ich" that dominates the entire work.

55. Psychologically, it is the linking of *ego* and triumph that constitute its appeal, not simply that it is "a pure expression of confidence in God" (S. Mowinckel, *The Psalms in Israel's Worship* [Oxford: Blackwell, 1962; Nashville: Abingdon, 1967]: 2.41; on p. 127 Mowinckel stresses the personal experience behind Ps 23).

Commentary

This reflects no pretention to produce a full-scale commentary, but some philological remarks are in order at the end of this poetic study. (Be it noted that, though no form of research is ever carried out in a vacuum, especially not research on so well-known a text as Ps 23, the poetic section of this paper was indeed actually redacted before this philological section.)

The first occurrence of the 1 c. s. suffix is "objective" and gives the tone to the entire work: "YHWH herds me," not "YHWH is a shepherd who belongs to me and who herds my sheep." If there were any doubt as to this interpretation, it seems to be dispelled by the following verbs + 1 c. s. pronoun, for the semantics of these verbs is linked closely with the tending of animals. The image of the deity as a shepherd is known from other Hebrew texts and from other ancient Near Eastern sources.[56] R. S. Tomback has shown recently that the combination of *rbṣ* and "green pastures" provides an image of peaceful security.[57] The precise sense of *mē*^{y} *mənūḥō*^{w}*t* is less clear: is this phrase "waters of repose" a "subjective genitive" denoting "quiet waters" or an "objective genitive" denoting "waters which produce repose"? The traditional answer has been "both": ovids/caprids prefer to drink from smooth-surfaced water, while in homiletic contexts, the interpretation must indicate the moral result, i.e., repose in YHWH.[58]

56. F. Asensio, "Entrecruce de simbolos y realidades en el Salmo 23," *Biblica* 40 (1959): 237–247; G. Rinaldi, "Il Salmo 23 (Volg. 22) (dominus regit me)," *Bibbia e Oriente* 3 (1961): 81–85; Merrill (N 14): 357–358; Milne (N 14): 239–241; Freedman, "Psalm" (N 13): 148–149; Mittmann, (N 4): 20–21. For a special emphasis on the shepherd motif in Egyptian, see D. Muller, "Der Gute Hirte: Ein Beitrag zur Geschichte ägyptischer Bildrede," *ZAS* 86 (1961): 126–141, accepted by D. B. Redford, "The Relations Between Egypt and Israel from El Amarna to the Babylonian Conquest," *Biblical Archaeology Today: Proceedings of the International Congress on Biblical Archaeology, Jerusalem, April 1984* (Jerusalem: Israel Exploration Society, 1985): 192–205, esp. p. 198.

57. "Psalm 23:2 Reconsidered," *JNSL* 10 (1982): 93–96. His comparison of the following phrase with an Akkadian incantation "in still waters be my oar, my god, in deep waters be my steering paddle" (p. 95) is considerably less illuminating because of the different motifs surrounding the "still waters" image. It may, however, provide a clue that the two cultures both saw "still waters" as an image of peace as opposed to the deadly connotations of "still waters" for deep-sea sailors!

58. This verse has been compared with the other biblical references to the rest afforded by YHWH to his people (Rinaldi [N 56]: 83) or has been linked more specifically to the Jerusalem tradition (Merrill [N 14]: 358, 359–360) or to the Exodus (Freedman, "Psalm" [N 13]: 150–151).

The meaning of the imagery of vs. 3 is difficult to pin down but, judging from the continuation of herding images in the following lines, it appears best to explain the terms as appropriate for animal husbandry.[59] *npšy* would refer, therefore, to the "throat" of the animal which is "brought back"[60] from the edge of death by the life-giving waters mentioned in the preceding verse. *ṣdq* in such a context surely refers to "right" ways, that is, safe ones for flocks to travel, but it also contains moral overtones[61] that will be reflected in the morally charged terms *ṭwb w ḥsd* in the final section of the poem. The following phrase, *l mᶜn šmw*, emphasizes the metaphorical side of *mᶜgly ṣdq* for it normally occurs in contexts of salvation expressed in non-bucolic terms.[62] The phrase in this case does not denote purpose but "correspondence to," the norm being YHWH's "name": he does what he is expected to do.

The "crisis" section is enunciated by the terms *ṣlmwt* // *rᶜ* and *yrᵓ*. The precise meaning of *ṣlmwt* is uncertain (*ṣl* + *mwt* or *ṣlm* + fem.pl. morpheme?) but in this case we can to a degree have

59. It appears to me, therefore, that Asensio abandons the *imagery* too early when he says that "En cuanto a *nefeš*-alma, no parece que, dado el ambiente metafórico de todo el salmo, haya razón para sustituírle con *nefeš*-garganta" (N 56): 241, n. 5 from p. 240). One must always pierce the meaning of a phrase before substituting (!) a metaphorical interpretation (my exclamation mark is intended to convey that Asensio has inverted the proper order of substituting). In the present case, though the poet is undoubtedly referring ultimately to the well-being of the king, he is at this moment presenting this well-being in terms proper to sheep and goats.

60. The translation offered above, "he gives me new life," is Meek's ([N 13]: 234; cf. Tournay [N 14]: 505 "il y refait mon âme"; Mittmann [N 4]: 3 "er erneurt meine Lebenskraft" [see his comment pp. 5–7]). It has the advantage of expressing the restoration to life implied by the verb *šb* without implying resurrection. Dahood's "Elysian Fields" (*Psalms I* [N 14]: 145) are out of the question here, in my estimation: the three phrases that could support such a statement, *napšīʸ yəšōʷbēb*, *ṣalmāwet*, and *ləᵓōrek yāmīʸm*, are all (part of) references to maintenance of life, not to resurrection, as the pastoral and royal imagery in general and the phrase *wəšabtīʸ bəbēʸt YHWH* in particular make clear.

61. One may accept that the phrase had such moral overtones without asserting that we have already passed from herding imagery to moral formulation (so Vogt [N 14]: 206–208).

62. Rinaldi (N 56): 82; Johnson (N 14): 259–260; Freedman, "Psalm" (N 13): 153–155; Mittmann (N 4): 8. At the risk of proving not to be one of "the discerning" who can appreciate the value of H. L. Ginsberg's emendation of *l mᶜn šmw* to *l šwrry* "because of them that lie in wait for me" ("Some Emendations in Psalms," *HUCA* 23/1 [1950–51]: 99–100), I must demur: it appears to me that Ginsberg has missed the salvific overtones which the other occurrences of the phrase indicate were a part of *l mᶜn šmw*.

our cake and eat it for the element *-māwet* can operate either by etymology or by punning.[63] The tricolon in vs. 4b is the pivot of this work, for its central segment contains two terms which, from the preceding images, should be expected to denote the shepherd's staff but the first of which, especially, is susceptible of being interpreted as the judge's rod or the king's scepter.[64] The turn in the direction of human concerns is made explicit by the verb *nḥm*, for flocks receive care rather than "comfort."[65] The attempt to dilute the shift in imagery by making the point of reference be the Exodus[66] does not really solve the problem of imagery, for the imagery shifts, no matter what the metaphorical application of the images be. The question is whether the entire body of imagery better fits the Exodus or royal concerns. Below, I will prefer the latter solution.

63. If the word is revocalized as *ṣalmūt* (cf. Asensio [N 56]: 242; Johnson [N 14]: 260; Freedman, "Psalm" [N 13]: 142), the pun is less clear. A revocalization *ṣəlāmôt*, equally plausible, would leave the pun clearer.

64. For an interpretation of the two terms grounded in *realia*, see Power (N 14): 434–442. Such a realistic interpretation does not, of course, invalidate, rather it provides a basis for other levels of interpretation: (1) poetic (half-line parallelism providing a cumulative effect); (2) literary (the royal overtones of *šēbeṭ*); (3) theological (YHWH as both guide and protector), etc. Mittmann's rejection of the imagery and of the line as poetry is unconvincing by its arbitrariness and reliance on outmoded perceptions of Hebrew poetic structure ([N 4]: 11).

65. It is obvious from this comment and from my previous remarks on structure, that the emendation of *nḥm* to *nḥh* (Dahood, *Psalms I* [N 14]: 147, without previous literature; cf. Tournay [N 14]: 504; Asensio [N 56]: 242–243; Ammassari [N 14]: 258) appears to me gratuitous, for it replaces rhetorical subtlety with morphological subtlety ("enclitic" *mem*). The new twist in Dahood's last statement on the topic combines adhesion to the verb *nḥh* with his new-found "destiny," of Eblaitic origin: *yanḥū mənī* "they guide my destiny" (*Biblica* 60 [1979]: 417–419). Freedman, "Psalm" ([N 13]: 154) adds a further argument regarding *yənaḥămūnī*^{y} that may or may not be valid: if this form were from *nḥh* it would constitute the only case of repetitive parallelism of a verb in this poem. The hesitation arises, of course, from *yəšō*^{w}*bēb*/*wəšabtī*^{y}, which may be a case of verbal repetitive parallelism (see above, note 14, and comment below to vs. 6). Even if one takes the two forms just cited as from one root, however, Freedman's argument regarding *yənaḥămūnī*^{y} is still persuasive for the first section of the psalm, vss. 1–4, for *yəšō*^{w}*bēb*/*wəšabtī*^{y} belong each to a different section. His semantic analysis, however, is not nearly so persuasive (*nḥm* = "protect, defend, vindicate") and is as much a misapprehension of the rhetorical purpose of the term as is that behind the emendation/reanalysis.

66. Milne (N 14): 244–245. Such an interpretational means of solving the problem of the shift in imagery is certainly, however, an improvement on far-fetched philological explanations which usually involve some form of emendation (for an overview, see Merrill [N 14]: 354–360).

Vss. 5 and 6 contain only imagery proper for human referents. It is both a reflection in palatial terms of the bucolic luxury of vss. 1–3 and, more specifically, imagery proper to a victor, for the word "adversaries" is used. The image is that of the victory banquet, one well known from Assyrian reliefs.[67] Most commentators have rejected attempts to "unify" the imagery of this work by making of *šlḥn* a word for a weapon, rather than the common word for table.[68] If the structure of the poem may be said to have its unity in royal imagery such philological sleight-of-hand is seen to be unnecessary (especially as several changes are needed to provide complete unity[69]). The term "adversaries" poses a particular problem for the narrow interpretation of this psalm as referring to the Exodus[70] for the motif of the "adversary" is not common to the Exodus stories.[71] I cannot believe that in a text so economically worded as this the word *ṣōrərāy* was not meant to contribute to the principal argument. The imagery is primarily royal, therefore, as Barré and Kselman have shown, and the only question is whether one can "justify the postulate of a reinterpretation of this imagery on the part of the poet in the direction of the new exodus/restoration theme."[72] I find their argument in favor of such a justification unconvincing: it requires a multi-levelled application, *by allusion*

67. For special emphasis on the royal victory aspect of this imagery, see Barré and Kselman (N 14): 104–106. Their change of heart recorded on pp. 121–22, viz., that *ṣrry* should be interpreted "bowels," requiring as it does an emendation of *ngd* to *ngr*, does not inspire confidence. *ngd* does not mean "in the sight of," as they translate (though it may imply proximity permitting observation), but "over against"—the emphasis is on opposition, not on proximity and certainly not on vision. The banquet interpretation is more convincing by the parallels cited by Barré and Kselman than is Merrill's explanation of the motifs in vs. 5 as referring to a coronation ceremony (N 14: 357, 359). Having grease rubbed in one's hair does not necessarily imply coronation, for the practice was followed in various situations (see my listing of the texts in *BiOr* 34 [1977]: 14–19, with citations of some of the literature).

68. Power (N 14): 434–442; accepted by Morgenstern (N 14): 15–16; Koehler (N 14): 233; rejected by Vogt (N 14): 197; Asensio (N 56): 243–244; Merrill (N 14): 355; Mittmann (N 4): 12–13.

69. The most consistent interpretation of Ps 23 as reflecting only herding imagery of which I am aware is Koehler's ([N 14]: 227–234), who profited by and took inspiration from the previous suggestions of Power and Morgenstern for reinterpreting certain terms and emending the recalcitrant ones. Rhetorical metricism.

70. Milne (N 14): 237–247; Freedman, "Psalm" (N 13): 139–166; Barré and Kselman accept much of the hypothesis but expand upon it and present the theological point of the exodus references as being the "new covenant" necessary for post-exilic restoration ([N 14]: 97–127).

71. As Freedman honestly admits ("Psalm" [N 13]: 160–161).

72. Barré and Kselman (N 14): 106.

only since there is no explicit reference to Exodus or post-exilic restoration, of royal motifs to the post-exilic community, with this community presented as a royal individual.[73] Is it not just as plausible to say that the lexical parallels in Jer 31:10–14[74] are reflections of the terminology of the royal psalms and thereby a partial reinterpretation of them (king standing for people; nostalgia for period of royalty, i.e., of political independence)? The key to the Exodus hypothesis (and its redevelopment by Barré and Kselman) is the phrase *taʿărōk ləpānay šulḥān*, for a very similar phrase is used in Ps 78:19 with reference to the Exodus. But to say that "of these passages [referring to the spreading of a table], only one sheds direct light on the meaning in Ps 23"[75] is rather prejudging the case in favor of the Exodus interpretation, for the other occurrences of *ʿrk* + *šlḥn* (Isa 21:5; 65:11; Ezek 23:41) show that the phrase can be used in quite disparate contexts and that it is not linked *literarily* to any one set of motifs. One may conclude that Ps 23:5 does not necessarily constitute a literary reflection of Ps 78:19 and that it must be interpreted from the angle of *ṣōrərāy* (i.e., as a royal victory motif) rather than from the specific context of Ps 78.

73. Barré and Kselman do not address adequately the literary problem of who the protagonist is meant to be. They state: "As the king prays in Ps 23:6 that he never be excluded from Yahweh's house, so the psalmist prays in the name of the exiles that they never again be excluded from the Promised Land" and "the psalmist here has artfully reworked the language, imagery, and motifs of royal psalmody and theology. The result is that . . . language once applied to the Davidic king (royal imagery) is now applied to the exilic community (restoration imagery)" (ibid., p. 113). But who is the "king" (the "I") of the post-exilic work? Were poets producing works in this period from the perspective of royalty, works which bear not a single explicit statement of origin and purpose? If a Judaean heard this work for the first time after 586, how was he to know whether it was an old (royal) work that he had happened not to hear before or a new (restoration) work full of allusions to the old situation? How was he to know that the *royal* references were really *community* references? Since I cannot determine how the post-exilic Judaean could have made such a decision, I *a fortiori* cannot make one. I can think of only one really plausible historical context for the production of this work with the implications that Freedman/Barré/Kselman would have it exhibit: it would be a work of a member of the royal family in exile or of a member of the royal entourage (a court poet in exile). The lack of specific statements would be owing to the political circumstances which would not have permitted overt assertions of royal restoration and revenge on the enemies of Judaean royalty.

74. Cited by Freedman, "Psalms" (N 13): 161; Barré and Kselman ([N 14]: 106) give as their principal text Isa 55:1–3 (important for the provisions motif but lacking the shepherd motif).

75. Freedman, "Psalms" (N 13): 159.

In verse 6 the terminology of divine benevolence towards human subjects, particularly *ḥsd*, is employed to set up a situation opposite to the dangerous *gyʾ ṣlmwt* and these virtues are said to dog the heels of the victor just as surely as his adversaries would have done had YHWH not protected the hero.[76] As vocalized in the Massoretic tradition, *wšbty* repeats the root by which the revival of life-giving water was expressed in vs. 3. If that analysis is correct, the hero is depicted as promising to return to the temple of YHWH on a regular basis for the rest of his days.[77] Only by stretching the

76. Barré and Kselman ([N 14]: 102–104) have cited biblical and extra-biblical parallels for the personification of weals and woes and have pointed out the reversal of polarity in this work (*rdp* usually is used in negative contexts). I doubt that this is an explicit reference to the new covenant (Jer 31), as they wish to have it, and this contention of theirs, even if accepted, does not rule out a quasi-demonic explanation of the terms (according to Dahood *ṭwb wḥsd* may be attendants on YHWH [*Psalms I* (N 14): 148; in *Psalms II* (1968): 51, he refers to such "attendants" as "demythologized" from an earlier status as Canaanite divinities; see the criticism by K. D. Sakenfeld, *The Meaning of Hesed in the Hebrew Bible: A New Inquiry* (Harvard Semitic Monographs 17; Missoula: Scholars Press, 1978]: 218–219, n. 6)]; according to Freedman *ṭwb wḥsd* would refer to "lesser divine beings" sent forth from YHWH, "demythologized . . . divine attributes," or "an early form of the later doctrine of guardian angels" ("Psalm" [N 13]: 162); G. J. Thierry earlier considered the possibility that they might be "protecting angels": "Notes on Hebrew Grammar and Etymology," *OTS* 9 [1951]: 1–17, esp. 14). Are such (de-)mythological interpretations necessary, however? Were ancient poets incapable of non-mythological personification? (Be it noted in passing that taking the two terms as angelic names is not a demythologization but a mythologization on another level!) Milne's attempt to set up a parallelism between *šibṭəkā ūʷmišʿantekā* and *ṭōʷb wāḥesed* ([N 14]: 238–239, 243–244), though somewhat weakened by the erroneous inclusion of *hēmmāʰ* (analyzed as an interjection, see above) as part of the structure, might lead one to identify *ṭōʷb wāḥesed* as the abstract equivalents of the concrete protectors *šibtəkā ūʷmišʿantekā* rather than as personifications. Tournay ([N 14]: 504) refers to both pairs of terms as personifications but makes no attempt to link the two sets.

77. Barré's and Kselman's explanation of the phrase *wšbty* as referring to preservation from the sort of illness that would prevent the king from entering the temple ([N 14]: 108–114) might be used as an argument for the phrase *wšbty* being interpreted as from *šb* "return" (though they do not do so). Alternatively, it may be from *yšb* and have the nuance of English "sit," or it may be taken hyperbolically, viz., the semi-divine status of the king means that ideologically he "dwells" in the temple even if in fact he does not do so. For such statements elsewhere in the Psalms, see Vogt (N 14): 209–210; Mittmann (N 4): 14–15; P. C. Beentjes, "Inverted Quotations in the Bible: A Neglected Stylistic Pattern," *Biblica* 68 [1982]: 506–523, esp. 512–513. In any case, the clear royal imagery of the rest of the poem precludes ascribing this one feature to a levitical origin (Tournay [N 14]: 504, 511), not even as a late revocalization—unless one be willing to accept that whoever revocalized this word pro-levitically had misunderstood the other motifs.

imagination to the limits can *ʾrk ymym* be taken to denote eternal life.[78] The "life" after death known very vaguely from the Ugaritic texts is both spatially and qualitatively different from earthly life: I know of no Ugaritic or Biblical text which would permit the inference that that the deceased "dwell" in the temple of the principal deity. At the limit, *wəšabtīʸ* could refer to the "return" of the king's shade when called up for some purpose.[79] Barré's and Kselman's interpretation of this verse as referring to protection from debilitation (see note 77) appears more plausible, however.

These various motifs are best summed up in one person, that of the king. He is the shepherd of his people but desires to receive himself the same form of care and is thus depicted in the first section as himself in need of a shepherd. He must face adversaries who are capable of causing him to descend to the underworld and his deity must be strong enough to enable him to win out over these adversaries and their deity. Once this is accomplished he can take his pleasures in a way fit only for humans and can praise his deity for the protection granted. The poem is best identified as royal and dated to the late royal period or perhaps to the exilic period;[80] in the latter case it is to be seen as a song expressing

78. Dahood, *Psalms I* (N 14): 149; accepted with some reservations by J. F. Ḥealey, "The Immortality of the King: Ugarit and the Psalms," *Orientalia* n.s. 53 (1984): 245–254, esp. 253. Johnson's position ([N 14]: 262–271) is more nuanced and eventually negative with respect to *ʾrk ymym* here denoting eternity (his example of "I'm forever blowing bubbles" as not denoting eternity is precious).

79. See my discussion of the Ugaritic king list (RS 24.257) in *Les textes para-mythologiques* (Paris: Editions Recherche sur les Civilisations, 1988).

80. In this relatively late dating I follow somewhat blindly the general argumentation of Barré and Kselman but admit freely to not having a settled opinion on the date. The very sophisticated poetic structure that I claim to have found here could be an argument for a relatively late date (I know of nothing like this in Ugaritic, for example) but for lack of data and for lack of specifically chronologically-oriented studies which would be attuned to the new methods of poetic analysis it is impossible at this juncture to say that this poem could not have been composed at any time in the first millennium B.C. before the formation of the psalter. As regards my relatively late dating, I would hold without hesitation that arguments for an early dating such as Ammassari's [N 14]: 257–259) are wholly specious: according to Ammassari, *raᶜ* in vs. 4 would be defective writing for *raᶜāʰ*; *ynḥmny* in vs. 3 would have enclitic *mem*; *ṣrry* in vs. 5 is written defectively; *wšbty* in vs. 6 would be a "forma contratta" of *wyšbty*. The first two have no basis in fact, Qal active participles are normally written defectively in MT, and even if *wšbty* is a byform or a contracted form of *yšb*, which I tend to doubt, there is no proof that such a form is particularly early.

confidence in the restoration of Judaean royalty.[81] Once the speaker is identified as royal, the use of the work as a rallying-point for the people becomes possible because of the king's status as representative of the people.[82] It is virtually impossible to devise a specific life-setting for so short a work which does not include specific historical allusions: it could be a conventional creation of a court poet of the pre-exilic period, it could have arisen from a specific crisis in the life of one of the kings, or it could have arisen from exilic aspirations for the restoration of the monarchy.

81. In the latter case, emphasis is to be kept on restoration of the king and not transferred to a hope for return of the people from exile without a king. As the immediately post-exilic writings show, the return from exile and the restoration of the monarchy were generally linked. Descriptions of the origin of this work which do not include the royal component (e.g., Morgenstern, [N 14]: 23-24; Vogt [N 14]: 195-211; Tournay [N 14]: 511-512) appear seriously deficient. See note 77 above.

82. Merrill (N 14): 357.

MAARAV 5–6 (Spring, 1990): 281–305

JONAH, THE RUNAWAY SERVANT*

ROBERT J. RATNER
EASTERN MONTANA COLLEGE, BILLINGS, MT

The story of Jonah is the story of a runaway servant. Jonah flees from his master, God.

2 Kings 14:25, the text recognized by many as the one from which the author of the book of Jonah derived his main character, presents the following notices: "He [Jeroboam II] restored the border of Israel from the entrance of Hamath as far as the Sea of the Aravah, according to the word of the Lord, the God of Israel, which he spoke by *his servant* Jonah the son of Amittai, the prophet, who was from Gat ha-Ḥefer."[1]

* I am indebted to the remark of S. Goitein in "Some Observations on Jonah," *JPOS* 17/1 (1937): 67: "Jonah flees as a servant from his lord," for stimulating my thinking on Jonah as a runaway servant.

This paper is a revised version of the first chapter of a thesis presented to the faculty of the Hebrew Union College-Jewish Institute of Religion, Cincinnati, titled "Studies in the Book of Jonah" (June, 1988). Thanks are intended to Professor David B. Weisberg, who acted as my thesis advisor, for his many insights and suggestions.

Prof. Weisberg brought to my attention the fact that the Septuagint to Jonah 1:9 has Jonah proclaim to the sailors: "I am a servant of the Lord." The present writer is not inclined to believe that this phrase is original to the text of Jonah. It is of interest, however, that certain textual traditions, certainly under the influence of 2 Kgs 14:25, desired to make explicit Jonah's servanthood to the Lord.

1. Among those who share this view are J. Wellhausen, *Die kleinen Propheten übersetzt und erklärt* (Berlin, 1898): 221; A. Feuillet, "Les sources du livre de Jonas," *RB* 54 (1947): 167; T. Fretheim, "Jonah and Theodicy," *ZAW* 70 (1978): 230; and the many critics who follow K. Budde's suggestion (*ZAW* 12 [1982]: 37–51, esp. 40–43) that the book of Jonah is a *midrash* inspired by 2 Kgs 14:25; cf. the partial list of these scholars given by G. Landes, "JONAH: A Māšāl?" *Israelite Wisdom: S. Terrien Festschrift* (J. Gammie *et al.*, eds.; Missoula, MT: Scholars, 1978): 150–151, notes 1 and 2.

The prophet Jonah, the son of Amittai, is spoken of as the Lord's servant. It is of some interest to note that Amos, who would have been Jonah's contemporary, also spoke of the Lord's prophets as his servants: "For the Lord will do nothing unless he has revealed his plan to *his servants*, the prophets" (3:7). The Lord's servants are called upon by God to act as messengers to his people Israel in particular, and to the people of the world in general.

We are told in 2 Kgs 14:25 that Jonah, the son of Amittai, carried out his appointed commission to Israel faithfully. His words were true and, by extension, he himself was a success. Jonah was a true servant of the Lord. The author of the book of Jonah, who sets out to compose a tract on the prophetic vocation, carefully selects this shadowy figure of antiquity right out of the pages of Israel's own history book. Our author now portrays Jonah as one unwilling to carry out his master's commission to a foreign nation, to the people of Nineveh. In this newly created scenario, the prophet will actually attempt to flee from his master for reasons that will not become clear until the final chapter of the book.

The author establishes the conflict without delay. The Lord addresses Jonah, saying: "Arise, go to Nineveh, that great city, and cry against it . . ." Jonah arises, but flees in the precisely the opposite direction. Will God allow Jonah to escape? Will he kill Jonah and commission another in his stead? In other words, if Jonah is indeed a runaway servant, what alternatives do Jonah's actions place before his master, God?

We would suggest that our author, in viewing Jonah as a runaway servant, may well have been guided in forming his narration by his knowledge of the legal customs pertaining to runaways of the society in which he lived. What was one obliged to do if he found a runaway? What was the view of those contemporaneous cultures surrounding Israel and of Israel herself toward the slave or servant who fled his master's service?

1. THE RUNAWAY IN THE ANCIENT NEAR EAST

In the case of the cultures round about Israel, all the extant evidence points in one direction: Runaways must return or be returned to their masters. The illustrative material presented below has been selected from ancient Near Eastern legal materials, letters, treaties, and wisdom literature. These texts were written in a variety of languages and derive from various times and places. They provide us with a general picture of the runaway servant/slave's status as well as that of the one who harbors him or her.

LAW

The ancient Near Eastern legal materials are of two kinds: (1) law codes and (2) legal documents, including purchase agreements, leases, records of court proceedings, and the like.

Codes

The law "codes"[2] which treat the runaway slave and the necessity of returning him were all written immediately prior to or in the second millennium B.C.E. This fact lessens, to some extent, the importance of these documents for our understanding of the legal milieu in which the writer of Jonah worked (mid-sixth–mid-fifth century B.C.E.). Nevertheless, these codes do testify to the serious threat posed to the economic system by runaways and those who harbored, aided, and abetted them.

The Code of Ḥammurapi (c. mid-eighteenth century B.C.E.), the classic legal formulation of the Old Babylonian period, treats the aider and harborer in paragraphs 15–16 and 19–20:

> [15] If a seignior has helped either a male slave of the state or a female slave of the state or a male slave of a private citizen or a female slave of a private citizen to escape through the city-gate, he shall be put to death.
>
> [16] If a seignior has harbored in his house either a fugitive male or female slave belonging to the state or to a private citizen and has not brought him forth at the summons of the police, the householder shall be put to death.
>
> [19] If he has kept the slave in his house (and) later the slave has been found in his possession, that seignior shall be put to death.

2. J. J. Finkelstein, *The Ox that Gored* (Philadelphia, 1981): 15 and n. 5, discusses the problem in using the term "code" to refer to these ancient documents. We will refer to them as codes hereafter merely for the sake of convenience. The codes that treat the runaway are Urnammu (14′, 21′), Lipit Ishtar (12, 13), Laws of Eshnunna (22, 23), Ḥammurapi (15–20), and the Hittite Laws (22–24).

> [20] If the slave has escaped from the hand of his captor, that seignior shall (so) affirm by god to the owner of the slave and he shall then go free.[3]

The amount of attention paid to slaves in the Code (§§15–20, 278–282) suggests that problems with them must have been common in the Old Babylonian period. These problems would be persistent throughout the long history of slavery in the ancient Near East, as we will see below. Aiding a runaway, from the perspective of the Code's writer, was seen as a most heinous crime.

Earlier laws are much more lenient in cases of harboring, requiring either the replacement of the slave or the payment of fifteen or twenty-five shekels of silver.[4] The punishment in Ḥammurapi's code is extremely harsh for those in the upper level of society, that is, for those most responsible, from the point of view of this legislation, for the maintenance of the society. Such punishment, though never encountered again in the legal literature of Mesopotamia, gives us ample evidence of the supreme importance of returning the runaway to the rightful owner. Without such cooperation among members of society, the slave system could not continue. Incentives were prescribed to nurture this cooperation. In §17, we read:

> If a seignior caught a fugitive male or female slave in the open and has taken him to his owner, the owner of the slave shall pay him two shekels of silver.[5]

The laws treated so far are well over one millennium older than the writing of Jonah and are not directly helpful in giving us a picture of the legal milieu which would have affected this writing. Of greater interest are the numerous legal documents of the Neo-Babylonian (626–539 B.C.E.) and Achaemenid (539–331 B.C.E.) periods, for it is during the time of the Exile (587/6–539 B.C.E.) or immediately after that the book of Jonah was written. The Exile

3. Translated by T. J. Meek, *Ancient Near Eastern Texts*, third edition with supplement, edited by J. Pritchard (Princeton, 1969): 166–167 (hereafter referred to as *ANET*³).

4. The Lipit Ishtar code, pars. 12 and 13, *ANET*³: 160, translated by S. N. Kramer and the Laws of Eshnunna, pars. 22 and 23, *ANET*³:162, translated by A. Goetze; cf. I. Mendelsohn, *Slavery in the Ancient Near East* (New York, 1949): 58, and note 137 on p. 143.

5. This stipulation finds its parallel in Urnammu, par. 14 and in the Hittite Laws, pars. 22, 23.

provided the context for direct contact between Israel and Babylonia, and Babylonian culture had every opportunity to influence that of Israel.

Legal Documents

We are greatly indebted to the monumental work of M. Dandamaev, *Slavery in Babylonia*, as well as to the scholars who have made this work available to the English-speaking world. Dandamaev has collected and organized the vast Babylonian material dealing with slavery from the middle of the first millennium B.C.E. Among the issues treated is the runaway.[6]

Slave sale documents witness to the frequency that slaves must have taken flight. In earlier periods, a clause might be written into the sale agreement providing a three-day escrow period during which an inquiry might be made into the slave's background. This protected the purchaser in the event the slave was in fact a fugitive, in which case the purchaser would be guilty of harboring and might have faced harsh punishment.[7] Under such circumstances, the sale became null and void.[8] In the Neo-Babylonian period and after, the seller often included a clause guaranteeing that the slave would not run away from the purchaser for 100 days.[9] The focus is no longer upon the harm that would be done to the purchaser, but rather upon the seller's obligation to guarantee the trustworthiness of the slave.[10]

6. M. Dandamaev, *Slavery in Babylonia*, rev. ed., tr. V. Powell, ed. M. Powell, D. Weisberg (DeKalb, Ill., 1984). The runaway is treated on pp. 220–228, 440–443, and 490–499.

7. An Old Babylonian document from the first half of the 17th century B.C.E. describes how a man purchased a slave girl from another man. This text ends as follows: "Three days are allowed for investigation (and) one month for epilepsy in order to clear her, *in accordance with the ordinances of the king*" (tr. T. J. Meek, *ANET*[3], text 5, pp. 218–219).

There are two points of interest here. First, we have evidence for the three-day waiting period. Second, this legal document seems to refer to the Code of Hammurapi (pars. 278 and 279). The present text demonstrates in a limited way that the code may, in fact, have been consulted or, at a minimum, that its contents were known to the scribe who took the proceedings of the court down.

8. Mendelsohn (N 4): 61.

9. Dandamaev (N 6): 184, 220.

10. Early in the second millennium, leases of slaves for work also included punitive damages to be paid by the leasee to the owner in the event one of his slaves got loose while outside his direct control; cf. Mendelsohn (N 4): 59f.

A document from the reign of Nabonidus (556–539 B.C.E.; probably written in 548 B.C.E.) relates the case of one Bariki-Ili who ran away several times.[11] Many years ago, it was suggested that this man was taken captive in the destruction of Jerusalem in 587/6 B.C.E. by Nebuchadnezzar.[12] While we can never be certain this, the man's name might betray his Judean background or it could simply be of a general West Semitic background.

The document under consideration is a record of Bariki-Ili's complaint to a court in Babylon. Bariki-Ili claimed that he was a free man, while his owners claimed him as their property. The court ordered him to produce the document testifying to his free status. He could not because there was none. He confesses:

> I have succeeded in running away from the house of my master two times and was not discovered for many days. I was afraid and I said: "I am a freeman." I have no free status. I am a slave who was redeemed for silver belonging to Gaga. She gave me to her daughter Nupta. Nupta legally transferred me to her son Zababa-iddin and her son Iddina. After the deaths of Gaga and Nupta, I was sold to Itti-Marduk-balaṭu son of Nabu-aḫḫe-iddin descendant of Egibi. I am a slave.[13]

Bariki-Ili admitted to having run away twice while under the ownership of Itti-Marduk-balaṭu (549 B.C.E.). The second attempt brought him into the service of one Bel-rimanni. Apparently, the rightful owners claimed him while he was with Bel-rimanni. The document does not mention any action taken against Bel-rimanni. The central issue is Bariki-Ili's status, and that having been determined, the slave must be returned to his rightful owner.

Some thirty years later in Babylon, we learn of the trouble the slave Nabu-kilanni caused his master, Nabu-apla-iddin, when he ran away.[14] After some time, the owner filed a complaint in court noting that he had seen his slave in the house of one Nabu-uballiṭ. This man changed the slave's name once he came into his possession. He called the slave Nabu-shepishu-shuzziz. The slave would be all the easier to sell with the new identity afforded him by the

11. Nbn 1113 (J. Strassmaier, *Inschriften von Nabonidu, König von Babylon* [Leipzig, 1889]); Dandamaev (N 6): 440–443. For the name, cf. Job 32:2, 6.

12. Dandamaev (N 6): 110, note.

13. Translated by Dandamaev (N 6): 442.

14. Darius 53 (J. Strassmaier, *Inschriften von Darius, König von Babylon* [Leipzig, 1897]); cf. Mendelsohn (N 4): 62 and Dandamaev (N 6): 223.

new name and, therefore, clean past. (It must have been difficult to sell slaves with a history of flight; see below, on the wisdom literature.) But the name itself is an instant give-away of the slave's tarnished past. It means, "O Nabu, stop his feet!" Despite this blaring warning, the slave's new owner was able to sell him.

Now we return to the court case brought by Nabu-apla-iddin, the original owner of the slave in question. He asked the court for permission to search the house of the one in whose possession he had seen his slave. The court granted him permission, stating that if his allegation proved true he could, "according the law of the king," take his slave back.

Two final points may be made with regard to this document. First, it is "the law of the king" that fugitives must be returned to their rightful owners. We, unfortunately, do not know what "the law of the king" refers to in this case. Second, no penalty is imposed upon the harborer of the runaway, supporting the view that in the Neo-Babylonian-Achaemenid periods the primary interest of the owner was in getting his property back.

This lenient treatment of the one in whose possession the slave of another was found extended even to the abductor.[15] In a document from the same period and provenience as the former, we learn that a Labashi abducted the slave woman of a member of the Egibi family. A member of that family forced Labashi to return the slave, but no punishment whatsoever was inflicted upon the abductor.

These many documents, combined with the evidence gleaned from the codes, establish a single fundamental legal principle with regard to the treatment of fugitives in the ancient Near East: The runaway must be returned to the rightful owner. This principle will also form one of the bases of the relations of one nation with others, as we learn from the many ancient treaties that have come down into our hands.

TREATIES

Treaties between nations of the ancient Near East were solemn oaths sworn between the signatories. Several outstanding examples of these treaties have been recovered that inform us of the stipulations the parties were obliged to carry out—in effect, evidence for what we might call ancient "international law." One frequent stipulation concerns the return of fugitive slaves.

15. Darius 207 (Strassmaier [N 14]); Mendelsohn (N 4): 62–63 and Dandamaev (N 6): 223.

Three documents will be cited. First, the treaty between Niqmepa of Alalaḫ and Ir-^{d}IM of Tunip (c. early fifteenth century B.C.E.):

> Seal of Ir-^{d}IM, king of Tunip. Text (of the agreement) sanctioned by an oath to the gods, between Niqmepa, king of Mukishḫe [and Alalaḫ], and Ir-^{d}IM, king of Tunip; Niqmepa and Ir-^{d}IM have now established [this agreement] between them as follows: [several stipulations]
>
> §5. If a fugitive slave, male or female, of my land flees to your land, you must seize and return him to me, (or), if someone else seizes him and takes him to you, [you must keep him] in your prison, and whenever his owner comes forward, you must hand him over to [him]. If (the slave) is not to be found, you must give him (the owner) an escort, and he may seize him in whatever town he (the slave) is found; (in any town where) he is not found, the mayor and five elders will declare under oath: "Your slave does not live among us and we do not conceal him"—if they are unwilling to take the oath, (but) eventually return his slave, [they go free], but if they take the oath and later he discovers his slave [among them], they are considered thieves and their hands are cut off, (moreover) they will pay 6,000 (shekels) of copper to the palace. [more stipulations, some concerning slaves]
>
> Seal of Niqmepa, king of Alalaḫ. Whosoever transgresses these agreements, Adad, [. . .] and Shamash, the lord of judgment, Sin, and the great gods will make him perish, [will make disappear] his name and his descendants from the lands, [. . .], they will make him forsake his throne and *scepter* [. . .][16]

Fundamental to right international relations is the return of fugitive slaves. Slaves often came from the booty taken in wars between both neighboring and distant states. If a slave were able to flee his master, he might just head home. To guarantee that such slaves would be returned to their rightful owners, stipulations such as this were created. I. Mendelsohn suggests that just such a treaty arrangement may have existed between Solomon and Achish of Gath, thus explaining the ease with which Shimei retrieved his slaves (1 Kgs 2:39–40;[17] see below).

We have evidence from among the documents of Alalaḫ that such stipulations carried weight in the arena of international relations. An extradition receipt reads:

16. Translated by E. Reiner, *ANET*^{3}: 531–532.
17. I. Mendelsohn, "On Slavery in Alalakh," *IEJ* 5 (1955): 65–72, esp. 70f.

> . . . 2 female (and) one male fugitives belonging to Pantarashshura in the presence of Niqmepa, Akiyya, the servant of Pantarashshura, of the city of Urume, has received them. Before Arnupar, the district overseer of the city of Aleppo.[18]

These slaves fled their master, Pantarashshura, an Alalaḫian of the city of Urume, and went to the foreign city of Aleppo. There they were captured and then delivered to king Niqmepa of Alalaḫ. He returned them to Pantarashshura's agent, his slave. We suspect that this Pantarashshura was a particularly important figure at Alalaḫ, for why else would Niqmepa himself have overseen the slaves' return? Though no reward for the return of these slaves is mentioned in this document, such was stipulated in another treaty from Alalaḫ.

As we saw in the law codes, rewards were to be paid to those who returned runaways to their masters. The short treaty between Idrimi and Pilliya, again from Alalaḫ (c. early fifteenth century B.C.E.) reads:

> Tablet of agreement. When Pilliya and Idrimi took an oath by the gods and made this binding agreement between themselves: they will always return their respective fugitives. . . . Anyone who seizes a fugitive and returns him to his master, (the owner) will pay as prize of capture 500 (shekels of) copper if it is a man, one thousand as prize if it is a woman. . . . From that day on it is decreed that fugitives have to be returned.[19]

The two treaties discussed so far are from the second millennium and from the West. The Sefire treaty, written in Old Aramaic in the eighth century B.C.E., is also from the West. One stipulation deals with fugitive servants of the king and the obligation to extradite them.

> If one of my officials or one of my brothers or one of my eunuchs or one of the people under my control flees from me and becomes a fugitive and goes to Aleppo, you must not pro[vide f]ood for them, and you must not say to them: Stay peacefully in your place, and you must not cause them to be disdainful of me. You must placate them and return them to me. If not, they shall [remain] in your

18. Mendelsohn, "Alalakh" (N 17): 69f.
19. Translated by E. Reiner (N 16).

> place to be quiet there until I come and placate them. If you cause them to be disdainful of me and provide food for them and say to them: Stay where you are and pay no attention to him, you will have betrayed this treaty.[20]

The language used here of the extradition of the king's servants is identical to that used of the extradition of slaves. Just as the slave's owner had complete control over his property, so the king had sovereign power over his servants.

In sum, the codes and the treaties (which in so many ways are interconnected with law) agree that slaves must be returned to their masters. The language of Idrimi's treaty is most emphatic on this point: "From this day on it is decreed that fugitives have to be returned!" We might, however, doubt the value of this information. Codes and treaties might have very little to do with the actual day-to-day lives of real people. But the legal documents also concur; they provide a check, for they are precisely from the workaday world. The legal documents are seconded by yet another reliable source of information about the way that people actually lived, letters.

LETTERS

A model letter for the instruction of schoolboys tells of a policeman's chase after two runaway slaves. He has now lost their trail and appeals to his colleagues in the south to inform him of the status of the search. This gendarme's view is presented in the Egyptian letter called by the modern translator "The Pursuit of Runaway Slaves":

> Another matter, to wit: I was sent forth from the broad-halls of the palace—life, prosperity, health!—in the third month of the third season, day 9, at the time of evening, following after these two slaves. Now when I reached the enclosure wall of Tjeku on the third month of the third season, day 10, they told [me] they were saying to the south that they [the slaves] had passed by on the third month of the third season, day 10. Now when [I] reached the fortress, they told me that the scout (?) had come from the desert [saying that] they had passed the walled place north of the Migdol of Seti Mer-ne-Ptaḥ—life, prosperity, health!—Beloved like Seth.

20. Translated by F. Rosenthal, *ANET*[3]: 660.

> When my letter reaches you, write to me all that has happened to [them]. Who found their tracks? Which watch found their tracks? What people are after them? Write to me about all that has happened and how many people you send out after them.[21]

In an Old Babylonian letter written by Kibri-Dagan, governor of Terqa, to his lord, Zimri-Lim, king of Mari, Kibri-Dagan gives the normal salutations and then states:

> Following (the receipt of) the message of my lord, I gave strict orders to my military posts on (both) the near and far banks [of the Euphrates river] concerning the fugitive slaves belonging to Turrunu-Gamil, (namely) Etel-pi-Shamash and his cohorts. I have not been negligent concerning this matter about which my lord has written me.[22]

Here a loyal servant of the king reports that every effort is being made to pursue and capture the fugitives in question. The tone of urgency and the pressure Kibri-Dagan felt highlight the tension raised when slaves took flight. Unlike stray cattle which can rarely succeed in vanishing without a trace, clever humans, if not captured soon after their escape, will never be seen again. These particular fugitives were apparently very important to someone close to the king, just as we had seen in the case of Pantarashshura of Alalaḫ, otherwise we could not explain his intervention in the matter at all.

A similar situation is found in a letter from the fifth century B.C.E., written in Aramaic from Arsham, an Egyptian high official, to Artawont, a lower official. Arsham informs Artawont of a case of runaway brigands and instructs him what is to be done to them. The high official acts in order to help his own officer:

> From Arsham to Artawont: I send thee much greetings of peace and prosperity. And [now];—one named Psamshek, son of Aḥ-Ḥapi [my officer] here has said thus: When I was coming to [my lord] . . . , (certain) slaves of Aḥ-Ḥapi my father [who were coming] in my train to my lord—[list of names of the slaves]—all (told) 8 men—took my property and fled from me. Now if it be good to my lord,

21. Translated by J. Wilson, *ANET*^{3}: 259.

22. G. Dossin *et al.*, *Archives Royal de Mari* XIII (Paris, 1964), text 118, lines 13–23, p. 123; my translation.

> let (word) be sent to Artawont [that, if] I present [those men] before him, the punishment which I shall give orders (to inflict) be inflicted upon them.
>
> Now Arsham [says thus]: (In regard to) that Psamshek-ḥasi and his fellows, the slaves of Aḥ-Ḥapi whom Psamshek will present before thee there—do thou issue an order that that punishment, which Psamshek shall [issue] an order to inflict upon them, be inflicted upon them.[23]

The letters make it abundantly clear that slaves ran away often, forcing their masters to turn to the police and government officials to help them recapture their property.

Men such as these, who might have had substance enough to hold slaves in the ancient Near East, would have been among those targeted for instruction by the wisdom literature. The best insurance against a slave becoming a fugitive is knowing how to treat him.

WISDOM LITERATURE

Ancient Near Eastern wisdom literature, like its counterpart from ancient Israel, counsels the student in proper behavior so that he may lead a clean, respectable, and prosperous life. One of the most famous collections of maxims, "The Words of Aḥiqar," written in Aramaic in the late sixth or early fifth century B.C.E., gives advice about the imposition of firm discipline upon slaves and the foolishness of acquiring runaways.

> A blow for a bondman, *a reb[uke]* for a bondwoman, and for all thy slaves dis[cipline. One who] buys a run[away] slave [or] a thievish handmaid *squanders his fortune* and [disgraces] the name of his father and his offspring with the reputation of his wantonness.[24]

According to this teacher, the firm hand is the key to keeping slaves in line. A slave who runs away is no good to anybody; he who purchases him is a fool. But more foolish is one who abandons discretion in dealing with his chattel and gives them means to take flight.

23. G. R. Driver, *Aramaic Documents of the Fifth Century B.C.* (Oxford, 1957): 24. This is Driver's translation.

24. Translated by H.L. Ginsberg, *ANET*³: 428; cf. J. Lindenberger, *The Aramaic Proverbs of Aḥiqar* (Baltimore, 1983): 55–56.

In sum, the ancient Near Eastern evidence is unanimous in its insistence that slaves must return or be returned to their rightful owners. Any who might incite, aid, or harbor a slave would, at a minimum, be betraying his role as a responsible member of a society whose economy was, in part, built upon slavery. The most intelligent stance was to give slaves no chance to get away in the first place. We, as moderns, naturally abhor the whole system of slavery, but we must recognize that it played an important role both in the ancient Near East and in ancient Israel itself.

2. THE RUNAWAY IN BIBLICAL PERSPECTIVE

We learn about biblical views concerning runaway slaves or servants from two kinds of sources: narratives, and a single statement in Deuteronomy. The outlook of the biblical narratives is entirely consistent with the ancient Near Eastern materials. Deut 23:16–17, however, presents a revolutionary attitude toward the treatment of runaways that would have been shocking to Israel's neighbors. Four narratives involve servants or slaves in flight from their masters.

The Hebrew word *ᶜebed* merits brief discussion before we turn to the biblical narratives. In Biblical Hebrew, *ᶜebed* "male servant" also means "slave" (also true for Hebrew *ʾāmāh/šipḥāh*, "female servant"). Biblical Hebrew shares this semantic range with the languages cognate to it, including Akkadian and Aramaic.[25] Underlying both meanings is "dependency"; the one bearing the title *ᶜebed* is to a greater or lesser degree, perceived to be dependent upon someone else. The determination of the degree of dependency, that is whether we are to render *ᶜebed* as "servant" or "slave," rests solely upon the context in which the word appears. It is context, then, that will guide us in our discussion of the biblical narratives.

Narratives

In Gen 16:2, we hear Sarai tell Abram: "Behold now the Lord has prevented me from bearing children. Go in to my maid. It may be that I will obtain children by her." Abram does exactly as he is

25. Cf. the discussion of Dandamaev (N 6): 81ff.

told. Hagar, Sarai's Egyptian slave girl, becomes pregnant and then taunts her mistress. Sarai becomes infuriated at the girl's behavior. Abram reminds Sarai that she may do to the handmaid as pleases her. Life, then, becomes unbearable for Hagar under Sarai's harsh treatment. The pregnant girl flees from Sarai and runs southward toward her home, Egypt. An angel of the Lord meets Hagar by a well. She confesses to the angel (v. 8): "I am fleeing from my mistress Sarai." The angel instructs Hagar (v. 9): "Return to your mistress and submit to her." The angel promises Hagar that the child she is bearing will be no man's slave. Hagar returns to her mistress as instructed and gives birth to Ishmael as promised.

The outstanding features of this story are two. First, slaves could be and were treated harshly by their masters. In the present case, Hagar provokes her mistress's anger by poking at Sarai's one sore spot: her infertility. But one power lost does not render the mistress powerless. Sarai makes the slave girl's life so miserable that Hagar flees. The reader wonders, "Is Hagar's affliction so great that she is justified in fleeing?" The answer to this question, provided in the text, underlines the second significant feature of this story for our investigation. Slaves must return or be returned to their masters no matter what motivated their flight. The Lord may have heard Hagar's affliction (v. 11), but he does not vindicate her. Instead, he instructs her to return to her mistress no matter what the consequences may be.

It is these consequences that bring fear to another Egyptian slave in 1 Sam 30. This slave of an Amalekite had been abandoned by his master and was found by David's troops who were about to take vengeance upon the Amalekites for the atrocity they committed at Ziklag (vv. 1–5). David asks that the slave lead him to the Amalekites. The slave adjures King David (v. 15): "Swear to me by God that you will not kill me or deliver me into the hands of my master, and I will take you down to this band." David apparently complies, is led down to the Amalekite camp, and routs them.

The Egyptian slave cleverly saves his own life twice because he can provide an essential service to his new lord, David. In the first place, he deserves to die at the hand of David for having participated in the brutal destruction of Ziklag (v. 14). Second, he knows that if David were to spare him and then capture his master in the ensuing battle, he would naturally be returned to him, even though his master had abandoned him. (In this respect, abandoned slaves were treated like runaways; they were still the chattel of their owners.) Under those circumstances, he would be a dead man for having broken his allegiance to his master and for having collaborated with the enemy. By agreeing to the slave's proposal, David lifts two sentences of death from the Egyptian's head.

The third biblical narrative concerning runaways, 1 Kgs 2:36–46, contains a story about runaway slaves within a story about a runaway servant. The servant is Shimei, the unrelenting adversary of King David (see 2 Sam 16:5–8; 19:16–23). The lord is David's son, King Solomon, who establishes his hold over United Israel by either eliminating his enemies or placing them in protective custody. It is into the latter condition that King Solomon places Shimei.

King Solomon summons Shimei and says to him (vv. 36–37):

> Build yourself a house in Jerusalem, and dwell there, and do not go forth from there to any place whatever. For on the day you go forth, and cross the brook Kidron, know for certain that you shall die; your blood shall be on your own head.

Shimei agrees to do as the king commands him: "What you say is good. As the king, *my lord,* has said, so will *your servant* do" (v. 38).[26] As we saw above in the Sefire treaty, a king's servants were of similar status to slaves. Shimei, having accepted his role as servant to his lord Solomon, obeys his king for the moment. The narrator continues (vv. 39–40):

> But it happened at the end of three years that two of Shimei's slaves ran away to Achish, son of Maacah, king of Gath. But when it was told Shimei, "Behold, your slaves are in Gath," Shimei arose, saddled an ass, and went to Gath to Achish to seek his slaves. Shimei went and brought his slaves from Gath.

The flight of Shimei's slaves forces him to act quickly. They must be returned to him, for he is their rightful owner! He could send agents to retrieve them, but he chooses to go after them himself. In so doing, he becomes a runaway servant from his lord Solomon. (The ease of the retrieval may be explained if Solomon in fact had an extradition treaty with Achish; see above.) Unlike the Egyptian slave who could bargain for his life by placing a king under oath,

26. The same language has prompted C. Carmichael to suggest that Jacob was a fugitive from his lord, Laban. This is dubious, however, because Jacob is, in fact, a hired worker. Cf. *The Laws in Deuteronomy* (Ithaca, 1974): 186–187.

Shimei, a servant who had taken a solemn oath on his very life from a king, must now forfeit his life in silence. The king, as the Lord's servant, must execute judgment against those who break oaths taken in the Lord's name (see v. 43).

Finally, we return to the narratives concerning David. In 1 Sam 25, the wealthy but ill-natured Nabal rebuffs David when he asks for food in return for the protection his forces have provided for Nabal. Nabal says (vv. 10–11):

> Who is David? Who is the son of Jesse? There are many servants nowadays who are breaking away from their masters. Shall I take my bread and my water and my meat that I have killed for my shearers, and give it to men who come from I do not know where?

From Nabal's point of view, David and his men are no better than runaway slaves—clearly to be understood as the most base men in society. We recall the statement in Aḥiqar, which emphasizes the corrupt reputation of the slave who habitually runs away. Wherever and whenever slavery existed, fugitives were an irritating problem and, unfortunately for their owners, a commonplace.[27] Laws were necessary to deal with this phenomenon.

Law

Remarkably, biblical law, in contrast with its counterparts from the ancient Near East, barely treats the problem of the runaway slave. The lone law is found in Deut 23:16–17:

> You shall not give up to his master a slave who has escaped from his master to you; he shall dwell with you in your midst, in the place which he shall choose within one of your towns, where it pleases him best; you shall not oppress him.

The first half of this law would appear to virtually undermine the institution of slavery! I. Mendelsohn has written, "If this law literally applied to any slave who had run away from his master, it certainly was unrealistic, for if put to practical use, it would have resulted in the immediate abolition of slavery."[28] The second half

27. Two other texts have implications for our discussion: (1) From the point of view of Pharaoh, Israel was a runaway after the tenth plague; (2) In light of Lev 25:42, Israel's insolent behavior toward God made her no less than a disobedient servant, but when she looked to foreign gods, it was as if she had crossed a border and become a runaway.

28. "Slavery in the Old Testament," *Interpreter's Dictionary of the Bible* (G. Buttrick *et al.*, eds.; Nashville, 1962): 4.389.

of the law seems to suggest, however, that the slave had been a foreigner. If the first half of the law is read in light of the second, the slave would be a fugitive from another country seeking asylum in the land of Israel and whose extradition is hereby prohibited. What cannot be determined with certainty is whether the slave himself is non-Israelite or Israelite.[29] If the interpretation of Deut 23:16–17 suggested here is correct, Israelite law virtually ignores the problem of the fugitive slave within Israel herself.

However this law is understood, it would have shocked and angered the members of the contemporaneous societies around Israel. As we noted already in our discussion of ancient Near Eastern treaty stipulations, signatories to such pacts were clearly obliged to return fugitives. Such seemingly humane behavior on Israel's part would certainly have placed significant barriers to "right" international relations between Israel and her neighbors.

Finally, though the wisdom literature of the canonical Hebrew Bible does not treat the runaway *per se*, it is of some interest to note that the apocryphal book of Ecclesiasticus, also known as the Wisdom of Joshua ben Sirach, does mention him. Much of the advice given here on the treatment of slaves could just as well have been recorded in any one of the many works of wisdom from the Near East, for it would have been of value to all in possession of slaves in the ancient world. Sirach 33:24–31 reads:

> Fodder and a stick and burdens for an ass; bread and discipline and work for a servant.
>
> Set your slave to work, and you will find rest; *leave his hands idle, and he will seek liberty.*
>
> Yoke and thong will bow the neck, and for a wicked servant there are racks and tortures.
>
> Put him to work, that he may not be idle; for idleness teaches much evil.
>
> Set him to work, as is fitting for him; and if he does not obey, make his fetters heavy.
>
> Do not act immoderately toward any body; and do nothing without discretion.
>
> If you have a [or "but one"] servant, let him be as yourself, because you have bought him with blood.

29. Jewish tradition recognizes both possibilities, cf. Rashi to Deut 23:16.

> If you have a [or "but one"] servant, treat him as a brother, for as your own soul you will need him. If you ill-treat him, and he leaves and runs away, which way will you go to seek him?

Servants ought to be kept busy, or else they might "seek liberty." Jonah prefers idleness to effort. Only when he is called upon to work does he flee. God will ultimately force him to return and get back to work. Finally, in chapter 4, Jonah will receive strong words of discipline from his master.

3. JONAH AS RUNAWAY

Faced with a commission by God that he does not want to undertake, Jonah takes flight from his master. Jonah's plan is to flee from the place over which he believes God has sovereignty. The fare paid, Jonah boards a ship bound for Tarshish. God responds to Jonah's insubordination by hurling a violent storm upon the sea. The ship threatens to break up from the force of the tempest. The vessel will remain in this precarious state throughout the action to follow. Why does God toy with the ship in this manner? Surely, if Jonah's god's anger is so intense against his rebellious servant, he could, in an instant, destroy the ship, thereby punishing Jonah for his arrogant behavior. However, the reader becomes convinced as the narrative unfolds that more is at stake here than simply the punishment of Jonah. The sailors increasingly become the story's focus, as Jonah, the scorner, refuses to learn a lesson from the hands of his master.

The storm serves two purposes simultaneously in the narrative. First, it is the means through which the sailors (and, by extension, the readers) learn profound lessons about God's power and nature. Second, the storm impedes Jonah's flight and, by means of his own words and deeds in response to the storm, Jonah will ultimately be returned to the master who pursues him so vigorously.

The mariners react to the tempest with a flurry of activity. Our author has aptly portrayed them as the superstitious lot we would expect them to be as heathen men of the sea. They cry out, each man to his own god, in hopes that they may appease whichever god may be angry (v. 5). They do not rely upon their prayers alone, however. They take action, too, by jettisoning whatever unnecessary ballast they can. These actions express their mild cynicism about placing full trust in often deaf and capricious gods.

The crew's concerted efforts and energetic response to impending doom find their complete contrast in the inactivity of our "hero." Jonah sleeps soundly. The captain wakes Jonah from his stupor and commands him, saying (v. 6): "Arise, call upon your god! Perhaps the god will give a thought to us, that we do not perish." If Jonah fled from God who gave him the command (v. 2), "Arise, go . . . cry out . . . ," would he be likely to obey the mere captain of a ship to "arise, cry out to" the selfsame god for help? The text informs us in its silence that Jonah did not carry out the order of the ship's supreme commander. Jonah's deliberate inactivity only serves to highlight the crew's sincere effort to save themselves.

Lots are cast so that the identity of the man on whose account they are all suffering might be revealed (v. 7). Once again, the reader is amused to witness the seemingly empty divinatory practices of superstitious heathen mariners. But the joke is on the reader! The lots fall on the right man. Could it be that Jonah's god has actually communicated with the heathen through the delicate manipulation of the lots? If so, this god makes every effort to speak to these men in an authoritative language he knows they will understand and heed. The seamen begin to learn more than they had set out to learn; the lesson of the lots will not be lost on them. They indeed heed the lots and turn directly to Jonah.

When questioned fully about his identity (v. 8), Jonah gives an incomplete, yet telling response: "I am a Hebrew. I worship/fear the Lord, God of heaven, who made the sea and the dry land" (v. 9). The reader is puzzled by several contradictions between Jonah's words and deeds. If he truly feared his Lord at first, why did he flee? If he is now in awe of the Lord, why does he refuse to cry out to God in repentance? If he is not simply repeating a traditional phrase by rote, does he not understand that a god who created both sea and land can certainly control them, as well as anything that moves upon them? If he understood this, why did he attempt to flee in the first place? Jonah neither hears nor understands what his own lips utter.

But the sailors do. They learn only now ("For the men knew that he was fleeing from the presence of the Lord because he had told them," v. 10b) that Jonah is fleeing from the god whom he just said he feared. This is yet a third time the reader is impressed by the author's realistic portrayal, building into his characters a knowledge of the law. They realize that *Jonah is a servant in flight from his master*. Jonah's flight has put the ship and its crew into mortal danger: They are harboring and transporting a runaway. The consequences could be dire, for his master is no mere mortal of flesh and blood. He is a god. Had their sin been committed in the human arena, governed by the laws of man, they might expect leniency. However, such an awesome god's vengeance might know no limitation. A deep fear grips the sailors. In a confused fury, the crew rebukes Jonah, asking (vv. 10–11): "What is this that you have done? What shall we do to you that the sea will quiet down from upon us?"

The question "What is this that you have done?" (and its variants) has a very specific usage in the narrative literature of the Bible. It is often uttered by a hurt, damaged, or wronged party to the one who inflicted the wrong, be it legal or moral. These words serve to rebuke the wrongdoer and, in some instances, to invite confession and repentance. One example from Genesis illustrates this usage.

In Gen 20, Abraham passes his wife, Sarah, off to the people of Gerar as his sister. Abimelech, the king, takes Sarah into his household. That night, God appears to Abimelech in a dream, informs him of the wrong he has committed and gives him an ultimatum: Return Sarah or die. On the morrow, Abimelech makes known to his servants all that transpired. A great fear grips them. We, then, read (vv. 9–10):

> Abimelech called Abraham, and said to him: "*What have you done to us?* And how have I sinned against you, that you have brought on me and my kingdom a great sin? You have done to me things that ought not to be done. . . . What were you thinking of that you did this thing?"

Abraham explains his motives and defends himself before the king. The females of the king's household, we later learn, had been afflicted with infertility so long as Sarah resided in their midst. It is only through the agency of Abraham, the prophet, that the women are healed. Abraham is rewarded with great riches for his intervention on behalf of Abimelech and his house.

This story illustrates well the usage as we have described it above. Abimelech, feeling himself and his household to have been brought unwittingly into sin by Abraham, rebukes Abraham and accuses him of willfully causing them to transgress. Abraham, in this case, believes that he has done nothing wrong, but does take the time to explain his actions to the king.[30]

The question "What is this that you have done?" functions in Jonah 1:10 in a very similar way to that found in Gen 20:9. After learning from the lots that the storm had befallen them because of Jonah (v. 7b), and then from Jonah's own mouth that he was a runaway servant from before his god (v. 10b), the sailors recognize cause and effect in Jonah's flight and the storm threatening them. They realize that Jonah has made them accessories to his crime by making them harborers of a fugitive. They cry out in rebuke: "What is this that you have done?" With these words they simultaneously accuse him of harming them unjustly and urge him to rectify their desperate situation.

The crew perceives that with each moment the sea's fury is becoming more intense (v. 11b). They realize that immediate action is needed; any delay could spell certain doom. They turn to Jonah and ask (v. 11): "What shall we do to you that the sea may quiet down for us?" The very question assumes the crew's sincere belief that Jonah can and will give them sound advice built upon his longstanding intimate knowledge of his god and how that god will behave. Jonah responds forthrightly to the sailors' urgent appeal for guidance. The prophet says (v. 12): "Lift me up and throw me into the sea so that the sea will quiet down from upon you, for I know that it is on my account that this storm has come upon you."

Jonah's guilt in fleeing his master jeopardizes the entire crew, but they refuse to accept Jonah's rash solution. Why? It is one thing to harbor, even aid and abet, a fugitive, but murder is murder. In taking such action, they would necessarily bring upon themselves guilt of the highest order. They decide to ignore Jonah's advice.

The sailors devise a plan of their own: They will turn the ship around and return Jonah directly home. This seems to be a rational approach. The crew has seen irrefutable evidence that Jonah's flight away from his master's service has brought calamity upon them. They will right Jonah's wrong for him by returning his body (with or without his consent) to his god's homeland. This god, they

30. Other examples of this usage may be found in Gen 3:13; 4:10; 12:18; 26:10; 29:25; 31:26; 44:15; Ex 1:19; 14:11; Num 23:11; Josh 7:19; Jdg 2:2; 8:1; 15:11; 18:3, 18; 1 S 13:11; 14:43; 2 S 3:24; 12:21; 1 Kgs 1:6.

believe, will surely approve. The runaway will be returned, a burden of guilt will be removed from their ship, and they will reap a significant reward: All will be as it was before they left Joppa.

But the harder they row in order to carry out their plan, the angrier the sea becomes (v. 13). Their effort is futile. The sailors recognize that the sea's rage directly reflects that of the one in control of it. Clearly, Jonah's god and master does not desire *this method* of returning the prophet. What method does he desire?

The crew recalls Jonah's earlier address to them (v. 12) and they now turn to him again. There could be no doubt now that Jonah had accurately described his god, the Lord, the God of Heaven as the one "*who made the sea* and the dry land." If the god who commissioned Jonah is powerful enough to create, control, and use the mighty sea to express his displeasure to the crew and if that god is subtle enough to communicate with the sailors by making the delicate lots fall upon Jonah, it may be that he has already communicated with them yet again, this time through his prophet: "Lift me up and throw me into the sea, then the sea will quiet down for you" (v. 12). (Prophets and prophecy were known to non-Israelites, and this assumption, made by the author, again makes us appreciate his craftsmanship.) The mariners now believe that perhaps Jonah, the prophet, speaks the truth. This understanding is a gamble on their part, to be sure, for there is no reason to trust Jonah. They hope that the prophet's words will be trustworthy.

The sailors hedge their bet with a prayer to the god whose words they now believe they have heard from Jonah's mouth. They pray that their understanding of the god's intention is correct and, therefore, that he will not hold them accountable for what they are about to do. They round off their petition with an affirmation of the fundamental principle they have learned: *God does as he pleases* (v. 14). The crew realizes that it is futile to flee their assigned task: This god desires that Jonah go overboard, and they are to be the god's agents in bringing this about.[31] The sailors now give no thought to their own devices and act obediently. They throw Jonah overboard. The almost verbatim repetition in v. 15 of the words found in v. 12 emphasizes their complete obedience to their new found master. How Jonah should have learned from their example!

31. Jonah recognizes this fact in his prayer (2:4).

The crew is rewarded immediately for their obedience. The sea quiets down the moment Jonah goes under. The sailors were correct: Jonah was a true prophet who communicated his god's will directly to them. This god now appears to them to be not only powerful, but fair. He is not capricious. This god merits fear and worship. The crew again complies.

As chapter one ends, we note Jonah's disappearance from the action. Jonah is nearly forgotten. The focal point has turned toward the sailors alone. The sailors had seen something profound in Jonah's words of advice. Yet Jonah's intent in giving that advice had been very different. He was entirely self-centered in his desire for self-destruction. Through his own death he would achieve the ultimate flight from God, thus thwarting God's designs altogether: Without anyone to warn them, the Ninevites would surely perish and Jonah, in death, would have victory over God.

But as we look back again at the words uttered by Jonah in v. 12, we note an important omission. Had Jonah actually understood that his words were intrinsically true because he was a prophet or that he had complete control over events, he might have said: "Lift me up, throw me overboard, *and kill me* . . ." Such was not to be his fate. Like his shipmates, Jonah will live, but unlike them, he will not have the benefit of learning that, in fact, he had spoken the truth.

God now appoints a new agent, the great fish, to return Jonah's body to the land. The fish is an obedient servant of its master (unlike Jonah) in carrying out an uncomfortable task. The fish completes its mission by returning Jonah to the place desired by his lord.[32]

Now Jonah must get back to work. God commands him again: "Arise, go to Nineveh . . ." (3:2). Utterly defeated, Jonah turns and drags his body to Nineveh. Obedient like the mariners and the fish? Yes, but only under extreme duress. Has he come to understand

32. Note Rashi's comment to Jonah 1:3: "He [Jonah] thought: 'I will flee to the sea, for the divine presence is not found outside the land of Israel.' The Holy One, Blessed be He, said to him: 'By your life, I have agents like you to send after you to bring you back from there.' This is analogous to the slave of a priest who fled from his master and entered a graveyard. [According to Jewish law, priests are forbidden from entering graveyards.] His master said to him: 'I have other servants just like you to send after you in order to bring you from there.'"

his god better, like the sailors, and has he (re)turned in repentance to his master? No. Jonah has much to learn.[33]

4. CLOSING REMARKS

The book of Jonah, as a tract on the prophetic office, is built upon Jonah's flight and its resolution. Jonah, we come to realize, is a negative model of prophetic behavior whom the audience is being admonished not to imitate. What Jonah is not, the reader is urged to be: a faithful, obedient servant.

God was concerned about the Ninevites. He desired to warn them of the doom that would befall them if they did not change their evil ways. He sent his servant Jonah the prophet to deliver his message. Jonah, however, fled his commission. His confession in 4:2 reveals the reason:

> I pray, O Lord, is this not what I thought when I was yet in my country? That is why I fled at first to Tarshish. For I know that you are a gracious God and merciful, slow to anger, abounding in steadfast love, and *repenting of evil.*

Jonah knows God's nature, and does not like what he knows. The prophet, Jonah believes, is doomed to humiliation when God goes back on the word he had sent his servant to deliver. Jonah knew God would *inevitably* relent of punishing the Ninevites if they repented, which they would inevitably do. So why go and be put to shame? To Jonah, such prophecy is a heavy yoke laid upon him by a cruel master. Jonah attempts to throw off this yoke and flee. He is returned against his will, watches all happen as he thought it would, and then brings his complaint before his master. The book's author ends his work by having Jonah silenced by a God who demands that Jonah's petty, selfish, and self-centered concerns are meaningless when measured against his own.

Jonah's aiders and harborers, the sailors, had learned precisely this point through their encounter with Jonah's god. They knew they had to return Jonah in order to save their own lives, but they could not accept the solution he proposed. The sailors, in devising a plan of their own, unknowingly acted disobediently toward the god

33. Cf. my article, "Jonah: Toward the Reeducation of the Prophets," *Dor le Dor* 17/1 (1988): 10-18.

who had spoken to them through his prophet. This realized, they confess (1:14): "For you, O Lord, have done as it pleased you." God does as he pleases. The sailors allow their collective will to bend to that of their new master. They learn what Jonah never could and become what Jonah never was: faithful, obedient servants.

Amos, the contemporary of the Jonah ben Amittai of 2 Kgs 14:25, called prophets servants of the Lord (3:7). Of prophecy, he declared: "A lion has roared [cf. Amos 1:2], who can but fear; the Lord has spoken, who can but prophesy?" (3:8) That gripping urgency felt by the first (and perhaps greatest) of the writing prophets, Amos, so seizes Jonah that he sleeps soundly in flight from God and utters five whole words in fulfilling his mission to the Ninevites. Finally, then, if Jonah's actions are the opposite of those expected of the obedient, faithful servant of the Lord, then the great prophet must ever yearn to enter God's presence and ever rush out zealously to teach, on God's behalf, the life-giving power of sincere repentance.

MAARAV 5–6 (Spring, 1990): 307–309

SOME OBSERVATIONS ON THE TEXT OF THE PSALMS

HELMER RINGGREN
UPPSALA UNIVERSITY, SWEDEN

Some of the observations made in preparing a new Swedish translation of the Psalms seem worthy of being brought to the attention of a wider public.

Ps 1:7 runs: "Therefore, the wicked shall not stand in the *mišpāṭ*, nor the sinners in the congregation of the righteous." *Mišpāṭ* is usually translated as "judgment," which suggests the Christian idea of the Last Judgment. But Old Testament religion does not know this concept. In addition, *mišpāṭ* is parallel with *ʿădat ṣaddīqīm*, which suggests that it denotes a body of people. The only probable solution is to assume that *mišpāṭ* here stands for the community, or society, in which law and order prevails. I therefore propose to translate: "The wicked shall not stand in the community of justice."

Ps 8:2, 3 contains several difficulties. First, *ʾăšer tənāh* is impossible from a grammatical point of view. It is also improbable that a hymn should begin with a relative clause, admitted that the refrain does not form part of the hymn proper. Most of the ancient versions seem to have read a perfect form of *nātan*, probably *nātattā*. The LXX might suggest a passive form of the verb *tānāh*, "to praise," attested only in Jud 5:11. But this again causes a new difficulty. A passive form should not be followed by an agent: "by the mouth of babes and sucklings." Or could a power or fortress (*ʿōz*) be "founded" from the mouth of small children—out of their praise? The LXX, followed by Matthew 21:16, avoided the problem by translating *ʿōz* as "praise," which is hardly a correct translation. And finally, how could all this be done "for the sake of the enemies"?

I see no other solution of the first problem than to follow the commentators who read *ᵓāšīrāh-nnā* instead of *ᵓăšer tənāh*. Dahood's suggestion *ᵓăšārətannāh*[1] is improbable because it has to assume a meaning for *šrt* which is not attested elsewhere. "I will sing" is a suitable introduction to a hymn.

If the founding of an *ᶜōz* has the enemies in view, it is possible to take *ᶜōz* in the sense of "refuge," or at least to find the idea of refuge inherent in the root *ᶜwz* reflected in the defectively written *ᶜōz*. Now, a refuge *from* something would naturally be expressed by a phrase with *min*. Is it possible that "the mouth of babes and sucklings" is something from which refuge has to be taken? It seems that the Ugaritic texts present a possible solution. In *KTU* 1.23:59, 61 we find the word *ynqm* applied to the two boys (gods? demons?) borne by the two wives of El. These two beings put "one lip to heaven, the other lip to earth" and devour everything that comes in their way, thus representing the evil forces in the world. That this myth was known in Israel is proved by Ps 73:9. If the *yōnəqīm* of Ps 8 represent the forces of chaos—*ᶜōləlīm* being only a parallel, poetic expression—it is quite plausible to speak of creating a refuge from them and to take *ṣōrərēkā*, *ᶜōyēb* and *mitnaqqēm* as other designations of the same evil beings, which once opposed the creation of the world. And this is the main subject of Ps 8.

Ps 10:10 is the *ṣade* strophe of the psalm, but the crucial word beginning with that letter is missing. It is usually assumed to be *ṣaddīq*, which would imply that the righteous one is crushed and sinks down. This, however, sounds awkward in the middle of a description of the activity of the wicked. It is interesting to note that the wicked one is compared with a lion which lurks in order to catch its prey. Now, the same comparison with much the same vocabulary occurs in Job 38:40, where it should be especially observed that *šḥḥ* refers to the crouching of the lion. In view of this, the possibility should be contemplated that the missing word is a form of *ṣādāh* "to lie in wait, to be after someone." The verse should then read: "He lies in wait, he crouches, and the hapless (?) falls by his might."

Ps 30:6 is usually translated: "His anger is but for a moment, but his favor is for a lifetime." But *ḥayyīm* does not usually denote the length of somebody's life; for this, expressions like *kol-yəmē ḥay-*

1. M. Dahood, *Psalms I: Introduction, Translation, and Notes* (AB 16, New York: Doubleday, 1965): 49.

yay are used. Furthermore, the traditional translation presupposes that the *bə* before *ʾappō* and *rəṣōnō* is the rare *bə essentiae.* The latter half of the verse must mean "there is life in his favor." Since *regaʿ* is parallel with *ḥayyīm*, it must denote something that is opposite to "life," possibly "unrest" or "fear" (which normally would have been expressed by a form of *rgz*). Or is the word related to Arabic *rağaʿa* "to return," i.e., return to dust = death?

Ps 31:12 "I have become the scorn of all my adversaries, and of my neighbors *məʾōd*" is impossible as it stands. If the author had wanted to say, "I have become the scorn of my neighbors, and very much so," the word order would have been different. However, *məʾōd* could be a derivative of the root *ʾwd* or *ʾyd,* which is not attested as a verb in Hebrew. In Prov 1:26f. we find the word *ʾēd* in parallelism with *paḥad* "terror," which suggests that the root was known in Hebrew in the sense of "fear" or "terror." It seems likely that *məʾōd* in our passage is derived from the same root and carries a similar meaning.

MAARAV 5-6 (Spring, 1990): 311-317

ON THE NATURE OF THE ORAL TRANSLATION OF THE BOOK OF EXODUS IN THE NEO-ARAMAIC DIALECT OF THE JEWS OF ZAKHO

YONA SABAR
UNIVERSITY OF CALIFORNIA, LOS ANGELES

The Jews of Kurdistan, like many other traditional Jewish communities, used the Bible, especially the Pentateuch, as the main corpus of instruction for the young boys in their traditional religious school.[1] After some basic preparation in the reading of the Hebrew text, the teacher would begin teaching the pupils the *šarḥ*, "commentary" (Arabic), i.e., the traditional Neo-Aramaic translation of the Bible. Usually, the teacher would read a verse or, when long, a part of it, in Hebrew, and then orally translate it into Neo-Aramaic, and then the pupil would repeat it after him. The instruction began, according to an old Jewish tradition, with the Book of Leviticus, continued with the Books of Numbers, Deuteronomy, Genesis, and finally Exodus.[2]

The traditional oral translation is usually a strict word-for-word translation of the Hebrew text.[3] However, there are many cases of deviation from this principle, some of them conscious, such as euphemisms, or translations based on midrashic (homiletic) commentaries, especially when the Hebrew text is obscure. Others may

1. See *EncJud* 4: 863-868, on the Bible translations in Jewish languages; cf. Sabar, *The Book of Genesis in Neo-Aramaic in the Dialect of the Jewish Community of Zakho* (Jerusalem: Magnes Press, 1983): 40 n. 2 of the introduction.

2. For other details, see E. Brauer, *The Jews of Kurdistan: An Ethnological Study* (Hebrew; Jerusalem: Palestine Institute of Folklore and Ethnology, 1947).

3. See many examples in Sabar, *Genesis* (N 1): 28-31 of the introduction.

be unconscious deviations, the result of misunderstanding or misreading the Hebrew text, or when everyday Neo-Aramaic patterns of speech creep into the translation.

In many cases of obscure text, the Neo-Aramaic translation is based on the old Aramaic translation, known as Targum Onkelos (TO), as well as the commentary of Rashi (Rabbi Solomon ben Isaac, 1040–1105 C.E.), both of which, as well as others, traditionally accompany the Hebrew text, and are known as *Miqraᵓot Gedolot*. However, there are also a few cases of unique interpretations which I could not find in the available traditional commentaries, and they may not be based on local traditions.

I found it interesting to compare the deviations from a strict literal translation with other translations as well, i.e., Saadiah Gaon's ("Rasag," 889–942 C.E.) Arabic translation, a Christian Neo-Aramaic translation, and the recent English translation by the Jewish Publication Society.[4]

This is a preliminary report, and a more detailed version (in Hebrew) has appeared in my book on the Neo-Aramaic translations of the Book of Exodus, published in the series of the Language Traditions Project of the Hebrew University, Jerusalem (Magnes Press, 1988). The informant for the recorded Neo-Aramaic translation in the Jewish dialect of Zakho was Ḥakham (Rabbi) Levi Amram, now in his late seventies, who served as a traditional teacher in Zakho till his emigration to Israel in 1950.

1. TRANSLATIONS BASED ON TRADITIONAL COMMENTARIES

ḤĀYÔṮ[5] (1:19) *šahraza* "smart," *yaḏōᵓe* "knowledgeable" (D); cf. TO *ḥakkîmān* "wise"; Rashi: *bəqîᵓôṯ* "expert"; Rasag: *baṣîrat* "smart"; but CNA: *ḥāyē* "lively"; JPS "vigorous."

YĀDAᶜ (2:25) *mrōḥimle* "had mercy"; cf. Rasag: *raḥamahum*; TO: "intended to save them"; Rashi and JPS: "took notice of them"; but CNA: *yḏeᶜle* "knew."

4. CNA = Bible in Christian Neo-Aramaic (Urmia), Beirut (The Bible Society in the Near East, 1966); Z = Zakho; D = A Bible manuscript in the Jewish Neo-Aramaic dialect of Dehok (in the National Library, the Hebrew University, No. 8° 712); JPS = Jewish Publication Society, *TANAKH, A New Translation of the Holy Scriptures According the the Traditional Hebrew Text* (Philadelphia, 1985); TO, Rashi, Rasag as in Miqraᵓot Gedolot.

5. The Biblical Hebrew word(s) appear(s) in capital letters, followed by the indication of chapter and verse (of Exodus), and then the Neo-Aramaic translation (in regular phonetic transcription), and its English translation in quotation marks.

*WĔLÔ*ʾ (3:19) *hakan la hōya* "unless it is"; cf. Rashi: "if I do not show him"; JPS: "only because."

DÔḎĀṮÔ (6:20) *brat ʾamōye* "daughter of his paternal uncle"; but all others: "his father's sister." This unique interpretation seems to be based on the common local custom of cousin marriage,[6] as well as the Biblical and Talmudic sanction against a marriage to an aunt.[7]

NĀḆÎʾ (7:1) *taljaman* "translator, speaker"; cf. TO, Rashi, and Rasag, but CNA and JPS: "prophet."

PĀSAḤTÎ (12:13) *bšafqēna* "I will have mercy"; cf. TO, Rashi, and Rasag, but CNA and JPS: "I will pass over you."

MIYYĀMÎM YĀMÎMĀH (13:10) *min šāta ʾil šāta* "from year to year"; cf. Rashi, Rasag, and JPS, but TO: *mizzəman lizman* "from time to time"; CNA: *min yumāne lyumāne* "from days to days."

ṬÔṬĀFÔṮ (13:16) *tifillin* "phylacteries"; cf. TO, Rashi, but Rasag: *manšūra* "stretched"; CNA: *ṭuṭaput* (leaving the Hebrew word untranslated); JPS: "symbol (or frontlet)."

NĔḆÛḴÎM (14:3) *mburbize* "scattered"; cf. JPS: "astray"; but TO, Rasag and CNA: "confused"; Rashi: *kəlûʾīm* "hindered, stuck."

MĔḤÔLÔṮ (15:20) *billūrat* "flutes"; but TO and CNA: "dances"; Rasag: "tambours"; JPS: "in dance with timbrels." The translation "flutes" appears also in a Neo-Aramaic manuscript from the 17th century, and seems to be based on the local custom of accompanying the drum with a flute; cf., however, Mekhiltot *ad versum*: *nāṭəlû tuppîn uməḥôlôṯ bəyāḏām* "they took drums and flutes (?) in their hands" (the meaning derived from the context).[8]

ʾANŠÊ ḤAYIL (18:21) *ṣaddiqîm*[9] "righteous men"; but TO, Rasag, CNA: "men of power"; JPS: "capable men"; Rashi: "rich men who do not need to flatter or be biased." Our unique translation seems to be based on context. However, the same words in 18:25 are translated as *nāšid ʿaskar* "men of army."

HĀʾĔLÔHÎM (21:6) *dayyānīm* "judges (in a religious court)"; cf. TO: *dayyānayyā*; Rashi: *bêṯ dîn* "court"; Rasag: *alḥākim* "the

6. Common in other Near Eastern societies; see R. Patai, *Society, Culture, and Change in the Middle East*³ (Philadelphia: Univ. of Pennsylvania, 1971): ch. 6 and pp. 413, 420–422; Sabar, *The Folk Literature of the Kurdistani Jews: An Anthology* (New Haven: Yale Univ. 1982): xiv.

7. See Lev 18:12; *B. Sanh.* 58b; *EncJud* 8: 1316.

8. For details, see Sabar, *Pešaṭ Wayhî Bĕšallaḥ, A Neo-Aramaic Midrash on Beshallah (Exodus)* (Wiesbaden: Harassowitz, 1976): 124 n. 145.

9. A Hebrew loanword in Jewish Neo-Aramaic; see others below.

judge"; CNA: *dayyāne* (*yan ʾalāha*) "judges (or God)"; JPS: "God (others: 'to the judges')."

YĔʿĀḎĀH (21:8) *mqādišla* "betrothes her," (21:9) *mbārixla* "marries her off"; but TO: *yəqayyəmah* "promises her"; JPS: "designated her."

BIFLÎLÎM (21:22) *bid xabir dayyānim* "by the word of the judges"; cf. TO, Rashi, and CNA; but Rasag: *biʾinṣāf* "justly"; JPS: "based on reckoning (others: 'as the judges determine')."

PAʿĂMÔṮ (25:12) *zingile* "bells"; but TO, Rashi, Rasag: "corners"; CNA and JPS: "feet."

ʿÊḎÛṮ (25:16) *tōra* "Torah"; cf. Rashi, but TO, Rasag, CNA: "testimony"; JPS: "[the tablets of] the Pact."

LEḤEM PĀNÎM (25:30) *laxma mare tre paswāsa* "bread of two faces (tops)"; cf. Rashi to 35:13, but the others translate literally; JPS: "bread of display."

BAMMARʾÔṮ HAṢṢÔVĔʾÔṮ (38:8) *bid rang ʿaskāre* "with the color of armies"; but TO, Rasag, CNA: "with the mirrors of women"; Rashi: "Daughters of Israel had in their hands mirrors"; JPS: "from the mirrors of the women who performed tasks (?)."

Some translations seem to be based on a folk etymology, i.e., a Hebrew word is translated by a Neo-Aramaic word of a similar sound, but not a real cognate, e.g.: *MISKĔNÔṮ* (1:11) "garrison or store cities" (JPS) *maskāne* "dwellings" (D); *GÔMEʾ* (2:3) "wicker basket" (JPS) *jāmi* "pine wood"; *HIṮʿALLALTÎ* (10:2) "I made a mockery" (JPS) *mtōʿilli* "I played"; *WĔHAMMÔṮÎ* (23:27) "I will throw into panic" (JPS; cf. TO and Rashi) *btēmēna* "I will annihilate"; *MĔNAQQIYYÔṮ* (25:29) "jugs" *qanye* "bamboo tubes, canes" (cf. Rashi: *ʾellū haqqānîm šemənaqqîn ʾôṯô* "these are the canes that clean it," etymologizing it as both *QNY* and *NQY*. In one case such a translation is induced by TO, i.e., *PAḤḤÊ* (39:3) "sheets (of gold)" (JPS), TO: *ṭassê*, Neo-Aramaic: *ṭasāsa* "plates, dishes."

2. TRANSLATIONS INDUCED BY EUPHEMISM

LĒʾLÔHÎM (4:16) *mgēb ʾilāha* "instead of God" (Z); *lʾistāḏa* "for a master" (D); cf. TO: *lərav*; Rashi: *lərav ûləsar*; Rasag: *ʾustāḏ*; but CNA: *lʾalāha*; JPS: "you are playing the role of God."

YHWH (4:24) *malʾax ʾistaz ʿōlām* "an angel of the Lord of the Universe"; cf. TO, Rasag; but CNA: *marya*; JPS: "the Lord."

HAMMAYMA (7:15) *ʾil reš māya* "to the water front," a euphemism for "to go to the rest room"; cf. Rashi; but all the other sources have a literal translation, "to the water."

ʾEṢBAʿ ʾĔLÔHÎM (8:15) *qudritid ʾilāha* "Omnipotence of God"; TO, Rashi, and Rasag: "plague from God"; but CNA and JPS: "the finger of God."

Note, however, that at times the Neo-Aramaic translation is literal even when others have a euphemism, e.g., *PĀNÎM ʾEL PĀNÎM* (33:11) *paswāsa ʾil paswāsa* "face to face," but TO: *mamlal ʿim mamlal* "speech against speech"; Rasag: *šafahan* "orally."

3. OBSERVATIONS ON MORPHOLOGY: NOUN

Collective nouns and nouns following a number, which in Hebrew are often in the singular, usually are translated by the plural, e.g., *BĀQĀR* (9:3) ("cattle") *tōre* "oxen"; *ʿĀRÔV* (8:17) *dahbe* "wild beasts"; *ṬAF* (10:24) *ṭifle* "little children"; *ḤAYIL* (14:4) *ʿaskāre* "armies"; *ŠIVʿÎM NĀFEŠ* (1:5) *šōʾi gyanāsa* "seventy souls"; *ŠNÊM ʿĀŚĀR MAṢṢĒVĀH* (24:4) *treʾsar dakanyāsa* "twelve stalls"; *ʾARBAʿ ṢÔʾN* (21:37) *ʾarba ʾirwe* "four sheep"; exceptions: *HADDĀGĀH* (7:18) *nunīsa* "fish" (sg.), but TO: *nūne* (pl.); *KINNĀM* (8:13) *qalma* "louse" (cf. TO: *qalmətā*, sg. as well). In two interesting cases Hebrew plural is translated by singular: *MĔRŌRÎM* (12:8) *mārōr* "bitter herb"; *TÔRÔṮ* (16:28) ("teachings") *tōra* "Torah"; in both cases a Hebrew loanword is known only in the sg. in Jewish Neo-Aramaic and other Jewish languages. On the other hand, Hebrew *PĀNÎM* "face," which has only the pl. form (in Biblical Hebrew) is always translated by *paswāsa*, a plural form, rather than by the common sg. form *pāsa*.[10]

Declined noun forms in the singular may be translated by the plural, and vice versa, partly due to the similarity of the forms, e.g.: *GĔVÛLEḴĀ* (10:4) ("your territory") *tixūbe dīdox* "your territories"; *ʿĂWÔNĒNÛ . . . ḤAṬṬAʾṮĒNÛ* (34:9) *ʿawōnōs dēni . . . xatāye dēni* "our iniquities . . . our sins"; *MAṬṬÔṮĀM* (7:12), pl., *ʿaṣṣa dōhun* "their rod" (cf. JPS: "each cast down his rod"); *MAʿĂŚEYḴĀ* (23:12), pl., *ṣaneʾta dīdox* "your work."

Usually, according to the principle of a strict literal translation, the gender of a Neo-Aramaic noun, when different, is often adjusted in accord with its Hebrew counterpart, e.g., *GÔY QĀDÔŠ* (19:6) *millita mqudša* "a holy (m.) nation (f.)"; *TĒṢĒʾ ʾĒŠ* (22:5) *mapqa nūra* "fire (m.) is started (f.)." An interesting case is the

10. As in Ladino (Judeo-Spanish): Hebrew *MAYIM, ḤAYYÎM* are translated as *aguas, vides* (in pl., to conform with Hebrew); Sabar, *Genesis* (N 1): 41 n. 14 of the introduction.

Hebrew loanword *šoḥaḏ* "bribe" which is m. in Hebrew but f. in Neo-Aramaic, because of its f. synonym *balṣa* (Arabic).

In spite of the strict literal translation, an indefinite article, an impersonal pronoun, and other particles are often added in the translation, e.g., *ᵓÊN ᵓÎŠ* (2:12) *lēs ču gōra* "not a person"; *LÔᵓ YÛḴAL LIRᵓÔṮ* (10:5) *la mṣe čuxa xāze* "none can see"; *ᵓŌMER* (16:16) *xa fitra* "a bushel"; *ᵓAḤAṮ BAŠŠĀNĀH* (30:10) *xa ga bid šāta* "one time in a year"; *YÔM YÔM* (16:5) *kud yōm kud yōm* "each day, every day"; strangely enough this is done even when Hebrew has an indefinite pronoun following the noun: *ṢINṢENEṮ ᵓAḤAṮ* (16:33) "a jar" *xa zawirta xa,* literally "a jar one"; *WĔᵓAḤĂRĀW* (10:14) "after it" *ubasre ši* "after it as well"; *HAPPAᶜAM* (9:27) "this time" *ᵓape naqla* "also this time"; *ᵓEḤAḎ* (9:6) *wala xa* (D) "not even one."

4. OBSERVATIONS ON MORPHOLOGY: VERB

In many cases, usually due to an ambiguous text, a Hebrew passive may be translated by a Neo-Aramaic active, and vice versa, e.g.: *NÔḎAᶜTÎ* (6:3) "I became known" *muyzeᵓli* "I made known"; cf TO: *hôḏāᶜit*; *WĔᵓIKKĀVĔḎĀH* (14:4) "I shall be honored" *mayqirēna* "I shall lie heavy"; *WAYYÛŠAV ᵓEṮ MÔŠEH WĔᵓEṮ ᵓAHĂRÔN* (10:8) "Moses and Aaron were returned" *mudᵓirre* "he (Pharaoh) brought (them) back"; *ᵓAZKÎR* (20:21) "I shall mention" *ᵓāse matxōre* "shall be mentioned"; *YĔRAPPĒᵓ* (21:19) "he should cure" *ᵓāse mbasōme* "he should be cured"; *WĔNEᵓĔḴAL* (22:5) "be consumed" *ᵓaxla* "it consumes"; cf. TO *wəyēḵûl.* Note that the Hebrew active participle, especially when the context suggests the past or preterite tense, is translated by the Neo-Aramaic passive participle, e.g.: *HABBĀᵓÎM* (1:1) *ᵓan ᵓisye* "who came"; cf. TO: *dəᶜallû*; *ᶜÔMĒḎ* (3:5) *ḥmīla* "have been standing"; *YÔṢĔᵓÎM* (13:4) *mpīqe* "have gone out" (but TO: *nâfəqîn* "going out"); *TÔᶜEH* (23:4) *tihya* "has wandered."

The perfect, imperfect, and other verb forms of Biblical Hebrew are usually adjusted to the Neo-Aramaic tense system according to the context, e.g.: *YĀḎAᶜTÎ* (3:19) *kiᵓēna* "I know"; *YIQQAḤ* (33:7) *šqille* "he took"; *WĔHĒVĒᵓṮÎ* (6:8) *mōsēli* "I have brought" (Z), but *mēṯēna* "I shall bring" (D); *WĔHAḴBĒḎ* (8:11) *muyqirre* "He hardened"; *HÔLĔḴÔṮ* (2:5) *gēzīwa* "were walking"; *BÔᶜĒR . . . WĔᵓÊNENNÛ ᵓUKKĀL* (3:2) *wēla biṭpāra . . . lēwa biqyāza* "was burning . . . (but) was not being consumed (by the fire)"; *WĔYAᶜAL* (10:12) *šud yāsiq* "let it go upon!"

A copula, unnecessary in Hebrew, is often added to nominal sentences, e.g.: *MÎ WĀMÎ* (10:8) *mani umanī-lu* "who and who are . . . ?"; *KÎ LÎ KOL HĀᵓĀREṢ* (19:5) *did ṭālī-la kulla ᵓarᵓa* "for mine is all the earth"; *ṬÔV* (14:12) *bisṭof-īla* "It is better."

Ambiguous and some uncommon verbal forms are mistranslated, e.g.: *NIQRAH* (3:18) and *NIQRAᵓ* (5:3) "happened" *ṣrixle* "called"; *TÔᵓSÎFÛN* (5:7) "you will add" *mjamᶜētun* "you will collect" (D); *NIRPÎM* (5:8) "weak" *bassīme* "healthy" (analyzing it as *RPᵓ* instead of *RPY*); *YIŠᶜÛ* (5:9) "indulge" *xalṣi* "be saved" (analyzing it as *YŠᶜ* instead of *ŠᶜY*); *LĒᶜĀNÔṮ* (10:3) "to humble oneself, to submit" (cf. TO, Rashi, JPS) *limjayōbe* "to respond"; *NEᶜERMÛ* (15:8) "heaped" *mgurgimlu* "roared" (analyzing it as *RᶜM* instead of *ᶜRM*); *ᵓĀRÎQ ḤARBÎ* (15:9) "I will bare my sword" (JPS) *mabirqēna sēpi* "I will flash my sword" (reading *ᵓĀRÎQ* as *ᵓAVRÎQ*?); *ᶜĀŠAN* (19:18) "was smoking" (verb) *tinna* "smoke" (noun); *WĔGĒRAŠTĀMÔ* (23:31) "you shall chase them" *bkardinnu* "I shall chase them"; *TIQREᵓNĀH* (1:10) "occur" (f. pl.?) *tafqālan* "occurs [f. sg.] to us" (cf. TO).

MAARAV 5–6 (Spring, 1990): 319–335

A DATABASE[1] APPROACH TO THE ANALYSIS OF HEBREW NARRATIVE

John H. Sailhamer
TRINITY EVANGELICAL DIVINITY SCHOOL, DEERFIELD, IL

0. INTRODUCTION

0.1. Computers provide an accurate and versatile means of forming lexical and grammatical indices to texts.[2] The personal computer has put the results within range of virtually any interested person. Although storing information in a computer is quite simple, making sense of it is another matter. As long as the work is carried out at the level of words and phrases—that is, within the clause—we can rely on the categories of traditional grammar, e.g., in Hebrew, tagging words as "perfect" or "imperfect." But when it comes to the storage and retrieval of relevant information beyond the level of morphology and inner-clausal relationships the need is apparent for exploring new systems of organization. The present article is an attempt to suggest some lines along which the personal computer can be used in the study of biblical Hebrew at a level beyond words and phrases. As such, it will attempt to describe an approach that is compatible both with a database management systems approach to syntactical analysis of biblical Hebrew and

1. The use of the term "database" is specifically related to the notion of database management systems (DBMS) and is to be distinguished from the related notion of information retrieval (IR). The primary difference between the two is that whereas DBMS work with structured data, that is, information that has been tagged and arranged in retrievable record files, IR systems, by contrast, work with unstructured data and pure texts. Edward A. Fox, "Information Retrieval: Research into New Capabilities," *CD Rom* (Microsoft, 1986): 144.

2. Robert A. Kraft and Emanuel Tov, "Computer Assisted Tools for Septuagint Studies," *Bulletin of the International Organization for Septuagint Studies* 14 (1981): 22–40.

the insights from recent studies in the field of textlinguistics.[3] It is with deep gratitude that I dedicate this work to Professor Stanislav Segert.

0.2. Stylistics and Textgrammar

Within the field of textlinguistics the goal of a textgrammar is to reconstruct a set of "rules"[4] governing the formation of texts. As such its attention is directed toward that which is obligatory and global. The rules apply to the generation of any and all texts. Stylistics,[5] on the other hand, is an attempt to describe the use of such obligatory rules in the formation of specific texts. Its focus is that which is optional and open to the choice of one generating a text.[6] Though these two levels of analysis are quite different, and should be kept distinct, the present article is intended to provide a basis for carrying out the separate tasks of both.

1. TAGGING THE CLAUSE

1.1 Clause Constituents

If the analysis is to carry on beyond the level of the clause, categories are necessary that will prove relevant for tagging clauses at that level. The clause will have to be approached from the top

3. Robert-Alain de Beaugrande and Wolfgang Dressler, *Introduction to Text Linguistics* (Longman, 1981); Gillian Brown and George Yule, *Discourse Analysis* (Cambridge University, 1983); Heinrich F. Plett, *Textwissenschaft und Textanalyse* (UTB, Quelle & Meyer, 1975); Siegfried J. Schmidt, *Texttheorie* (UTB, Wilhelm Fink, 1976); Teun A. van Diyk, *Some Aspects of Text Grammars* (The Hague: Mouton, 1972).

4. "The global task of a T(ext)-grammar is thus the formulation of the rules forming and relating semantic structures with phonological structures of all the well-formed texts of a language," van Diyk (N 3): 11. In order to avoid "an unduly rigid application of notions from 'exact' sciences" (de Beaugrande and Dressler [N 3]: XIV), the concept of "rules" in text grammar is to be understood in light of the warning of de Beaugrande and Dressler, "We should work to discover regularities, strategies, motivations, preferences, and defaults rather than rules and laws . . . It is the task of science to systemize the fuzziness of its objects of inquiry, not to ignore it or argue it away" (de Beaugrande and Dressler [N 3]: XV).

5. Eduard König, *Historisch-Comparative Syntax der Hebräischen Sprache* (Leipzig: J. C. Hinrichs, 1897): 620.

6. "Despite the diversity of approaches, nearly all work reflects the conviction that style results from the characteristic selection of options for producing a text or set of texts" (de Beaugrande and Dressler [N 3]: 16).

down. Only those constituents of the clause that point beyond the clause itself will be considered in formulating analytical categories for tagging the biblical text. The following is a list of such categories with a minimal rationale for each.

1.1.1. The presence or absence of the WAW

It has long been recognized that the presence or absence of a WAW with a clause plays an important role in the function of the clause at higher levels.[7] In light of such unanimity on the importance of the WAW, we suggest that the occurrence of the WAW with a clause be a marked feature of all tagged clauses. Within our database, then, the first major constituent of a clause will be marked as either "W," representing the presence of the WAW with a clause, or "0," representing its absence.

1.1.2. The Position of the Predicate

The position of the predicate within a verbal clause may be motivated by *inner*-clause factors.[8] It is, however, widely held that *inter*-clause factors also play an important role.[9] W. Richter has given an extended discussion of the importance of marking the position of the predicate within the verbal clause.[10] A somewhat modified version of his notation system is offered here for tagging the *inner*-clause relationships.

The first position[11] within a verbal clause is marked for whether or not it is occupied by a predicate. If the first position is occupied

7. Rudolf Meyer *Hebräische Grammatik. III: Satzlehre* (Berlin: de Gruyter, 1972): para. 112; W. Richter, *Grundlagen einer althebräischen Grammatik. B. Die Beschreibungsebenen III. Der Satz (Satztheorie)* (St. Ottilien: EOS, 1980): 7; F. I. Andersen, *The Sentence in Biblical Hebrew* (The Hague: Mouton, 1974): 36; C. Brockelmann, *Grundriss der vergleichenden Grammatik der semitischen Sprachen* (Berlin: Reuther & Reichard, 1913): 2.475f, 498; E. König (N 5): 489ff; P. Joüon, *Grammaire de l'hebreu biblique* (Rome: Institut Biblique Pontifical, 1923): §177; E. Kautzsch, *Gesenius' Hebrew Grammar* (Oxford: Oxford Univ., 1910): §154.

8. E.g., negation (*lʾ*) results in the predicate being put in a non-initial position.

9. W. Gross, "Syntaktische Erscheinungen am Anfang althebräischer Erzählungen: Hintergrund und Vordergrund," *Supplements to Vetus Testamentum* (Leiden: Brill, 1981): 131–145; K. Schlesinger, "Zur Wortfolge im Hebraischen Verbalsatz," *VT* 3 (1953): 380–390.

10. Richter, *Grundlagen* (N 7): 207ff.

11. For sake of consistency in tagging, the WAW is not considered a nuclear member of the clause. By "nuclear member" is meant a *Syntagma* (Richter, *Grundlagen* [N 7]: 209).

by a predicate, the type of verbal predicate is given, e.g., QATAL or YIQTOL.[12] If the first position is not occupied by the predicate of the clause, the position is marked with an "X." The function of the notation "X" is merely to mark the non-initial position of the predicate. The actual clause constituent occupying that position is not marked.[13] For example, the clause *brᶜšyt brᶜ ᶜlhym* (Gen 1:1) is tagged as 0 + X + QATAL. The absence of the WAW is marked by "0." The non-initial position of the predicate (the initial position is occupied by *brʾšyt*) is marked by the "X." The predicate (*brʾ*) is marked by QATAL.[14]

The difficulty of marking the predicate in the Hebrew nominal clause is well known.[15] Two approaches to tagging the predicate are suitable for analyzing nominal clauses at an *inter*-clausal level. The simpler approach is merely to mark such clauses as nominal with the notation "NC," leaving the question of the identification of the predicate and its location undecided. Such an approach would allow a "text-level" descriptive tagging of nominal clauses, corresponding to the tagging of verbal clauses, yet without forcing the question of the identification of the nominal predicate. For example, the clause *wḥšk ᶜl pny thwm* (Gen 1:2), is tagged as "W + NC." The WAW is marked by "W" and the nominal clause simply by "NC." If such an approach to tagging the nominal clauses is taken, the relevant particulars of the clause constituents can be recorded at another point in the database record.[16] In this way such details can be kept separate from the clause analysis itself and the tagging of both the verbal and nominal clauses allowed to remain descriptive.[17] A more detailed approach to tagging nominal clauses is based on J. Hoftijzer's suggestion that the constituents of the nominal clause are better described by form than by function. Rather than attempting to identify the "subject" and "predicate" of a nominal clause, one could note the relative positions of grammatically marked nominal constituents within the clause, e.g.,

12. See footnotes 19ff.

13. The type of clause constituent, e.g., Richter's (1. Sy) . . . (11. Sy) (*Grundlagen* [N 7]: 93), can be recorded at another point in the database record.

14. See note 19 below.

15. J. Hoftijzer, "The Nominal Clause Reconsidered," *VT* 23 (1973): 446–510.

16. It is convenient to include a field called "Notes" within the record system which can contain any number of miscellaneous data.

17. The question can be raised here whether the nominal clause with a participial predicate is to be considered with the nominal clauses, as in traditional grammars, or whether it should be given its own classification, e.g., "PTC." (Gross [N 9]: 135 n. 14).

whether the first position is occupied by a definite noun, an indefinite noun or a prepositional phrase (see note for a complete listing of nominal constituents).[18] Thus the clause tagged above as W + NC, can be tagged as W + inn-pp, meaning it is a clause connected by a WAW and having an indefinite noun in the first position and a prepositional phrase in the second position.

1.1.3. Type of Verbal Predicate

To avoid making assumptions about the semantics of the Hebrew verbal system, the following notation of the type of verbal predicate is useful: QATAL,[19] YIQTOL,[20] WAYYIQTOL,[21] YAQOM,[22] QETOL.[23] The verbal stems, such as NIPHAL, PIEL and HIPHIL, can be noted in a separate part of the database record, but they are not marked as a clause constituent here because their relevance does not extend beyond the clause.

1.2. Clause Type

Hebrew grammarians generally recognize three primary types of clauses: Nominal, Verbal and Inverted Verbal.[24] Since it is also

18. "d" = definite, "i" = indefinite, "da" = definite with an article, "ds" = definite with a suffix, "ic" = indefinite construct state, "dc" = definite construct state (e.g., "dca" = construct state with article on nomen rectum), "pr" = pronoun, "dpn" = proper noun, "pl" = particle, "pp" = prepositional phrase, "nn" = nomen (any substantive), "nm" = numeral, "pt" = participle, "if" = infinitive. (I would like to thank two of my students, Francois D. E. Blokland and Steve Hall, for suggestions and help with regard to these sigla.)

19. Perfect or Suffixed form.

20. Imperfect or Prefixed form.

21. Waw-consecutive. We need not decide whether the WAW here is an *inner*- or *inter*- clause level WAW. For convenience sake, it can be treated as a separate type in opposition to QATAL and YIQTOL. Thus, we need not mark it as 0 + WAYYIQTOL + X. The simple notation WAYYIQTOL marks all the relevant points: presence of the WAW (1.1.1); position of the predicate (1.1.2); and type of verbal predicate (1.1.3).

22. 3rd and 1st person Volition moods, viz., Jussive and Cohortative.

23. 2nd person Volitional mood, viz., Imperative.

24. The "Inverted Verbal" clause is the "zusammengesetzte Nominalsatz" (Meyer [N 7]: 14; Diethelm Michel, *Tempora und Satzstellung in den Psalmen* [Bonn: H. Bouvier u. Co., 1960]: 179). The question of the ultimate status of such a clause (whether verbal or nominal in nature) need not be decided here (cf. GKC §140f). There is consensus enough among grammarians that a third type of Hebrew clause does exist: " . . . there is an essential distinction between verbal-clauses, according as the subject stands before or after the verb" (GKC §142a).

generally recognized that the choice of one of these clause types is often motivated by constraints beyond the clause itself, a text-linguistically based analysis should tag each clause according to its type: "V" for verbal clause with Predicate-Subject;[25] "I" for inverted clause with Subject-Predicate; and "N" for nominal clause.[26]

1.3. Summary

The following tagged clauses from Genesis 1:1–5 demonstrate the appearance of a database containing the analysis of a Hebrew clause. Each line represents the data of a single record containing three fields describing the clause: Reference, Clause Constituent, Type.

Reference	Clause Const	Type
ge01.01al	0 + X + QATAL	V
ge01.02a1	W + X + QATAL	I
ge01.02a2	W + NC	N
ge01.02b1	W + NC	N
ge01.03a1	WAYYIQTOL	V
ge01.03a2	0 + YAQOM + X	V
ge01.03b1	WAYYIQTOL	V
ge01.04a1	WAYYIQTOL	V
ge01.04b1	WAYYIQTOL	V
ge01.05a1	WAYYIQTOL	V
ge01.05a2	W + X + QATAL	V
ge01.05b1	WAYYIQTOL	V
ge01.05b2	WAYYIQTOL	V
ge01.05b3	O + NC	N

2. TAGGING BEYOND THE CLAUSE

Once we move beyond the clause there is little help available from traditional grammars in shaping categories for analysis.[27] Andersen's notion of the "sentence"[28] is helpful, though, by the

25. Or P + (1. Sy) in Richter's notation.

26. The nominal clause could be divided between "N," for nominal predicates, and "P," for participial predicates.

27. E.g., GKC concludes with a discussion of various kinds of subordinate clauses.

28. "For a start we shall say that there are some constructions in which two clauses are related to each other in certain ways and which we propose to call sentences" (Andersen [N 7]: 24).

nature of the case, his approach is limited to only certain kinds of clauses.[29] R. Longacre's application of Tagmemic categories to biblical narrative texts has also proven helpful,[30] but unfortunately such categories are not "text immanent" to the biblical narratives.[31] The following analytical system is taken primarily from the text-linguistical approach of E. Gülich and W. Raible.[32] Its value lies in its providing descriptive, text immanent categories for parceling a text into units larger than individual clauses.

Put simply, beyond the level of the clause and its constituents, a text can be viewed along two axes. It can be viewed vertically as a set of non-intersection planes of discourse and it can be viewed horizontally as a set of contiguous segments. Thus an analysis of a text can proceed both vertically, down through embedded levels of text, and horizontally, across a series of textual units.

2.1. Vertical analysis (Text Planes)

Viewed vertically, a text contains layers of communicational planes.[33] Each level of discourse has its own set of referents and world within which the reference is carried out.[34] Each level is a text-world in its own right.

29. E.g., "The sequential coordination of clauses on paragraph-level by means of WP and WS 'consecutive' verb constructions is only marginal to sentence grammar," (Andersen [N 7]: 61).

30. E.g., see especially, Robert Longacre and Stephen Levinsohn, "Field Analysis of Discourse," *Untersuchungen in TextTheorie* (Göttingen: Vandenhoeck & Ruprecht, 1977): 103–122.

31. This is not a criticism of Longacre since the basis of a Tagmemic approach is the fact that it allows categories that go beyond "text immanent" descriptions. For a helpful analysis of Tagmemics see Elisabeth Gülich and Wolfgang Raible, *Linguistische Textmodelle: Grundlagen und Möglichkeiten* (München: Wilhelm Fink, 1977): 97–115.

32. Elisabeth Gülich and Wolfgang Raible, "Überlegungen zu einer makrostrukturellen Textanalyse: J. Thurber, The Lover and His Lass," *Untersuchungen in Texttheorie* (Vandenhoeck & Ruprecht, 1977): 132–175.

33. Gülich and Raible call such levels the "Ebenen der Kommunikation" and the markers that distinguish them the "Gliederungsmerkmal." Ibid.: 137.

34. "Teilt ein Sprecher S1 einem Hörer H1 in einer Kommunikationssituation etwas mit, so sprechen wir von einer Mitteilung auf der ersten Ebene der Kommunikation. Das Modell sprachlicher Kommunikation kann nun rekursiv angewendet werden. Das heisst, dass im Bereich der Gegenstande und Sachverhalte wieder ein Sprecher und ein Hörer auftreten konnen, die sich etwas mitteilen. Teilt innerhalb der Mitteilung, die S1 an H1 richtet, ein weiterer Sprecher S2 einem weiteren Hörer H2 etwas mit, so ist diese Mitteilung eine Mitteilung auf der zweiten Ebene der Kommunikation, in der Regel eine in eine Mitteilung auf der ersten Ebene der Kommunikation eingebettete 'direkte Rede'. Ein einschlägiges Beispiel

In biblical Hebrew, meta-communicational planes are usually marked with clauses such as "and he said . . ." (*wayyôʾmer*). Gülich and Raible call such clauses "meta-communicational clauses" or "hyper-clauses."[35] The function of such markers is to signal the beginning and end of a communication act within a narrative and to establish the context (world) within which "reference" is made in the communication act. In the case of *wayyôʾmer* the meta-communicational plane is marked by an explicit signal, namely the presence of the term *wayyôʾmer*. However, some meta-communicational planes are only implicitly signaled in the narrative. For example, although *wayyôʾmer* marks explicitly the beginning of an act of communication, there is no explicit marker to signal the *end* of a meta-communication plane begun with *wayyôʾmer*.[36] The effect of the meta-communication markers, then, is to bisect the narrative into primary spheres of communication: (1) that occupied by the author and reader of the narrative and (2) that occupied by the actants within the narrative. At the level of the first sphere of communication, the author can refer to the reader directly (e.g., Gen 13:10b), indirectly (Gen 2:24) or simply by virtue of the communication act implied in the existence of the narrative itself. At the second level of communication within the narrative, a communication act is established between two or more actants in the story (e.g., Gen 6:13ff).

In a database approach to text analysis, the operation of a clause at higher levels of the text should be monitored and registered within its specific communication plane. Every clause should be tagged to mark its meta-communicational level. Thus, for each clause, the level (McLEVEL) is either "1," representing the first level of communication between the text and the reader; or "2," representing the next level of communication, namely that between two actants of the first level; or "3," representing the third

---

wäre eine Rahmenerzählung, in die auf einer zweiten Ebene der Kommunikation eine Binnenerzählung eingebettet ist, die von einem im Rahmen eingefuhrten Sprecher erzählt wird" (Gülich and Raible [N 32]: 137).

35. "Metakommunikative Satze" or "Hypersatze" (Gülich and Raible [N 32]: 138).

36. Unlike English and other languages which have a closed quotation sign ["]. Occasionally in biblical narrative, a quotation will have no explicit introduction and will be recognized as such only by internal clues such as pronominalization, e.g., Gen 4:25b, where the first person pronoun *ly* is the only marker that the clauses are a quote. Another example of an *implicit* marker is the *beginning* of narrative. It is not customary to begin a narrative act of communication between an author and a reader with an explicit marker. The onset of the text itself is usually sufficient to establish the communication relationship.

level, namely an act of communication reported at level "2" by actants in level "1"; and so on.[37]

2.2. Horizontal Analysis (Text Segments)

A horizontal analysis of the role of a clause within a text is based on a conceptualization of the text as a series of functional units or segments. Gülich and Raible call such functional units "text-segments" ("Teiltexte").[38] Each segment represents a specific unit of narrative and has a particular *function*[39] with respect to the text as a whole.

2.2.1. Text-Segment Markers

The "markers" of distinct segments within a text are likely to be both *thematic*[40] and *formal.*[41] The concern of this section is the formal markers, that is, the "signals" within a text that allow the reader to divide and arrange the text into meaningful and manageable units in the process of reading. Within our database, then, the clause will have to be tagged with respect to its position along this axis.

2.2.2. Kinds of Text-Segment Markers

There are three kinds of text-segment markers in narrative texts, each of which bears a relationship to one of three "dimensions"

37. An example of how complicated such "layers of reference" within a single narrative can become is the narrative of Jer 26:1–6, where at the conclusion of verse 6 in many English translations, the quotation marks (" ' ") show that at least three distinct levels of discourse have been at play within the narrative: (1) the Lord speaks to Jeremiah, commanding him to (2) speak to the people, saying (3) thus says the Lord (to them). Each level has its own sphere of time, space and reference.

38. Gülich and Raible [N 32]: 133.

39. Ibid.

40. A Thematic marker is one found within the ideas or subject matter contained in the text. For example, the Book of Genesis can be segmented on the basis of its subject matter into such text-segments as "creation," "fall," "flood," or "primeval period" and "patriarchal period." See S. Bar-Efrat, "Some Observations on the Analysis of Structure in Biblical Narrative," *VT* 30 (1980): 168ff.

41. A formal marker is one that is actually signaled by a constituent of the text and is not contingent on the specific subject matter. The most obvious example of such a marker is the system of chapters and verses inserted into the biblical narratives, though, of course, they were inserted long after the texts were written and hence do not necessarily represent the author's own segmentation.

within a narrative. The first marker is the purely linguistic clue. This type of marker relates to the essentially linguistic nature of a text and is language-specific, it follows the "rules" of the language in which the text is written. An author may use whatever linguistic devices are available within a given language to signal a break in the text. The most common variety of such devices in English is its system of "punctuation." *Commas, periods, indentation,* all enable the reader to follow the "breaks" in the narrative that are intended by the author. Like most such signals, there is a hierarchical order of value to the English system, e.g., a *period* represents a higher order of break within a sentence than a *comma.*

Biblical Hebrew apparently did not have an original system of punctuation that operated at the level of the largest units of narrative. It did, however, have a number of linguistic devices that enabled the author to signal "breaks" at appropriate moments in the narrative. Some or all of these may have been operative only when the text was heard aloud (oral). There may have been graphic markers as well.[42]

A second type of text-segment marker belongs to the "narrative world" within the narrative. Since that world is one in which there are "breaks" and movements from one "scene" to another or from one "time" to another, such breaks also provide important points of segmentation in the reading of the narrative. For example, the break between Gen 2:24 and 2:25ff is marked by a change in the narrative "scene" from the place of Adam's "deep sleep" to that of the place of the "temptation."

Since biblical narrative is a *reproduction* of the real world, its "narrative world" is a *facsimile* of that world and thus follows the rules of the real world. Consequently, elements that assure "breaks" or segmentation in the "narrative world" are the same as those that exist in real life. Thus a third type of segmentation marker in narrative texts is derived from markers which are a part of the "real world" itself. If within a narrative two actants end a conversation and part ways, there will be a "break" in the narrative, *just as in "real life."* Such a break will usually mark a significant

42. In the Aramaic texts from Deir ᶜAlla red ink is used to mark important breaks in the narrative, see J. Hoftijzer and G. van der Kooij, *Aramaic Texts from Deir ᶜAlla* (Leiden: Brill, 1976): 184: "This makes it probable that in this kind of text an introductory clause and a clause (/clauses) introducing a new and important aspect were written with a special kind of (red) ink to bring out clearly their special character."

segmentation in the narrative, e.g., Gen 18:33 ("And the Lord left as he finished speaking to Abraham and Abraham returned to his place") marks a major break in the narrative, as also 20:1 ("And Abraham went away from there towards the land of the Negev"). Not only do such changes in *place* mark a break in the narrative, but also changes in *time* (e.g., Gen 15:1, "After these things the word of the Lord came to Abram . . .") and changes in *persons* (e.g., Gen 19:1. "And the two messengers came to Sodom . . ."). Common signals of "breaks" in the real world are thus, (1) changes in persons, (2) changes in time, and (3) changes in place. A change in any of these variables in the real world, signals a break or segmentation in the communication act. When they are *mimicked* in narrative they are also likely to signal a change in a text segment.

Text-segment markers that stem from the narrative world and the language of the text are text-internal markers, whereas those that stem from the real world are text-external markers. Gülich and Raible suggest that although the analysis of written texts must depend primarily on text-internal markers, the distinction between text-internal and text-external markers can provide a basis for establishing a *hierarchy* of text markers within a written text. This may be done by drawing a distinction between text-segment markers for which there is an analogy in the text-external field and those for which there is no analogy. For example, in real life, when a person begins to speak it usually marks a break from some previous action. Either someone else was speaking and the new speaker has marked the end of that speech, or there was silence and the new speech thus marks the beginning of the new action. Such breaks in "real life" actions are *mimicked* in Hebrew narrative by means of the simple clause, "and he said . . ." (*wayyôʾmer*). Thus the expression "and he said" is a narrative feature (text-internal marker) that is formed by analogy to the segmentation markers in the real world. On the other hand the use of a Waw in biblical Hebrew, is an example of a narrative feature (text-internal marker) that has no analogy to any segmentation markers in the real world. Gülich and Raible suggest that *in realistic narrative, priority should be given to those markers that simulate "breaks" in real life over those markers which do not.*[43] The reason is that the goal of realistic narrative is to *mimic* the real world, namely, to

43. Gülich and Raible [N 32]: 137.

take on important characteristics of that world. Thus, segmentation features of the real world that are *mimicked* in the narrative should be afforded a higher level of importance in segmentation than those that do not.[44]

Since priority is to be given to those text-segments which show an analogy to text-external communication acts, a likely source of top level markers is the "world" depicted in the narrative. Like the "real world," the "world" of realistic narrative is one that unfolds in *time* and *space*. Events of the *narrative world* are *time* and *space* events. When it is understood that these events are carried out by narrative *characters (actants),* all the essential components of the *narrative world* come into view:

ACTANTS:	Subjects of events in *time* and *space*.[45]
ACTIONS:	Events in *time* and *space* performed by or upon ACTANTS.
TIME:	Relative sequence of events.
PLACE:	Relative location of events.

Just as in the "real world," segmentation of the *narrative world* is marked by variations in these components. "Actions can take place 1) at different times in different places; 2) at different times in the same place; 3) at the same time in different places."[46] Each of these three types of segmentation can be further divided by a change in the actants and thus provide a helpful schematic for tagging clauses within a database.[47]

44. Ibid.

45. Ibid.: 139.

46. Ibid.: 140.

47. "Die lokalen Parameter eines dargestellten Handlungsablaufs sind prinzipiell ebenso wichtig wie die zeitlichen. Denn einerseits verandert sich bei Geschehens- und Handlungsablaufen mit Notwendigkeit die Zeit, während der Ort gleichbleiben kann. Auf der anderen Seite bedeutet jede Veranderung des Ortes bei ganz order teilweise identischer Konstellation der Handlungstrager automatisch auch Veranderung in der Zeit, so dass in diesem Falle die Merkmale, welche die Ortsbefindlichkeit anzeigen, zugleich auch eine Veranderung in der Zeitbefindlichkeit bedeuten. Die betreffenden Merkmale können dann nicht nur—wie oft—gemeinsam auftreten, sondern das Vorhandensein des einen impliziert das des anderen. Berucksichtigt man weiter, dass eine Veränderung der Zeit in Geschehens- und Handlungsablaufen auch von einer Veranderung in der Konstellation der Handlungstrager unabhangig ist, so ergibt sich, dass solche Merkamale, welche die Zeitbefindlichkeit und/oder die Ortsbefindlichkeit anzeigen, in der Hierarchie der Gliederungsmerkmale über den Merkmalen stehen, die eine Veränderung der Personenkonstellation anzeigen." Ibid.: 140.

2.2.3. "Change in time" as a Text-Segment Marker

Along with the Text-segment marker of a "change in place," the marker of a "change in time" receives the highest priority among the text-segment markers which are derived from an analogy with the segmentation of events in the "real world." "Change in time," therefore, is an important clue to the structural segmentation of narrative.[48]

The use of a change in time in biblical narrative is common for both absolute and relative changes in time. Without raising the question of how to distinguish between the relative and absolute use of change in time in biblical narrative, the following examples are offered:

Genesis 16:15–16	Genesis 17:1
And Abram named the son Hagar bore to him Ishmael; and Abram was 86 years old when Hagar bore Ishmael.	And Abram was 99 years old and the Lord appeared to Abram.
Genesis 14	Genesis 15:1
Abram defeated the kings of the East and delivered Lot and his possessions.	After these things the word of the Lord came to Abram in a vision saying. . . .

2.2.4. "Change of place" as a Text-Segment Marker

"Change of place" in the "real world" nearly always marks a segmentation of a communication act and is frequently associated with change of time. Such is the case in the world of the narrative as well. Change of place marks a change from one state or sphere of spacial uniformity to another.

48. Change of time, however, can mark various levels of segmentation within a narrative. According to Gülich and Raible, change in time can mark an absolute change as well as a relative change within a narrative. An absolute marker signals a change to a major new section of a narrative, e.g., a new episode. A relative marker signals a change within a smaller unit of narrative, e.g., within an episode. Ibid.: 143.

Genesis 4:1–16	Genesis 4:17
Cain and Abel: the Lord gave a sign to Cain that whoever might find him would not slay him.	And Cain went out from before the Lord and dwelt in the land of Nod, east of Eden.

Genesis 12:9	Genesis 12:10
And Abram sojourned toward the Negev, pitching his tent along the way.	And there was a famine in the land and Abram went down to Egypt to sojourn there.

2.2.5. "Change of actant" as a Text-Segment Marker

A change in the characters (actant)[49] within a narrative can signal minor segments within a narrative text.

Genesis 12:15a	Genesis 12:15b
And the servants of Pharaoh saw her and praised her to the Pharaoh.	And the woman was taken into the house of Pharaoh.

A change in character along with a change in place and consequently a change in time, however, is likely to be a signal of the beginning of a major text-segment, as it would be in the "real world."

Genesis 19:36–38	Genesis 20:1
Story of the two daughters of Lot	And Abram went from there to the land of the Negev . . .

2.2.6. Summary of Horizontal Analysis (Text Segments)

The above notion of text segments provides a relevant system of tagging Hebrew clauses for their role within large spheres of text. Without deciding beforehand which segment markers are hierarchi-

49. Not all characters in a narrative are actants. In so far as it is relevant for marking text-segments, an actant is a character occupying the principal role in the text-segment—usually the subject of all the story-line verbs (e.g., WAYYIQTOL).

cally first and second, etc., each clause can be tagged for its role with respect to a change of actant, time and place within the narrative text. The following notation system incorporates all the relevant variables: "A" marks a change in actant, "=" marks the actant as the same as that of the previous clause, and "a" marks the actant as the same as that of the previous clause and that it is explicitly "renominalized"[50] as such within the clause. "T" marks a change in time, "+" marks the time as the same as that of the previous clause, and "t" marks the time as the same as that of the previous clause and that it is explicitly mentioned in the clause as such. "P" marks a change in place, "$" marks the place as the same as that of the precious clause, and "p" marks the place as the same as that of the previous clause and that it is explicitly mentioned in the clause as such.

ge01.01a1	O + X + QATAL	V NAR 1 ATP
ge01.02a1	W + X = QATAL	I NAR 1 A ==
ge01.02a2	W + NC	N NAR 1 A ==
ge01.02b1	W + NC	N NAR 1 A ==
ge01.03a1	WAYYIQTOL	V NAR 1 A ==
ge01.03a2	O + YAQOM + X	V DIS 2
ge01.03b1	WAYYIQTOL	V NAR 1 A ==
ge01.04a1	WAYYIQTOL	V NAR 1 A ==
ge01.04b1	WAYYIQTOL	V NAR 1 a ==

3. EXAMPLE OF RETRIEVABLE TEXT DATA

Once the information has been entered and stored in the computer, it is retrievable in any number of combinations involving the tagging discussed in this article. The versatility of the computer will allow the results to be printed on screen or stored in a file to be edited or printed.[51] The following is a printed example of a request for O + X + QATAL/I/NAR, that is, all the clauses in Genesis that do not begin with a WAW (= O), have a predicate in non-initial position (= X in first position), have a perfect as the verbal predicate (= QATAL) have inverted order (+ I) and are in narrative (= NAR) texts—as opposed to discourse.

50. Ibid.: 155ff.

51. The Hebrew texts in this example were read directly from the Michigan-Claremont BHS data files supplied by the Computer Assisted Tools for Septuagint Studies (CATSS).

1. ge03.20b1 O + X + QATAL I NAR 1 A==
כִּי הִוא הָיְתָה אֵם כָּל־חָי

2. ge04.20b1 O + X + QATAL I NAR 1 A==
הוּא הָיָה אֲבִי יֹשֵׁב אֹהֶל וּמִקְנֶה

3. ge04.21b1 O + X + QATAL I NAR 1 A==
הוּא הָיָה אֲבִי כָּל תֹּפֵשׂ כִּנּוֹר וְעוּגָב

4. ge06.04a1 O + X + QATAL I NAR 1 Atp
הַנְּפִלִים הָיוּ בָאָרֶץ בַּיָּמִים הָהֵם

5. ge07.08a1 O + X + QATAL I NAR 1 A=P
מִן הַבְּהֵמָה הַטְּהוֹרָה וּמִן הַבְּהֵמָה אֲשֶׁר
אֵינֶנָּה טְהֹרָה וּמִן הָעוֹף וְכֹל אֲשֶׁר רֹמֵשׂ
עַל הָאֲדָמָה שְׁנַיִם שְׁנַיִם בָּאוּ

6. ge07.22a1 O + X + QATAL I NAR 1 A==
כֹּל אֲשֶׁר נִשְׁמַת רוּחַ חַיִּים בְּאַפָּיו מִכֹּל
אֲשֶׁר בֶּחָרָבָה מֵתוּ

7. ge08.19a1 O + X + QATAL I NAR 1 A=P
כָּל הַחַיָּה כָּל הָרֶמֶשׂ וְכָל הָעוֹף כֹּל רוֹמֵשׂ
עַל הָאָרֶץ לְמִשְׁפְּחֹתֵיהֶם יָצְאוּ מִן הַתֵּבָה

8. ge10.08b1 O + X + QATAL I NAR 1 A==
הוּא הֵחֵל לִהְיוֹת גִּבֹּר בָּאָרֶץ

9. ge10.09a1 O + X + QATAL I NAR 1 A==
הוּא הָיָה גִבֹּר צַיִד לִפְנֵי יְהוָה

10. ge11.27a2 O + X + QATAL I NAR 1 A==
תֶּרַח הוֹלִיד אֶת אַבְרָם אֶת נָחוֹר וְאֶת הָרָן

11. ge13.12a1 O + X + QATAL I NAR 1 A=p
אַבְרָם יָשַׁב בְּאֶרֶץ כְּנָעַן

12. ge14.03a1 O + X + QATAL I NAR 1 A=P
כָּל אֵלֶּה חָבְרוּ אֶל עֵמֶק הַשִּׂדִּים

13. ge15.17a2 O + X + QATAL I NAR 1 At=
הַשֶּׁמֶשׁ בָּאָה

14. ge19.23a1 O + X + QATAL I NAR 1 A=P
הַשֶּׁמֶשׁ יָצָא עַל הָאָרֶץ

15. ge24.15a2 O + X + QATAL I NAR 1 AT=
הוּא טֶרֶם כִּלָּה לְדַבֵּר

16. ge25.19b1 O + X + QATAL I NAR 1 A==
אַבְרָהָם הוֹלִיד אֶת יִצְחָק

17. ge34.27a1 O + X + QATAL I NAR 1 A=P
בְּנֵי יַעֲקֹב בָּאוּ עַל הַחֲלָלִים

18. ge36.02a1 O + X + QATAL I NAR 1 A==
עֵשָׂו לָקַח אֶת נָשָׁיו מִבְּנוֹת כְּנָעַן אֶת עָדָה
בַּת אֵילוֹן הַחִתִּי וְאֶת אָהֳלִיבָמָה בַּת עֲנָה
בַּת צִבְעוֹן הַחִוִּי

19. ge36.13b1 O + X + QATAL I NAR 1 a==
אֵלֶּה הָיוּ בְּנֵי בָשְׂמַת אֵשֶׁת עֵשָׂו

20. ge37.02a2 O + X + QATAL I NAR 1 AT=
יוֹסֵף בֶּן שְׁבַע עֶשְׂרֵה שָׁנָה הָיָה רֹעֶה אֶת אֶחָיו בַּצֹּאן

21. ge44.04a1 O + X + QATAL I NAR 1 a=P
הֵם יָצְאוּ אֶת הָעִיר

22. ge47.26b1 O + X + QATAL I NAR 1 A==
רַק אַדְמַת הַכֹּהֲנִים לְבַדָּם לֹא הָיְתָה לְפַרְעֹה

23. ge50.23b1 O + X + QATAL I NAR 1 A==
גַּם בְּנֵי מָכִיר בֶּן מְנַשֶּׁה יֻלְּדוּ עַל בִּרְכֵּי יוֹסֵף

MAARAV 5–6 (Spring, 1990): 337–344

PHOENICIAN *NBŠ/NPŠ* AND ITS HEBREW SEMANTIC EQUIVALENTS

ZIONY ZEVIT
UNIVERSITY OF JUDAISM, LOS ANGELES, CA

I

Phoenician *npš* is attested in *KAI* 37:B:5, an inscription from Kition, Cyprus, *lnpš bt ʾš lʾštt*, "for the personnel of the temple who are by the ?" It occurs in two inscriptions with the sense "grave stone": (1) *KAI* 128:3, a Neo-Punic inscription from Libya, *circa* 1st century C.E., . . . *ḥwʾ š*[*ʾ*]*nt šmn*[*m*] *šš npš mt*, "he lived eight(y)-six years. A grave stone of the dead."[1] (2) *KAI* 136:1, a Neo-Punic inscription from Tunisia, *circa* 1st century C.E., *nʾpš šʾdyt*, "the grave stone/stele of Adit."[2]

The word also occurs in *KAI* 24:13, from Zinjirli, *circa* 830–825 B.C.E., *whmt št nbš km nbš ytm bʾm*, where its sense is somewhat more difficult to establish. The following translations have been suggested for this passage:

1. " . . . so dass sie (mir) eine Gesinnung zeigten, wie die Gesinnung der Waise zu ihrer Mutter."[3]
2. " . . . and gave them an affection (for me) like the fatherless for his mother."[4]

1. This sense of *npš* is attested in Jewish-Aramaic, Syriac, Palmyrene, Nabatean, and Arabic (cf. *KAI* II: 133; *DISO*: 183–184). The more common Phoenician word with a similar sense is *mṣbt* (e.g., *KAI* 34:1; 35:1). In Neo-Punic, *ʾbn* is attested with a similar sense (*KAI* 133:1; 135:1).

2. J. Hoftijzer, "Notes sur une épitaphe en écriture Neopunique," *VT* 11 (1961): 344–348.

3. M. Lidzbarski, *Ephemeris für Semitische Epigraphik* III (Giessen: Topelmann, 1915): 238.

4. C. C. Torrey, "The Zakir and Kilamua Inscriptions," *JAOS* 35 (1915): 365; cf. also S. Segert, *A Grammar of Phoenician and Punic* (München: Beck, 1976): 295, where *nbš* is rendered "soul, feeling."

3. "... et eux, ils ont disposé leur âme comme l'âme de l'orphelin à l'égard de sa mère."[5]
4. "They were disposed (toward me) as an orphan is to his mother."[6]
5. "Und sie fühlten eine Gisinnung wie die Gesinnung der Waise gegenüber der Mutter."[7]
6. "Ils montaient (envers moi) une disposition comme la disposition d'un orphelin de père vers sa mère."[8]
7. "... and as for them, (each) placed himself as the desire of an orphan for its mother."[9]
8. "... and they behaved (towards me) like an orphan towards (his) mother."[10]

Most of these translations concur that the Phoenician describes a psychological state, "Gesinnung, âme, disposition, affection" and all, without saying so explicitly, agree that the Phoenician here is idiomatic. This explains the different circumlocutions employed in the various translations to express similar ideas and the non-literal rendering of the verb *št*, "zeigen, disposer, be disposed, fühlen." Characteristic of all these translations except the last two is that they appear to work backwards from the expression *km nbš ytm bʾm*, "like the *nbš* of an orphan for its mother" which is taken to be a picturesque way of describing affection, kindness or the like, to the expression *whmt št nbš* which is then translated to fit in with the last half of the line.[11] None have attempted to work out the exact sense of the idiom and none have sought parallels in related languages that can throw light on the Phoenician. M. Lidzbarski, whose translation was presented in first position above, noted that the nuance of *nbš* could only be characterized through comparative study.[12] Since Lidzbarski wrote in *Ephemeris III*, in 1915, this

5. A. Dupont-Sommer, *Les Araméens* (Paris: A. Maisonneuve, 1949): 43.

6. F. Rosenthal, in *ANET*^{2}: 501.

7. *KAI* II: 31.

8. *DISO*: 183.

9. R. S. Tomback, *A Comparative Semitic Lexicon of the Phoenician and Punic Languages* (SBLDS 32; Ann Arbor: SBL, 1978): 218.

10. J. C. L. Gibson, *Textbook of Syrian Semitic Inscriptions* III (Oxford: Clarendon, 1982): 35.

11. The translation of *ytm* by "orphan" must be clarified. In BH, *yātōm* clearly refers to the fatherless (cf. Lam 5:3) but nowhere is it clear that the word applies to someone both of whose parents are dead. In Mishnaic Hebrew, however, it seems to be used of the parentless (*T. Sanh.* 19b) and of the motherless (*M. Bek.* 9:4). I assume that *ytm* here is used with the sense "parentless." Cf. l. 10, "I was a father ... I was a mother." This is the sense that best complements Kilamuwa's hyperbole.

12. Lidzbarski (N 3): 234–235.

task has been left unattended. One of the objectives of this essay in honor of Prof. St. Segert is to limn the nuances of this vocable.

II

An expression similar to *št nbš* is BH (= Biblical Hebrew) *šît lēb*, "pay attention" (2 Sam 13:20; Jer 31:21; Ps 48:14; Job 7:17; Prov 22:17; 24:32; 27:33). Also similar is BH *śîm* (*ʾet*) *lēb/lēbāb*, "pay attention" (Deut 32:46; 1 Sam 9:20; 25:25; Hag 1:5, 7; 2:15, 18). Slightly removed is the idiom *śīm ʿal lēb*, "place on heart," i.e., "to know, to remember, to consider," which occurs first in Jeremiah and then thereafter only in post-exilic texts (Is 42:25; 47:7, 57:11) and may be considered a post-sixth century B.C.E. idiom.[13] These expressions should be translated literally "place the heart" and "place on the heart," which make sense only when it is recalled that in Hebrew *lēb*, "heart," refers to the mind and will, the rational aspect of man's personality (Deut 7:17; 8:7; 1 Sam 21:13; 1 Kgs 2:44; Is 6:10; Jer 51:50).[14] In all of these examples of *šīt lēb, śīm (ʾet) lēb*, and *śīm ʿal lēb*, the *lēb* is always that of the subject of the verb *šīt/śīm*. Only in Jer 12:11 and Mal 2:2 does the expression *śīm ʿal lēb* occur without this agreement and seems to mean "to pay attention" rather than "to remember."

In BH, *nepeš* refers, among other things, to the appetites and emotions. It is hungry and thirsty (Ps 107:9; 42:3; 63:2), happy and sad (Ps 86:4; Is 38:15).[15] In Deuteronomy and in Deuteronomic writings from the 7th–6th centuries B.C.E., *nepeš* occurs many times

13. Cf. P. Joüon, "Locutions hebraiques avec le preposition *ʿl* devant *lb, lbb*," *Biblica* 5 (1924). He writes: "Mais le sens litteral être sur le coeur suggère ici très fortement le sens figure être dans la mémoire . . ." (49). Joüon also suggests that *bāʾ, ʿalā* + *lēb* developed by analogy to *śīm ʿal lēb* (50). It should be noted, however, that *śīm ʿal lēb* and *ʿālā ʿal lēb* both occur first in pre-exilic Jeremiah (Jer 12:11; 3:16; 7:31), while only *bāʾ ʿal lēb* is exclusively post-exilic (2 Chr 7:11). However, the expression *bāʾ ʿal lēb* in the Chronicles passage corresponds to *ḥāpēṣ*, "desire," in 1 Kgs 9:1 and is thus differentiated semantically from the other expressions.

14. C.-F. Jean, "Notules de semantique hebraique," *Mélanges Syriens Offerts à Monsieur René Dussaud* II (Paris: Geuthner, 1939): 703–722. Jean notes that the use of *lēb* to indicate "will, intelligence, and memory" is paralleled somewhat by Egyptian *ib* (715). For Akkadian parallels to Hebrew uses of *lēb* and *nepeš*, see E. Dhorme, *L'emploi metaphorique des noms de parties du corps en Hebreu et en Akkadien* (Paris: Libraire orientaliste Paul Geuthner, 1923): 18, 123–124.

15. C. A. Briggs, "The Use of *npš* in the Old Testament," *JBL* 10 (1897): 17–30. See also A. Murtonen, *The Living Soul. A Study of the Meaning of the Word naefaeš in the Old Testament Hebrew Language* (Helsinki, Societas Orientalis Fennica, 1958). The meaning "mind"—on which see below—and the use of *nbš* in Phoenician were overlooked in this study.

in an idiom, *bəkol ləbābəkā ūbəkol napšəkā*. In this idiom it may be interpreted either as referring to the rational aspect of the personality and therefore semantically equivalent to *lēb*/*lēbāb* or to the irrational aspect—emotions and appetites—and part of a merismus (e.g., Deut 4:29; 6:5; 10:12; 11:13; etc., 1 Kgs 2:4; 8:48). In a few other passages *nepeš* may refer to the rational center of the personality, e.g., Gen 23:8: *ʾim yēš ʾet napšəkem liqbōr ʾet mētī milləpānay*, i.e., "if your thought is . . ." or "if your desire is . . ." See also 2 Kgs 9:15; Isa 42:1; 66:3; Ps 77:3. Coordinated with *šīt*/*śīm* it occurs only in the expression *śīm nepeš bəkap*, "to place one's life in one's own hand" (Judg 12:3; 1 Sam 19:5; 28:21; Job 13:14). There is no undisputable Hebrew example of *nepeš* referring to the mind or rational aspect of a person.

In *KAI* 24:13, the line under discussion describes the response of the *Mškbm* to the largesse and support of Kilamuwa. Bearing in mind the similarity of the constructions *št nbš* and BH *šīt*/*śīm lēb*, we hypothesize that they are similar in meaning and that in the context of this inscription, *nbš* refers to the rational aspect of the personality, corresponding semantically to Hebrew *lēb*/*lēbāb*, and possibly to some rare uses of Hebrew *nepeš*.

This hypothesis is supported tangentially in the Aramaic Sefire inscriptions where the idiom *tʾmr bnbšk* (*KAI* 223:B:5) corresponds to BH *ʾāmar bəlēbāb*/*bəlēb*, "to think" (Deut 8:17; 9:4; Eccl 2:1; 3:17, 18).[16]

The Phoenician expression may then be translated tentatively "and they remembered, like the mind of an orphan, a mother," or "and they remembered as an orphan (remembers) a mother." If this interpretation be accepted, then it is obvious that the second half of the line, *km nbš ytm bʾm*, is written elliptically. A verb with the sense "remember" or a form of the verb *št* must be understood after the word *ytm*.[17] This is clear from the preposition *b* which lacks a governing verb and is bolstered by the fact that in BH, another Canaanite dialect, the object of mental acts is often indicated by the preposition *b*: *heʾĕmīn bə* (Gen 15:6; Ex 14:31; 1 Sam 27:12; Mic

16. The complete expression is *hn tʾmr bnbšk wtʿšt blbbk*, "if you think and plot." Cf. J. C. Greenfield, "Stylistic Aspects of the Sefire Treaty Inscriptions," *Acta Orientalia* 24 (1965): 6; J. Fitzmyer, *The Aramaic Inscriptions of Sefire* (Rome: PBI, 1967): 81. Greenfield points out that *ḥāšab bəlēbāb* in Zech 7:10, 8:17 is the semantic equivalent of Aramaic *ʿšt blbb* in Sefire. Both *nbš* and *lbb* here refer to the mind.

17. I hypothesize an original sentence similar to the following from which our expression developed: **km nbš ytm št bʾm*.

7:5); *bāṭaḥ bə* (Deut 28:52; Judg 9:26; Isa 30:12); *zākar bə* (Jer 3:16); *šāmaᶜ bə* (Gen 27:5; 22:18; 2 Sam 19:36; *KAI* 14:6). The nuance of the deleted verb must be discerned from the context. The preceding expression *št nbš* in the first part as well as the noun *nbš* delimit and describe the sense of what is to be understood.

The test of this hypothesis resides in its ability to enhance our understanding of the inscription as a whole.

The remembering motif of line 13 is related to line 14 of the inscription which we translate: "And (concerning) whoever of my sons who rules in my stead, (should) he damage this inscription, may the *Mškbm* not honor the *Bᶜrrm* and may the *Bᶜrrm* not honor the *Mškbm*." The kindness of Kilamuwa towards the *Mškbm* mentioned in ll. 10–13 is the reason he expects and adjures them to act on his behalf in the future. Clearly, their actions in the future vis-à-vis his request depends on their remembering their obligations. Thus the idiom in l. 13 is a crucial pivot between ll. 9–12 that deal with Kilamuwa's past acts of largesse and ll. 14–16 that deal with a possible scenario in the future.

The same motif functioning in the same way is found in a more extensive 7th century B.C.E. Hebrew text. Remembering past favors or kindnesses obligates Israel to YHWH (Deut 8:2, 18; and see Ezek 16:22), and the injunction that Israel remember the treachery of the Amalekites is inseparable from the command to extirpate them (Ex 17:14; Deut 25:17–19).

It is also found in the Sefire inscriptions. The treaty between Matiel and Bar-Ga'yah was written as a *zkrn*, reminder, to the children and grandchildren of Matiel of their obligations (*KAI* 222:C:2–3). This is the self-same term used in the aforementioned Ex 17:14: "Write this as a *zikkārōn*, reminder, in a scroll . . . that I will blot the *zēker*, remembrance, of Amalek from under heaven." (Compare Deut 25:17–19: "*zākōr*, remember, . . . you shall blot out the *zēker*, remembrance, of Amalek . . . you shall not forget.")

Elsewhere in Phoenician, "to remember" is expressed by *skr* in an inscription from Lapethos, Cyprus, from the 3rd century B.C.E.: *wyskrn mlqrt*, "and may Milqart remember me" (*KAI* 43:18). This is cognate to BH *zkr*.

In stark contrast to Hebrew usage, Phoenician *lb* refers only to the emotional center of the personality: *KAI* 26:A1:12–13: *bṣdqy wbḥkmty wbnᵓm lby*, "because of my righteousness, my wisdom, and my goodness of heart"; *KAI* 145:11, *bᵓšr lb*, "happiness of heart," i.e., delight, satisfaction, and *KAI* 26:A18; II:8, 14, *nḥt lb*, "calmness of heart."

III

The Hebrew term that corresponds to Phoenician *npš* with the sense "servitors, personnel" of a temple is *məšārēt* (Ez 44:11, 19), while the semantic equivalents of Phoenician *npš*, "grave stone," are *maṣṣēbā*[18] (Gen 35:20) and *yād* (2 Sam 18:18; Isa 56:5). In Mishnaic Hebrew, however, *nepeš* is used to indicate a grave stone (*M. Šeqal.* 2:5)[19] and a tomb marker (*M.ᶜErub.* 5:1[?]; *M. ᵓOhol.* 7:1)[20] and is attested in the inscription from the Bene Hazir tomb from outside Jerusalem, *qbr whnpš*, "tomb and memorial."[21]

IV

Because Phoenician *nbš* is a *hapax legomenon* in the attested corpus, only a few tentative remarks may be ventured about its orthography/phonology. It is obviously cognate to *npš* but exhibits a unique semantic development when compared with Hebrew (and Ugaritic) usages. However, since it is found at Zinjirli where Aramaic may have been the spoken language and where Kilamuwa's descendants left inscriptions in Aramaic, it is possible that *nbš* is an Aramaic loanword into the local Phoenician. What data support this conclusion?

Old Aramaic regularly used *nbš* for a wide range of meanings paralleling much of the semantic field covered by Hebrew *nepeš*. It is attested, for example, in the inscriptions of Haddad, lines 17, 21,

18. In BH, *maṣṣēbā* also refers to pillars set up for worship, to mark the site of a theophany, and to pillars set up as covenant memorials (Gen 28:18, 22; Gen 31:44–45; Ex 24:4). Cf. B. D. Eerdmans, "The Sepulchral Monument *mṣbh*," *JBL* 30 (part II; 1911): 109–113. *Yād*, in addition to the cited sense, refers also to a stele of undisclosed purpose (1 Sam 15:12) and perhaps to a border stone (1 Chr 18:3). Concerning Isa 56:5, see the study of G. Robinson, "The Meaning of *yād* in Isaiah 56:5," *ZAW* 88 (1976): 281–284, where the author argues unconvincingly that the vocable does not mean "memorial" but "portion." The *yād wāšēm* is promised there not to the foreigners, introduced in v. 6, but to the eunuchs, introduced in v. 4, incapable of having children to memorialize them. They are like Absalom who sired no male children to take care of such matters and so built a memorial for himself.

19. See also the references in B. Maisler, *Beth Shearim I: Report on the Excavations During 1936–1940* (Hebrew; Jerusalem: Jewish Palestinian Exploration Society, 1944): 120–122. The language of these inscriptions is, however, late Mishnaic Hebrew, i.e., a form of Hebrew used by people who were most likely no longer native speakers.

20. *M. ᶜErub.* 5:1: *napāšōt šeyyēš bāhen bēt dīrā*, "tombs in which there are living quarters." S. Krauss, *Talmudische Archäologie* (Leipzig: Fock, 1910): 80, suggested that this referred to a mausoleum.

21. N. Avigad, "The Inscription in the Bene Hazir Tomb" (Hebrew), *Yediot* 12 (1945–46): 57–61; cf. p. v of the English summary.

22 and Panammu, line 18, in the Sefire inscriptions (cited above), and in the Tell Fekherye inscription, line 7, with the sense "life" corresponding to *napšātišu* in the Akkadian.[22] Thus, since it is attested in both western and eastern dialects of Old Aramaic, it must be considered the original, common form while *npš*, with the voiceless, bilabial plosive, found in the younger Aramaic dialects remains to be explained.[23] In addition, since it is posited for common Old Aramaic, the form may be assumed in the Aramaic dialect that Kilamuwa spoke. Finally, in light of the fact that of all the contemporary related Canaanite dialects and Northwest Semitic languages only Aramaic *nbš* demonstrates the semantic nuance of "mind," it must be the source of this word in Kilamuwa's Phoenician. In light of the Aramaic orthography/phonology of the word, it is possible, as suggested above, that the word was borrowed into Phoenician and that we are not dealing with a semantic calque on a Phoenician word.[24]

V

These observations lead to two conclusions: 1) Were both a Phoenician and Israelite asked "What word in your language refers to the seat of the emotions and what to the seat of the intellect?," the

22. J. C. Greenfield considers the Samalian dialect proto-Western Aramaic ("Dialect Traits in Early Aramaic," *Leshonenu* 32 [1968]: 364), while T. Muraoka implies that Fekherye may be considered proto-Eastern ("The Tell Fekherye Bilingual Inscription and Early Aramaic," *Abr-Nahrain* 22 [1983–84]: 108).

23. Muraoka (N 22): 89 suggests that all cases of *b* where etymological *p* should appear are to be explained as due to assimilation from a preceding vowel. If so, this does not clarify why $b < p$ should become *p* again in younger dialects. His explanation proposes a solution to the synchronic problem but not to the diachronic one. In any event, Muraoka's work is highly suggestive.

L. Grabbe has demonstrated conclusively, in my opinion, that the various examples of what appear to be *b/p* interchanges in Northwest Semitic must all be considered independent of each other ("Hebrew Paᶜal/Ugaritic BᶜL and the Supposed B/P Interchange in Semitic," *UF* 11 [1979]: 312), while W. R. Garr has shown, at least for Ugaritic, that the phenomenon follows a regular, predictable, and describable pattern ("On Voicing and Devoicing in Ugaritic," *JNES* 45 [1986]: 45–46, 52). The data in Hebrew and Phoenician, however, are less tractable. See, conveniently, S. Gevirtz, "On Hebrew *šēbeṭ* = 'Judge,'" in G. Rendsburg *et alia*, eds., *The Bible World. Essays in Honor of Cyrus H. Gordon* (New York: Ktav, 1980): 62–63. At least 15 occurrences of *b/p* variants are attested in Mishnaic Hebrew, a dialect usually overlooked by investigators. Cf. J. N. Epstein, *Introduction to the Text of the Mishnah*[2] II (Hebrew; Jerusalem: Magnes, 1964): 1220–1223.

24. In addition to its attestation in Sefire, the nuance may be present in Ahiqar, l. 187: *npšy lʾ tdᶜ ʾrḥh*, "my mind doesn't know its way."

Phoenician would respond, "Emotions, *lb*; intellect, *nbš*." The Israelite would respond, "Emotions, *nepeš*; intellect *lēb*." 2) The first conclusion clarifies the meaning of l. 13 in the Kilamuwa inscription and helps elucidate the inscription's structure by bringing it into the orbit of the somewhat conventional ancient Near Eastern notion of treaty and of Northwest Semitic treaty terminology.

MAARAV 5–6 (Spring, 1990): 345–384

BIBLIOGRAPHY OF THE WRITINGS OF STANISLAV SEGERT*

1946

Contribution to Book

"Učitel z milosti Boží" [A charismatic teacher], pp. 6–9 in L. Brož, ed. *Miscellanea exigua . . . J. B. Souček dicata* (Prague: Spolek posluchačů Husovy . . . fakulty).

1948

Review

K. Hoenn, *Artemis*. *LF* 72: 42–44.

1949

Reviews

Písmo, II: Nejstarší věštci. *Slovesná věda* 1:171ff.

M. Bič, *Stopy po drobopravectví v Jisraeli. Palestina od pravěku ke křesťanství, I*. *Křesťanská revue* 16: 29–31.

* The following bibliography was compiled from Prof. Segert's own bibliographical records, and owes its relative completeness to that fact. Besides the customary abbreviations in scholarly literature, the following should be noted: *AAst* = *Asian and African Studies* (Bratislava); *CV* = *Communio viatorum* (Prague); *DLZ* = *Deutsche Literaturzeitung* (Berlin); *LF* = *Listy filologické* (Prague); *NO* = *Nový Orient* (Prague); *NOB* = *New Orient Bimonthly* (Prague); *Th př KR* = *Theopříloha Křesťanské revue*. Publishers: NČSAV = Nakladatelství Československé akademie věd (Prague); SNKLU = Státní nakladatelství krásné literatury a umění (Prague); VSAV = Vydavatel'stvo Slovenskej akadémie vied (Bratislava).—ED.

1951

Articles

"A Discovery of Hebrew Manuscripts near the Dead Sea," *ArOr* 19: 610–611.

"Nálezy rukopisů u Mrtvého moře," *Evangelický kalendář 1952* 32: 85–93.

1952

Contribution to Book

"Nálezy u Mrtvého moře," *Evangelický kalendář na rok 1953*. Prague: Kalich.

Article

"O Starém zákonu," *Evangelický kalendář 1953* 33: 76–80.

1953

Articles

"Zur Habakuk-Rolle aus dem Funde am Toten Meer, I," *ArOr* 21: 218–239.

"Ein alter Bericht über den Fund hebräsicher Handschriften in einer Höhle," *ArOr* 21:263–269.

"Indogermanisches in den alphabetischen Texten aus Ugarit," *ArOr* 21: 272–275 (with L. Zgusta).

"Vorarbeiten zur hebräischen Metrik, I–II," *ArOr* 21: 482–542.

"Život a dílo Bedřicha Hrozného," *Evangelický kalendář 1954* 34: 74–78.

Reviews

A. Dupont-Sommer, *Aperçus préliminaires sur les manuscrits de la Mer Morte. ArOr* 21: 470–471.

G. Ryckmans, *Les religions arabes préislamiques. ArOr* 21: 479–480.

1954

Articles

"Zur Habakuk-Rolle aus dem Funde am Toten Meer, II–III," *ArOr* 22: 99–113, 444–459.

"Bemerkungen zur *Semitistik I*," *ArOr* 22: 588–596 (with K. Petráček).

"Septuaginta a rukopisy z Ain Fašcha," *LF* 77: 293–294.

Reviews

C. H. Gordon, *Introduction to Old Testament Times. ArOr* 22: 143–145.

H. H. Rowley, *The Zadokite Fragments and the Dead Sea Scrolls. ArOr* 22: 145–146.

H. Bardtke, *Die Handschriftenfunde am Toten Meer. ArOr* 22: 146–147.

A. Dupont-Sommer, *Nouveaux aperçus sur les manuscrits de la Mer Morte. ArOr* 22: 147–149.

J. Z. Lauterbach, *Rabbinic Essays. ArOr* 22: 149–152.

A. Rumpf, *Archäologie, I. ArOr* 22: 484–485.

M. Noth, *Die Welt des Alten Testaments. ArOr* 22: 485–486.

I. al-Yasin, *The Lexical Relation between Ugaritic and Arabic. ArOr* 22: 485–488.

G. Beer and R. Meyer, *Hebräische Grammatik, I. ArOr* 22: 488–490.

O. Muneles, *Bibliographical Survey of Jewish Prague. ArOr* 22: 490–491.

A.-G. Barrois, *Manuel d'archéologie biblique, II. ArOr* 22: 602–603.

F. M. Cross and D. N. Freedman, *Early Hebrew Orthography. ArOr* 22: 603–605.

T. H. Robinson and F. Horst, *Die Zwölf Kleinen Propheten. ArOr* 22: 605–606.

A. Bea, ed. *Canticum Canticorum Solomonis. ArOr* 22: 606.

O. Eissfeldt, *Der Gott Karmel. ArOr* 22: 607–608.

A. Bentzen, tr. M. Bič, *Mesiáš—Mójšé redivivus—Syn člověka. ArOr* 22: 608.

M. A. Beek, *Wegen en voetspoeren van het Oude Testament. ArOr* 22: 608–609.

F. A. W. van't Land and A. S. van der Woude, *De Habakuk-rol van ʿAin Fašḫa*. *ArOr* 22: 609.

L. Nemoy, *Karaite Anthology*. *ArOr* 22: 609–611.

1955

Contributions to Books

"Die Gütergemeinschaft der Essäer," pp. 66–73 in *Studia Antiqua A. Salač*. Prague: NČSAV.

"The Unity of the New Covenant—The Unity of Brethren," pp. 71–80 in *Jewish Studies: Essays . . . G. Sicher*. Prague.

Articles

"Zur Habakuk-Rolle aus dem Funde am Toten Meer, IV–VI," *ArOr* 23: 178–183, 364–373, 575–619.

"Zu einigen assimilierten Verba im Hebräischen," *ArOr* 23: 183.

"Zum Übergang ā > ō in den kanaanäischen Dialekten," *ArOr* 23: 478.

"Z esejských chvalozpěvů," *Th př KR* 22: 1–4.

"De inscriptione Latina CIL III 4327 denuo reperta," *LF* 78: 171–173, 1 pl. (with L. Vidman).

Reviews

Studia Orientalia Ioanni Pedersen . . . ArOr 23: 226–231.

A. S. Kapelrud, *Baal in the Ras Shamra Texts*. *ArOr* 23: 235–236.

A. van Selms, *Marriage and Family Life in Ugaritic Literature*. *ArOr* 23: 236–238.

A. Alt, *Kleine Schriften zur Geschichte Israels, I–II*. *ArOr* 23: 238–241.

L. A. Weigle, ed. *An Introduction to the Revised Standard Version*. *ArOr* 23: 241–242.

V. Christian, *Untersuchungen zur Laut- und Formenlehre des Hebräischen*. *ArOr* 23: 242–247.

H.-J. Kraus, *Gottesdienst in Israel*. *ArOr* 23: 247–249.

Y. Kaufmann, *The Biblical Account of the Conquest of Palestine*. *ArOr* 23: 249–250.

W. Kornfeld, *Studien zum Heiligkeitsgesetz*. *ArOr* 23: 250–252.

W. Eichrodt, *Krisis der Gemeinschaft in Israel*. *ArOr* 23: 252–253.

H. Bardtke, *Hebräische Konsonantentexte*. *ArOr* 23: 253–254.

The Jewish People Past and Present, III. *ArOr* 23: 254–256.

E. R. Goodenough, *Jewish Symbols in the Greco-Roman Period, I–III*. *ArOr* 23: 256–262.

J. Leipoldt and S. Morenz, *Heilige Schriften*. *ArOr* 23: 262–269.

W. H. Rossell, *A Handbook of Aramaic Magical Texts*. *ArOr* 23: 263–264.

R. Köbert, *Textus et Paradigmata Syriaca*. *ArOr* 23: 264–265.

F. Altheim and R. Stiehl, *Das erste Auftreten der Hunnen. Das Alter der Jesaja-Rolle. Neue Urkunden aus Dura-Europas*. *ArOr* 23: 265–268 (with O. Klíma and P. Poucha).

H. Volavková, *The Pinkas Synagogue*. *ArOr* 23: 319–320.

G. B. Roggia, *Le religioni dell'Oriente antico*. *ArOr* 23: 487–488.

S. A. Birnbaum, *The Hebrew Scripts*. *ArOr* 23: 488.

Neutestamentliche Studien für Rudolf Bultmann. *ArOr* 23: 488–489.

Neutestamentliche Studien für Rudolf Bultmann. *Th př KR* 22: 116.

1956

Books

With O. Klíma: *Mluvnice hebrejštiny a aramejštiny* [A Grammar of Hebrew and Aramaic]. Prague: NČSAV. (SS: Úvod, pp. 7–17; Literatura k studiu aramejštiny, pp. 20–21; Mluvnice aramejštiny, pp. 237–302). 308 pp.

Píseň písní [Song of Songs]. Přeložili St. Segert a J. Seifert. Ilustrace M. Váša. Prague: V. Picka. 40 pp.

Contribution to Book

"Die Versform des Hohenliedes," pp. 285–298 in *Charisteria Orientalia J. Rypka*. Prague: NČSAV.

Articles

"Zu einigen assimilierenden Verba im Hebräischen," *ArOr* 24: 131–134 (with K. Petráček).

"Neue aramäische Texte aus Ägypten," *ArOr* 24: 284–291.

"Aramäische Studien, I," *ArOr* 24: 383–403.

"Zur methode der alttestamentlichen Literarkritik," *ArOr* 24: 610–621.

"Bemerkungen zur *Semitistik II-III*," *ArOr* 24: 476–484 (with K. Petráček).

"Památce Albrechta Alta a Carla Brockelmanna," *Th př KR* 23: 149–151.

Reviews

F. Kotalík, *Ras Šamra-Ugarit*. *ArOr* 24: 151–152.

W. F. Albright, *The Bible after Twenty Years of Archaeology*. *ArOr* 24: 153–155.

G. Beer and R. Meyer, *Hebräische Grammatik, II*. *ArOr* 24: 155–156.

S. Moscati, *I Manoscritti ebraici del Deserto di Giuda*. *ArOr* 24: 155–156.

F. Spadafora, *Collettivismo e individualismo nel Vecchio Testamento*. *ArOr* 24: 156–157.

E. R. Goodenough, *Jewish Symbols in the Greco-Roman Period, IV*. *ArOr* 24: 157–160.

Donum natalicium W. S. Nyberg oblatum. *ArOr* 24: 160–163 (with O. Klíma and I. Hrbek; St.S.: 162–163).

M. H. Pope, *El in the Ugaritic Texts*. *ArOr* 24: 335:337.

S. A. Birnbaum, *The Hebrew Scripts*, fasc. 2. *ArOr* 24: 337.

S. Moscati, *Oriente in nova luce. ArOr* 24: 491–492.

E. S. Mulder, *Die teologie van die Jesaja-Apokalipse. ArOr* 24: 492–493.

A. Rumpf, *Archäologie, II. ArOr* 24: 642.

S. Moscati, *Il sistema consonantico delle lingue semitiche. ArOr* 24: 642–644.

E. L. Sukenik, ed. *'Ocar ha-mgilot ha-gnuzot. ArOr* 24: 644–646.

J. C. Dancy, *A Commentary on I Maccabees. ArOr* 24: 646–647.

W. Brandenstein, *Griechische Sprachwissenschaft, I.* O. Hoffmann, *Geschichte der griechischen Sprache, I.* A. Debrunner, *Geschichte der griechischen Sprache, II.* F. Stolz, *Geschichte der lateinischen Sprache. Th př KR* 23: 91–92.

M. Dibelius and W. G. Kümmel, *Paulus. Th Př KR* 23: 123–124.

1957

Contribution to Books

The following items in A. Novotný, ed., *Biblický slovník, I–II* (Prague: Kalich): "Izaiáš" (pp. 253–254), "Izaiášovo proroctví" [Prophecy of Isaiah] (254–255), "Izrael" (257–264, with additions by M. Bič and J. B. Souček), "Král" [King] (348–350), "Ozeáš" (576–578), "Pentateuch" (616–620), "Píseň Šalomounova" [Song of Solomon] (632–634), "Přísloví (jako literární druh)" [Proverbs as a literary genre] (754–755), "Přísloví (jako SZ kniha)" [Proverbs as an OT book] (755–757; with additions by M. Bič), "Rut 2: Kniha R." [Ruth 2: The Book of R.] (814–815), "Samuelovy knihy" [The books of Samuel] (851–852), "Sofoniáš 1. Prorok" (936–937), "Soudců kniha" [The book of Judges] (943–945), "Starý Zákon" [Old Testament] (970–983), "Zachariáš (prorocká kniha)" (1268–1269), "Zjevení Janovo" [Revelation] (1–10; 1301–1303), "Zorobábel" (1318), "Žalm (jako slovesný druh)" (1335–1336), "Žalmy (Kniha žalmů)" [Psalms, book of] (1336–1342), "Žaltář" [Psalter] (1343), "Mapa VIII: Dnešní Palestina" [Map VIII: Today's Palestine].

Articles

"Aramäische Studien, II," *ArOr* 25: 21–37.

"Vorarbeiten zur hebräischen Metrik III," *ArOr* 25: 190–200.

"Textkritische Erwägungen . . . zu den Chronikbüchern," *ArOr* 25: 671–675.

"Z Písně Písni," *Host do domu* 1957: 49–50 (with J. Seifert).

"L. Köhler a jeho význam pro hebrejskou lexikografii" [L. Köhler and his importance for Hebrew lexicography], *Th př KR* 24: 116–119.

"Za profesorem Rudolfem Růžičkou," *Th př KR* 24: 263–265.

"Řecké zlomky Dvanácti proroků z Judské pouště (De Prophetarum minorum fragmentis Graecis in Iudaico deserto repertis)," *LF* 80: 31–35.

"Starověké způsoby dojení s hlediska moderní fysiologie" [Ancient methods of milking from the viewpoint of modern physiology], *NO* 12: 155, 3 fig. (cover, p. 3; with Jan Bílek).

"Žalozpěv nad zkázou města Jeruzaléma" [Lamentation on the destruction of the city of Jerusalem], *NO* 12: 2–3 (with V. Závada).

"Rímsky sarkofág CIL III 4327 v evanjelíckom a.v. kostole v Komárne" [Roman sarcophagus CIL III 4327 in the Evangelical A.C. Church in Komárno], *Slovenská archeológia* 5: 240–244.

Reviews

W. F. Albright, *Recent Discoveries in Bible Lands. ArOr* 25: 163.

M. Burrows, *The Dead Sea Scrolls. ArOr* 163–165.

F. Stier, *Das Buch Ijjob, Hebräisch und Deutsch. ArOr* 25: 295–297.

G. Lisowsky, *Konkordanz zum hebräischen Alten Testament. ArOr* 25: 297–298.

G. R. Driver, *Semitic Writing. ArOr* 25: 298–299.

A. von Selms, *De verscheurde Stad. ArOr* 25: 299–300.

A. Jirku, *Die Ausgrabungen in Palästina und Syrien. ArOr* 25: 502–503.

Melilah, Vol. V. ArOr 25: 503–504.

Z. Vilnay, *Ha-ʾarec ba-miqraʾ. ArOr* 25: 504–505.

Čtyři knížky o řeckém a latinském jazyce. LF 81: 124–128 (F. Stolz, A. Debrunner, O. Hoffmann, W. Brandenstein).

Z. Svobodová, *Dobrovský a německá filologie. OLZ* 52: 20–21.

J. Gray, *The Krt Text in the Literature of Ras Shamra. ThLZ* 82: 106–108.

1958

Book

Pět svátečních svitků. Přeložil St. S. za básnické spolupráce J. Seiferta, V. Závady, V. Kubíčkové. Prague: SNKLHU. 300 pp., 8 pl. [Translation of Five Megilloth from Hebrew into Czech in co-operation with Czech poets, provided with introductions and notes, with contributions of Czech orientalists.]

Contributions to Books

"Die Schreibfehler in den ugaritischen literarischen Keilschrifttexten," pp. 223–241 in *Von Ugarit nach Qumran. Beiträge . . . O. Eissfeldt.* BZAW 77: Berlin: de Gruyter.

"The Writing and Its Development—L'écriture et son evolution—Die Schrift und ihre Entwicklung—Escritura et su desarollo." *Calendary of Artia for 1959.* Prague: Artia.

"Nálezy u Mrtvého moře po deseti letech" [Finds at the Dead Sea after ten years], pp. 55–61 in *Židovská ročenka 5719.* Prague.

Articles

"Ugarit und Griechenland." *Das Altertum* (Berlin) 4: 67–80.

"Altorientalische Arten des Melkens vom Standpunkt der modernen Physiologie," *Archiv für Tierzucht* (Berlin) 1: 185–188 (with J. Bílek).

"Charakter des westsemitischen Alphabets," *ArOr* 26: 243–247.

"Altorientalisches Material zum Alten Testament," *ArOr* 26: 498–505.

"Aramäische Studien, III–V," *ArOr* 26: 561–584.

"Noch zum Charakter des westsemitischen Alphabets," *ArOr* 26: 657–659.

"Bis in das dritte und vierte Glied," *CV* 1: 127–134.

"Aufgaben der biblisch-aramäischen Grammatik," *CV* 1: 127–134.

"Ninetieth Anniversary of Alois Musil's Birth," *CV* 1: 184–186.

"Die Methoden der hebräischen Metrik," *CV* 1: 233–241.

"Die Gemeinschaft von Qumrān und das Urchristentum," *CV* 1: 275–285 (review article).

"David—král a básník" [David—king and poet], *NO* 13: 53–54.

"Píseň písní" [Song of songs], *NO* 13: 105.

Reviews

C. H. Gordon, *Ugaritic Manual. ArOr* 26: 302–307.

G. D. Young, *Concordance of Ugaritic. ArOr* 26: 307–308.

P. Fronzaroli, *Leggenda di Aqhat. ArOr* 26: 309.

P. Fronzaroli, *La fonetica ugaritica. ArOr* 26: 309–311.

S. Moscati, *I predecessori d'Israele. ArOr* 26: 311–313.

G. Widengren, *Sakrales Königtum im Alten Testament und im Judentum. ArOr* 26: 313–315.

G. Fohrer and K. Galling, *Ezechiel. ArOr* 26:315–317.

W. Zimmerli, *Ezechiel* (Lief. 1–3). *ArOr* 26: 317–318.

H. H. Rowley, *Jewish Apocalyptic and the Dead Sea Scrolls. ArOr* 26: 318.

J. van der Ploeg, *Fondsten in de Woestijn van Juda. ArOr* 26: 318–319.

Ch. Rabin, *Qumran Studies. ArOr* 26: 319–322.

E. R. Goodenough, *Jewish Symbols in the Greco-Roman Period, V–VI. ArOr* 26: 322–326.

P. Kahle, *Opera Minora. ArOr* 26: 516–519.

H.-J. Kraus, *Klagelieder. ArOr* 26: 519–520.

O. Eissfeldt, *Einleitung in das Alte Testament,* 2d ed. *ArOr* 26: 520–523.

G. R. Driver, *Canaanite Myths and Legends. ArOr* 26: 523–526.

G. R. Driver, *Aramaic Documents of the Fifth Century B.C. ArOr* 26: 670–672.

H. Schmökel, *Heilige Hochzeit und Hoheslied. ArOr* 26: 672–674.

B. Svoboda and D. Končev, *Neue Denkmäler antiker Toreutik. ArOr* 26: 674–676.

M. Ingholt, H. Seyrig, J. Starcky, eds., *Recueil des tessères de Palmyre. ArOr* 26: 675–676.

Hollenberg—Budde—W. Baumgartner, *Hebräisches Schulbuch. ArOr* 676–677.

F. Dornseiff, *Antike und Altes Orient. ArOr* 26: 678–680.

C. Brockelmann, *Hebräische Syntax. ArOr* 26: 695–698.

B. Schindler, ed. *Gaster Centenary Publication. ArOr* 26: 697–698.

H. H. Rowley, *The Faith of Israel*; Th. C. Vriezen, *Theologie des Alten Testaments in Grundzügen. CV* 1: 71–73.

G. Fohrer, *Elia. CV* 1: 73.

M. Noth, *Amt und Berufung. CV* 1: 291.

O. Eissfeldt, *Die Genesis der Genesis. CV* 1: 291–292.

E. L. Ehrlich, *Geschichte Israels von dem Anfang bis zur Zerstörung des Tempels. CV* 1: 292–293.

J. Hempel, *Heilung als Symbol und Wirklichkeit*... *CV* 1: 293–294.

H. H. Rowley, *Prophecy and Religion in Ancient China and Israel. DLZ* 79: 586–590 (with M. Velingerová).

L. Matouš, tr., *Epos o Gilgamešovi. Náboženská revue církve československé* 29: 281–283.

Ch. Burchard, *Bibliographie zu den Handschriften vom Toten Meer, I. OLZ* 53: 351–353.

M. Martin, *The Scribal Character of the Dead Sea Scrolls, I. RQ* 1: 517–533.

M. Martin, *The Scribal Character of the Dead Sea Scrolls, II. RQ* 2: 99–111.

H. J. Kraus, *Geschichte der historisch-kritischen Erforschung des Alten Testaments. Th př KR* 25: 86–88.

Biblický komentář k Starému zákonu. [Biblischer Kommentar—Altes Testament.] *Th př KR* 25: 90–92.

1959

Contribution to Book

"Poznámky k transkripci orientálních jmen," in *Th. Mann, př. P. Eisner, Josef a bratří jeho.* Prague: SNKL.

Articles

"New Books on the Dead Sea Scrolls," *ArOr* 27: 447–462 (review article).

"Makkabäer und Hussiten," *CV* 2: 50–60.

"Der Messias nach neuen Auffassungen," *CV* 2: 348–353 (review article).

"Dobrovského Hebraica v Národním Museu. *Časopis Národního musea,*" Odd. věd společenských 128: 175–179.

"Die Schreibfehler in den ugaritischen nichtliterarischen Keilschrifttexten," *ZAW* 71: 23–32.

Reviews

K. M. Kenyon, *Digging Up Jericho. ArOr* 27: 163–165.

L'Ancien Testament et l'Orient. ArOr 27: 165–167.

M. F. Unger, *Israel and the Aramaeans of Damascus. ArOr* 27: 167–168.

E. Balla, *Die Botschaft der Propheten. ArOr* 27: 168–169.

A. Bertsch, *Kurzgefasste hebräische Sprachlehre. ArOr* 27: 169–172.

J. T. Milik, *Dix ans de découvertes dans le Désert de Juda. ArOr* 27: 172–174.

A. Murtonen, *Materials for a Non-Masoretic Hebrew Grammar. ArOr* 27: 347–348.

J. Levý, *Theorie českého překladu. ArOr* 27: 349–350.

O. Eissfeldt, *Enno Littmann. ArOr* 27: 349–350.

J. Weingreen, *Classical Hebrew Composition. ArOr* 27: 350.

L. Koehler and W. Baumgartner, *Lexicon in Veteris Testamenti Libros, Supplementum ad . . . ArOr* 27: 496–498.

H. Bardtke, *Zu beiden Seiten des Jordans. ArOr* 27: 498–499.

O. Eberhard, *Aus Palästinas Legendenschatz. ArOr* 27: 701–702.

K. G. Cereteli, *Chrestomatia sovremennogo assirijskogo jazyka. ArOr* 27: 702–703.

E. Galbiati, *La struttura letteraria dell'Esodo. ArOr* 27: 703–704.

A. Jepsen, *Die Wissenschaft vom Alten Testament. CV* 2:93.

G. von Rad, *Theologie des Alten Testaments, I. CV* 2: 362–364.

S. H. Hooke, ed. *Myth, Ritual, and Kingship. CV* 2: 364-366.

H. W. Wolff, *Immanuel. CV* 2: 366-367.

B. E. Metzger, *Introduction to the Apocrypha. CV* 2: 367-368.

G. Baumbach, *Qumran und das Johannes-Evangelium. CV* 2: 368-369.

A. Vögtle, *Das öffentliche Wirken Jesu auf dem Hintergrund des Qumranbewegung. CV* 2: 369-370.

Gott und die Götter: E. Fascher Festgabe. CV 2: 370-371.

1960

Contribution to Book

"Problems of Hebrew Prosody," pp. 282-291 in *Congress Volume Oxford 1959. Supplements to VT* VII. Leiden: Brill.

Articles

"À l'occasion du soixante-dixième anniversaire du Professeur Ján Bakoš," *ArOr* 28: 1-4.

"Das hebraistische Werk von Josef Dobrovský," *ArOr* 28: 72-90.

"Considerations on Semitic Comparative Lexicography," *ArOr* 28: 470-487.

"Semitistischer Cercle," *ArOr* 28: 657, 666.

"Palästina im Spiegel der neueren Darstellungen der biblischen Geographie," *CV* 3: 73-86 (review article).

Reviews

Cl. F.-A. Schaeffer and Ch. Virolleaud, *Le Palais Royal d'Ugarit, II. ArOr* 28: 151-153.

J. Aistleitner, *Die mythologischen und kultischen Texte aus Ras Schamra. ArOr* 28: 153-154.

J. Gray, *The Legacy of Canaan. ArOr* 28: 155-157.

O. Kaiser, *Die mythische Bedeutung des Meeres in Ägypten, Ugarit und Israel. ArOr* 28: 157–158.

M. du Buit, *Geographie de la Terre Sainte. ArOr* 28: 159.

R. Meyer, *Hebräisches Textbuch. ArOr* 28: 349–351.

W. Leslau, *Ethiopic and South Arabic Contributions to the Hebrew Lexicon. ArOr* 28: 515 (with K. Petráček).

D. W. Thomas, ed. *Documents from Old Testament Times. ArOr* 28: 527–528.

C. H. Gordon, *Adventures in the Nearest East. ArOr* 28: 691–692.

R. de Vaux, *Les Institutions de l'Ancien Testament, I. ArOr* 28: 692–693.

O. Eissfeldt, *Das Lied Moses . . . und das Lehrgedicht Asaphs. ArOr* 28: 693–694.

H. Gese, *Der Verfassungsentwurf des Ezechiel. ArOr* 28: 694–695.

H. Gese, *Lehre und Wirklichkeit in der alten Weisheit. ArOr* 28: 695–696.

J. Scharbert, *Solidarität im Segen und Fluch im Alten Testament, I. ArOr* 28: 696–698.

G. Lisowsky, L. Rost, *Konkordanz zum hebräischen Alten Testament.* S. Loewenstamm and J. Blau, *ᵓOṣar lešon ha-Miqraᵓ. ArOr* 28: 698–700.

A. Sperber, ed., *The Bible in Aramaic, I–II. ArOr* 28: 701–704.

E. R. Goodenough, *Jewish Symbols in the Greco-Roman Period, VII–VIII. ArOr* 28: 704–707.

D. J. Wiseman, *Zwischen Nil und Euphrat. CV* 3: 87–88.

F. F. Bruce, *Biblical Exegesis in Qumran Texts. CV* 3: 88.

Gottes ist der Orient. CV 3: 88–89.

W. Brandenstein, *Griechische Sprachwissenschaft, II. LF* 84(8): 173–174.

B. Syrový, *Vývoj stavebnictví a architektury v starověku. NO* 15: 71–72.

J. van der Ploeg, *Le Rouleau de la Guerre. RQ* 2: 454–458.

1961

Articles

"Úloha archeologie při zkoumání kumránských nálezů (Le rôle de l'archéologie dans l'étude des trouvailles de Qumrân)," *Archeologické rozhledy* (Prague) 13: 587–591.

"Semitische Marginalien," *ArOr* 29: 80–118.

"Die Sprache der moabitischen Königsinschrift," *ArOr* 29: 197–267.

"Překlady z orientálních jazyků" [Translations from Oriental languages], *Dialog* (Prague) 1961, 1.

"Zamečanija o svitke 'Vojny' iz Kumrana" [Some comments on the Qumran War Scroll], *Narody Azii i Afriki* 6: 150–159.

"Tři sta let od narození Daniela Arnošta Jablonského," *NO* 16: 50.

"Další Bar Kochbovy dopisy" [Further letters of Bar Kochba], *NO* 16: 170, 192.

Reviews

W. Baumgartner, *Zum Alten Testament und seiner Umwelt. ArOr* 29: 156–157.

Congress Volume Oxford 1959. ArOr 29: 157–158.

P. E. Kahle, *The Cairo Geniza*, 2d ed. *ArOr* 29: 159–160.

E. Täubler, *Biblische Studien: Die Epoche der Richter. ArOr* 29: 160–161.

S. Holm-Nielsen, *Hodayot: Psalms from Qumran. ArOr* 29: 351–352.

O. Eissfeldt, *Der Beutel der Lebendigen. ArOr* 29: 483–484.

A. Dupont-Sommer, *Les écrits esséniens. ArOr* 28: 483–486.

M. Martin, *The Scribal Character of the Dead Sea Scrolls, I–II. ArOr* 29: 486–487.

H. Jensen, *Die Schrift in Vergangenheit und Gegenwart. ArOr* 29: 508–510.

Textus, Vol. I. C. Rabin, ed. *ArOr* 29: 510–512.

J. A. Février, *Histoire de l'écriture. ArOr* 29: 677–680.

K. M. Kenyon, *Excavations at Jericho, I. ArOr* 29: 680–683.

S. Moscati, *Le antiche civiltà semitiche. ArOr* 29: 683–684.

R. de Vaux, *Les institutions de l'Ancien Testament, II. ArOr* 29: 684–685.

E. Y. Kutscher, *Hlšwn whrq*[c] *hlšwnj šl mgjlt Jš*[c]*jh . . . ArOr* 29: 685–687.

M. Philonenko, *Les interpolations chrétiennes des Testaments des Douze Patriarches et les manuscrits de Qumrân. ArOr* 29: 687–289.

F. Muzika, *Krásné písmo ve vývoji latinky. LF* 84(9): 194–196 (with P. Spunar).

P. Benoit, ed., *Les grottes de Murabba*[c]*ât. LF* 84(9): 338.

Rylcem i trzciną (Warszawa 1959). *NO* 16: 170, 192.

K. G. Kuhn, *Rückläufiges hebräisches Wörterbuch. RQ* 3: 143–145.

K. G. Kuhn, *Konkordanz zu den Qumrantexten. RQ* 3: 145–148.

1962

Contribution to Book

"A Preliminary Report on a Comparative Lexicon of North-West Semitic Languages," pp. 383–385 in *Trudy dvacat'pjatogo meždunarodnogo kongressa vostokovedov.* Moskva. I.

Articles

"Concerning the Methods of Aramaic Lexicography," *ArOr* 30: 505–506.

"Počátky a předlohy řecké abecedy" [Origin amd Patterns of the Greek Alphabet], *LF* 85: 1–9.

"The Alphabet Conquests the World," *NOB* 3: 136–139, 186–190.

"Hérődés zvaný Veliký" [Herodes called Great], *NO* 17: 36–37.

"Hanibal, vojevůdce mírumilovných" [Hannibal, the commander of the peaceful], *NO* 17: 108–109, 1 fig.

"Masinissa—sjednotitel Numidů" [M., unifier of the Numidians], *NO* 17: 156–157.

"Odkud pochází jméno Afrika" [The name of Africa], *NO* 17: 176–177.

"Jugurta—král Numidů" [J., king of the Numidians], *NO* 17: 230–231, 1 fig.

"Zur Etymologie von *lappīd*, 'Fackel'," *ZAW* 74: 323–324.

Reviews

G. Tchalenko, *Villages antiques de la Syrie du Nord, I–III. Byzantinoslavica* (Prague) 23: 89–91.

F. Pfister, *Alexander der Grosse in den Offenbarungen. . . . Byzantinoslavica* (Prague) 23: 317–318.

M. Cohen, *La grande invention de l'écriture et son évolution, I–III. DLZ* 83: 100–103.

G. Schöne, *Jerusalem. LF* 85: 402–403.

A Novel on the Qumran Cave: H. A. Stoll, *Die Höhle am Toten Meer. NOB* 2: 60–61.

1963

Contribution to Books

"Die Sprachenfragen in der Qumrān-Gemeinschaft," pp. 315–319 in H. Bardtke, ed., *Qumrān-Probleme.* Berlin: Academie-Verlag.

"Použití matematických strojů pro semitskou lexikografii" [Use of computers in Semitic lexicography], pp. 32–38 in *Orientalistický sborník*. Bratislava: VSAV.

"Staroegyptská literatúra" [Ancient Egyptian Literature] and "Kenáanske literatúry" [Canaanite Literature], pp. 17–21, 22–34 in M. Pišút, ed., *Dejiny svetovej literatúry* [History of World Literature]. Bratislava.

Articles

"Zur Orthographie und Sprache der aramäischen Texte von Wadi Murrabaʿāt," *ArOr* 31: 122–137.

"Zu den altorientalischen Motiven in 'Tausend und einer Nacht,'" *ArOr* 31: 630–634.

"Altaramäische Schrift and Anfänge des griechischen Alphabets," *Klio* (Berlin) 41: 38–57.

"Za překladatelem 'Růže ran'" [Obituary of E. A. Saudek], *Th př KR* 30: 201–202.

"Klasická filologie a orientalistika" (Klassiche Philologie und Orientalistik), *LF* 86: 1–8.

"Řecké papyry ze sedmé jeskyně kumránské" [Greek Papyri from Qumran Cave 7], *LF* 86: 336–337.

"Kolik písmen měla nejstarší abeceda?" [How many letters had the oldest alphabet?] *NO* 18: 144–145.

"Poklady měděného svitku" [Treasures of the Copper Scroll], *NO* 18: 170–172, 3 fig.

"Jeskyně pokladů" [The Cave of Treasures], *NO* 18: 292.

"Hebraistické počátky a práce Václava Fortunata Durycha" [Hebraistic origins and works of Václav Fortunat Durych], *Slavia* (Prague) 32: 47–53.

"Počátky abecedy podle nových objevů" [The beginnings of the alphabet according to new discoveries], *Vesmír* (Prague) 42: 173–176, 8 fig.

Reviews

Ch.-F. Jean and J. Hoftijzer, *Dictionnaire des inscriptions sémitiques de l'Ouest*. *ArOr* 31: 333–336.

S. Wagner, *Die Essener in der wissenschaftlichen Diskussion. ArOr* 31: 336–338.

R. de Vaux, *L'archéologie et les Manuscrits de la Mer Morte. ArOr* 31: 505–506.

G. et C. Charles-Picard, *La vie quotidienne à Carthage au temps d'Hannibal. ArOr* 31: 507–508.

R. J. H. Shutt, *Studies in Josephus. ArOr* 31: 508–509.

J. van Goudoever, *Biblical Calendars,* 2d ed. *ArOr* 31: 509–511.

A. Alt, *Kleine Schriften zur Geschichte Israels, III. ArOr* 31: 689–692.

P. Humbert, *Opuscules d'un hébraïsant. ArOr* 31: 692–694.

K. G. Kuhn, *Konkordanz zu den Qumrantexten. ArOr* 31: 694–695.

K. Rudolph, *Die Mandäer, I. ArOr* 31: 695–699.

E. Segelberg, *Maṣbūtā. ArOr* 31: 700–701.

O. Klíma, *Manis Zeit und Leben. NO* 18: 287–288.

M. Baillet et al., eds., *Les "Petites Grottes" de Qumrân. RQ* 4: 279–296 (with addendum by J. B. Pelikán, pp. 296–297).

H. A. Stoll, *Griechische Tempel. Zprávy Jednoty klasických filologů* (Prague) 5: 70–71.

1964

Book

Píseň písní: Přeložili J. Seifert a St. S. Ilustrace A. Paderlík. [Translation of Song of Songs from Hebrew] Prague: SNKLU. 72 pp.

Contribution to Book

"Contributions philologiques à l'histoire carthaginoise," pp. 7–12 in *Mnema Vladimír Groh.* Prague: NČSAV.

Articles

"Zur Schrift und Orthographie der altaramäischen Stelen von Sfire," *ArOr* 32: 110–126.

"Nejstarší město světa" [The oldest city in the world], *Lidé a země* (Prague) 13: 4–7, 1 fig., 1 map.

"O překládání ze skuteične mrtvých jazyků" [Translating from really dead languages], *Dialog* 4: 1–12.

"M. Luther, List o překládání" [Translation from German, with E. Skála, of M. Luthers *Sendbrief vom Dolmetschen*], *Dialog* 4: 93–109.

"Nálezy řeckých textů v jižní části Judské pouště" [Discoveries of Greek texts in the southern part of the Judean Desert], *LF* 87: 198.

"Juba II., spisovatel na trůně" [Juba II, writer on the throne], *NO* 19: 26–27.

"Po stopách Bar Kochby" [In the steps of Bar Kochba], *NO* 19: 154–155.

"Archeologie pod mořem" [Archeology under the sea], *Vesmír* 43: 329–330.

Reviews

G. Tchalenko, *Villages antiques de la Syrie du Nord, I–III. ArOr* 32: 323–325.

P. Kahle, *Der hebräische Bibeltext seit Franz Delitzsch. ArOr* 32: 325–326.

F. Rosenthal, *A Grammar of Biblical Aramaic. ArOr* 32: 326–327.

Z. Kallai, *Gbwlwtjh hṣpwnjjm šl Jhwdh. ArOr* 32: 327–328.

S. Loewenstamm and J. Blau, *ʾwṣr lšwn hmqrʾ. ArOr* 32: 339–340.

J. Maier, *Die Texte vom Toten Meer, I–II. ArOr* 32: 339–340.

*Abr-Nahrain, 1, 1959–1960. ArOr*32: 340–341.

M. Noth, *Die Ursprünge des alten Israel im Lichte neuer Quellen. ArOr* 32: 341–342.

Oriens Antiquus I/1, 1962. ArOr 32: 342–343.

J. J. Koopmans, *Aramäische Chrestomathie, I–II. ArOr* 32: 454–455.

Hebrew and Semitic Studies Presented to G. R. Driver. ArOr 32: 455–457.

H. J. Franken and C. A. Franken-Battershill, *A Primer of Old Testament Archaeology. ArOr* 32: 457–458.

M. Avi-Yonah, *Oriental Art in Roman Palestine. ArOr* 32: 458–459.

S. Yeivin, *Mḥqrjm btwldwt Jśrᵓl wᵓrṣw. ArOr* 32: 459–460.

E. Jacob, *Ras Shamra-Ugarit et l'Ancien Testament. ArOr* 32: 460–461.

Wm. B. Stevenson and J. A. Emerton, *A Grammar of Palestinian Jewish Aramaic. ArOr* 32: 461–462.

D. Baramki, *Phoenicia and the Phoenicians. ArOr* 32: 654–655.

A. Sperber, ed., *The Bible in Aramaic III. ArOr* 32: 657–658.

O. Eissfeldt, *Kleine Schriften I. ArOr* 32: 657–658.

M. Mansoor, *The Thanksgiving Hymns. ArOr* 32: 658–659.

F. A. Rice and M. F. Saᶜid, *Eastern Arabic. ArOr* 32: 659–660.

H. Bardtke, *Vom Roten Meer zum See Genezareth. ArOr* 32: 660.

E. G. Clarke, *The Selected Questions of Ishō bar Nūn on the Pentateuch. OLZ* 54: 482–484.

1965

Book

Ugaritskij jazyk [Monograph on the Ugaritic language, translated from the author's German original into Russian by A. A. Zvonov]. Moscow: Izdatelstvo "Nauka." 104 pp.

Contribution to Books

St. Segert, ed., *Studia Semitica philologica necnon philosophica Ioanni Bakoš terquinque lustra complectenti dicata.* Bratislava: VSAV (includes "Das wissenschaftliche Werk von Ján Bakoš," pp. 13–21; "Zur Geschichte der Orientalistik in der Slowakei," pp. 23–27; "Der wissenschaftliche Nachlass von Ján Lajčiak," pp. 51–53; "Ugaritisch und Aramäisch," pp. 215–226).

"Židovská válka a její dějepisec" [The Jewish War and its Historian]; "Poznámky" [Notes] (with L. Vidman); "Geografický index" in *Flavius Josephus, Válka židovská.* Přeložili J. Havelka a J. Šonka. Prague: SNKLHU.

Articles

"Aspekte des althebräischen Aspektsystems," *ArOr* 33: 93–101.

"Sprachliche Bemerkungen zu einigen aramäischen Texten von Qumrān," *ArOr* 33: 190–206.

"Zur literarischen Form und Funktion der Fünf Megilloth," *ArOr* 33: 451–462.

"Kann das Ostrakon von Nimrud für Aramäisch gehalten werden?" *AAst* 1: 147–151.

"Juba II., the Writer King," *NOB* 4: 11–12.

"Dead Cities and Living Villages," *NOB* 4: 70–73, 2 pl.

"Klíč k tajemství etruštiny" [Phoenician Inscription of Pyrgi], *NO* 20: 110.

"Aim and Terminology of Semitic Comparative Grammar," *Rivista degli Studi Orientali* (Rome) 40: 1–8.

"Osídlení kumránské oblasti v Judské poušti ve světle nových nálezů" [Settlement of Qumran area in the Judean Desert in the light of new discoveries], *Sborník Čs. společnosti zeměpisné* (Prague) 70: 277–281, 2 pl. (with O. Pokorný).

Reviews

Ch.-F. Jean and J. Hoftijzer, *Dictionnaire des inscriptions sémitiques de l'Ouest, III. ArOr* 33: 121–122.

H. Donner and W. Röllig, *Kanaanäische und aramäische Inschriften, I. ArOr* 33: 122–123.

S. Moscati, A. Ciasca, G. Garbini, *Il Colle di Rachele.* Y. Aharoni, *Excavations at Ramat Rahel. ArOr* 33: 123–125.

M. Noth, *Die Welt des Alten Testaments. ArOr* 33: 125–126.

U. Cassuto, *The Documentary Hypothesis. ArOr* 33: 126.

H.-J. Kraus, *Psalmen. ArOr* 33: 126–128.

V. Vellas, *Hē epidrasis tēs Hellēnikēs philosophias epi tou bibliou tēs Sophias Solomōntos. ArOr* 33: 128.

A. Kuschke, ed., *Verbannung und Heimkehr, W. Rudolph. ArOr* 33: 1282129.

P. E. Kahle, ed. R. Meyer. *Die Kairoer Geniza. ArOr* 33: 129–130.

A. Adam, ed., *Antike Berichte über die Essener. ArOr* 33: 130–131.

H. L. Strack and P. Billerbeck, ed. J. Jeremias, *Kommentar zum Neuen Testament aus Talmud und Midrasch, VI. ArOr* 33: 131–132.

G. Eichholz, *Landschaften der Bibel. ArOr* 33: 131–132.

M. Liverani, *Storia d'Ugarit. ArOr* 33: 658–660 (with H. Freydank).

K.-H. Bernhardt, *Das Problem der altorientalischen Königsideologie im Alten Testament. ArOr* 33: 660–662.

J. Hempel, *Weitere Mitteilungen über Text und Auslegung der am Nordwestende des Toten Meeres gefundenen hebräischen Handschriften. ArOr* 33: 662–663.

E. Y. Kutscher, *Mlym wtwldwtyhn. ArOr* 33: 663.

G. Morawe, *Aufbau und Abgrenzung der Loblieder von Qumrān. ArOr* 33: 664.

K. Michalowski, *Palmyre, I–IV. ArOr* 33: 664–666.

H. Chyliński, *Wykopaliska w Qumran a pochodzenie chrześciánstwa. ArOr* 33: 667.

P. Matthiae, *Ars Syra. ArOr* 33: 667–668.

E. Oswald, *Das Bild des Mose in der kritischen alttestamentlichen Wissenschaft. ArOr* 33: 669–670.

H. G. May, ed., *Oxford Bible Atlas. ArOr* 33: 670.

Cambridge Ancient History, I–II. (Gadd, Hinz, Labat). *LF* 88: 95.

H. Frost, *Under the Mediterranean. NOB* 4: 30.

1966

Contribution to Books

"Starověk: Severní Afrika" [Antiquity: North Africa] and "Znalosti o Africe u starověkých národů" [Knowledge of Africa among the ancient peoples] in I. I. Hrbek, ed., *Dějiny Afriky, I.* Prague: Svoboda.

"Ugaritská literatura," pp. 139–152 and "Aramejské literatury," pp. 153–156 in O. Král, ed., *Z dějin literatur Asie a Afriky, I.* Prague: Universita Karlova.

Article

"Some Phoenician Etymologies of North African Toponyms," *Oriens Antiquus* 5: 19–25.

Reviews

H. H. Rowley, *From Moses to Qumran. ArOr* 34: 118–119.

Congress Volume Bonn 1962. ArOr 34: 119–120.

M. Ellenbogen, *Foreign Words in the Old Testament. ArOr* 34: 120–122.

Sh. Morag, *The Vocalization Systems of Arabic, Hebrew, and Aramaic. ArOr* 34: 122–123.

J. M. Solá-Solé, *L'infinitif sémitique. ArOr* 34: 123–124.

L. Alonso Schökel, *Estudios de poetica hebrea. ArOr* 34: 246–249.

W. Tyloch, *Rękopisy z Qumran nad Morzem Martwym. ArOr* 34: 249–250.

R. Gradwohl, *Die Farben im Alten Testament. ArOr* 34: 250–251.

S. Gevirtz, *Patterns in the Early Poetry of Israel. ArOr* 34: 251–253.

A. Malamat, ed., *Bymy byt r'šwn: Mlkwywt Yśr'l wYhwdh. ArOr* 34: 253–254.

Ch. Rabin and Y. Yadin, eds., *Mḥqrym bmgylwt hgnwzwt (In memory of E. L. Sukenik). ArOr* 34: 254–255.

M. V. David, *Les débats sur les écritures et l'hiéroglyphe au XVIIe et XVIIIe siècles. ArOr* 34: 255–257.

M. Dunand, *Byblos*. E. J. Wein and R. Opificius, *7000 Jahre Byblos*. *ArOr* 34: 430–431.

O. Eissfeldt, *Kleine Schriften, II*. *ArOr* 34: 432–433.

I. J. Gelb, *A Study of Writing*. *ArOr* 34: 433–434.

D. Harden, *The Phoenicians*. *ArOr* 34: 434–435.

G. L. Harding, *Baalbek*. *ArOr* 34: 435–436.

S. Moscati, *Historical Art in the Ancient Near East*. *ArOr* 34: 436–437.

A. Ungnad and L. Matouš, *Grammatik des Akkadischen*. *ArOr* 34: 437–438.

J. Aistleitner, *Die mythologischen und kultischen Texte aus Ras Schamra,* 2d ed. *ArOr* 34: 649–650.

H. Eggers, ed. *Erstes Kolloquium über Syntax natürlicher Sprachen und Datenverarbeitung*. *ArOr* 34: 650–651.

A. Jirku, *Kanaanäische Mythen und Epen aus Ras Schamra*. *ArOr* 34: 651–652.

Moses in Schrift und Überlieferung. *ArOr* 34: 652–653.

M. Mansoor, *The Dead Sea Scrolls*. *ArOr* 34: 653–654.

G. Jeremias, *Der Lehrer der Gerechtigkeit*. *ArOr* 34: 654–656.

W. Caskel, *Der Felsendom und die Wallfahrt nach Jerusalem*. *ArOr* 34: 656.

K. G. Cereteli, *Sovremennyj assirijskij jazyk*. *AAst* 2.

O. Eissfeldt, *Einleitung in das Alte Testament,* 3d ed. *DLZ* 61: 460–462.

B. H. Warmington, *Carthage*. *NOB* 5: 62.

1967

Books

Orientalistik an der Prager Universität. Erster Teil. 1348–1848. Prague: Universita Karlova (with K. Beránek). 266 pp., 2 pl.

Grígórios Abulfaradž Barhebraeus, Kratochvilná vyprávění. [Translation of the Book of Laughable Stories from Syriac into Czech.] Prague: Odeon. 203 pp.

Contribution to Books

"Zur Bedeutung des Wortes *nōqēd*," pp. 279–283 in *Hebräische Wortforschung. Festschrift W. Baumgartner. Supplements to VT* XVI. Leiden: Brill.

"Surviving of Canaanite Elements in Israelite Religion," pp. 155–161 in *Studi sull'Oriente e la Bibbia, offerti al . . . G Rinaldi.* Genova.

Seventy-four short articles about Ugaritic, Syriac, and Hebrew writers and literary monuments in J. Průšek, ed., *Slovník spisovatelů Asie a Afriky* [Dictionary of Asian and African Writers]. Prague: Odeon.

"Husův zájem o hebrejský jazyk" [John Huss's interest in the Hebrew language], pp. 69–72 in *Husův sborník.* Prague: Komenského evangelická fakulta bohoslovecká.

"Bratří a Starý Zákon" [Unitas fratrum and the Old Testament], pp. 90–93 in R. Říčan, ed., *Bratrský sborník.* Prague: Komenského evangelická fakulta bohoslovecká.

Articles

"Some Trends in Qumran Research," *ArOr* 35: 128–144 (review article).

"A la mémoire du Professeur Ján Bakoš," *ArOr* 35: 181–182.

"Semitistischer Cercle III," *ArOr* 35: 292–293.

"Contribution of Professor I. N. Vinnikov to Old Aramaic Lexicography," *ArOr* 35: 463–466.

"A New Source of Knowledge on the Christian Jews," *NOB* 6: 82–82.

"Nový pramen o židovských křesťanech" [New sources on the Judaeo-Christians], *NO* 22: 93–94.

"Firmus, bojovník za svobodu Maurů" [F., fighter for Maurs' freedom], *NO* 22: 276–277.

Reviews

La Bible—L'Ancien Testament, ed. Éd. Dhorme. *ArOr* 35: 316–318.

K. Cereteli, *Materialy po aramejskoj dialektologii, I. ArOr* 35: 492–493.

M. Dunand and R. Duru, *Oumm el-ᶜAmed, I–II. ArOr* 35: 668–671.

H. B. Rosén, *A Textbook of Israeli Hebrew. ArOr* 35: 671–674.

H. Ringgren, *Israelitische Religion. ArOr* 35: 674–675.

W. M. W. Roth, *Numerical Sayings in the Old Testament. JSS* 12: 130–131.

H. Volavková, *Příběh židovského muzea. NO* 22: 96.

H. Volavková, *Schicksal des Jüdischen Museums in Prag. NOB* 6: 125.

Ch. Burchard, *Bibliographie zu den Handschriften vom Toten Meer, II. OLZ* 62: 38–40.

J. Assfalg, *Syrische Handschriften. OLZ* 62: 45–48.

1968

Book

Kniha Jóbova. Přeložili V. Závada a St. Segert. Prague: Československý spisovatel. [Translation of the Book of Job from Hebrew into Czech, with postscript, pp. 107–123, and notes, pp. 124–130, 131–134.] 134 pp.

Contribution to Books

"Die Bedeutung der Handschriften von Qumrān für die Aramaistik," pp. 183–187 in *Bibel und Qumrān. Beiträge . . . H. Bardtke.* Berlin: Evangelische Haupt-Bibelgesellschaft.

"Tendenzen und Perspektiven der semitischen vergleichenden Sprachwissenschaft," pp. 167–174 in *Studia Orientalia in memoriam C. Brockelmann.* Halle. (= WZ, Spr.-Ges. R., Heft 23, Jg. 18).

Articles

"Semitischer Circle," *ArOr* 36: 468.

"Recent Progress in Ugaritology," *ArOr* 36: 443–447 (review article).

"Gildó, pán nad Afrikou" [G., the ruler of Africa], *NO* 23: 97–102.

Reviews

D. Barthélemy, *Les devanciers d'Aquila. ArOr* 36: 160–163.

H. Donner, *Israel unter den Völkern*. *ArOr* 36: 163–164.

Ch.-F. Jean and J. Hoftijzer, *Dictionnaire des inscriptions sémitiques de l'Ouest*. *ArOr* 36: 164–167.

J. Wellhausen, *Die kleinen Propheten*. *ArOr* 36: 167.

J. A. Fitzmyer, *The Genesis Apocryphon of Qumran Cave I: A Commentary*. *JSS* 13: 281–282.

K. Beba, *"Tajemný" Orient*. *NO* 23: 256.

1969

Book

Píseň písní. Přeložili Jaroslav Seifert a St. S., 3 vyd. Prague: Odeon. [Translation of Song of Songs from Hebrew into Czech.] 72 pp.

Sabatino Moscati, *Staré semitské civilizace*. [Translation of *Le antiche civiltà semitiche* from Italian into Czech, with translator's postscript, pp. 336–342.] Prague: Odeon. 352 pp.

Contribution to Books

"Le rôle de l'ougaritique dans la linguistique sémitique comparée," pp. 461–477 in *Ugaritica VI*. Paris: Geuthner.

"Hebrew Bible and Semitic Comparative Lexicography," pp. 204–211 in *Congress Volume Rome 1968*. *Supplements to VT* XVII. Leiden: Brill.

"Die Arbeit am vergleichenden Wörterbuch der semitischen Sprachen mit Hilfe des Computer IBM 1410," pp. 714–717 in *XVIII. Deutscher Orientalistentag 1968, Vorträge, Teil. 2*. Wiesbaden: Steiner.

Articles

"Die Deutungen des Namens Qumrān," *ArOr* 37: 189–195.

"Phoenician Background of Hanno's Periplus," *Mélanges offerts à M. Maurice Dunand, I = Mélanges de l'Université Saint-Joseph* 45, 1969: 499–519 (fasc. 30, 1–21).

"Versbau und Sprachbau in der althebräischen Poesie," *Mitteilungen des Instituts für Orientforschung* 15: 312–321 [in the issue dedicated to R. Meyer].

"Bar Hebraeus, Kniha kratochvilných vyprávění," *NO* 24: 67, 70, 74, 77, 79, 80, 32–83.

1970

Book

Synové světla a synové tmy: Svědectví nejstarších biblických rukopisů. Prague: Orbis. [Book on Qumran Scrolls.] 230 pp., XXIV pl.

Contribution to Book

"Franz Rosenzweig, Písmo a Luther," pp. 367–392 in J. Čermák et al., eds., *Překlad literárního díla.* Prague: Odeon. [Translation from German into Czech of "Die Schrift und Luther."]

Articles

"První hláskové písmo" [The first alphabet], *NO* 24: 248–253, 4 fig.

"Rozhovor o biblistice a semitské filologii. Zapsal V. Sadek" [Conversation on Biblical studies and Semitic philology. Recorded by V. Sadek], *NO* 24: 257–259.

Reviews

J. Finegan, *The Archaeology of the New Testament. American Historical Review* 1970: 2024–2025.

H. Donner and W. Röllig, *Kanaanäische und aramäische Inschriften, II–III. ArOr* 38: 223–225.

E. Speiser, ed., *At the Dawn of Civilization. ArOr* 38: 225–227.

G. Fohrer, *Überlieferung und Geschichte des Exodus. ArOr* 38: 227–230.

J. C. Trever, *The Untold Story of Qumran. ArOr* 38: 230–231.

J. Hempel, *Geschichten und Geschichte im Alten Testament bis zur persischen Zeit. ArOr* 38: 348.

G. A. Williamson, *The World of Josephus. ArOr* 38: 349.

H. Maundrell, ed. D. Howell, *A Journey from Aleppo to Jerusalem in 1697. ArOr* 38: 349–350.

K. Koch, *Was ist Formgeschichte? ArOr* 38: 491–492.

O. Eissfeldt et al., *Religionsgeschichte des Alten Orients, I. ArOr* 38: 492–494.

1971

Book

Starověké dějiny Židů [History of the Jews in Antiquity]. Set by Svoboda, Prague, 1970. Photo-copied from the proofs, Los Angeles, 1971. 208 pp.

Contribution to Book

"The Ugaritic Texts and the Textual Criticism of the Hebrew Bible," pp. 413–420 in H. Goedicke, ed., *Near Eastern Studies in Honor of W. F. Albright*. Baltimore: Johns Hopkins.

1972

Contributions to Books

"Zur Bezeichnung der Frauen in den aramäischen Verträgen von Elephantine," pp. 619–621 in *Studi in onore di E. Volterra, VI*. Milano.

"Starověká Fénicie a Kartago" (pp. 120–126) and "Jednotlivec a společnost ve starověkém Izraeli" (pp. 127–136) in L. Balcar and V. Cvekl, eds., *Historia Magistra, 1*. Prague: Svoboda. [Anonymous.]

Reviews

H. Donner and W. Röllig, *Kanaanäische und aramäische Inschriften, I–III,* 2d ed. *JSS* 17: 137–139.

J. Lindblom, *Erwägungen zur Herkunft der josianischen Tempelurkunde*. *JSS* 17: 267–268.

J. Fitzmyer, *The Genesis Apocryphon of Qumran Cave I: A Commentary*. *JSS* 273–274.

1973

Book

Phénicie-Carthage. Introduction bibliographique à l'histoire du droit et à l'éthnologie juridique publiée sous la direction de J. Gilissen: A/4. Éditions de l'Université de Bruxelles. 17 pp.

Contributions to Books

"Form and Function of Ancient Israelite, Greek and Roman Legal Sentences," pp 161–165 in *Orient and Occident: Essays Presented to C. H. Gordon*. Kevelaer/Neukirchen-Vluyn.

"A Computer Program for Analysis of Words according to Their Meaning (Conceptual Analysis of Latin Equivalents for the Comparative Dictionary of Semitic Languages)," pp. 149–157 in G. Buccellati, ed., *Approaches to the Study of the Ancient Near East . . . offered to I. J. Gelb = Orientalia* 42/1–2 (with J. R. Hall; St. S.: 149–152).

1974

Contributions to Book

Sixty-one items in J. Průšek, ed., *Dictionary of Asian Writers, Vol. I.* (J. Bečka, ed.) London/New York: Allen & Unwin/Basic Books.

1975

Book

Altaramäische Grammatik mit Bibliographie, Chrestomathie und Glossar. Leipzig: Enzyklopädie. 555 pp., 1 map.

Contribution to Book

"Some Remarks Concerning Syncretism," pp. 63–66 in B. Pearson, ed., *Religious Syncretism in Antiquity*. Missoula: Scholars Press.

Article

"Verbal Categories of Some Northwest Semitic Languages: A Didactic Approach," *Afroasiatic Linguistics* 2/5: 83–94.

Reviews

E. Vogt, *Lexicon Linguae Aramaicae Veteris Testamenti. JAOS* 95: 110.

J. Blau, *On Pseudo-Corrections in some Semitic Languages. WZKM* 67: 265–267.

O. Eissfeldt, *Adonis und Adonaj. WZKM* 67: 267–268.

S. Schechter, *Documents of Jewish Sectaries. WZKM* 67: 268–270.

D. Barthélemy and O. Rickenbacker, *Konkordanz zum hebräischen Sirach. WZKM* 67: 170–172.

Jakob von Sarug, tr. S. M. Grill, *Die Kirche und die Forschung—Ausgewählte Briefe. WZKM* 67: 272–273.

P. Grelot, *Documents araméens d'Égypte. WZKM* 67: 273–275.

W. Selb, ed., *ᶜAbdīšōᶜ Bar Bahrīz, Ordnung der Ehe und der Erbschaften . . . WZKM* 67: 275–277.

L. Bernhard, *Die Chronologie der syrischen Handschriften. WZKM* 67: 277–279.

1976

Book

A Grammar of Phoenician and Punic. München: C. H. Beck. 330 pp.

Article

"Genres of Ancient Israelite Legal Sentences: 1934 and 1974," *WZKM* 68: 131–142.

Reviews

B. Porten, *Jews of Elephantine and Aramaeans of Syene. WZKM* 68: 216–217.

Sh. Morag, *The Book of Daniel. WZKM* 68: 217–218.

J. H. Charlesworth, *The Odes of Solomon. WZKM* 68: 219–220.

1977

Article

"The Origin of the Greek Alphabet," *Archaeology at UCLA* 1/11 (May 1977), 1–4.

1978

Contribution to Book

"Rendering of Ugaritic Phonemes by Cuneiform Syllabic Signs in the Quadrilingual Vocabularies from Ras Shamra," pp. 257–268 in B. Hruška and G. Komoróczy, eds., *Festschrift Lubor Matouš.* Budapest.

Article

"Vowel Letters in Early Aramaic," *JNES* 37: 111–114.

Reviews

M. Sokoloff, *The Targum to Job from Qumran Cave XI. JAOS* 98: 145–146.

J. Blau, *A Grammar of Biblical Hebrew*. *JSS* 23: 105–111.

E. Y. Kutscher, *Studies in Galilean Aramaic*. *WZKM* 70: 114–115.

1979

Article

"Ugaritic Poetry and Poetics: Some Preliminary Observations," *UF* 11: 729–738 [in the volume dedicated to Cl. F.-A. Schaeffer].

1980

Contribution to Book

"Syntax and style in the Book of Jonah: Six Simple Approaches to Their Analysis," pp. 121–130 in J. A. Emerton, ed., *Prophecy: Essays presented to G. Fohrer*. *BZAW* 150. Berlin: de Gruyter.

Article

"Sto let od narození Bedřicha Hrozného" [A hundred years since the birth of Bedřich Hrozný], *Proměny* (Washington, D.C.) 17: 70–74.

Reviews

L. Schlimme, *Der Hexaemeronkommentar des Moses bar Kepha, I–II*. *WZKM* 72: 171–174.

W. Strothmann, *Das Sakrament der Myron-Weihe in der Schrift "De ecclesiastica hierarchia."* *WZKM* 72: 174–175.

W. Strothmann, ed., *Syrische Hymnen zur Myron-Weihe*. *WZKM* 72: 175.

W. Strothmann, ed., *Codex Syriacus Secundus*. *WZKM* 72: 176.

E. Lipiński, *Studies in Aramaic Inscriptions and Onomastics, I*. *WZKM* 72: 176–179.

J. L. Cunchillos, *Quando los angeles eran dioses*. *WZKM* 72: 179–181.

J. Hoftijzer and G. van der Kooij, eds., *Aramaic Texts from Deir ʿAlla*. *WZKM* 72: 182–189.

R. Macuch, *Zur Sprache und Literatur der Mandäer*. *WZKM* 72: 189–191.

1981

Review

Neue Ephemeris für semitische Epigraphik, Band 3. JAOS 98: 451.

1982

Reviews

G. Saadé, *Ougarit, Métropole canaanéenne. WZKM* 74: 237–238.

P. Xella, *I testi rituali de Ugarit I. WZKM* 74: 239–241.

K. Ehlich, *Verwendung der Deixis beim sprachlichen Handeln. WZKM* 74: 241–245.

1983

Book

Altaramäische Grammatik, 2d ed. Leipzig: Enzyklopädie. 555 pp., 1 map.

Contributions to Books

"Ethiopian and Hebrew Prosody: Some Preliminary Observations," pp. 337–350 in St. Segert and A. J. E. Bodrigligeti, eds., *Ethiopian Studies Dedicated to Wolf Leslau on the Occasion of his Seventy-Fifth Birthday.* Wiesbaden: Harassowitz.

"Decipherment of Forgotten Writing Systems: Two Different Approaches," pp. 131–156 in K. Ehlich and F. Coulmas, eds., *Writing in Focus* (Trends in Linguistics: Studies and Monographs 24). Berlin: de Gruyter

"Prague Structuralism in American Biblical Scholarship: Performance and Potential," pp. 697–708 in Carol L. Meyers and M. O'Connor, eds., *The Word of the Lord Shall Go Forth: Essays in Honor of David Noel Freedman.* Philadelphia/Winona Lake: American Schools of Oriental Research/Eisenbrauns.

Articles

"Parallelism in Ugaritic Poetry," *JAOS* 103/1: 295–306. (Special issue: Studies . . . dedicated to Samuel Noah Kramer).

"The Last Sign of the Ugaritic Alphabet," *UF* 15: 201–208.

"Polarity of Vowels in the Ugaritic Verbs II /ʾ/," *UF* 15: 219–222.

Reviews

Maria-José Fuentes Estañol, *Vocabulario Fenicio. WZKM* 206–208.

L. H. Vilsker, *Manuel d'araméen samaritain. WZKM* 75: 208–209.

R. Macuch, *Grammatik des samaritanischen Aramäisch. WZKM* 75: 209–213.

S. Rummel, ed., *Ras Shamra Parallels, Vol. III. JSS* 28: 361–364.

1984

Book

A Basic Grammar of the Ugaritic Language with Selected Texts and Glossary. Berkeley/Los Angeles /London: Univ. of California. xxvi, 213 pp.

Contribution to Book

"Semitic Poetic Forms in the New Testament," pp. 1433–1462 in W. Haase, ed., *Aufstieg und Niedergang der römischen Welt II* 25.2. Berlin: de Gruyter.

Articles

"Paronomasia in the Samson Narrative in Judges XIII–XVI," *VT* 34: 454–461.

"A Controlling Device for Copying Stereotype Passages? (Amos I 3–II 8, VI 1–6)," *VT* 34: 481–482.

Reviews

J. W. Welch, ed., *Chiasmus in Antiquity. CBQ* 46: 336–338.

1985

Contribution to Book

"Hebrew Poetic Parallelism as Reflected in the Septuagint," pp. 133–148 in N. Fernandez Marcos, eds., *La Septuaginta en la investigación contemporanea. (V Congreso de la IOSCS).* Textos y estudios "Cardinal Cisneros," 34. Madrid: Instituto "Arias Montano."

Reviews

A. Abou-Assaf, P. Bordreuil, A. R. Millard, *La statue de Tell Fekherye et son inscription bilingue assyro-araméenne. AfO* 31: 90–94.

G. Del Olmo Lete, *Mitos y leyendas de Canaan según la tradición de Ugarit. AfO* 31: 94–96.

K. P. Jackson, *The Ammonite Language of the Iron Age. BASOR* 260: 85–86.

V. Brugnatelli, *Questioni di morfologia e sintassi dei numerali cardinali semitici. JAOS* 105: 730.

K. Cereteli, *Aramejskij jazyk. JAOS* 105: 731.

H. Schweizer, *Metaphorische Grammatik: Wege zur Integration von Grammatik und Textinterpretation in der Exegese. JAOS* 105: 800.

Y. Sabar, *spr brʾšyt bʾrmyt ḥdšh. ZAW* 97: 153–154.

1986

Book

Altaramäische Grammatik, 3d ed. Leipzig: Enzyklopädie. 555 pp, 1 map.

Contribution to Books

"Symmetric and Asymmetric Verses in Hebrew Biblical Poetry," pp. 33–37 in *Proceedings of the Ninth World Congress of Jewish Studies: Division A, The Period of the Bible.* Jerusalem: World Union of Jewish Studies.

"Renderinig of Parallelistic Structures in the Targum Neofiti: The Song of Moses (Deuteronomy 32: 1–43)," pp. 515–532 in D. Muñoz-Leon, eds., *Salvación en la Palabra: Targum-Derash-Berith. En memoria del Profesor Alejandro Díez Macho.* Madrid: Cristianidad.

"Jan Hus's Reform of Czech Orthography: A Hebraist's Contribution," pp. 343–350 in *Essays in the Area of Slavic Languages, Linguistics and Byzantology: A Festschrift in Honor of Antonín Dostál = Byzantine Studies* 8, 11, 12/1982, 1984, 1985.

"An Ugaritic Text Related to the Fertility Cult (*KTU* 1.23)," pp. 217–224 in A. Bonanno, ed., *Archaeology and Fertility Cult in the Ancient Mediterranean.* Msida: Univ. of Malta.

Reviews

A. Lemaire and J.-M. Durand, *Les inscriptions araméennes de Sfire et l'Assyrie de Shamshi-ilu. AfO* 33: 104–106.

V. Collado and E. Zurro, eds., *El misterio de la Palabra: Homenaje al . . . Luis Alonso Schökel. CBQ* 48: 155–157.

J. R. Miles, *Retroversion and Text Criticism: The Predictability of Syntax in an Ancient Translation from Greek to Ethiopic. ZAW* 98: 318–319.

1987

Contribution to Books

"'Live Coals Heaped on the Head,'" pp. 159–164 in J. H. Marks and R. M. Good, eds., *Love and Death in the Ancient Near East: Essays in Honor of Marvin H. Pope.* Guilford, Conn.: Four Quarters.

"Phonological and Syntactic Structuring Principles in Northwest Semitic Verse Systems," pp. 543–557 in H. Jungraithmayr and W. W. Müller, eds., *Proceedings of the Fourth International Hamito-Semitic Congress, Marburg, 20–22 September, 1983.* Amsterdam/Philadelphia: Benjamins.

Articles

"Words Spread Over Two Lines," *UF* 19: 283–288.

"The Ugaritic *nqdm* after twenty years: A note on the function of Ugaritic *nqdm*," *UF* 19: 409–410.

Reviews

G. Del Olmo Lete, *Interpretación de la mitología cananea. AfO* 34: 87–88.

Adele Berlin, *The Dynamics of Biblical Parallelism. AfO* 34: 89–91.

W. Baumgartner and J. J. Stamm, *Hebräisches und Aramäisches Lexikon zum Alten Testament.* 3. Aufl. *WZKM* 77: 230–233.

K. Beyer, *Die aramäischen Texte vom Toten Meer. WZKM* 77: 233–237.

F. Werner, *Die Wortbildung der hebräischen Adjektiva. WZKM* 77: 238–240.

M. Sokoloff, eds., *Arameans, Aramaic and the Aramaic Literary Tradition. WZKM* 77: 240–242.

Y. Sabar, *The Book of Genesis in Neo-Aramaic. WZKM* 77: 242–244.

1988

Contributions to Books

"Writing," pp. 1136–1160 in G. W. Bromiley et al., eds., *The International Standard Bible Encyclopedia, Revised, Vol. IV.* Grand Rapids: Eerdmans.

"Observations on Poetic Structure in the Songs of the Sabbath Sacrifice," pp. 215–223 in F. García Martínez and É. Puech, eds., *Mémorial Jean Carmignac* (= *RQ* 13/49–52). Paris: Gabalda.

"Die Orthographie der alphabetischen Keilschrifttafeln in akkadischer Sprache aus Ugarit," pp. 189–205 in P. Xella, ed., *Cananea Selecta: Festschrift für O. Loretz (= Studi epigrafici e linguistici* 5). Verona: Essedue.

Articles

"Two Whales of Petr Chelčický," *CV* 31: 127–134.

"Diptotic Geographical Feminine Names in the Hebrew Bible," *Zeitschrift für Althebraistik* 1: 99–102.

"Ugaritic as a Tool in Teaching Hebrew Language and Literature," *Bulletin of Higher Hebrew Education* 3: 1–6.

Reviews

J. Hoftijzer, *The Function and Use of the Imperfect Forms with Nun Paragogicum in Classical Hebrew. JAOS* 108: 157–158.

E. Qimron, *The Hebrew of the Dead Sea Scrolls. CBQ* 50: 308–309.

P. Bordreuil, *Catalogue des sceaux ouest-sémitiques inscrits . . . ZAW* 100: 311.

1989

Review

W. Eckardt, *Computergestützte Analyse althebräischer Texte. CBQ* 51: 320–321.

Works in Press

Contributions to Books

"Une inscription phénicienne trouvée à Ras Shamra," *Ugaritica*. Paris.

"Parallelism in the *Qolasta*." *Studia Semitica necnon Iranica Rudolpho Macuch . . . dedicata*. Wiesbaden: Harrassowitz.

"Northwest Semitic Postvelar /ǵ/ in Correspondence to Dental Phonemes," *Proceedings of Fifth International Hamito-Semitic Congress,* ed. H. Mukarovsky. Amsterdam: Benjamins.

"History and Poetry: Poetic Patterns in Nehemia 9:5–37," *Soggin Volume*, ed. F. Israel. Rome.

"Ancient Near Eastern Traditions in the Thousand and One Nights," *Proceedings of the Twelfth Levi Della Vida Conference,* ed. G. Sabagh. Los Angeles.

"Forms of Gnostic Poetry: A Preliminary Survey," in W. Haase, ed., *Aufstieg und Niedergang der römischen Welt, II.* Berlin: de Gruyter

"Phoenician Linguistic and Traditional Substratum in North African Christianity," in W. Haase, ed., *ANRW.*

"Hebrew and Aramaic," *International Encyclopedia of Lexicography.* Berlin: de Gruyter (with Y. Sabar).

"Other Languages of the Ancient Near East" (with Françoise Grillot, V. Haas, J. A. Brinkman), *International Encyclopedia of Lexicography.*

Articles

"The Ugaritic Voiced Postvelar in Correspondence to the Emphatic Interdental." *UF.*

"Masoretes and Translators—Karaites and Czech Brethren," *Bulletin des Études Karaïtes.* Paris.

Reviews

A. V. Hunter, *Biblical Hebrew Workbook, CBQ.*

A. Murtonen, *Hebrew in its West Semitic Setting. Part One, Section A. WZKM.*

R. Alter and F. Kermode, eds. *The Literary Guide to the Bible. WZKM.*

Works in Manuscript

Articles

"New Editions of Ancient Aramaic Texts" (review article), *Maarav.*

"An Eighteenth Century Czech Manuscript about Jews."

"Letter about Book Reviewing."

"Unitas fratrum and the Old Testament."

"Assonance and Rhyme in Hebrew Poetry."

"Non-alphabetic evidence for the Ugaritic Language" (review article).

"Formulas in the Book of Haggai."